BEYOND URBAN BIAS
IN AFRICA

BEYOND URBAN BIAS IN AFRICA

URBANIZATION IN AN ERA OF STRUCTURAL ADJUSTMENT

Charles M. Becker
The Economics Institute

Andrew M. Hamer
The World Bank

Andrew R. Morrison
Tulane University

HEINEMANN
PORTSMOUTH, NH

JAMES CURREY
LONDON

Heinemann
A division of Reed Elsevier Inc.
361 Hanover Street
Portsmouth, NH 03801-3912

James Currey Ltd
54b Thornhill Square
Islington
London N1 1BE, England

First published 1994

The authors and publisher wish to thank those who granted permission to reprint previously
published material:

Excerpts from "The Demo-Economic Impact of the AIDS Pandemic in Sub-Saharan
Africa" by Charles M. Becker, *World Development*, Dec. 1990, reprinted with permission from
Pergamon Press Ltd, Headington Hill Hall, Oxford OX3 0BW, UK.

Excerpts from "The Determinants of Urban Population Growth in Sub-Saharan Africa" by
Charles M. Becker and Andrew Morrison, *Economic Development and Cultural Change*,
36(2):259–78. © 1988 by The University of Chicago. All rights reserved.

Excerpts from "Observational Equivalence in the Modeling of African Labor Markets and
Urbanization" by Charles M. Becker and Andrew Morrison, *World Development*, April 1993,
reprinted with permission from Pergamon Press Ltd, Headington Hill Hall, Oxford
OX3 0BW, UK.

Library of Congress Cataloging-in-Publication Data
Becker, Charles M.
    Beyond urban bias in Africa : urbanization in an era of structural adjustment /
Charles M. Becker, Andrew M. Hamer, Andrew R. Morrison.
        p.   cm.
    Includes bibliographical references and index.
    ISBN 0-435-08091-1 (Heinemann : cloth). — ISBN 0-435-08093-8
(Heinemann : pbk.)
        1. Structural adjustment (Economic policy)—Africa, Sub-Saharan.
    2. Africa, Sub-Saharan—Economic conditions.   3. Urbanization—
Africa, Sub-Saharan.   I. Hamer, Andrew Marshall.   II. Morrison,
Andrew R.   III. Title.
HC800.B42   1994
307.76'0973—dc20   93-32405
                                                                         CIP

British Library Cataloguing-in-Publication Data
Becker, Charles M.
    Beyond Urban Bias in Africa: Urbanization
    in an Era of Structural Adjustment
    I. Title
    307.76096

ISBN 0-435-08091-1 (Heinemann Cloth)
ISBN 0-435-08093-8 (Heinemann Paperback)
IBSN 0-85255-148-7 (James Currey Cloth)
ISBN 0-85255-147-9 (James Currey Paperback)

6   5   4   3   2   1   BB   94   95   96   97

Dedication

There are only a handful of economists who work primarily on cities and urban labor markets in developing countries. One of the most promising was Vibhooti Shukla of the University of Texas at Dallas, who died in a tragic accident in August 1992. Vibhooti was a fine economist, whose estimates of agglomeration economies in Indian cities are a unique and important contribution to the field. She was also a kind and caring person, with a fine sense of humor.

It is to her memory that we dedicate this book.

Contents

Acknowledgments

So many people have provided insights and assistance that it is hard to know where to begin. This volume has been underway for a long time, giving us the opportunity to distill the wisdom of others as the "received knowledge" evolved.

During the past several years, we have benefited from outstanding research assistance from Chris DeBodisco at Vanderbilt University, Jennifer Woodward and Chris Grewe at the University of Colorado, and Dipak Ghosh at Tulane University. Chris Grewe and Jennifer Woodward were painstakingly conscientious in working with census data, and we owe a great deal to their creativity and cleverness in reconciling often incomplete data series.

Our colleagues in economics and demography have contributed greatly toward the present work, though they bear no responsibility for its shortcomings. In particular, we have been influenced by and received helpful comments and criticism from Dale Adams, Gary Gaile, Michael Greenwood, Subbiah Kannappan, Allen Kelley, Edwin Mills, Jacques Ledent, Carl Liedholm, Michael Lipton, Lubuele Luan'Sende, Robert Lucas, William Milne, Elizabeth Peters, Andrei Rogers, Richard Rogers, Vibhooti Shukla, Boubacar Traore, Gasper Urriyo, John Weeks, and Jeffrey Williamson. Jean-Marie Cour was extremely generous in sharing the invaluable data on urbanization that he compiled.

Finally, our publishers, John Watson of Heinemann and James Currey, have been exceptionally patient and understanding. Neither we nor they realized when we first came to terms in 1986 that the patterns of urban growth in Africa were on the verge of a major shift. They nonetheless persevered as we tried to grapple with new facts, paradigms, and models. For this they have our enormous gratitude and, we hope, a far better book.

Charles Becker, Boulder, Colorado
Andrew Hamer, Washington, DC
Andrew Morrison, New Orleans, Louisiana

1

African Economic Development and Urbanization

1.1 Introduction

The population of urban Africa is increasing at a stunning rate. Sub-Saharan Africa's urban population is doubling every twelve years (UNDP and World Bank [1992]), and the urban populations of the lowest income sub-Saharan countries are growing at an even faster rate. Dealing with this growth is of paramount importance, as it imposes severe budget constraints on virtually all African governments. At the same time, rapid urbanization has generated important demand shifts, largely toward goods with high import contents during an era of continent-wide foreign exchange crises. Declining or weak agricultural sectors also have been a standard feature, and consequently, so have been disastrous export performances. Thus, the factors associated with rapid urban growth in Africa are also strongly associated with its macroeconomic problems.

These high and possibly accelerating growth rates of African cities and towns emerge as a natural consequence of economic growth, but also result largely from the particular public policies followed. Despite the urbanizing impact of much public policy, nearly all African nations have sought to restrict their urban growth rates, and some have imposed quite severe policies to achieve this end.[1] Yet virtually nowhere have these policies succeeded in stemming the tide of urban growth, perhaps because the full impacts of macro policies were not recognized. Consequently, it is critical to consider the unintended spatial effects of macro and other public policies; at the same time, it is essential to determine whether rapid urban growth is in fact undesirable.

Indeed, although nearly one-third of the region's population lives in cities or towns and over half of Africa's gross domestic product (GDP) is generated in urban centers, little attention has been focused on the contributions made by the urban economy to overall national development. This is surprising, given the substantial

1

effort devoted to identifying bottlenecks and suggesting solutions to the economic difficulties facing sub-Saharan Africa.

We argue in favor of harnessing the human and financial resources of the African city as part of a strategy to ensure greater and more widespread economic development. We further suggest that certain initiatives at the subnational level are necessary if macroeconomic measures are to be successful. The urban sector can no longer be considered merely as a social sector. The urban agenda goes well beyond physical planning and shelter: it also includes aspects of agricultural development, industrialization, regional transportation, resource mobilization, investment planning, pricing reforms, and institution building. In each area, the efficiency with which the urban sector performs a range of tasks will be vital to the success of policies elsewhere.

In building this argument, we seek first to understand the nature of African urban growth. What roles do urban areas play in Africa? What forces have caused their rapid growth in recent years? What determines the structure of incomes within urban areas, and their level relative to rural incomes? What public policies matter, and how do they affect urban growth and living standards? In addressing these questions, we will be able to suggest appropriate urban and macro policies, and also to assess likely patterns of future urban growth.

1.2 The Challenge Created by Africa's Macroeconomic Constraints

According to U.N. estimates, Africa is expected to continue to be the world's most rapidly urbanizing region for some time. To be able to understand—and evaluate—these estimates, it is necessary to understand the process of urbanization and the factors that affect it. In particular, we argue that the fundamental change in the types of macroeconomic policies pursued by African governments will alter and probably slow urban growth below levels that have been predicted.

The economies of sub-Saharan Africa vary enormously in scope. Of the forty-five nations that comprise the area, nine had fewer than 1 million inhabitants in 1990, while Nigeria had roughly 100 million.[2] As of 1987, thirteen nations had gross domestic products (GDPs) of less than US$1 billion, while four nations had GDPs of roughly $10 billion or more.

Nevertheless, there are certain commonalities among these nations which, as a whole, have a 1990 population of 480 million, and a GDP of about $140 billion (1987), implying a per capita income of $340. After a post-Independence decade of economic promise, a majority of countries have experienced either a decline or virtual stagnation in per capita output. Only ten countries (discussed in World Bank [1984a]) managed to improve their GDP growth rate from 1973 to 1983 compared with the previous decade; with eight minor exceptions, all states also experienced increases in population growth rates over the period, compounding the problem. African economies, in general, continued to deteriorate remarkably in the early and mid-1980s. Per capita food production fell in twenty-five of thirty-five countries for which data are available (see Table 2.3). Nor was this miserable agricultural performance offset by prosperous manufacturing sectors. Manufacturing wages fell an average of 1.2 percent per year in the ten-year period 1974–84, with most of this decline concentrated in the 1980s. The absolute value of manufacturing output fell in over one-third of the countries (see Table 2.7).

This deterioration in economic performance has affected not only agricultural and industrial output, but also the quality of infrastructure services and the financial and managerial viability of key development institutions. What, then, were the common macroeconomic problems?

The situation faced by each country in the region has its own individual features, but World Bank reports (World Bank [1981] and [1984a]; Krumm [1985]; Nellis [1985]) suggest that the difficulties often have similar exogenous and domestic causes. Exogenous factors include: the oil price hikes of 1973 and 1979, the boom-bust cycle affecting the prices of many primary exports, and the aggressive international lending practices of private banks in the 1970s and early 1980s that accompanied the rapid growth of the Eurodollar market. These factors interacted with one another. The commodity price boom that followed the 1973 oil price increase encouraged African governments to sharply boost expenditures at home and borrowing abroad. Once commodity prices fell, there was additional recourse to external credit. Many countries had thus exhausted their external borrowing potential by the time the 1979 oil price crisis occurred. The event was followed by a world recession, an increase in international interest rates, and widespread political instability and drought across much of Africa, all of which inflicted further damage. The world disinflation of the 1980s caused further problems for countries with large amounts of long-term debt. World Bank reports suggest that the national adjustment policies undertaken in the late 1970s and early 1980s were insufficiently comprehensive and were not enacted sufficiently early to avoid a serious debt-servicing problem. This forced the adoption of restrictive import policies, compounding an already serious slowdown in economic activity.

Studies of African macroeconomic problems point as well to endogenous factors. Many countries—probably the vast majority—experienced an over-extension of central government beyond limits of its financial and managerial capability, as attempts were made to command and regulate a large share of economic activity. Market signals, such as interest rates, foreign exchange rates, and relative prices often were controlled. These controls curtailed incentives for private production, especially among primary producers. Many governments felt the necessity to expand their involvement in marketing and productive activities, partly through the use of parastatal enterprises. To finance these ventures and to build infrastructure projects, large public investments were undertaken that in retrospect appear ill-advised, especially as many yielded very low short- and medium-run returns.

African economic collapse was accompanied by continued deficits in balance of payments—deficits which were not sustainable without a continuing flow of external (mainly public) financing. By 1989, *nonconcessional* African debt had reached 253 percent of exports and 63 percent of GDP; the *ex ante* ratio of debt service to exports for the continent was an extraordinary 46 percent (and, in fact, above 100 percent in Guinea-Bissau, Mozambique, Sao Tome and Principe, Somalia, and Sudan). Sub-Saharan African countries were forced at various times in the 1980s to take what to the majority of leaders was a distasteful step: implementation of stabilization programs suggested by the International Monetary Fund, and later, the World Bank.

The basic features of stabilization packages are well known. The policy advice from international organizations and bilateral donors has involved two goals: increased production of output for both domestic and foreign markets and the reduction of central government activities to more sustainable levels. These objectives have resulted in the advocacy of several major reforms for the region's economies. The Bank-Fund reforms include drastic devaluation to improve the balance of trade and removal or reduction of tariff and nontariff barriers, combined with either cuts in government spending or increases in taxation, in order to produce a more balanced government budget. The first instrument—devaluation—is assigned to the balance of payments target, while the reduced government deficits and import liberalization are designed to reduce inflation.

These broad policies typically are accompanied by complementary measures. First, the World Bank and other donors have urged that market signals and private producers be given a greater role. Secondly, African countries have been pressured to abolish or curtail their parastatal sectors, with those remaining in existence advised to receive assistance in financial management and manpower training. Third, the slimmed-down public sector has been pushed to give priority to expenditures for operations and maintenance of essential infrastructure and public services, with increased private sector participation. This has been accompanied by selective rehabilitation and removal of bottlenecks, to allow fuller use of existing capacity. In practice, there also has been pressure to shrink public employment and social services, and to attempt to recover services' costs by introducing fees. Finally, international donors and lenders have stressed financial liberalization to generate more domestic savings, and limitations on wage increases in order to combat inflation.

Since the mid-1980s, many African nations have gradually accepted these "structural adjustment programs" (SAPs). In large part, this acceptance reflects a lack of alternatives, plus an understanding that international support will occur only if reasonable adherence to SAPs occurs. But much of the acceptance is also genuine, and, in any event, there is no doubt that policy modifications during the past six years have been far more profound than in the period 1973–83.

Structural adjustment policies may *slow* the pace of urbanization significantly, especially in the medium term. One major reason involves the impact of reduced government expenditures on education on migration flows. Migrants from rural to urban areas tend to be better educated than their nonmigrating peers. Several explanations have been offered for this stylized fact, including the role that education plays in reducing the uncertainty (and hence cost) of a move and the fact that better-educated migrants will be able to more successfully compete for jobs in urban labor markets. The balanced budgets mandated by structural adjustment programs have reduced all types of social sector spending, including spending for education. Unable to obtain education—especially postprimary schooling—many individuals who previously might have migrated may stay at home.

Another impact of reductions in government spending mandated by structural adjustment programs involves the tightening of parastatal enterprises' budgets. Government-owned firms are particularly important in Africa, contributing between 12–14 percent of GDP in the mid-1980s (based on an unweighted average of twelve countries). Parastatals have frequently been managed with objectives other than profit maximization; one of these has been to provide employment for a large number of individuals. Parastatals' wage policies also have been designed to curry political favor rather than minimize labor costs. This was possible because parastatals traditionally have faced rather soft budget constraints, and workers' demands were accommodated by additional transfers from the central government if such transfers were feasible. Much of this rent-sharing behavior may have been reduced with the introduction of structural adjustment policies. To the extent that above-market salaries in parastatal enterprises lured potential migrants, the attractiveness of this lure has declined as real wages have dropped and employment possibilities worsened during the past fifteen years.

Devaluation and trade liberalization also may slow urbanization. Devaluation will increase migration to areas in which export production takes place. Traditional exports from sub-Saharan countries are agricultural and mineral goods. While some value added in these activities is produced in urban areas, a significant proportion is produced in rural areas. Trade liberalization, in contrast, is unambiguous in its effect on urbanization. Reduction in tariffs and nontariff barriers will reduce output and employment in import-substituting industries. If wages are downwardly flexible in these industries, potential migrants will be discouraged by both lower wages and a lower probability of finding a job. If wages are not flexible, lower employment probabilities will still dissuade some potential migrants. Furthermore, the declines in value of production in urban manufacturing will have demand-linkage and income-spending effects that cause employment to fall in the service sectors and in small-scale manufacturing.

On the other hand, devaluation can be expected to result in expanded exports, and hence greater availability of foreign exchange. In economies where foreign exchange is scarce and is allocated in a non-market fashion, import shortages will accompany export stagnation. These shortages will affect urban industries particularly severely, causing them to curtail output and employment. To the extent that SAPs generate growing exports (or simply growing foreign exchange availability, since the international community has tended to be fairly generous with aid to those countries that agree to implement SAPs), they may generate renewed urban growth, especially in the long run. Our belief, however, is that this effect probably is not as strong as the many growth-restricting effects, especially in the short run.

Unfortunately, the policies prescribed by the international donor/lender community generally have ignored urban areas and the local institutions that must manage them. This lack of attention is truly problematic, for most problems and most solutions transcend sectoral and geographic boundaries. Even problems usually considered "rural" in nature often involve cities and towns.

Among the historical antecedents of the present crisis that are ignored, for example, is the evolution of local government in sub-Saharan Africa. The conventional wisdom in the region following Independence was that centralized decision making was the key to rapid socioeconomic change and to development freed from parochial self-interest. Local autonomy was identified with the notion of competing centers of power and patronage, at a time when pluralism was increasingly unacceptable. Finally, the concern with local administrative inefficiency was addressed not by an active defense of local institutions, but by a strategy that assumed such shortcomings could be avoided by centralization. Instead, the result was waste and ineffective governance, and a massive neglect of local infrastructure networks and services, without which the other "sectors" of the economy cannot operate effectively.

To resolve Africa's economic problems, a new sensitivity is needed, among donors and governments alike, concerning the role of cities and towns. The degree to which the urban environment is supportive of productive activities will affect significantly the attainment of agricultural and industrial sector objectives. Efforts to increase resource mobilization, cut subsidies, and redirect expenditures will encounter severe difficulties unless the urban agenda is addressed.

More generally, it is important to understand the linkages between macro and urban policies. Macroeconomic policies affect rural-urban migration by altering differences in returns to economic activities in different regions, and by altering relative living costs. Food and commodity pricing policies have particularly important differential impacts on the residents of rural and urban areas. Urban housing and infrastructure policies affect the relative attractiveness of urban life (and hence migration rates); they also affect the rate of public capital formation, the government's budgetary position, and the delivery of services to rural areas. Urban employment creation programs affect the same variables. Location and decentralization policies affect the productivity of modern sector firms, thereby influencing the viability of the industrial sector and rate of capital formation.

It is especially important to design urban sectoral policies that further national economic growth and improve standards of living for the poor in both rural and urban areas. Appropriate industrial location policies, coordination of infrastructural planning with major investment projects, promotion of urban areas that serve the needs of a healthy agricultural sector, and policies that improve the integration of urban areas with labor and other markets in their hinterlands are among the key topics that must be addressed. A particularly difficult problem involves the reduction of effective subsidies in food pricing and social services that benefit skilled and many unskilled workers in urban Africa, as removal of these privileges may provoke violent reactions from those who lose their benefits.

In summary, urban policies have important impacts on short- and medium-run macroeconomic outcomes, while short-run macroeconomic policies also effectively delimit urban policies. At the same time, there are important long-run linkages between urbanization and economic growth, and these also need to be understood. Furthermore, these linkages must be incorporated into long-run economic models of African nations, and also into long-run policy plans.

1.3 The Theory of Urbanization and Long-Run Development

Volumes of statistics and many studies provide strong evidence that increased urbanization typically accompanies economic development. It is no surprise, then, that the world's less developed countries are becoming progressively more urban over time, and Africa is no exception to this trend. The positive correlation between levels of urbanization and economic development is intriguing, although the direction of causality is far from clear. Does increased urbanization cause increases in per capita income and other measures of economic welfare? Or does increased income lead to urbanization?

Cases can be made for both arguments. Urbanization—when driven by rural-urban migration—tends to move workers to higher productivity occupations. Urban service, commerce, and manufacturing sectors, for example, may have significantly higher labor productivity than found in low-surplus agriculture.[3] In practice, however, care must be taken in assessing the productivity benefits of rural-to-urban migration, since productivity calculations take rural-urban relative prices as a given and these prices may be systematically distorted in favor of urban activities. Unfortunately, macro analysts generally have ignored this problem, and in consequence have been biased toward policies that redistribute resources to (urban) sectors with price distortions that make their output appear more valuable than would be the case at world prices.

Urbanization also will create agglomeration economies. Agglomeration economies are cost advantages that accrue to firms that locate in close geographic proximity to one other. Urban economists typically distinguish between two types of agglomeration economies: *localization economies*, which benefit only firms within a specific industry, and *urbanization economies*, which benefit all firms located in an urban area. Factors such as better or cheaper access to intermediate inputs or specialized labor pools and communication among specialists involved in production fall under the heading of localization economies. Urbanization economies may involve such factors as better-developed insurance and banking services, high-quality public infrastructure (roads, communication links, ports), and well-developed public services (sewerage, electric service). In addition, within individual firms average costs of production may fall over a considerable range of output and employment: that is, most African enterprises, especially in manufacturing, have substantial scope to realize *scale economies*.

Urbanization also may contribute to economic development in more subtle ways. Urbanization (and, unquestionably, extensions of female schooling associated with urbanization) may lead to lower levels of fertility, which in turn permit faster growth in per capita income for a given rate of total income growth.[4] Mortality will decline as well, as individuals will benefit from closer access to health care providers. Urbanization—and the increased population density that it creates—may make economically feasible the production of goods that previously could not be produced because of prohibitive transportation costs.

The political consequences of urbanization may also foster economic development. Urbanization is typically accompanied by the expansion of the middle class, as bankers, engineers, doctors, and other professionals find a market for their services. This middle class is a powerful political constituency which may demand more intelligent and enlightened development policy choices.

But it is also possible to argue that urbanization is a consequence rather than the cause of economic development. Changes in demand patterns that often accompany economic development stimulate demand for urban-produced goods. The limited increase in demand for agricultural products in response to increases in income levels causes the agricultural sector to shrink relative to the nonagricultural sector during the development process.

There are many natural forces of economic development that make cities more attractive over time, and thus pull in rural migrants. With economic development, demand patterns shift toward urban products, and capital formation occurs at higher rates in urban activities. Employment opportunities therefore grow more rapidly in urban areas. Education and other modern services can be provided more efficiently in densely populated areas; those seeking them will migrate as well. As a nation's skilled labor force grows, costs in skill-intensive urban industries will fall, making them more competitive, and inducing them to expand. Efficient use of much infrastructure also necessitates dense populations, so that it too is concentrated in cities. As infrastructure expands, production costs again fall for urban industries and services.

Perhaps the most likely explanation is that urbanization is both cause and consequence of economic development. But whatever the direction of causality, one thing is clear: urbanization is a key part of the development process.

The question remains, though, as to whether urbanization is of particular economic importance in Africa. At first glance, Africa seems a singularly peculiar region to use as material for the study of urbanization. Africa is, after all, one of the least urbanized of the world's regions. According to U.N. projections, 39 percent of Africa's population will live in urban areas in the year 2000. This compares with over 76 percent in Latin America, and 75 percent in North America and in Europe. Only Asia is projected to have comparably low levels of urbanization, with 35 percent of its population living in urban areas.

While possessing one of the world's lowest urbanization levels, however, Africa has by far the most rapid rate of *urban population growth*. The United Nations projects an annual growth rate of urban population of 4.5 percent for the years 2000–2005.[5] This continent-wide average conceals some regional diversity; central Africa's urban population is projected to grow most rapidly (5.6 percent), while southern Africa's urban population is projected to grow most slowly (3.2 percent). It is somewhat startling to note that the urban population of southern Africa nonetheless is expected to grow more rapidly than that of any other continent. Asian urban population is projected to grow at 3.0 percent per year, and Latin American, North American, and European urban populations at much slower rates (see Tables 2.5 and 2.6 for more detail on international comparisons).

Africa's extraordinarily rapid urban population growth in the past three decades has had important economic impacts. Of great concern to African policymakers is the budgetary strain placed by demands for expanded provision of public services. Increased levels of negative externalities, such as congestion and pollution, also are undesirable by-products of urbanization. The per unit cost of providing public services also may rise after some particular city size is surpassed. Some economists have argued that it is possible to calculate an optimal city size at which the unit costs of infrastructure and public services are at their minimum. Unfortunately, calculations of optimal city size have shown great sensitivity to the parameters used to compute them, and the estimated range for optimal size consequently has been quite large (see Wheaton and Shishido [1981], Henderson [1988], and Shukla and Stark [1990]). In addition, such naive calculations ignore the benefits of living and working in cities of different sizes.

Other important—if difficult to quantify—effects of urbanization have been positive. To the extent they have been realized, agglomeration economies have undoubtedly lowered the cost of doing business for urban firms. As writing on city systems has made clear, larger cities produce a wider variety of goods and services than smaller cities. Increased choice of consumer goods and services, other factors being equal, increases the welfare of residents of larger urban centers relative to the welfare of smaller urban centers and rural areas.

Africa's rapid urbanization during the 1970s and 1980s is in itself likely evidence that this growth was welfare enhancing. Migrants continued moving to Africa's cities despite increases in open unemployment and underemployment rates. As has been shown in the economic migration literature, such behavior is entirely consistent with rational, utility-maximizing migrants. If migrants move because expected earnings are higher in urban areas, some will lose this bet and instead suffer unemployment or severe underemployment. On average, nonetheless, migrants must be better off in urban areas, or rural-urban migration flows would slow. The only possible slip between migration flows and welfare improvement would be if migration flows produced large enough negative externalities that were not incorporated into migrants' decision calculus. In such a case, migration could be individually optimizing but socially undesirable.

1.4 Other Issues in African Urbanization

Structural adjustment will be an important determinant of African urbanization in coming years. And when structural adjustment policies are replaced by some alternate set of macroeconomic policies, these new policies will affect migration flows and urbanization. The moral is clear: macroeconomic conditions are powerful determinants of urbanization patterns. But other forces matter as well.

To begin with, *demographic trends* will also affect urbanization rates. Africa possesses one of the youngest population pyramids of any region in the world. As birth rates slowly drop, the rate of growth of the pool of young adults—those individuals at greatest risk to migrate—will also slow.

The existing *structure of African national city systems* also will condition the evolution of these very systems. Very decentralized city systems (e.g., Nigeria) will not become centralized ("primate") overnight, nor will primate systems become rapidly decentralized. City systems have evolved in response to a complex set of influences, including European colonization patterns, geographical features of the national terrain, long-standing trading routes, and a host of other factors. Macroeconomic policies and demographic trends will influence the evolution of these systems but will not transform them instantaneously.

While all African urban areas have grown rapidly, the largest cities typically have grown most rapidly. In 1980, some 36 percent of the urban population in a typical African nation lived in the largest city—an increase from 28 percent in 1960. Urban populations as a whole are growing at an annual rate of nearly 6 percent, but capital cities have been averaging roughly 8.5 percent. This growing primacy has been of considerable concern to governments, which have responded with plans to decentralize industry and employment. It is far from obvious that decentralization itself is desirable. But given the clear political desire for a reduction in urban primacy, it is important to investigate means of decentralization that do not greatly sacrifice productivity and capital formation.

The *structure of factor markets* also will influence migration and urbanization trends. The structure and behavior of urban formal and informal labor markets are of crucial importance in determining urbanization trends. Are urban minimum wages set at above equilibrium levels? How much mobility is there between urban formal and informal sectors? How do migrants gauge the relative probability of employment in the two sectors? The usual focus in migration analysis is on the struc--

ture of labor markets, but capital market conditions may also influence migration decisions (Stark [1991]). In particular, credit market segmentation that denies smallholders access to loans may stimulate migration from rural areas.

Employment growth in predominately urban occupations also has been slow in most of Africa. In particular, the percentage of the labor force working in industry has been almost stagnant since the mid-1970s (with a few notable exceptions). The share of Africans living in cities rose from 14 percent in 1965 to 22 percent in 1980; during this period the proportion of the labor force in industry rose from 6 percent to 8 percent. Since 1980, urban growth has slackened little, while the industrial employment share probably has stagnated. It is not surprise, then, that industrial employment and production growth is a primary concern of African policymakers.

Weak "formal" sector employment growth has given rise to increasing (if often unenthusiastic) awareness of the *potential of "informal" or "intermediate" sector employment*, especially in cities and towns. The extent to which such activities can accommodate productive employment needs, provide adequate incomes, and provide spillover benefits to other sectors demands careful examination. It is also important to design macroeconomic and sectoral policies that are not strongly biased against the informal sector.

Finally, the *roles of price distortions and trade policy* also merit attention. Internal and international relative prices are viewed in neoclassical economic theory as being critical determinants of behavioral incentives, and hence outcomes. In a partial equilibrium setting, it is clear that overvalued exchange rates and low agricultural prices favor the growth of urban areas; in a general equilibrium setting the outcome is not quite so obvious.

1.5 Five Urban Policy Themes

Thus far, we have outlined how urbanization affects economic performance in Africa, and how macroeconomic policies affect urban growth. The remaining analytical task in this chapter is to discuss the effects of urban policies that are common in Africa. There are, of course, many such policies, but for the sake of brevity we consider five major themes or tenets that have been common to policymakers throughout the continent. These themes are discussed here at the outset only briefly, but will be referred to frequently in the coming pages.

Population Densities

A striking feature of African cities is their low population densities relative to those of Asia or Latin America. Moreover, while many of the poor live on the periphery of urban areas in much of the Third World, this feature seems to be particularly prevalent in Africa. Central areas often are modern, (neo-) colonial enclaves, with a distinct area usually reserved for modern industrial activity. Much of the urban poor and working class live in fairly isolated ghettos, often far from the city center or industrial areas (detailed examples are provided in the *Southern African Economist* [1990]).

These low urban densities are likely to result in unnecessarily high unit costs of urban infrastructure. As we argue in the following chapters, the high unit costs of transport and utilities have exerted an underappreciated drag on African industries. Decentralization will also prevent many urban residents from enjoying access to various amenities.

The causes of this low population density are not entirely obvious. Part of the problem is the inherited colonial legacy, which sought to encourage racial segregation and keep the indigenous African population under "control." A pervasive planning mentality also may be partly responsible, as may be a desire by officials to restrict access to public services. But poorly defined land markets and other property rights also may have been important, since uncertainty discourages density-increasing investments (or sales) by people currently occupying urban space. In any event, though, African governments have taken many steps that effectively limited population density, and few that raised densities. These policies must be reexamined.

Excessive Urbanization

A common view is that the rate of urbanization is excessive, as is the rate of growth of the urban population. The belief in part stems from concern over and fear of the large proportion of visibly unemployed or underemployed individuals in many African cities. A common conclusion drawn is that rural-urban migration is excessive and should be curtailed.

In the following chapters, we argue that urbanization is an inevitable consequence of successful urban economic development and of rural stagnation. It certainly is inappropriate to regard migration as an undesirable force that must be suppressed. Migration instead should be recognized as an equilibrating response to disequilibrium elsewhere in the economy. Africans migrate to cities because they believe the opportunities to be better there. Nor is there any evidence that African migrants are mistaken in their belief. The highest urbanization rates in 1987 (World Bank, [1989a]) were associated with countries that had experienced periods of rapid economic growth (Côte d'Ivoire, 44 percent urban; Cameroon, 46 percent; Congo, 41 percent; Gabon, 43 percent) or had undergone dramatic rural declines (Liberia, 42 percent urban; Mauritania, 38 percent; Somalia, 36 percent; Central African Republic, 45 percent), or experienced rural neglect (Zambia, 53 percent urban).

African cities also grow rapidly because the entire population is growing rapidly, and because conditions continually foster far more rapid growth of economic and educational opportunities in most urban than in most rural areas. As capital cities tend to be the most favored cities, they grow more rapidly still.

Even successful agricultural growth may give rise to urbanization.[6] In each of the major success stories of African agriculture over the past thirty years the urban population grew more rapidly than the continental average (Cameroon, 8.6 percent per annum between 1973 and 1980; Kenya 8.5 percent; Malawi, 7.9 percent; Côte d'Ivoire, 7.3 percent; versus an African average of 5.7 percent). Agricultural growth generates needs for agricultural implements and services; it also creates opportunities for agricultural processing industries, and for the production of consumer durables for farmers. In some instances, labor-saving biases in agricultural technological improvements also may release labor to urban areas.[7] Perhaps most importantly, agricultural growth means growing exports, and hence increasing capacity to import the goods needed to run urban industries.

Nevertheless, many inducements to migrate do not derive from natural economic forces, but are instead due to public policies that unintentionally and inappropriately favor urban areas. Pricing policies, wage policies, and employment maintenance policies all favor urban formal sector activities, as does the provision of urban services. On the other hand, the tendency for many African governments to pursue industrial policies that generate little employment growth may have had the side effect of stemming urbanization.

Excess Primacy

Another strongly held view is that current city-size distributions are too primate—that is, that their urban populations are too concentrated in a few large cities. African policymakers, like those in Latin America and Asia, are particularly interested in restricting the growth rates of their largest cities. These cities, including most capitals, are indeed growing more rapidly than the urban population as a whole. Furthermore (see Chapter 3), many African countries do have city-size distributions that are extraordinarily primate by world standards. Sierra Leone, Malawi, Côte d'Ivoire, Zimbabwe, and Cameroon are all exceptionally primate, but Botswana, Niger, Nigeria, and Lesotho all have unusually unconcentrated urban populations.

The desire to decentralize is driven by many factors. In an overwhelmingly rural continent, it is important to create an urban structure capable of handling the marketing and other needs of rural areas, and such considerations make some spatial diffusion of the urban population desirable. This has given rise to the policy of creating "growth centers," medium-sized cities in agricultural areas charged with providing basic agricultural processing industries as well as services to nearby rural areas (see Gaile [1988b] and [1990], Gaile and Aspaas [1991], and Rondinelli [1982] and [1983]). Political considerations may require regional policies that distribute scarce resources to an inefficiently large number of urban areas and ethnic groups.

Other forces that give rise to concerns of excessive primacy include 1) the presumed high level of unemployment spawned by rapid urbanization, 2) concerns about the largest cities exceeding their optimal sizes, and 3) the supposed "need" for a balanced city system. The concern about unemployment is a reasonable one, given that even the most rapidly growing African economies are unlikely to generate sufficient urban modern sector employment to absorb all aspirants to modern sector employment. Unfortunately, no easy policy options exist. Neither Tanzania's strategy during the mid-1970s of "eliminating" unemployment by returning unemployed rural-urban migrants to their village of origin nor Kenya's recent bulldozing of squatter settlements is appropriate policy. Urban modern sector job creation is expensive and may attract more new job seekers than the number of individuals removed from unemployment. Food subsidies and urban incomes policies are also unwieldy policy tools, and are out of the financial reach of poorer African governments. But problems with other policies do not imply that curtailing growth of the largest cities is desirable.

Concerns about the continent's largest cities exceeding their optimal size are misguided for the simple reason that optimal size calculations are extraordinarily imprecise. If, for example, the optimal size is found to be (as is often the case) between 100,000 and 1,000,000 inhabitants, policy implications for a large number of cities falling within this range are unclear. Should further growth be encouraged or discouraged?

It is also far from obvious that African nations lack balanced city systems. It is important to note that even the largest African cities are not large by international standards, and only four cities (Brazzaville, Dakar, Cotonou, and Conakry) contained more than 15 percent of their national populations in the mid-1980s. At least on the basis of naive international comparisons, African city systems do not seem overly primate.

Nor is there generally a clear "optimum" city-size distribution. In their analysis of India's decentralization schemes, Mills and Becker (1986) find little reason to suspect that such policies enhance any reasonable measure of social welfare. City-size distributions that evolve do so in response to market- and government-generated incentives. If government chooses its spatial production decisions so as to minimize the costs of producing its desired bundle of services, then the resulting endogenous city-size distribution will be an efficient one.[8] While there are many externalities and income distribution considerations that warrant public sector intervention in the economy to restore socially efficient production patterns, none of these considerations involve direct restrictions on urban growth as a first-best policy. It is, for example, better to deal with the problems of urban congestion by better transport management than by limiting the sizes of large cities. If large cities such as Lagos require huge investments in transport infrastructure, then in principle its road users should be compelled to meet these costs, rather than being arbitrarily limited in number. Similarly, income transfers caused by increased land prices are best dealt with through the tax system. Migration restrictions and land-use controls are second-best policies that may impose significant costs in other areas in order to achieve the primary objective.

Maintaining Standards

Africa's colonial cities were characterized by a high level of social services for the expatriate population, and a very low level for the indigenous African population. With Independence, there was a broad mandate to extend services to the previously unfavored African urban working classes. Urban infrastructure commitments soared. By the mid-1970s, increases in government expenditures on social services *excluding* education had come to exceed growth in government expenditures on agriculture in all but the semiarid countries.

But expanding urban social services made cities all the more attractive, and induced further rural-urban migration. The proportion of urban populations living in squatter settlements failed to decline despite a flurry of public housing projects. Standards of education and social services could not be maintained at close-to-European levels. In fact, as virtually all African nations have come to realize, even the level of services provided to the relatively small and favored urban working and middle classes in the 1960s could not be maintained, given the massive urban growth rates that have occurred.

How important have been expenditures on urban social infrastructure? It is difficult to generate an accurate estimate, but some indications are available. If we assume that the urban share of all noneducation social services is half of the national total (almost certainly an understatement), then just over 9 percent of central government expenditures would on average be devoted to urban social amenities and infrastructure. Yet even in Tanzania, which has avoided excessive provision more effectively than most countries, the stated goal of the Second Five Year Plan (United Republic of Tanzania [1969: vol.1, p.185]) was to keep "public resources for urban infrastructure . . . below ten percent of the total central government budget." As a rough guess, then, it seems likely that the average African government may spend 10–15 percent of central expenditures on urban services and social infrastructure, excluding education.

African governments thus have spent large portions of their budgets on urban services, largely in an attempt to provide unsustainably high service levels to a small segment of the national population. These policies began to be reversed in the 1980s (and, in several countries, expenditures on urban services virtually collapsed), but are far from dead. Many countries' social service policies are inegalitarian and inefficient. Because extensive services cannot be provided universally, only a favored few can benefit. And since these services are concentrated in the largest urban areas, migrants are drawn to these cities by the possibility of receiving some of the government's largesse, in addition to being drawn by normal market forces. Consequently, the largest cities grow even faster than they would otherwise. Finally, government service expenditures drain resources from employment-creating investment projects, thereby lowering national productivity growth.

Many governments have attempted to maintain relatively high wages for their formal sector workers as well. Many also have made commitments to expand formal sector employment, or at least to maintain it during periods of economic recession. These well-intentioned efforts also have undesirable side effects, and lead to real urban/rural wage gaps that until recently were far higher than elsewhere in the developing world. These wage gaps induced further rural-urban migration, and quite likely a higher urban unemployment rate than otherwise would have prevailed. Again, because the urban formal sector is concentrated in the largest cities, it is they that experience the highest in-migration rates.

Wage and employment support policies also severely reduce parastatals' profits, and thereby reduce rates of capital formation. At least in Zambia, those public enterprises able to shed excess labor during its prolonged depression were often the relatively profitable ones (Becker [1985]). Nor does there appear to be a link at the margin between employment growth and output growth across Zambia's parastatals.

Private sector firms subject to government wage policy are also likely to avoid further expansion of employment, or will extract effective compensation from the government for the additional wage burden. African economists such as Rweyemamu (1973) have claimed that multinationals' investments, as a consequence of these unnecessarily high labor costs, tend to be biased toward production of import substitutes for the internal market behind a high tariff wall. Since most African countries have small markets, the industrial sector thus has come to be characterized by inefficient monopolies, with high wages and capital-intensive techniques. This cannot possibly be a desirable pattern of industrial production.

In summary, African government efforts to maintain service and wage standards have had many undesirable effects, and may have been counterproductive as well. High wage standards have prevented employment growth. Excessive hiring in response to government exhortations to increase formal sector employment may have worked in the short run, but its curtailment of profits and hence reinvestment have led to reduced labor demand in the long run. Labor-saving innovations in response to high wages have further restricted employment growth. These innovations remain in place even now that real wages have fallen steeply across the continent. Nor has Africa's ailing industrial base been able to provide growing tax revenues, thus tightly constraining government social expenditures.

Distrust of the Informal Sector

A final pervasive article of faith in African governments' urban sector policies has been a distaste for economic activities outside the formal sector. Perhaps because of the difficulty in taxing this sector, the small-scale manufacturing and service activities that comprise the informal or "microenterprise" sector are viewed by government officials as being incapable of self-sustaining economic growth.

In reality, the informal sector enjoys a largely symbiotic relationship with the modern manufacturing and service sectors. The informal sector mainly produces consumer durables, nondurables and services, and some intermediate goods and repair services for the formal sectors. Consequently, its demand is a derived one, and depends on formal sector incomes.

Many consumer goods produced in the informal sector, however, compete directly with modern sector production and with imports. Since local content is much higher in informal sector production, though, domestic resource cost ratios (an indication of international competitiveness) will be far lower than in the modern sector, unless the economies of scale realized by the latter are quite great.

In sum, most African informal sectors are relatively efficient producers of many goods, including a wide range of import substitutes. They are also a critical source of employment, particularly for those without the skills or connections to obtain a formal sector job. As its investments are self-financed, informal sector growth is unlikely to reduce significantly investable resources from other sectors (at least not the urban formal sector). The sector is also a spawning ground for indigenous entrepreneurial talent.

In view of these considerations, it seems highly inappropriate to suppress or discourage the informal sector. Urban sector policies such as land-use controls, combined with various licensing requirements and weak small-scale credit markets, do have a constraining effect, though. Unreasonably high standards for materials used by government or in government-funded projects (especially self-help housing projects) also reduce demand for informal sector goods.

1.6 The Agenda

Thus far, we have established the connections between urbanization and economic growth, both in the short and longer terms, along with the possibility that African urban policies may have been seriously misguided. The remainder of this book examines the evolution of African city systems, charting the contribution of migration and other factors to urban growth. The structure of urban labor markets will receive special attention, as will models attempting to explain why rural-urban migration flows occur. Armed with this analysis, we will then be in a position to assess future African urbanization patterns, and to suggest macroeconomic and urban sector policies that will interact effectively.

Chapter 2 begins by exploring the role of urban centers in African economies. What roles do cities play in economic development? The urban sector's share of GDP growth is likely to exceed its share in output, largely because technological gains are likely to be concentrated in modern market sector activities. Typically, all sectors purchase urban-produced goods. Agricultural production uses manufactured inputs, even in very poor countries. Consumption goods will include some domestically produced manufactures and many specialized services that are produced in the urban sector.

Emphasizing the contribution of urban production to national output is not the same as a plea for urban-biased policies; neglect of the agricultural sector is a major policy error. One reason is that the rural poor—the poorest of all Africans—will suffer if small-scale agriculture declines. Not only the rural poor suffer when agriculture is neglected, though; due to pervasive urban-rural links, the welfare of the vast majority of the population is linked, directly or indirectly, to agricultural performance. These links between urban and rural sectors are investigated in section 2.2.

Section 2.3 compares Africa's urbanization levels and rates with those found in other regions of the world. World Bank and U.N. data show Africa to be the most rapidly urbanizing region in the world. Section 2.4 then proceeds to document the pattern of urban productive activities in Africa. One important stylized fact is the importance of informal sector activities in urban production, even in the largest cities. Survey evidence indicates that over 50 percent of the urban labor force is typically found in the informal sector in the region's capital cities. Thus, labor force participation numbers argue for attention to the urban informal sector, but there is an equally potent reason for policymakers to focus on the urban informal sector: as structural adjustment proceeds, government subsidies to and protection of the modern sector will diminish, and a decreasing percentage of labor force entrants will be able to find work there. The informal sector is 1) already accustomed to responding to market-determined relative prices, 2) adept at providing for human capital accumulation via apprenticeships, 3) efficient at mustering savings via the reinvestment of small firms, and 4) able to satisfy a growing demand for customized and/or low-cost goods and services.

The rebirth of African modern sectors, as well as the growth of traditional sectors, is dependent upon progress in improving conditions that currently stifle their growth. Infrastructure must be improved (section 2.5), and land and capital markets must function more efficiently. Strategies for achieving these ends are outlined in sections 2.6 and 2.7. Finally, section 2.8 discusses policies to reinforce and develop the links between urban and rural sectors. Simply "getting (relative) prices right" is insufficient, since farmers react to an entire set of incentives, most of which are linked to the adequacy of urban-based infrastructure and services. Transportation networks between rural hinterlands and urban regional centers are also a key to establishing strong rural-urban links.

Chapter 3 analyzes the characteristics of African city systems and urban growth. It begins with an examination of the myth of overurbanization in section 3.1. A more careful analysis of the concentration within city systems is presented in section 3.2, which provides some standard measures of urban concentration. The results from this section are mixed; according to some measures of concentration African city systems are somewhat more primate than city systems of other less-developed countries, while according to others, African city systems are not particularly concentrated.

While the summary measures of urban concentration provide a convenient but highly simplified snapshot of a nation's urban system, they provide no explanation for why this urban structure evolved as it did. Section 3.3 addresses this concern, analyzing and applying theories of urban location such as central place theory, geographical explanations hinging on terrain and climate, and historical explanations. Section 3.4 builds on section 3.3, delineating factors that contribute to city growth and changes in city systems.

Finally, section 3.5 applies two important theories from the international trade literature to analyze the impact of the capital intensivity of production on a nation's city system. The maintained hypothesis is that the more capital intensive production is in a country, the greater the percentage of large cities it will possess. Empirical tests reveal only a weak relationship between the two variables. This section also reports more extensive tests of the economic determinants of urban concentration.

Chapter 4 examines the role of migration in African urbanization. A major focus of this chapter is the analysis of the social (section 4.2.1), economic (sections 4.2.2 through 4.2.6), and demographic (section 4.2.7) factors determining the magnitude of migration flows. Important social factors include desire to improve social status or, in the case of women, to escape the weak social position of childless women in traditional cultures.

The economic factors are presented in systematic fashion by identifying those variables included in various theories of urbanization and migration. The urban bias thesis (section 4.2.2) suggests that urban producers and consumers are favored in governments' allocation of public spending and service provision; simultaneously, rural residents are hurt by pricing and tax policy. Evidence suggests that such biases have been quite common in Africa. The Harris-Todaro migration model, which posits that migrants move in because of higher expected wages in urban areas, is presented in section 4.2.4. This model focuses attention on the role of urban minimum wages, adjusted for the presence of open unemployment in urban areas, in determining migration flows. The labor turnover model (section 4.2.5) modifies the Harris-Todaro model to take account of the fact that urban modern sector jobs are quite difficult to obtain. Because workers who obtain such employment are likely to remain in these jobs for a long time, labor turnover is quite low. This means that new migrants will find few vacancies in the modern sector and thus redirects our attention to conditions in urban informal sector labor markets as an important determinant of migration flows. Section 4.2.6 presents a queuing model of migration. Because in many African countries the supply of educated workers has expanded more quickly than the demand for skilled labor, educated workers have begun to "filter down" into low-skill jobs. This model focuses our attention on the education profile of migrants and the role that education plays as a screening device in hiring decisions.

Demographic factors (section 4.2.7) are also crucial determinants of the size of migration flows and pace of urbanization. The demographic approach emphasizes that the educational, age, and sex composition of populations "at risk" to migrate is an important determinant of the size of migration flows. Specifically, populations which are more heavily male, young, and better educated will have higher migration rates.

After identifying the principal factors determining the size of migration flows, Chapter 4 turns to an analysis of the consequences of rural-urban migration (section 4.3). Migration will affect labor supply in both source and destination regions. Financial flows often link migrants with relatives who remain in source regions; initially the flow of resources is to the migrant to support his job search activity, but later flows are remittances from successful migrants to relatives. In destination regions, increased migration generally will give rise to higher unemployment and greater strain on municipal and national budgets. At the national level, migration typically will affect fertility rates, although there is debate about how much fertility will be lowered. From an economic viewpoint, perhaps the most important national consequence of migration is its effect on output. Since most capital accumulation occurs in large cities, labor is likely to have a higher marginal productivity there, and the transfer of labor from rural to urban areas typically will raise measured output (subject to the caveats about price distortions mentioned above).

Policy responses to migration are analyzed in section 4.4. Policies to 1) reduce the stock of potential migrants, 2) decrease the flow of migrants by inducing potential migrants to remain in source regions, 3) create attractive alternative destinations, and 4) successfully absorb migrants into their preferred destinations are examined in this section. Finally, section 4.5 assesses the effect of World Bank and other international agencies' macroeconomic and sectoral policies on urbanization, while section 4.6 examines more closely the shifts in migration incentives stemming from the introduction of structural adjustment policies.

Chapter 5 analyzes employment growth and the wage structure in African urban formal and informal sectors. Recent trends in employment and wages are charted, and the effect of interventionist state policies on formal sector labor markets is assessed. Structural adjustment has reduced the wage gap between formal and informal sectors in most countries, although absolute wages in both sectors typically have fallen. Despite the existing wage gap, some evidence suggests that total factor productivity is higher in informal sectors.

Section 5.3 turns from formal-informal wage gaps to rural-urban wage gaps. Two salient characteristics of rural-urban wage gaps deserve emphasis. First, the size of the rural-urban gap varies greatly across countries. As an extreme example, estimates for the 1970s ranged from 1:6 in Sierra Leone to 1:1 in Senegal (see Table 5.7). Second, available evidence supports the contention that rural-urban wage gaps have been falling over time; such an outcome is to be expected in an era of structural adjustment. Finally, section 5.4 examines the effect of the AIDS pandemic on African labor markets and economic growth. This analysis suggests that while the human costs of AIDS will be staggering, the economic costs may not be that large.

Chapter 6 returns to the theme of migration. If intelligent policy is to influence migration streams, policymakers must be confident that they understand the causes of these streams. To address this concern, this chapter presents several competing migration models and assesses their ability to capture African reality. The "candidate" models include a neoclassical model of migration, a rent-seeking model in which urban formal sector workers are able to capture a share of economic rents, and a demographic cohort shift model that disaggregates migration flows by important demographic and human capital characteristics. Some support is found for all three models, but the rent-seeking model seems a better description of African reality than the neoclassical model. The demographic cohort shift model is especially useful in predicting the future evolution of migration streams.

Chapter 7 concludes the book by offering an integrated set of macroeconomic and urban strategies. The chapter focuses on achieving balanced growth, with output gains in both rural and urban areas. It also emphasizes the need to increase rates of capital accumulation, and to modify industrial development strategies to accommodate continued rapid population growth and urbanization. Microeconomic policies involving increased local autonomy and improved factor market operations are also analyzed.

This book is a lengthy document, and each chapter has important lessons for policymakers. It might be useful to summarize some of the more important results in one place at the outset; more detail, of course, is offered in later chapters.

Perhaps the most fundamental conclusion of this book is that the old, comforting wisdoms about African urbanization have little relevance today. Urbanization in many cases has not been excessive, and it is impossible to define an optimal city size; city systems cannot be classified as too primate, since an "optimal" degree of primacy cannot be identified; colonial standards for urban wages and public services cannot and should not be maintained; governments' distrust and suspicion of activities taking place outside of the formal sector is unwarranted and unwise, since these activities may be particularly dynamic, enjoy a symbiotic relationship with the formal sector, and use input combinations that are more consistent with national factor endowments.

If the old, conventional wisdoms cannot guide informed policy, what can? An important first step toward intelligent policy-making is recognition of the heterogeneity of African urban centers, both within a given country and between countries. The percentage of urban labor force working in small enterprises is quite large. This is one reason why policymakers should concern themselves with microenterprises. But the fact of the matter is that policymakers may have little choice in the matter: with the continuing implementation of SAPs the protection of large-scale, formal enterprises will become a policy of the past. Nor should such a policy change be lamented. There is some evidence that total factor productivity is higher for informal firms than for formal sector firms. In addition, the urban informal sector has absorbed much of the growth of the labor force in the 1970s and 1980s.

In contrast, African formal sectors—especially manufacturing sectors—have had quite mediocre employment performance over the 1970s and 1980s. Manufacturing sectors in several of the larger countries suffered absolute declines in employment in the early and mid-1980s. Aside from limited employment growth, African formal sectors have a host of other unattractive attributes: dominance by parastatal firms, low-capacity utilization, high dependence of imported intermediate and capital goods, and low levels of efficiency due to insulation from foreign competition. Not surprisingly given the slow employment growth in formal sectors, only a small portion of urban population growth rates can be explained by employment growth in the urban formal sector. Dependence on imported intermediate and capital goods has certainly played a key role here; as traditional export sectors were ignored in development programs focused on import substitution industrialization, the growth of import-dependent formal sectors was limited by a lack of availability of foreign exchange. But as is argued in more detail in the following chapters, the policy response to this situation should not simply be a reactivation of traditional export activities in order to finance continued import substitution industrialization.

Real wages in the formal sector have fallen substantially during the 1970s and 1980s. Interestingly, some of these declines preceded the onset of SAPs. It is not surprising—given the collapse in formal sector real wages—that there was significant narrowing of formal/informal sector wage gaps during the 1980s. Not only wages have become more similar: security and stability of formal sector employment has declined as labor legislation has become less binding and the region's economic crisis has become more severe.

The conventional wisdom has been that the urban informal and formal sectors are linked only very tenuously. In one sense, the conventional wisdom is correct: informal firms sell relatively little output to formal sector firms. But the two sectors are linked in another way: formal sector workers are a key component of demand for goods and services produced in the informal sector. Thus, expansion of the formal sector is likely to have important multiplier effects on the informal sector, despite the paucity of productive linkages.

Mirroring the decline in formal/informal sector wage gaps, the wage gap between urban and rural areas has declined in most countries. This does not mean that there are not rural areas that continue to suffer severe poverty. The gaps have been narrowed largely because of the collapse of formal sector wages, not because of increases in real incomes in rural areas. We should note that further compression of urban formal sector wages is unlikely, however, since these wages are anchored by rural wages.

Many models of rural-urban migration focus on differences in expected wages as the prime determinant of the magnitude of migration flows. On the basis of these models, the reduction in urban/rural wage gaps should be expected to slow urbanization rates. Other factors clearly matter as well. Urban-biased policies quite clearly have contributed to Africa's rapid urbanization. We define a sectorally biased policy to be any policy that raises a sector's value added at domestic prices above that which would prevail at international prices. One particularly damaging form of urban bias has been the concentration of administrative decision-making and taxing powers at the national level. Such a policy favors the country's capital and largest urban centers, at the expense of small- and medium-sized cities and rural areas.

Urban-biased policies are under attack by the SAPs in place in most of the region. Devolution of decision-making and taxing authority by itself will not produce the hoped-for outcomes. The World Bank and other international agencies must take seriously the "institutional support components" of their projects. But the heaviest burden—and most responsibility—lies with African governments to provide the skilled labor with the educational characteristics needed to run these streamlined, new bureaucracies.

In sum, urban bias is neither statically nor dynamically efficient, and we advocate a balanced development policy. This definition seems to clash with Hirschman's (1961) notion of unbalanced development. It does not. Imbalances should be determined by market forces and returns, not by government edict.

National governments must formulate urban policies that consist of more than just a commitment to reduce urban bias. The fact of the matter is that urban areas are crucial to national economic development. Depending on the country, urban areas generate between 25 and 75 percent of GDP. Even if these figures are somewhat overstated by vestiges of urban bias in pricing policies, it is clear that urban economies must grow if there is to be significant expansion of national output.

In order to make such growth possible, governments must take certain steps. Perhaps the two most important are the provision of the infrastructure needed by urban firms and the correction of distortions and failures in factor markets. The provision of urban infrastructure is a task that can be postponed no longer; much vital infrastructure has fallen into disrepair due to inappropriate tax policies, lack of planning, and political instability. Productive infrastructure deficiencies (*e.g.*, water and electricity) directly lower firms' productivity. Other infrastructure deficiencies (*e.g.*, communications and transport) affect production indirectly by raising the cost of doing business. Firms can compensate for the lack of infrastructure, of course, but this adjustment almost always entails higher costs than the value of taxes to provide the infrastructure. The policy conclusion that governments must increase their tax effort and tax collection capability in order to provide appropriate infrastructure is far from glamorous. Yet failure to do so will carry a high cost in foregone economic growth.

Factor markets often have significant distortions in African economies. Labor markets have been addressed above; here the focus is on land and capital markets. The lack of a well-functioning market for urban land hinders urban development by increasing costs and uncertainty for both firms and individuals. There are often conflicting claims to parcels of urban land, and the possibility that another claimant may appear at some future date is a powerful disincentive to making capital improvements on a plot of land. The policy prescription to remedy this situation is straightforward: municipal governments must initiate progressively upgradable land information systems which record (at a minimum) the name of the owner, owner's agent, and occupant. The registration and titling of land is essential for urban economic growth to occur.

Distortions in capital markets must be eliminated ruthlessly. Subsidized loan programs generally keep credit from those very groups that they are designed to help. In sum, it is important to distinguish between capital scarcity (characteristic of almost all less-developed countries) and the inefficient allocation of the financial capital that is available. Capital markets should function efficiently, and equity concerns should be addressed by designing transfer programs that aid disadvantaged groups. SAPs have gone a long way toward eliminating loans at negative real interest rates. Positive real interest rates allow lending institutions to recoup funds that can then be lent to other individuals or firms.

SAPs seem to be slowing Africa's urbanization rate significantly. The explanations for such an effect are clear. Reductions in spending on social services curbs rural-urban migration, since these services tend to be concentrated in urban areas. Reductions in spending on educational programs reduce the pool of individuals "at-risk" to migrate, since educational attainment is strongly correlated with migration. The devaluations universally present in SAPs simultaneously boost rural agricultural and mineral production while decreasing the output of urban firms producing import substitutes. In the longer run, however, SAPs may create conditions necessary for renewed urban growth. Infrastructure revitalization will boost the productivity of urban firms, and to the extent that SAPs succeed in relieving foreign exchange bottlenecks, import-substituting firms may once again have access to the hard currency needed to import intermediate and capital goods. More generally, renewed economic growth will be urbanizing. Increasing incomes will boost the demand for urban-produced goods more than the demand for rural-produced items.

One must be a strong optimist to focus on the long-run positive impacts of SAPs. In the short run, the effect of SAPs on GDP growth rates is not as clear as the World Bank and the International Monetary Fund would have us believe. The higher growth rates reported for countries undertaking SAPs vis-à-vis those countries without SAPs may be little more than a direct result of the increased capital inflows which initially accompany the signing of a letter of intent with the International Monetary Fund. We cannot discard the potentially important impact of structural reforms, but it is hard to determine the relative importance of reforms versus capital inflows.

As of the early 1990s, in fact, the prospects for Africa's cities appear to be exceptionally bleak. Services have decayed terribly; no country can provide formal sector employment to match the growth in job seekers; industrial productivity is shockingly low; any increased dynamism of the private sector remains on the distant horizon; and social problems, including rising crime and HIV incidence, have become increasingly pervasive. In short, urban living standards have fallen greatly in the past decade, both for the poor and for many of the wealthy.

But the forces driving these problems are not mysterious; rather, because there are so many, they must be analyzed and treated in a comprehensive fashion. If they are, there is ample reason to believe that the coming decades will witness a gradual revival of Africa's cities, along with commensurate growth in its rural areas.

2

Urban Centers in African Economies

Why have urban centers arisen in sub-Saharan Africa? Are they central to the process of economic development, or does their growth in fact deter development? This chapter addresses these questions in an economic context, and, more generally, examines the economic roles played by African cities.

It is important to begin by stating a central finding from the empirical results generated by our demographic and economic models: African cities grow extremely rapidly, but do so for readily explicable reasons. Put differently, the forces driving patterns of growth and development of African cities are similar to those elsewhere, although the magnitudes are often vastly different—and differ across regions within Africa.

The fundamental economic rationale for the existence of urban areas is that they permit the realization of scale economies either within a production unit or external to it (in which case they are termed "agglomeration economies"), or they are driven by access to a spatially concentrated scarce resource. Chapter 2 translates this rather abstract statement into an examination of the roles played by African urban centers. Sections 2.1 and 2.2 examine the role of cities in economic development. Section 2.3 then considers the importance of linkages between rural and urban areas. Section 2.4 discusses characteristics of African urban growth, while Sections 2.5 and 2.6 focus on the characteristics of the sectors that comprise African urban economies. Sections 2.7 then evaluates some of the key bottlenecks facing urban sectors, while the final section examines economic policies designed to spur urban economic growth by reducing these bottlenecks.

2.1 The Role of the Urban Sector in the National Economy

One way to characterize African economies is to divide economic activity into non-marketed production (mainly for own-household consumption) and marketed production. Typically, though hardly uniformly, African households will participate in both sectors. Moreover, even in countries that have not experienced rising per

23

capita incomes, the importance of marketed production has been rising rapidly. Using this characterization, then, economic growth can come from technological gains in either the nonmarketed "subsistence" sector or in the market sector. Alternatively, it can result from shifts from low productivity nonmarket to higher productivity market sector activities.[1]

Especially in the absence of economic policies favorable to smallholder agriculture, subsistence sector productivity gains may well be limited and derived from the application of market sector technologies. Consequently, in the absence of dramatic labor shifts from the subsistence sector, recorded African economic growth will stem primarily from market sector productivity gains. As urban activities are disproportionately "modern" and marketed, the urban sector's share of increments to output is likely to exceed its share of total output. To reiterate, since urban activities provide close to a majority of market sector output, it is inevitable that measured African economic growth is inextricably linked to urban productivity gains.[2]

Nor is the link between economic development and urbanization limited to Africa. In general, however, an economy will not evolve without continuous spatial restructuring; people and jobs cannot simply increase in situ. The reason for this spatial transformation can be found by analyzing the emergence and increasing dominance of the market economy. In the pure subsistence economy without trade (an economy that exists almost exclusively as an abstract construct), all activity is for own household consumption. In such a subsistence setting, economic roles are largely undifferentiated and there are few, if any, incentives to live in cities and towns. Economic development implies the increasing specialization of economic activity undertaken by individuals, and the growth of production for sale. This specialization of activity and the resulting monetization requires some spatial concentration, as 1) specialization results in the realization of scale economies, and 2) specialization implies the need to trade, and hence creates costs to producing and living far from markets and other consumers. These forces thus give rise to the formation of cities and towns—that is, permanent groupings of specialized households and firms concentrated in limited areas.

These forces have resulted in urban economies that, even in very poor African nations, account for a substantial portion of total economic activity. Agricultural production uses manufactured inputs, even in very poor countries. Consumption as well includes some essential manufactures and many specialized services. Furthermore, a reasonably high proportion of these manufactured goods and specialized services will be produced domestically, especially in economies with large markets, such as Nigeria. And since most manufactures and services exhibit some scale and/or specialization economies, these goods typically will be produced in an imperfectly spatially dispersed fashion. Their production, moreover, gives rise to the production of other goods and services to meet the demands of those active in the "basic" sectors.

Systematic estimates of the share of urban activities in gross domestic product (GDP) are not available for a broad spectrum of African countries. Some tentative estimates have been made, though. A recent World Bank mission to Madagascar estimated that 45 percent of value added was produced in urban areas in 1988, despite the fact that only 25.6 percent of national population resided in urban areas (World Bank [1991d: 4-6]). If one is willing to impose some very restrictive simplifying assumptions, it is possible to derive estimates of the urban sector's share in GDP for a larger number of countries. These estimates are presented in Table 2.1. Columns 4 and 5 of Table 2.1 assume that 75 percent of industrial activity is urban based, as is 50 percent of all services and 5 percent of agricultural production.[3] Alternatively, urban shares can be calculated from estimates of the ratio of urban/rural per capita incomes (columns 6–9). A survey of these ratios indicates that the urban/rural gap is far greater in Africa than elsewhere, and that until fairly recently the ratio may have been as high as 4:1 or more.[4] Estimates by Van der Hoeven (1984) confirm the magnitudes presented in Table 2.1. Using the 1976 Zambian household survey, he found that urban areas accounted for 59 to 64 percent of GDP. His unadjusted urban/rural per capita income ratio is 2.21, while after adjustments for taxes, distributed profits, and an imputed value for own produce, this ratio rises to 2.82.

Even if the per capita income gaps are only around 2.0, it is clear that Africa's urban sectors contribute a disproportionately large share of total recorded GDP. Their share tends to exceed one-third for all but a very few low-income countries, and averages 45–50 percent for the middle-income nations. In countries such as Zambia or Gabon, the share may be as high as two-thirds. Estimates derived from sectoral share figures are roughly consistent with those generated by income gap estimates. The unavoidable conclusion is that although only 29 percent of Africa's population lives in urban areas, a much higher proportion of output is generated there.[5]

The other striking feature of Table 2.1 is the apparent decline in the percentage of GDP generated in urban areas for Africa as a whole, from 45 percent (in 1980) to 42 percent (in 1990). This result is driven by the decline in industry's contribution to GDP, which fell from 33 percent in 1980 to 28 percent in 1987. Whether or not urban GDP share actually fell cannot be determined from such a simple exercise, but it is certainly possible that it might have done so in a period of economic deterioration in the modern sector, followed by the austerity of structural adjustment programs.

While it is clear from Table 2.1 that the urban sector is crucially important to African economies, it is almost certainly true that these statistics overstate the urban economy's true importance. The disproportionately large urban share in GDP relative to population share in part stems from the extraordinary degree of relative price distortions prevailing in many African countries. It is important to recognize that the figures in Table 2.1 are based on income gaps calculated at *domestic* prices, not *world* prices.

A sense of the magnitude of domestic price distortions can be obtained from the results of the international real income comparison project (Summers and Heston, 1988 and 1991). Their study reports purchasing power parities (PPPs) per U.S. dollar (i.e., the exchange rate that would convert the domestic item's price into the prevailing U.S. dollar price) in 1975 for a wide variety of items. The ratio of two goods' PPP exchange rates is an indicator of the extent to which domestic relative prices diverge from U.S. and, roughly, international prices. If we take the PPP exchange rate of "bread and cereals" to be the closest approximation possible to the true rural PPP exchange rate, we can get an idea of the extent of protection for the various "urban" goods in the three African nations in Kravis' study. These data are reported in Table 2.2.

TABLE 2.1. The Urban Sector's Contribution to African Gross Domestic Product (GDP)

			Percentage of GDP Generated by Urban Activities					
	Percentage Urban		(a) Assuming That 75% of Industrial, 50% of Services, and 5% of Agricultural Activity Output is Urban		(b) Assuming Urban/Rural Per Capita Product Ratio of:			
					2.0		4.0	
(1) Country	(2) 1980	(3) 1990	(4) 1980	(5) 1990	(6) 1980	(7) 1990	(8) 1980	(9) 1990
Low income, semiarid								
Burkina Faso	7	9	35	40	13	17	23	28
Somalia	30	38	21	23	45	55	63	71
Other low income								
Kenya	16	24	41	41	28	39	43	56
Uganda	9	10	18	17	17	18	28	31
Zaire	34	40	44	44	51	57	67	73
Zambia	43	56	53	54	60	72	75	84
Middle-income oil importers								
Lesotho	14	20	46	48	25	33	39	50
Senegal	35	38	48	47	52	55	68	71
Zimbabwe	22	28	53	56	36	44	53	61
Oil exporters								
Cameroon	35	49	44	48	52	66	68	79
Gabon	36	46	62	55	53	63	69	77
Nigeria	27	35	49	47	43	52	60	68
Africa	22	29	45	42	36	45	53	62

Source: UNDP/World Bank (1992).

TABLE 2.2. "Urban" Commodities' Purchasing Power Parity (PPP) Exchange Rate Relative to "Bread and Cereals' " PPP Exchange Rate

	Nation		
Urban Commodity	Malawi	Kenya	Zambia
Beverages	1.76	2.40	5.02
Tobacco	1.26	1.06	6.21
Clothing and Footwear	1.81	1.85	3.35
Transport and Communications	3.05	2.09	5.14
Capital Formation	1.61	1.96	3.02
Government	0.59	0.87	1.59

(PPP exchange rate = units of domestic currency per dollar at which U.S. and domestic prices are identical).

Source: United Nations (1988).

For a country like Zambia, rural per capita value added measured in *international* prices may differ little from urban per capita value added. Since food is the primary component in the expenditures of unskilled workers, if prices of processed urban food relative to rural food are comparable to the beverages/ cereals or tobacco/cereals ratios (5.02 and 6.21, respectively), then the wage gaps recorded may mostly reflect vastly higher prices in urban areas for basic consumption goods that are more important in the consumption baskets of urban than rural dwellers.[6]

In general, prices of Africa's urban manufactures are maintained far above world levels by high tariffs or quotas. The monopolistic structure of domestic production ensures that prices will remain high even if local production is efficient and demand is adequate to exhaust scale economies—two large qualifications in the African milieu. Prices of modern urban services also tend to be at best distantly related to domestic opportunity costs and international competition.[7] At the same time, overvalued exchange rates depress cash crop prices in the local currency, while food prices also tend to be kept below market levels by a variety of government policies.

These urban/rural gaps and, consequently, the share of GDP generated by urban economic activities have been declining with the adoption of structural adjustment programs (SAPs) in most sub-Saharan countries. SAPs have included 1) cuts in high-wage urban civil service and parastatal employment, 2) reductions in subsidies for publicly provided urban services, 3) exchange rate devaluation, causing increases in the costs of imported intermediates and consumer goods used especially intensively in urban activities, and 4) increases in food prices and in the prices of many rural cash crops. All of these forces will work to reduce real urban incomes, and hence urban GDP shares and urban/rural income gaps. It is true that SAPs also have focused on export promotion and industrial rehabilitation, but significant results have been far slower in these areas.

2.2. Urban-Rural Economic Links

Although economic development is unlikely to be rapid without urban productivity gains, neglect of the agricultural sector (and rural nonagricultural activities) is a major error. Economic growth in Africa will be hindered unless food crop production is given top priority in development strategies, and unless incentives and research efforts are restructured to reflect this reorientation. In some but not all cases, export crop promotion is highly desirable as well.

The need for emphasis on food production stems from several factors. Most critically, food production growth has been dismal in all but a few African nations. Food production per capita declined at an average rate of 1.2 percent per annum in low-income Africa over 1970–82 (World Bank [1984] and [1989a]). This decline undoubtedly is reflected in a decrease in living standards for the rural poor as well.[8]

Nor have most African countries experienced expanding per capita food production during the 1980s (see Table 2.3; also the World Bank [1989b]). Only nine African nations have experienced increases in per capita food production, while twenty-four countries have experienced declines; moreover, several of the countries (principally Uganda and Ghana) in which per capita food production increased are in this category only because production in the base period (1979–81) was abnormally low. With such a lackluster performance, it is not surprising that food imports have hovered around 15 percent of all African import spending in the mid- and late 1980s, little different from the 14 percent and 17 percent shares in 1965 and 1960, respectively.[9] While the percentage of foreign exchange spent on food is not abnormally high by world standards, Africa's vast tracts of available arable land, the high proportion of its population working in agriculture, and the existence of some "success stories" suggest that the continent could do far better.

In virtually all African countries, the welfare of the vast majority of the population is linked to agricultural performance. Food is of course produced in agriculture, and, outside of the mineral-producing economies, so is most of the foreign exchange needed to import food. Africa's population is still predominately rural, too, so that incomes are closely tied to agricultural performance. Furthermore, given many countries' export dependence on agricultural products, the fate of urban manufacturing activities (and the consumption standards of the elite) depend critically on the efforts by peasants and plantation workers to produce cash crops for export (or defray food imports), since urban activities are almost universally import-dependent.

The linkages among different economic groups is discussed in analytical terms in Chapter 6. For present purposes, however, a few salient points need to be made. *First, the welfare of the urban and rural poor are closely linked.* An economic shock that affects the cities will result in return migration to rural areas and a decline in remittances, plus reduced demands for rural goods. Each of these effects reduces rural incomes.

Second, the type of agricultural growth experienced will have a critical impact on the incomes of different rural and urban groups. The degree of rural inequality will depend on a country's main crops—whether they are predominately food or nonfood crops, the extent to which they are labor-intensive, and the extent to which they have forward linkages (Hirschman [1961]).[10] In general, both the urban proletariat and the rural poor will benefit from an economic policy aimed at food crop production, since rapid food output growth will keep prices of the most important consumption good low.

Third, rural prosperity will be greatly affected by the nature of the "modern sector development strategy" chosen. In principle, highly import-dependent manufacturing

TABLE 2.3. Trends in Per Capita Food Production,
1979–81 to 1986–88 (1979–81 = 100)

	1984–86	1986–88
Uganda	111	121
Burkina Faso	112	116
Benin	114	110
Ghana	109	108
Senegal	102	106
Ivory Coast	105	104
Nigeria	103	103
Chad	100	103
Sierra Leone	97	101
Burundi	98	100
Somalia	98	100
Zaire	100	98
Cameroon	94	97
Mali	101	97
Gabon	98	97
Madagascar	98	97
Zambia	96	96
Guinea	93	93
Liberia	99	92
Congo	93	92
Ethiopia	87	89
Kenya	87	89
Mauritania	88	89
Tanzania	92	89
Sudan	96	89
Togo	91	88
Angola	90	87
Central African Rep.	94	87
Malawi	90	85
Mozambique	85	83
Niger	85	83
Rwanda	87	82
Zimbabwe	92	81
Lesotho	82	80
Botswana	76	69
Unweighted Average	95.5	94.3

Sources: World Bank, *World Development Report 1988*
(New York: Oxford University Press, 1988).

United Nations Development Programme, *Human Development Report 1991* (New York: Oxford University Press, 1991).

sectors and bureaucracies should give rise to low exchange rates, and hence high prices for rural cash crops. In African reality, a more frequent result is rationing of foreign exchange and a dearth of manufactured implements and consumer goods available to the countryside, plus a collapse of national infrastructures. On the

TABLE 2.4. Food Imports as a Percentage of Total Imports in 1960, 1978, and 1986

	1960	1978	1986
Benin	17	15	16
Burkina Faso	21	19	20
Uganda	6	8	6
Ghana	19	9	7
Ivory Coast	18	13	15
Nigeria	14	14	11
Senegal	30	23	10
Mali	20	19	13
Chad	19	15	17
Zaire	—	17	16
Liberia	16	17	21
Burundi	—	23	12
Gabon	—	12	21
Madagascar	17	17	13
Somalia	27	25	15
Sierra Leone	23	21	32
Sudan	17	19	21
Zambia	—	6	4
Cameroon	20	10	11
Central African Rep.	15	17	16
Congo	18	21	19
Guinea	—	—	12
Tanzania	—	11	4
Zimbabwe	—	2	12
Togo	16	8	23
Angola	—	—	—
Malawi	—	5	7
Mauritania	5	—	25
Ethiopia	—	6	22
Kenya	12	7	9
Rwanda	—	—	12
Mozambique	—	—	—
Niger	24	10	18
Lesotho	—	—	—
Botswana	—	—	—

Note: Data are not available for all countries for all years; missing data are denoted by —.

Sources: World Bank, World Development Report 1988 (New York: Oxford University Press, 1988).

World Bank, Accelerated Development in Sub-Saharan Africa (Washington: World Bank, 1981).

other hand, mineral export booms may lead to the "Dutch disease" of overvalued exchange rates and depressed agricultural economies (Nigeria is the most glaring example: see Nafziger [1988: Ch. 12] and Collier [1983]). These two unhappy outcomes are not the only possibilities, though, and alternatives are considered below.

Fourth, rural development generates growth in demand for urban products that is essential for any viable industrialization strategy. Rapid rural growth is accompanied by growth in the demand for many nonagricultural products: agricultural implements and other inputs, marketing services, transport equipment, clothing, furniture, and other consumer durables. Growth of this sort may generate urban production growth in industries very different from those that currently dominate much of African manufacturing. While demand for luxury consumer items is unlikely to decline, rural-based growth can be expected to shift demand to relatively unskilled labor-intensive, foreign exchange–saving goods.[11] Perceptible if not dramatic declines in the sophistication of the typical technology employed (resulting mainly from shifts within sectors to the production of more labor-intensive goods consumed by the poor) and the degree of standardization needed should be observed as well. The presence of a mass demand base for a fairly limited number of items should enable competitive urban enterprises to realize available scale economies even while producing only a fraction of total domestic demand. Conversely, the failure of most African manufacturing industries to realize scale economies is a critical (but hardly the sole) reason for the very high costs present in many plants.

Thus, rural growth greatly influences both the extent and the structure of urban production growth. African modern sector industrialization to date largely has involved the production of luxury goods of little value to the urban or, especially, rural poor. Modern urban services tend to be dominated by the public sector bureaucracy. The net result is that many "modern" goods and services produced are of little value to most of the populace, and are made using skilled-labor-intensive techniques, high import contents, and low value-added shares. The expenditure patterns of modern sector workers also have high import and luxury good contents, thereby reducing the linkage effects between the protected modern urban sector and the rest of the economy. As the capacity for further easy import substitution is very limited, the future expansion of this type of urban economic activity will be very slow in most African nations. However, urban growth based on growing demands from a dynamic rural economy and from export industries is far less constrained.

The historical record bears out these points clearly. As agriculture in general and food production in particular have stagnated, real export values have declined. After expanding at an annual rate of 6.0 percent in the 1960s, low-income countries' export volumes contracted at a rate of 2.5 percent per annum between 1970 and 1982 (World Bank [1984]).[12] Imports also declined, contributing substantially to the industrial depression in much of Africa. The typical African manufacturing enterprise is highly dependent on imported intermediates, spare parts, and capital goods. Expansion of capacity in the 1960s thus led to import needs for replacement of worn machinery and for continued production in the 1970s; to this was added the needs of newly constructed plants. This growth in effective import demand, combined with inelastic export supply and foreign exchange earnings, has resulted in shockingly low rates of capacity utilization in a capital-scarce continent.[13]

Finally, it is important to recognize that rapid rural development need not imply a reduction in rural-urban migration rates. What happens to migration will depend on the importance of "Engel's effects" in demand structures, and the extent to which new crops and technologies are laborsaving.[14] Urban population growth will depend as well on the extent to which urban production shifts to more labor-

TABLE 2.5. World Urbanization Levels by Region (Percentage of Population Living in Urban Areas)

Region	1970	1980	1990	2000
Africa	22.5	27.0	32.6	39.0
Eastern Africa	10.3	15.1	21.5	28.4
Middle Africa	24.8	31.6	39.7	47.7
Northern Africa	36.5	39.9	44.6	50.6
Southern Africa	44.1	49.6	55.3	60.9
Western Africa	17.6	22.2	27.9	34.9
Americas	64.7	68.9	72.9	76.1
Latin America	57.4	65.4	72.1	76.8
Northern America	73.8	73.9	74.3	74.9
Asia	23.9	26.6	29.9	35.0
East Asia	26.9	28.1	29.5	32.9
South Asia	21.3	25.4	30.2	36.5
Europe	66.7	70.2	72.8	75.1

Source: United Nations, *World Population Trends and Policies, 1987 Monitoring Report* (New York: United Nations, 1988).

intensive activities. If a renewed emphasis on rural development results in exchange rate devaluation and more realistic prices for credit in urban areas, the relative price of capital will rise, inducing firms to hire more workers per unit of capital. Furthermore, purchasing power will shift from high-income skilled workers and the urban "labor aristocracy" (and government) to unskilled labor; as claimed above, this shift probably will result in demand shifts toward more unskilled labor-intensive urban products. Consequently, urban population growth may well increase as a result of this employment growth. Finally, rural households with rising incomes may well invest part of their savings by financing the schooling or job search activity of a child, thus further increasing migration.[15]

2.3. The Changing Level of Urbanization in Sub-Saharan Africa

Africa still contains many of the least urbanized nations in the world, reflecting, among other factors, colonial policies that restricted free movement of the indigenous population. From projections based on purely demographic variables, the United Nations (1988a:176) estimates that 39.0 percent of all Africans will be living in urban areas in the year 2000. This compares with a world average of 46.6 percent, and regional averages of 75.1 percent for Europe, 76.8 percent for Latin America, and 74.9 percent for North America. Only south and east Asia are projected to be less urbanized than Africa in the year 2000. These projections are summarized in Table 2.5.

But while Africa's absolute level of urbanization is low, its urban population growth rate is among the highest in the world. Recent World Bank estimates ([1989b: 224–25]—but, one should note, based on data of mixed quality) indicate that for the period 1980–87, Africa's urban population grew at an annual rate of 6.9 percent (or, if one prefers the numbers in the UNDP/World Bank [1992], 5.7

percent).[16] No other region of the world had such rapid urban population growth, except for the People's Republic of China, with an annual urban growth rate of 11.0 percent, but where city growth had been severely repressed during the previous thirty years. The Bank's projections for south Asian urban population growth is 4.1 percent, and for Latin America only 3.2 percent per annum. Current international agency estimates of urban growth rates for African countries and for the rest of the world's regions are shown in Table 2.6. Note that both within Africa and other continents, there is significant regional variation in urban population growth rates. But the most striking data from WDR 1989 (World Bank [1989b: 224–25]) concerning the urbanization experience of the early and middle 1980s are the tiny number of non-African nations reported as having city growth equal to the African weighted *average*. Only five other countries are listed with 1980-87 urban growth rates above 6.9 percent: China (11.0 percent), Oman (8.8 percent), Yemen Arab Republic (8.4 percent), Nepal (7.8 percent), and Libya (7.0 percent). The next highest non-African urban growth rates are for Laos (6.1 percent), Saudi Arabia (6.0 percent), Bangladesh (5.8 percent), Honduras (5.8 percent), Jordan (5.3 percent), Kuwait (5.2 percent), Malaysia (5.0 percent), Indonesia (5.0 percent), and Ecuador (5.0 percent). Twenty of the largest thirty-four African nations listed in WDR 1989 (and twenty-four of the forty-three African countries for which data were available: see World Bank [1989b:278–9]) had growth rates above the Laotian 6.1 percent; only twelve of forty-three (and eight of the largest thirty-four) African countries had city growth rates below 5.0 percent. Obviously, unless World Bank data are completely erroneous, the pace of urbanization in sub-Saharan Africa is dramatically greater than in all but a few countries elsewhere in the world. And while the United Nations predicts (albeit in a mechanistic fashion on the basis of extremely scanty evidence) that African growth rates will fall continuously into the next century, the African urban population growth rate is projected to drop below 4 percent only after the year 2010.

A frequent criticism of U.N. and World Bank urbanization estimates is that these data reflect individual nations' widely divergent definitions of "urban." Fortunately, the French demographer Jean-Marie Cour has recomputed urban population growth statistics using a consistent definition of urban residence. Cour's study reveals that the population of African cities and towns rose from 28 million to 103 million between 1960 and 1980.[17] The rate of growth was twice as fast as that for the population as a whole, and the percentage residing in urban areas doubled to 29 percent. Cour's implied urban growth rate for Africa is 6.7 percent, a figure noticeably *greater* than World Bank estimates (around 5.6 percent) for the same period. Cour also forecasts that by 2000 the African urban population will have tripled compared to 1980 totals, with 46 percent of the region's population living in cities or towns.

While the U.N.'s and Cour's predictions of urban population for the year 2000 may differ due to different definitions of what constitutes an urban area, they agree that between 1980 and 2000, the urban population will triple. Population growth in sub-Saharan Africa from 1980 to 2000 will add between 160 million (U.N.) and 200 million (Cour) new residents to the region's cities and towns. On the other hand, if the World Bank estimates are correct and 1980–87 urban growth continues through the remainder of the century, then Africa's urban areas will quadruple between 1980 and 2000. For several reasons explained in Chapter 6, however, we be-

TABLE 2.6.   Rates of Urban Population Growth by World Region (Percentage Per Year).

Region	1970–75	1980–85	1990–95	2000–2005
Africa	4.4	4.8	4.8	4.5
Eastern Africa	6.5	6.8	6.3	5.6
Middle Africa	5.0	5.1	4.9	4.4
Northern Africa	3.3	3.7	3.6	3.2
Southern Africa	3.5	3.7	3.6	3.2
Western Africa	5.3	5.4	5.6	5.3
Americas	2.5	2.3	2.0	1.7
Latin America	3.9	3.3	2.7	2.1
Northern America	1.1	1.0	0.9	0.8
Asia	3.4	2.8	3.0	3.0
East Asia	2.0	1.6	2.0	2.4
South Asia	4.2	3.9	3.8	3.4
Europe	1.3	0.7	0.6	0.4

Figures for 1990–95 and 2000–2005 are U.N. forecasts.

Source: United Nations, *World Population Trends and Policies, 1987 Monitoring Report* (New York: United Nations, 1988).

lieve that all of these estimates are implausibly high, barring a reversal of the continent's political and economic fortunes.

Though many may lament the pace of African urbanization, it is actually rather unlikely that a more efficient macroeconomic or sectoral policy environment would decrease *long-run* urbanization levels. In fact, when Montgomery and Brown (1985) regress urbanization levels against explanatory factors such as per capita national income, sub-Saharan Africa appears to behave in ways comparable to other regions. By and large, the countries the World Bank identifies as having low incomes also have low levels of urbanization, and usually these fall below the 29 percent region-wide level for 1980 identified in Cour's study. Moreover, the exceptions, including Somalia, Zaire, Central African Republic, and Ghana, have all experienced drastic rural economic declines.[18] Put differently, *structural adjustment should have a one-time negative impact on urbanization, but the ensuing growth stemming from more appropriate macroeconomic management will itself be highly urbanizing.*

The middle-income oil-importing countries, with an average urbanization rate slightly above Cour's regional average, seem to experience levels of urbanization comparable to similar countries in other regions. If anything, there are several cases of countries with unusually low levels of urbanization. Zimbabwe, with only 24 percent (Cour's 1980 estimate; the 1987 World Bank estimate is 26 percent) of its population living in urban areas, is about twenty percentage points below its per capita income peers.[19] This has as a proximate cause the colonial and neocolonial government policy of restricting black African access to urban areas, and of bottling up the majority in so-called Tribal Trust or communal areas. In studies of Zimbabwe, and even of other countries like Kenya, one finds concern that urbanization may not proceed fast enough to meet rural development objectives:

> If the annual rate of employment growth in the urban areas [over the next twenty years] were only 3.5 percent, then effectively the [communal ar-

eas] . . . may still have to support over twice their present population in 20 years time, implying per capita incomes falling to only 66 percent of their present level.[20]

Finally, among the middle-income oil exporters, there appear to be no surprises. Nigeria's apparent low level of urbanization may well be a statistical artifact: from Cour's uniform definition, it appears that Nigeria's urban population already accounts for 46 percent of the total population, a level matched by other oil-exporting nations.

2.4. An Overview of Urban Productive Activities in Africa

In discussions of African economic development, the concern for rehabilitating the agricultural sector sometimes leads analysts to implicitly slight the importance of the nonfarm economy. Yet the 2,900 African cities and towns with populations of five thousand or more (Cour [1985]) play a major role in the region's development. At the lower end of the settlement spectrum, rural nonfarm enterprises foster the growing specialization of their area's economy.[21] As monetization and specialization proceed, farm and village household production for own use gives way to market exchanges.[22] In Africa, as recently as the late 1970s up to two-thirds of all nonfarm employment was in rural areas, either in rural areas themselves or in towns of up to twenty thousand to thirty thousand residents.[23] Moreover, Haggblade and Liedholm (1991) and Haggblade and Brown (1989) have concluded that, if anything, *rural nonfarm employment has generally increased over time.* In such areas, roughly 40 percent of all workers work principally in nonfarm activities. Given the undeveloped nature of rural infrastructure (roads, power, water) and the dispersed nature of the population at large, small cities and towns are critical hubs of local economic development. It is also here that households with access to little or no agricultural land find the closest opportunity for supplemental income, thus adding an equity dimension to such rural and small-town development.

The force behind growing nonfarm rural area employment is the high income elasticity of demand for rurally produced, nonfarm commodities among farmers.[24] Apart from marketing services, these town dwellers produce plows, irrigation pumps, and motors; they repair equipment; and they provide final consumer goods and services, including clothing, leather goods, furniture, and metal products. It is important to emphasize that a large part of these "urban" commodities are actually produced at the local (rural and small-town) level, since the markets for the products of the dominant suppliers, small enterprises, are highly localized (Page [1979]).[25] For both goods and services, marketing depends basically upon personal exchanges between the businessman and the final customer. It is also clear, especially relative to large-scale, formal sector enterprises, that small enterprises are both labor-intensive and foreign exchange saving.

As one travels up the size hierarchy of smaller cities and towns, enterprises are exposed to new potential benefits. The concentration of population tends to reduce unit costs of public utilities, education, and health and social services, making their provision more affordable, and, therefore, more likely. In each of these cases, there exist substantial fixed costs of operation that generate scale economies and make the services very expensive to provide in low-density areas. Small manufacturers, crop processors, and repair and service facilities begin to adapt to the availability of piped water and electrification (Anderson [1978]). Many activities begin to experience cost reductions when other activities, external to the enterprise, are in close proximity.[26] It becomes easier to assemble the appropriate package of inputs, labor of varying skills, business services, and credit. Even the scope of the market expands, as road and communication links are improved, and each town's hinterland widens. Consequently, one begins to find firms of more substantial size capturing a greater share of output.

Nevertheless, the importance of smaller-scale firms continues to be felt. Even large cities have an important percentage of their labor force working in small, usually unregistered enterprises. Survey results suggest that approximately 60 percent of the employment in Lagos can be classified as traditional, informal, or unregistered (Wilber Smith Associates et al. [n.d.]). For Abidjan, the total so classified equals perhaps 55 percent.[27] In Kinshasa, virtually the same proportion applies for the unregistered sector (Gozo [1985]). For Bamako, fully 68 percent of all workers are excluded from the "modern" economy (Direction du Projet Urbain de Mali [1984]). In Dakar, the informal sector captures 56 percent of employment (World Bank [1983c]). In Nairobi, up to 44 percent of the labor force is employed in unregistered, small-scale activities (House [1981]), while the proportion in Lusaka approaches 40 percent (Sandbrook [1982]).

Policymakers in sub-Saharan Africa should concern themselves with the informal or "microenterprise" sector for reasons other than the relative share of the labor force involved. The alternative formal or "modern" sector has, in the past, been protected and subsidized by the central government. With the introduction of the structural adjustment process, this type of assistance has declined in scope, and is bound to decline further. Unless economies surge in response to liberalization and privatization, only a small share of new labor force entrants into the labor force will be able to rely on formal sector jobs in the 1990s.[28] This has also been the case since the mid-1970s. As Table 2.7 shows, manufacturing employment has varied greatly in Africa, but the median growth rate is roughly equal to the labor force growth rate (between 3.0 and 4.5 percent). Table 2.7 also shows the gloomy trend in real manufacturing earnings per worker, which has been declining in a slight majority of countries for which data are available.

The informal sector, on the other hand, is already accustomed to working within a framework of more appropriate price signals, and thus is geared toward labor-intensive production methods. The informal sector is also capable of providing an efficient mechanism for "on-the-job" training, through its apprenticeship system. While expanding the stock of human capital in the cities, the informal sector helps attract savings that bypass financial institutions, thus increasing the supply of physical capital as well.

Finally, the informal sector deserves attention because it satisfies a large and growing demand for customized and/or low-cost goods and services by an urban population that, on average, spends at least half of its income on food alone.[29] Especially among low-income households, the outputs of small-scale firms are likely to be more appropriate, in quality and in price, than the production of most larger firms.

TABLE 2.7. African Manufacturing Employment, Earnings and Output Growth (1980 = 100)

Country	Year	Real Earnings →		Real Ouput /Empl.	Year	Real Earnings		Real Output /Empl.	Annual Growth Rates		
		Empl.	/Empl.			Empl.	/Empl.		Emp.	Ern	Out
Benin	1974	95	102	96	1985	124	—	134	2.5%	—	3.1%
Botswana	74	60	85	137	85	177	81	68	11.4	−0.5%	−6.8
Burkina Faso	74	92	56	84	85	107	107	106	1.4	6.1	2.1
Burundi	74	72	190	97	83	139	133	135	7.6	−3.9	3.7
Cameroon	74	84	69	61	85	111	197	215	2.6	10.0	12.1
CAR	74	235	61	77	85	176	103	80	−2.6	4.9	0.3
Côte d'Ivoire	74	64	106	76	82	94	105	92	4.9	−0.1	2.4
Ethiopia	74	75	152	75	85	118	79	113	4.2	−5.8	3.8
Gambia	75	164	45	—	85	108	137	—	−4.1	11.8	—
Ghana	74	92	363	184	83	74	48	76	−2.4	−20.1	−9.4
Kenya	74	75	117	70	85	123	76	90	4.6	−3.8	2.3
Lesotho	74	97	68	55	85	105	161	151	0.7	8.2	9.6
Madagascar	74	114	103	87	84	122	62	56	0.7	−4.9	−4.3
Malawi	74	66	103	121	83	92	105	92	3.8	0.2	−3.0
Mali	74	56	161	90	81	98	98	126	8.3	−6.8	4.9
Mauritius	74	64	91	157	85	134	112	104	6.9	1.9	−3.7
Nigeria	74	43	91	79	83	75	86	112	6.4	−0.6	4.0
Senegal	74	69	134	133	85	114	101	102	4.7	−2.5	−2.4
Somalia	74	71	170	166	85	150	69	68	7.0	−7.9	−7.8
Swaziland	73	60	94	—	83	105	95	—	5.8	0.1	—
Tanzania	74	69	175	132	85	107	45	74	4.1	−11.6	−5.1
Togo	74	93	—	45	82	104	—	121	1.4	—	13.2
Zambia	74	92	135	124	85	107	95	103	1.4	−3.1	−1.7
Zimbabwe	74	92	93	99	85	103	142	113	1.0	3.9	1.2
unweighted averages									3.4	−1.2	0.8

Source: World Bank. *World Tables, 1988–89 Edition*. Baltimore: Johns Hopkins University Press, 1989c.

Yet the smaller-scale enterprise cannot shoulder the full burden of supplying nonagricultural goods and services. And it is in the larger cities that one finds the bulk of medium to large businesses. The reasons for this are many. The opportunities for agglomeration economies are largest in such cities. In addition, during the early stages of economic development, the ease of access to the national and international monetized economy will vary drastically from one center to another, favoring large cities privileged by reason of history and/or geography (e.g., possession of an excellent transshipment point such as a deep-water port). Furthermore, during the long stage of development when investment funds are extraordinarily scarce relative to demand (which certainly characterizes most of Africa today), governments are likely to concentrate infrastructure—including power, water, roads, telecommunications, and education and health facilities—in a few large places, so that at least those economic "city-states" can service the widest possible range of enterprise demands.[30] The differential availability of infrastructure will act to restrict the range of settlements available for the location of many types of economic activity, compared with what would be available at a more advanced level of development. Finally, larger cities and towns serve as transport hubs and centers of transshipment; combined with the presence of a relatively large market, large cities are often the natural sites for medium- and large-scale enterprises.

Only as development proceeds—and once variations in settlement size and density are no longer associated with major differences in public service quality and ease of access to markets—will a portion of formal sector productive activities decentralize their operations away from very large urban centers, where rents and congestion costs exceed the clustering advantages and scale economies that some enterprises can reap. Until then the formal sector's health will be tied to large cities.

One can get a good grasp of the magnitude of these big city economies by examining their contributions to national output. Careful studies suggest, for example, that without Nairobi, Kenya's GDP would be cut by one-third; without Abidjan, half of the Ivory Coast's GDP would not exist; without Bamako, Mali's economy would shrink by one-third; without Lagos, fully one-fifth of Nigeria's output would vanish; without Kinshasa, one-third of Zaire's output would disappear; and without Greater Dakar, Senegal's output would fall by one-half.[31] Much of this output is produced by the regulated, formal sector, despite the significant proportion of labor involved in the unregulated economy.[32] And the formal sector contributes heavily to making such large centers the most diversified local economies in their countries.

While structural adjustment may weed out some of the weaker modern sector firms, many existing industrial firms, and the specialized business services they foster, will survive the adjustment process and be joined by additional firms in an increasing number of industrial sectors (see, for example, Keesing [1984] and [1985]). As Keesing's regional review (1984) notes:

> A number of the larger countries in Sub-Saharan Africa have built up enough industry and acquired enough industrial experience so that they are already into the middle phases of industrial development. Their further success depends on building up large-scale, low-cost intermediate goods industries (in addition to cement and other building materials al-

ready being made), and increasing the competitiveness of a wide range of manufacturing industries including those making engineering products of various kinds, while at the same time expanding the overall economy despite foreign exchange, agricultural, and other constraints. Countries already into these middle phases include . . . Nigeria and Zimbabwe . . . [the] Ivory Coast and Kenya followed in some ways by Zambia.

Beyond these countries, most of the remainder—smaller and poorer—face a challenge in building up even basic manufacturing industries. Taken as a group, however, the sub-Saharan countries have been projected to increase industrial output by at least 50 percent by 2000, or as much as 250 percent under more optimistic scenarios (again, see Keesing [1984]). Whether either of these figures will be realized is unclear, but they accurately reflect the latent potential.

2.5 The Magnitude and Impact of Infrastructure Deficiencies on the Productivity of Cities

What type of problems thwart the development of sub-Saharan Africa's nonfarm sector? In essence, they are problems requiring solutions at a subnational or local level to complement measures being taken at the macroeconomic level. Policy changes are needed to remove impediments and to take advantage of growth opportunities. These changes require recasting the role of the public sector, encouraging it to do things that only it can do, and to cease doing many things that it does inefficiently. In our view, the end result would be a pared-down public sector, a lesser *central* government role, and an expanded role for municipalities.[33] It would not necessarily involve any increase in central government expenditures devoted to urban problems. Some issues facing cities require few extra resources; others involve more effective use of existing resources; yet others necessitate more self-financing of urban activities. In all cases, resources would be directed increasingly to initiatives showing very high rates of return.

One of the major problems facing the urban economy in Africa is the state of local infrastructure. This, in turn, is merely a symptom reflecting the neglect of local government throughout the continent, as well as the failure to mobilize resources at the local level. How bad are infrastructure conditions in Africa's cities?[34] As a rough indication, in virtually all African countries, at least 50 percent of the urban population in 1980 lived in slums without basic services (Cohen [1982]). Also as a rule of thumb, conditions are likely to be best in the very largest cities, such as capitals and major ports. Detailed city studies of smaller centers are rare, but one can assume that poorly functioning large cities are matched by deficiencies in the rest of the urban hierarchy.

For example, in Nigeria, major secondary centers such as Ibadan, Kano, Kaduna, Benin City, and Port Harcourt suffer serious service and infrastructure deficiencies similar to those identified in Lagos. In Ghana, the problems faced by Accra are also found in Kumasi. Like Kinshasa, virtually all the small urban centers in Zaire, including Kisangani and Bukavu, are in a state of disrepair that reflects twenty years of neglect. Conversely, when infrastructure conditions are good in the largest city (Harare in Zimbabwe), they are generally reasonably good elsewhere as well. This is true not only in Bulawayo, with 450,000 inhabitants, but also

in Kwekwe and Marondera, each with fewer than 50,000 residents. A review of the
state of urban services and infrastructure in major African cities is therefore revealing. As a starting point, emphasized in *Southern African Economist* [1990], virtually
all countries have experienced a deterioration in urban infrastructure in the past
decade, and at least most do not foresee major improvements as imminent.

Virtually all major African urban centers have a core area (but often tiny in
proportion to the city's total size), inherited at Independence, where infrastructure
conditions are tolerable to good in spite of the cities' need to accommodate much
higher population densities than was originally foreseen.[35] Elsewhere within the
main cities, as a rule, the situation is more alarming. For the very largest cities,
such as Kinshasa and Lagos, conditions are unusually serious only because of the
scale of the problem. They provide a vivid illustration of what many of tomorrow's
African cities will look like if the politics of neglect continue to prevail. Kinshasa,
with a population of three million, has increased in size from six thousand hectares
in 1960 to twenty-five thousand hectares today (Bureau d'Etudes d'Amenagements
Urbains [Kinshasa] [1984]). Yet the paved road network has remained virtually un-
changed over that period. Paralleling these deficiencies is the absence of storm
drains or the obstruction of existing drains with uncollected solid wastes. These
problems contribute to severe flooding in the rainy season and accelerate the deterioration of existing streets. As a result, the potential coverage provided by public
transit facilities is severely limited. Workers living in districts developed after 1960
are forced to walk long distances to reach a bus or their workplaces.

The case of Lagos (population 4.5 million) is also illustrative. The problem can
be detailed subsector by subsector (World Bank [1983d]):

> (a) *Water:* "In addition to bottlenecks in the transmission and distribu-
> tion systems, much of the city lacks adequate tertiary networks; those that
> do exist are in poor condition."
> (b) *Storm Drainage:* ". . . much of Lagos is inadequately drained or not
> drained at all. Most drains are not maintained and have, for lack of main-
> tenance, become dysfunctional. Consequently about 8,400 hectares of the
> city are subject to frequent and often severe flooding. . ."
> (c) *Roads:* "large land areas are often serviced by a single arterial or col-
> lector road and there is a lack of adequate arterial and collector facilities
> for cross-town trips. . . . Many of the major routes suffer considerable
> pavement distress."[36]
> (d) *Communications:* "The communications system in Lagos is character-
> ized . . . by few telephones, much frustration and many delays in placing
> calls.

Kampala's infrastructure has deteriorated significantly since the 1960s, largely
as a result of neglect and Uganda's political strife. While many elements of basic
infrastructure are lacking, the situation with regard to electric power is especially
acute: "At present, daily power outages are common in Kampala, which is relatively well supplied compared to the rest of Uganda. Overall only about 6 percent
of the population has access to electricity" (World Bank [1991b: 20]).

Accra (population 1.4 million) provides an example of a city that has lost its
once proud status of a well-equipped city. Half the population now lives in areas
where little infrastructure is available. The state of the remaining infrastructure is
now poor:

Due to lack of maintenance in recent years the condition of the [road] network, particularly the heavily traveled paved roads, has deteriorated and suffers from various degrees of pavement distress, moderate to extensive, over much of the paved network. . . . The remaining pavement life is, on average, five years. This deterioration . . . and missing network links causes extensive delay in the movement of goods and services (particularly to and from the ports), damage to vehicles and equipment, [and] very high vehicle operating costs. . . . Due to the lack of routine maintenance, the drainage system has also deteriorated to the point of ceasing to function in many places, and flooding during the rainy season causes extended road blockages and further deterioration of the road network. (World Bank [1984b]).[37]

Many centers of even relatively moderate size suffer from similar problems. Bamako (population 675,000) is described in one World Bank report as follows:

The organized city has only a minimum of facilities and overexploits a deteriorating infrastructure while nearly all the new areas expand without even makeshift equipment and infrastructure. (World Bank [1985a])

Even more dramatic are the descriptions of conditions in Douala (population 740,000), Cameroon's main port and industrial center:

The lack of drainage facilities in most of the newly urbanized areas and the severe deterioration or even complete destruction of existing networks in older districts cause severe flooding during most of the year. Mud flows and accumulations, indiscriminate garbage disposal, and squatter settlements in natural streams have combined to worsen already minimal environmental conditions. . . .
The road network has not kept pace with the expansion of residential areas, and an inefficient transport system is responsible for considerable loss of productivity and it increasingly affects the functioning of vital sectors such as the port and the railways system. (World Bank [1984c])

Unfortunately, these descriptions are representative rather than extreme, particularly for cities in the poorer African nations. The *Southern African Economist's* (1990) survey of urban conditions makes this clear, as the following (again, fairly random) comments indicate:

Dar es Salaam: "There is only one serviceable fire tender to fight the 272 fires that break out every year."
Maputo: "Maputo's public transport now consists of just 25 buses. Yet in 1985, when there were many fewer people, there were 196 buses. At least 60 percent of the commuters rely on the informal sector."
Lusaka: "The shortage of foreign exchange has made it impossible to replace passenger [bus] fleets or get hold of spare parts. . . . Under 'normal' circumstances, Lusaka would require 80 vehicles of various types for refuse collection. But it is trying to operate with only eight trucks— and these are over ten years old."

Conakry, Guinea, suffers from severe infrastructure deficiencies. When the Second Republic came to power in 1984, "most infrastructure was in a state of utter disrepair. Large urban areas lacked basic services, and extremely poor living and working conditions affected the productivity of urban acitivities" (World Bank [1990a]: 46). No sectors were in good repair:

(a) *Roads:* "Road investment had been insignificant over two decades and the 1984 network barely exceeded the one that existed at Independence."

(b) *Garbage disposal:* "Lack of suitable road access deprived large portions of the urban centers of the possibility of any garbage collection service. Even in serviced areas, collection was at best erratic, and only one-fifth of waste produced daily was actually collected."

(c) *Public transport:* "Public transport companies had virtually ceased to operate in Conakry."

(d) *Electricity:* "Power supply was plagued by chronic breakdowns which severely affected the functioning of economic activities."

In some countries, however, progress has been made toward rehabilitating or constructing necessary infrastructure to accommodate some or most of the population growth. One example of such progress is the Republic of Guinea. The World Bank (World Bank [1990a: 47]) reports that the situation has improved steadily under the Second Republic (1984–present):

Priority roads and drainage rehabilitation programs have been implemented. Conakry municipal services have been stenghtened to carry out systematic maintenance and repairs of the drainage network as well as garbage collection over most of the urbanized area . . . [but] continuous efforts are indispensable to make up for the accumulated backlogs in the provision of essential urban infrastructure and services. . . .

Notwithstanding these recent gains, Guinea has a long way to go. Other "partial success stories" include Nairobi (population 1.2 million), Abidjan (population 2.0 million), and Dakar (population 1.6 million).

Nairobi's infrastructure network is relatively complete. There is an extensive network of paved roads with associated drainage facilities, power and piped water are readily available, and public transport facilities are reasonably good. However, the recent period of national austerity has led to policies of deferred road and drainage maintenance which threaten to create important new investment requirements simply to repair the results of neglect. Solid waste collection is also emerging as a serious problem because maintenance of collection and disposal equipment has been deferred for so long.

Abidjan is characterized by generally good road infrastructure which, combined with careful attention to traffic management, allows public transport to perform effectively in spite of the growing separation of job centers from areas of high residential growth. Water supplies are plentiful, and telephone service is satisfactory. Less developed services include electricity and storm drainage. In addition, Abidjan has a problem in preserving the gains it has made since Independence, because, like Nairobi, maintenance functions have been neglected.[38]

Dakar has a weaker infrastructure base. Electricity supplies are adequate, but much other infrastructure is deficient. Out of seven hundred kilometers of roads, only about two hundred are paved, and most are located in the ex-colonial core. This network is even less effective than it might be because little attention has been paid to traffic management (streetlights, one-way streets, bus lanes). Like Abidjan, Dakar is experiencing ever longer average commuting times, as jobs remain tightly clustered in older core locations. Water supplies are constrained; telephone service is poor. Solid waste disposal procedures are deficient, which leads to the dumping of garbage into an already poorly maintained drainage system.

The major cities of Zimbabwe have the best conditions in Africa, largely because urban population growth was controlled until 1980 through in-migration restrictions. As the World Bank's *Zimbabwe Urban Sector Review* notes:

> . . . primary infrastructure is already in place at a high standard. Water and sewerage reticulation is complete, even in low-income areas. Major surplus capacity exists in most of the municipal streets. . . . Zimbabwe is in the unusual situation . . . of requiring infrastructure investment only for the increment of population, starting from a solid base. (World Bank [1985])

Namibia, Botswana, and Swaziland are other African countries with reasonably strong infrastructures. These situations, however, are exceptional. The earlier examples suggest the norm.

Three characteristics of this general deficiency in the supply of infrastructure and services should be underlined.[39] First, *different forms of infrastructure and services have differing impacts in the efficiency of economic activity.* Some types of infrastructure (road access, drainage) are prerequisites for land development. Other public services (public transport, telecommunications, solid waste removal, public safety) affect daily business operations and production indirectly. Yet others (power, water) act as direct inputs into production process.

Second, enterprises will differ in their dependence on particular services. Large- and medium-sized enterprises are likely to see all basic infrastructure as necessary, while very small businesses may operate without telecommunications and often power facilities. They are also relatively less dependent on infrastructure such as transport and water than are formal sector enterprises. But these differences are less important than they may seem at first because smaller enterprises do depend on the efficiency of larger enterprises. Large-scale enterprises often import or produce goods utilized by small businesses (e.g., factory-made yarns and dyes, metal goods, plastics, rubber, and leather: see O'Connor [1983]). In addition, many of the small business workers learn their trade and/or accumulate their initial capital while working for larger firms (Sandbrook [1982]). Finally, the wage incomes generated by larger firms help create demand for commodities marketed by small-scale firms.

A final characteristic of these deficiencies is that they can be compensated for, but at considerable cost, and that cost usually exceeds the value of the taxes and user charges needed to finance public provision of such services.[40] Businesses can develop private infrastructure networks, investing in generators, borehole wells, water purification equipment, private employee transport, security guards, walkie-talkies, and otherwise unnecessarily large inventories. If this financial burden is impossible to assume, there are only two remaining alternatives: to do without the service (e.g., operate with manual tools instead of powered machinery) or, more likely for any sophisticated operation, to forego the investment opportunity. In either case, there are serious costs to the economy as a whole.

The fact that this appears to be a self-evident area for priority action does not mean, however, that the policymakers of multinational and bilateral development agencies—whose priorities increasingly will affect what strategies are actually followed in Africa—fully understand its importance. As an example, two recent studies on private business prospects in Africa, when listing ways to promote economic development, devote virtually no attention to the heavy burdens imposed by poor urban infrastructure.[41] Part but far from all of this neglect reflects an ideological distrust (buttressed by ample historical experience of poor performance) of the public sector. Another part reflects the (inaccurate, in our view) perception that urban infrastructure is inessential for economic growth, at least in the short run; and a third part also reflects the not entirely unfounded belief that urban infrastructural projects tend to favor the relatively wealthy, and divert resources from the rural poor. On the other hand, however, it may also be the case that cessation of infrastructure projects will be highly inegalitarian, since the relatively wealthy are already serviced, while squatter settlements on the periphery of cities are not.[42] Finally, it should be noted that international agencies' plans for financing and maintaining infrastructure and other public services are often far from realistic, largely because skilled labor and institutional constraints are frequently ignored.[43]

2.6. Additional Constraints on Urban Business Activity: The Issue of Land Markets

A major problem facing the business community involves distortions in the markets for complementary inputs like land. Land markets across Africa's cities tend to be disorganized, with conflicting, often unrecorded ownership claims and unclear boundaries characteristic of most parcels of land. Without an adequate system for measuring and recording the boundaries of land parcels, and without the registration of legal rights to such plots, it is impossible for a potential entrepreneur to go to any one or two sources in a city and find out what land is available for sale, what prices prevail in the market, and who the owners are.[44] Property transfers are fraught with long-term risks. Transactions are time-consuming and may involve payments to several purported owners. These types of obstacles clearly impede publicly sponsored development projects as well.

Examples of these problems are found in a number of World Bank and non-Bank reports. A study of Monrovia, Liberia (World Bank [1981a]), notes that

> although most land is privately owned, there is often a proliferation of conflicting deeds for the same or overlapping properties involving government, tribes, organized community groups, institutions, families and individuals. . . .
> The lack of clear ownership of urban land has created a number of problems. . . . It has prevented development of any effective system of mortgages, inhibited land sales and building construction, discouraged improvement and maintenance of existing structures, and undermined the establishment of effective real estate taxation. Property in Monrovia is rarely bought or sold and when it is, prices fluctuate dramatically.

In Kinshasa, Zaire, only 10 percent of the parcels are officially registered, while the rest have been acquired informally. Such plots are sold by customary chiefs and "validated" by local government commissioners, who grant "livrets de logeur." These permits are based on a colonial system that has since been abolished; they therefore have no legal standing (see Prud'homme [1985] and Mbuyi [1989]). A report on urban conditions in Cameroon (World Bank [n.d.]) suggests that the new titles issued each year represent less than 10 percent of the demand.

Those who wish to obtain a title must wait two to seven years, depending on the "persuasiveness" of the applicant. In Kampala, Uganda, "about 20 percent of transactions are officially recorded and fully documented while about 80 percent take the form of verbal agreements, all technically illegal, which initially save time and money but which often lead later to disputes" (O'Connor [1983]). In Accra, Ghana, the prevalence of customary land law is blamed for impeding the expansion of the central business district and for discouraging construction investments across the city (O'Connor [1983]). Finally, in Dakar, Senegal, where the land tenure status of about 60 percent of urban dwellings is unclear, "the authorities are unable to inform a private individual within a reasonable time of the whereabouts of sites approved for building or whether he even is eligible to obtain title to the land" (World Bank [1983c]).

Land information systems and formalization of property rights facilitate private and public real estate transactions, increase the opportunity for using land as loan collateral, and undergird any system of local real property taxation.[45] The existing situation, in contrast, represents a vicious circle: to paraphrase Cohen (1982:16), most households pay no property taxes; do not register with municipal institutions; ignore regulations governing informal trade, health, transportation and sanitation; and in turn receive virtually no municipal services and suffer from many negative external economies imposed by their neighbors, whom they adversely affect in turn. What is needed, above all, is the political commitment to develop a continuously updated system and to institute streamlined procedures for transferring land rights and titles. That, in turn, depends on the recognition that such systems are "as much a part of basic infrastructure as roads or electric grids: an essential element to expedite virtually all other forms of development" (Doebele [1983]).

2.7. Bottlenecks Created by the Failure of Capital Markets

Small- and medium-sized enterprises also face serious problems created by the fragmented nature of capital markets in urban areas (Hugon [1980] and Sethuraman [1981]). Typically, "formal" market funds are available to large establishments from commercial banks or specialized development finance institutions. Often these funds are lent at subsidized rates, which means that excess demand for the funds will exist, and loans will be rationed according to bank officials' and political leaders' preferences. Smaller enterprises, aside from benefiting from token, officially sponsored "small business" efforts, are restricted to their own resources, funds borrowed from friends or relatives, or money raised (typically at very high cost) from informal money lenders. Economic activities with very high rates of return but in capital-starved sectors are therefore either underfunded or not undertaken at all.[46] Both project-specific jobs and employment indirectly stimulated by such projects may be foregone. Opportunities to mobilize personal and family savings through the availability of matching loan funds also are diminished.

Studies on the informal sector conducted across African cities suggest that the latent demand for loans is very high.[47] The cited studies also suggest that the type of loan demanded (fixed capital, working capital) differs according to type of informal activity. Manufacturing activities, for example, generally require more start-up capital than commerce and services; often land may have to be purchased, structures built, and tools and machinery bought. In one survey of activities in Abidjan, Côte d'Ivoire, the fixed capital requirements of manufacturing enterprises are at least ten times those for commercial or service firms (de Miras [1980]). This finding is confirmed in work on Freetown, Lagos, and Nairobi. Whatever the type of loan desired, the same sources confirm that formal financial institutions play a negligible role in promoting informal sector business development. Thus, capital market fragmentation serves as a special deterrent to growth in small- and medium-scale manufacturing owned by indigenous capitalists, who also lack the connections of expatriate communities or minority ethnic groups with strong commercial traditions. Not surprisingly, small- and medium-scale, indigenously owned manufacturing firms are especially scarce in much of Africa.

2.8. Neglected Opportunities: Policies to Reinforce Rural-Urban Links

The exploration of rural-urban links has become an object of increasing attention among students of development.[48] A brief review of the subject cannot delve into the degree of specificity that agriculture and rural development specialists might prefer, given the enormous number of commodities involved, each with its own characteristic production, processing, and distribution features. Nevertheless, it is worth emphasizing those spatial aspects of the production and marketing cycle shared by most commodities.

Broadly speaking, each rural household involved in agricultural production can draw on nearby towns, and the network of cities and towns connected to them, for a variety of products and services. Input requirements met through the urban network include market information, improved seeds, fertilizer, machinery and tools, spare parts, repair services, and credit. Once produced, outputs must be marketed. Nearby towns act as transportation and communication hubs that can reach out to regional, national, and international markets. This marketing function involves various operations, including grading, storage, assembly for shipment, distribution to wholesalers, and sales by retailers. These same towns are often the centers of daily or periodic markets directed at local regional consumers. The production and sale of agricultural commodities is not an end in itself—there must be "incentive" consumer goods and services, as well as savings and investment opportunities. While not every option need come from local urban centers, those locations may be far more accessible than the rest of the urban system, and thus play an important role in shaping rural household perceptions on available goods, services, and investment opportunities.

The public services provided by these small urban centers also are accessible, at relatively low cost, to the region's rural community. Urban-based schools and health facilities can service a large number of farms and villages. Local municipal authorities can help to maintain area roads feeding into the urban centers, providing a form of asset maintenance otherwise hard to come by. The availability of power and piped water in the region's towns opens new options for agribusinesses, especially those involved in processing activities. These, in turn, can provide farmers with a service, and potentially for some, an outlet for savings. The provision of residential, transportation, and communications infrastructure in urban centers can also create an appropriate local base for skilled workers who must be attracted to provide specialized services, such as extension work or credit institutions.

A substantial proportion of the urban population in sub-Saharan Africa derives its livelihood primarily by serving the rural producer, directly or indirectly. One estimate (Cour [1985]) suggests that up to 90 percent of the labor force in towns of five thousand to twenty thousand is so engaged; while, on a regional basis, seven out of every ten urban residents are linked, in some degree, to the primary sector.

One final linkage bears mentioning. *Across sub-Saharan Africa there is evidence that rural-urban migration forms part of a rural household strategy to diversify sources of income* (for an excellent and detailed discussion of rural-urban social ties, see Clark [1985]; for the basic theory see Stark [1991] or Collier and Lal [1984]; see also Lucas and Stark [1985], O'Connor [1983], and Jamal and Weeks [1988]).[49] The central idea is that rural households or extended families will seek to reduce the riskiness of their income streams by sending one or more family members to work in cities, often bearing some of the migrant's (or migrants') urban set-up and job search costs. The increase in "job portfolio diversification" enables the household to engage in risky but high expected yield farm investments (and urban job search), and to hedge against crop failure. Thus, employment diversification and migration effectively substitute for well-functioning capital and insurance markets.

A review of existing data suggests that most migrants regularly remit goods or money to rural areas, and that these remittances represent between 10 percent to 20 percent of migrants' estimated household income.[50] In a 1982 survey of smallholders living in Central Province, Kenya, it was found that 68 percent of migrants sent remittances to rural relatives; the amounts sent averaged 19.6 percent of the full sample's earnings, and 23.5 percent of the incomes of those that did choose to remit (Hoddinott [1992]).[51]

The relative weight of the remittances in rural household income also varies; in some cases, notably the communal farming areas of Zimbabwe (World Bank [1983e]) or the villages of southeast Senegal (Venard [1985]), remittances can literally double annual rural household income. This income stream is more than an insurance scheme; it can play a major role in promoting farm innovation and the purchase of off-farm inputs. Collier and Lal (1984) (also see Stark [1980]), reviewing evidence from three provinces in Kenya, suggest that rural factor markets do not work very well. As a result, the adoption of innovations (including the associated capital and operating expenses) is often foregone, because self-financing out of current income is impossible and credit is difficult to obtain. Remittances associated with town and city employment help attenuate the perceived risk of innovation, while providing a means of servicing loans used to switch production to cash crops, improved livestock, hybrid maize, and a high level of purchased inputs.

A proxy for measuring the impact of remittances on rural development can be found by examining the behavior of rural-urban migrants who return to the countryside, especially in areas that are relatively accessible to urban markets.[52] Return migrants in Zambia, for example, tend to own larger farms than nonmigrants, and to make greater use of improved agricultural practices and technology (Chilivumbo [1985]). Capital from migration allows farmers without access to prohibitively expensive credit to invest in farm improvements, while giving others a chance to qualify for formal sector loans. Return migrants also help to inject cash resources into the rural economy, and to develop the bulk of nonfarm rural entrepreneurial ventures. In each case, the earnings and savings of the return migrant constitute the major source of funds for such activities. Adepoju (1983) confirms that the Zambian example is not unusual:

> Return migrants are known to serve as agents of cultural, social, and economic diffusion. They often influence the home community, on a macro level, by their personal example. By introducing new crops or improved varieties of existing ones, by employing new or improved techniques of production, and by encouraging education and organization, they serve as agents of change, opinion leaders and innovators. The ripple effect of their expenditures and investments in housing construction, trade, commerce, large-scale farming, and the introduction of new varieties of high-yielding seeds may directly promote rural development. . . .

This wide variety of rural-urban linkages does not appear automatically. In fact, sub-Saharan Africa is full of examples of policies and institutions which short-circuit these interactions to the detriment of both farm and town. A prime culprit is the macroeconomic environment that has typified conditions across much of the region. Inadequate price incentives also have been a common complaint among African farmers, especially in the prestructural adjustment era. With exceptions of countries where farm organizations have a strong organized lobby (Côte d'Ivoire, Zimbabwe, Kenya), farmers have faced onerous price controls often backed by attempts to suppress unofficial private trading or, in the case of food goods, by efforts to flood the market with subsidized imports.[53] Often, these policies are accompanied by a protectionist trade regime and an overvalued currency, whose combined impact is to raise the prices of consumer goods to levels well above what they would otherwise be.

Many economists therefore recommend "getting the prices right" as the principal means of solving sectoral problems. However, World Bank and other sources provide repeated evidence that price incentives alone are insufficient. In his study of the impact of price and exchange policies on agriculture in the region, Cleaver (1985) concludes that the price and exchange rate policies followed since Independence have had an impact on agriculture production, and that impact has usually been negative. However, he finds that these policies are not the most important reason for the poor agricultural performance registered by so many of the region's economies. Instead, farmers react to a whole package of incentives, most of which are linked to the adequacy of urban-based activities.[54] The World Bank's agricultural sector report on Kenya [1984e] asserts, for example:

> Without additional measures to improve input delivery and incentives, it is unlikely that the Government's ambitious agricultural development programs will be effective, as input availability may well be as important to smallholders as price incentives in influencing production decisions.

Bryceson's (1984) study of Tanzanian agriculture seconds this, reporting that improved rural production cannot be achieved without effective urban development policies on the one hand, or urban manufactured goods and services on the other. Nor can it be achieved without adequate rural infrastructure, part of which is provided by urban dwellers and institutions, and which boosts peasants' productivity:

> The urban-provisioned rural infrastructure would have to involve an improvement of transport as well as increased productivity in urban manufacturing and services, thereby lowering the costs of consumer and producer goods and social services for the rural population.

Finally, there is a detailed illustration of disrupted urban-rural links to be found in the World Bank (1988) *Zaire Urban Sector Mission Report*, with its review of regional development in Kivu province:

> The major bottleneck of the agricultural sector does not seem to be on the production side but on the marketing side. Food productivity (quantity of food produced per farmer) is mostly determined by the size of the market, which is to say by the demand for food by non-farmers, beyond local self-consumption.
>
> This means that the prerequisite to an increase in agricultural output is an expansion of accessible market(s). . . . The size of the urban market for food projects develops at a low rate because urban population itself grows at a low rate, because urban incomes are low, and because accessibility to the urban market of Kivu and to other regional markets is very poor (unpredictable state of roads, high transport costs, inadequate marketing facilities and other services, lack of credit).

This last example is worth elaborating. Cour (1985) has pointed out that ready access to urban markets is a major factor in explaining the productivity of the farm community. In fact, one can conceive of a network of urban centers whose demand impact on farmers in any locality is proportional to each city's size and inversely proportional to the difficulty of reaching it. Around major urban centers one usually finds a prosperous farm belt specializing in such perishable, high value-to-weight produce as vegetables and fruits, as well as raising chickens and producing dairy products. At great distances from urban centers, isolation results in little more than subsistence farming. In between, the degree to which farmers produce for sale will vary with the state of local and interregional transport links. This suggests that both rural and urban development investment decisions are best undertaken in a coordinated fashion with transportation plans for each region.

In Zambia, for example, a review of rural development (Chilivumbo [1985]) found that a strong correlation existed between a province's access to the network of urban centers and its level of agricultural development (a point obvious to anyone with even a passing familiarity with the Zambian economy). The Southern province has the best market access and the most developed farm system. The Eastern province is far less accessible to urban centers and transport facilities and is correspondingly less developed. The Western and Luapula provinces are isolated and have thus participated minimally in cash crop production.

Isolation from national urban markets also explains the fate of the town of Matam (population twelve thousand) in eastern Senegal. That area's farmers are cut off from the bulk of potential buyers due to the absence of all-weather interregional roads. As a result, Matam can do little but wait. A bilateral donor who financed an abattoir in Matam has erected little more than a monument to excessive optimism. To a lesser degree, the urban centers of the Great Lakes region of central Africa (Kivu province, Zaire; Burundi; Rwanda) face demand constraints that can only be fully removed through more investment in interregional or international transport links. The potential rate of return in new transport facilities in these areas can be gauged by the fact that farmers in Kivu province export produce to Kinshasa by air, while cement is flown in the opposite direction.[55]

In other cases, the problems restricting urban-rural links are susceptible to resolution at the regional or local level, but only after an appropriate reform in intergovernmental relations initiated at the national level. In Zaire and Côte d'Ivoire, for example, any infrastructural investment of more than very modest dimensions is decided by the central government. Localities cannot, on their own, mobilize substantial resources at the local level to finance, directly or through loans, infrastructure programs that will provide electric power, piped water, improved schools, and better local area roads. As a result, cities like Oume (population twenty-six thousand) in Côte d'Ivoire or Beni (population forty thousand) in Zaire's Kivu province cannot translate their earnings from coffee production into additional infrastructure that will allow the urban economic base to expand. Conversely, a city like Marondera (population twenty thousand) in Zimbabwe has grown within an environment that has allowed it to invest in its own development. As a result, it has a full spectrum of public services and infrastructure, mostly geared to satisfying the requirements of its agricultural hinterland.

Whatever the proximate cause, there are widespread reports across Africa of communities that cannot develop the infrastructure base necessary to stimulate private investment. As a result, the money generated by commercial farming transactions and by remittances does not attract more than a small fraction of the potential volume of local urban economic activity. The local multiplier effect is thus weakened (Prindle [1984], McNulty [1985]), further stunting the development of secondary towns and commercial agriculture in rural areas.

As Cleaver's (1985) review of the factors behind poor agricultural performance points out, some of the bottlenecks appear to have been caused by deliberate government attempts to replace the private sector operating in cities and towns with highly centralized and vertically integrated parastatals. As a result, the urban system fails to support agriculture, and farmers are forced to rely on the parastatals which are, as a rule, very poor substitutes.

An excellent example of an inefficient parastatal is the Senegalese SAED,[56] which is charged with the development of irrigated rice areas in the northeast. Studies prepared for the Commission of the European Communities emphasize the total detachment of the area's rice production system from the network of cities and towns:

> The transporters, the artisans, the merchants, the local banks—none are called upon, because all credit or inputs, all marketing activities follow the integrated circuit of the parastatal. (Champand, Lombard, and Sivignon [1984]; authors' translation).

> The parastatal's functions are developed in a featureless plain characterized only by conditions linked to soil quality, to climate, and to water management. At the limit, one would think that the immense zone controlled by SAED is only populated by canals and a "work force." (Bissiliat and Fenet-Rieutord [1984]; authors' translation).

As part of the structural adjustment process, SAED is to be largely dismantled. A review of urban functions in the Senegal River delta suggests that one center, Richard Toll (population 20,000), has the potential to grow to 100,000 inhabitants in twenty years. This would come about largely because of the dismantling of SAED. Already, private firms are emerging to cultivate, process, and market rice using Richard Toll as a base. Input suppliers that previously serviced parastatals from Dakar, like the Societe Senegalaise des Produits Chimiques, are beginning to open facilities in Richard Toll to reach the small-scale purchaser (Venard [1985]).

It is clear that, to a greater or lesser extent, lessons such as this one can be documented across sub-Saharan Africa. The synthesis of country studies prepared for the Commission of the European Communities (Wetheimer, Becq, and Gaveau [1984]) puts the case as eloquently as any. It reports that most parastatals are based in the capital; even if branches are located in secondary centers, they often are mere satellites de-linked from all local activity:

> Modern equipment, fertilizers and pesticides are supplied by the agencies themselves not by the town, stocks of inputs being transported direct from the center; heavy equipment, including tractors, is owned by the agencies or by central enterprises.
>   . . . the banking function, which is so important for a town, has to a large extent been supplanted by a closed system, of centralized origin, which supplies inputs for free against a promise that the produce will be marketed. Funding comes directly from the center, is changed into inputs and exchanged for produce, which represents a very low velocity of circulation.

As a result, the network of towns has a moribund commercial and manufacturing sector, there is little financial intermediation through local institutions, and the centers have few resources with which to develop themselves. Neither locally held savings nor locally established financial institutions will flourish, nor will their potential backward and forward linkages be able to operate.

The international donor community has, in the past, been guilty of supporting these types of parastatals.[57] In addition, there is evidence that even rural development projects financed with donor aid have ignored the urban network:

> Usually, the foreign and local management personnel take up temporary residence on site or in the nearest town, bring in their own vehicles, have their own stock of inputs and independent means of equipping the project.
>   It is rare for the secondary town to be explicitly included in the operation and for measures to be taken, within the context of the project, to stimulate its supply of services and its demand for products, or, in other words, to organize mutual aid reciprocal enrichment. (Wetheimer et al. [1984])

Because the institutional structure prevalent until now has been inefficient and damaging to marketed agricultural output, it is under review in many countries. The structural adjustment process often has as one of its objectives the abolition or drastic restructuring of the agricultural parastatals. As a result, the private sector, operating from cities and towns, could gain new importance. As noted, Senegal's SAED is to be stripped of most of its present functions. Ghana's Cocoa Board is now committed to reducing its staff by twenty thousand workers, while being reorganized as a for-profit, commercial operation; the streamlined corporation will be far more reliant on the private sector than in the past. In Zambia, the National Agricultural Marketing Board (NAMBOARD) has been reduced to undertaking interprovincial trade of maize and fertilizer and the holding of national grain reserves. In Uganda, there is broad agreement that the role of the main export crop marketing boards should be limited to the purchase of the processed crop and the transport to port for export. These types of actions are likely to be repeated across the continent as the structural adjustment process intensifies.

As institutional changes and reforms in pricing and trade regimes promise to restructure incentives, the question arises about the future course of the agricultural sector. There is broad agreement on two major points: 1) the sector must generate much more commercial production than it has in the past; and 2) such increases will be made possible in part by a change in technology, which will be more input- and equipment-intensive than is true on average today. Both counts suggest that the relative importance of the subsistence farmer—who has little use for a town—will diminish and that commercial operations will become more significant.[58] Thus, the fact that future economic growth will occur within the context of an agriculture-led development strategy in no way diminishes the role of cities and towns in the future. The pervasive links between cities and rural areas documented in this chapter indicate the crucial importance of urban centers to any successful rural development strategy.

3

African City Systems and Urban Growth

3.1 The Spectre of Overurbanization: Myths and Realities

Fears about urbanization frequently are but proxies for concern about the size and growth rates of very large cities. This may explain much of the concern about African urbanization, since the continent's urban growth has been disproportionately concentrated in capital cities and major ports. Section 3.1 focuses on three areas that have been of particular concern to both economists and African policymakers: the presumed high level of unemployment in large cities, the assumed upper limits to a city's optimal size, and the apparent need for a balanced system of cities, often reflecting the purported optimality of the "rank size rule."[1]

There is a limited substantive basis to each of these concerns, but in no case does the problem warrant restricting economic or population growth of Africa's very large cities. Of the three issues, the most severe real problems surround urban unemployment.

The remaining sections of the chapter address statistical measures of urban concentration and primacy, as well as the forces shaping the present patterns of African urban systems. The chapter concludes with an econometric examination of Africa's existing urban systems and the predictions of neoclassical economic trade theory.

3.1.1. Unemployment and the Growth of Large Cities

There can be little doubt that substantial open unemployment and severe underemployment characterize most large African cities today. As is documented in Chapter 5, formal sector job growth has at best equalled the national population growth rate in most countries since 1974. This has resulted from stagnant public sector employment and low manufacturing employment growth rates of around 3–4 percent. Moreover, it is obvious that small formal sectors can absorb only a portion of potential labor force entrants even if economic performances improve considerably, since Africa's urban population growth rates are typically in the 5–7 percent range. To make matters worse, both the national and urban populations of

53

TABLE 3.1. Annual Growth Rates of Population by Age Groups: National and Urban Estimates (percent)

Age Group:	National population			Urban population		
	all	20–24	25–29	all	20–24	25–29
1. Botswana, 1971–81						
Female	4.8	6.5	5.6	9.3	12.3	11.3
Male	5.4	9.4	7.3	10.3	15.0	12.5
2. Kenya, 1969–79						
Female	3.5	4.3	2.8	5.5	7.4	5.6
Male	3.3	4.1	3.9	4.9	6.4	4.7
3. Zambia, 1974–80						
Female	3.1	7.3	3.4	9.7	9.3	8.6
Male	3.3	7.7	5.2	7.9	8.2	7.7

Source: United Nations, Demographic Yearbook, various years.

teenagers and young adults—who will be the main labor force entrants—generally are growing more rapidly still (see Table 3.1). With respect to national populations, the twenty- to twenty-four-year-old age group grew 2–4 percent more rapidly in Botswana, 0.8 percent more rapidly in Kenya and about 4 percent more rapidly in Zambia. A smaller but still positive difference exists for the twenty to twenty-five year cohort, excluding the inexplicably (and probably implausibly) slow growth of Kenyan women in this group. A considerable positive difference also exists for young urban groups with respect to total urban population growth, although here it appears mainly for the twenty to twenty-four year cohort. In any event, it is unreasonable to expect that even an economy as vibrant as Botswana's will be able to easily generate employment for its young adults in the urban formal sectors, and it is quite clear that moribund economies like Zambia's will not.

Nor can it be expected that highly productive informal sector employment will absorb all of the rest. Informal sector activities rely heavily on demand generated by formal sector workers: economy-wide recessions and foreign exchange crises almost certainly have reduced informal sector incomes as well.

On the other hand, it has not been shown conclusively that unemployment is worse in big cities than in small cities and towns, although most observers probably believe this to be the case.[2] In the absence of reliable data, though, there are several reasons to believe that unemployment rates are highest in larger cities. To start with, large cities tend to have more institutions of higher education and more young educated people: assuming plausibly that the return to job search activities rises with skills, then overt unemployment also will rise with education (at least until very scarce skills are exhibited). Sheer size also increases the complexity of the labor market, and the amount of information to be gathered, implying again that returns to search activity—and hence unemployment—will rise with city size.

For the most part, though, assuming that such an unemployment gap does exist between Africa's largest cities and its smaller urban areas, it is likely to be due to policies that concentrate opportunities in the largest urban centers, and to other labor market imperfections (see Chapter 5 for a more detailed analysis). An impartial observer might urge that governments address the structural causes of unemployment rather than the symptoms—unemployment, after all, is clearly an endogenous variable, not a direct policy variable. It is also important to recognize, however, that unemployment in big cities carries with it more potential for political instability than does unemployment and underemployment elsewhere, so that governments may be rational in trying to control big city population growth and unemployment.

But without denying that the present economic crisis has created unemployment problems in urban areas, most visibly in large cities, the fact remains that prolonged unemployment is not an option except for secondary household members and school-leavers from relatively affluent households.[3] Migrant household heads, once they have worn out their welcome with kin (though this may involve a lengthy stay), must either work or move again, and are thus unlikely to create an unemployment problem for cities, large or small.[4] This is especially true in countries with lagging agricultural performance, as rural families are able to finance only short spells of urban job search for migrant family members. Most new labor force entrants become employed in "informal" activities or small-scale enterprises rather than in large, capital-intensive offices and factories, in part because the search period is much shorter for informal employment.[5] These informal activities may offend some sensitivities, but this sector's growth in no way merits the retaliatory action (banning certain activities and licensing others) that some countries have taken. In fact, the informal sector may (or, at least in principle could) provide formal sector enterprises an efficient source of inputs that permit them to compete with imported goods and, in some cases, to export their products. Even more importantly, the earnings differential (once adjusted for demographic and skill factors) between formal and informal sector workers undoubtedly has fallen markedly in the structural adjustment era.[6]

Nor is there merit in steps taken to directly limit the growth of large cities. Shipping the unemployed back to the countryside, as Tanzania has done at times (discussed in Stren [1982] and [1989]), or bulldozing squatter settlements, as the Kenyan government did in the spring of 1990 (and which has been common in many Third World countries), temporarily removes evidence of desperate poverty from the capital cities.[7] But neither poverty nor the poor vanish; rather, assuming that those prevented by various means from living in the cities would have lived there out of economic self-interest, the consequence is to worsen their plight. Squatter clearance also destroys the small amount of savings (in the form of housing stock) that those affected have managed to accumulate.

Other standard remedies for urban unemployment are problematic as well. *Urban formal sector job creation* measures are extremely expensive and generally ineffective. Few African governments can possibly afford to provide a sufficient number of such jobs so as to substantially reduce urban unemployment. But most have tried, and the result has been abysmally low government savings rates (and often alarmingly high rates of money supply growth), coupled with parastatals rendered less competitive than ever because of their needlessly large wage bills. Even to the extent that new jobs are created, though, urban unemployment may not fall. As Harris and Todaro (1970) pointed out long ago, new job creation will attract migrants from the countryside in search of urban opportunities, and the number attracted may well exceed the number of new jobs.

Nor are *food subsidies aimed at improving the welfare of the urban poor* a generally viable option, although they may be appropriate if narrowly focused at target groups. Subsidies tend to be prohibitively expensive if not targeted, and in countries such as Sudan have led to macroeconomic havoc. Moreover, once in place these subsidies are difficult to remove. But the alternative preferred by many governments—to suppress food prices by imposing a monopsony on peasant food grain deliveries, and by maintaining an overvalued exchange rate to keep food imports cheap—is as bad or worse. Price suppression policies reduce peasant incomes and marketed surpluses, while overvalued exchange rates deter commercial food and nonfood production further.

Finally, *urban incomes policies* aimed at reducing poverty among unskilled formal sector workers are a misguided effort. To the extent such policies work, their effect is largely to create a "labor aristocracy" rather than to alleviate poverty generally. These policies also ensure high costs for parastatals. Ironically, these policies may well increase urban unemployment for the standard Harris-Todaro reasons. Because of the distortions they entail, especially by inhibiting urban formal sector job creation, these incomes policies represent a very expensive way to transfer incomes to the formal sector unskilled.[8]

The policies sketched above may (or may not) reduce urban unemployment and poverty. Wealthier governments can engage in skills training and food subsidy programs to improve the lot of the urban poor, but should be aware of these policies' indirect effects on migration, production, and government finances. But for weaker African states, these options often are not viable. Rather, the best policy for these nations is likely to involve a labor-using, high-growth strategy. Although there is not uniform agreement on the importance of demand structure, we believe that the evidence suggests that shifting demand toward labor-intensive goods matters. While one might normally not expect demand structure to be critical in what are essentially supply-constrained economies, two forces modify this general principle. First, many African countries are very small, and have very poor transport infrastructure, so that demand expansion may be necessary for producers to realize scale economies, even in the informal sector. Secondly, there is great variation in the capital intensity of different productive sectors in African economies, so that there is considerable scope for achieving both more egalitarian income distribution and expansion of (capital- and import-saving) activities in which a country has a comparative advantage.

Efforts to raise incomes of the poor while simultaneously concentrating on policies that generate supply expansion of their main consumption items will also be important. Ironically, as Becker, Williamson, and Mills (1992) have found for India, one of the most important consumers of capital-intensive goods (and employers of skilled labor, thereby skewing further the income distribution) is government.[9] Government has an important role to play throughout Africa in terms of molding incentives and institutions and in providing infrastructure, but, in many cases, its size is a direct determinant of the degree of income inequality and urban bias. Furthermore, African governments certainly should not be restricting urban growth—either of large or small cities—in order to combat unemployment.

3.1.2. Is There an Optimal City Size?

A popular misconception that often appears in discussions of "excess primacy" is the notion of optimal city size. A simple argument in support of this hypothesis posits that, as cities grow, infrastructure and public service unit costs first fall, then bottom out, and rise. The minimum unit cost point is thus associated with the optimal city size. Usually this size is estimated as being between one hundred thousand and one million inhabitants.[10]

There are several fatal problems with this "optimal" size argument. First, it ignores the *benefits* associated with working and living in cities of different sizes. Unit cost minimization is no substitute for maximizing net benefits (i.e., benefits minus costs).[11] A similar problem exists with arguments in favor of controlling city size in order to minimize pollution or congestion costs for the urban or national populations.

Second, the argument over cost is itself flawed. The observed pattern of infrastructure costs across cities reflects both unit costs and the income levels; these two factors are important determinants of the quality or standards of investments. From the demand side, certain types of households (especially the relatively wealthy) that dominate larger cities may desire higher levels of public services, and, being politically powerful, may get them. If their wishes are met, the apparent greater cost of providing urban services in large cities may simply reflect quality differentials (and, if public service supply curves are upward sloping, the cost will reflect this fact as well). If different urban populations recognize the supply curve's shape and if they demand different quantities nonetheless, no inefficiency results from higher per capita public service expenditures, as long as households are willing to and do themselves pay for a given level of service (Tiebout [1956]).[12]

Third, the unit cost curves of different services (one for each level of quality) will begin increasing at different hypothetical city sizes. How then can planners decide how to weigh all the various "optima" (one for bus networks, one for standpipes, one for paved roads, one for power . . .)? A fourth problem is that the optimal size argument is essentially applicable only in a static environment. In reality, of course, external conditions, and hence optimal city sizes, change constantly. But since investments in urban infrastructure are largely irreversible, public policies aimed at reaching an optimal city size are likely to be frequently misguided.

Finally, unit costs of different services can be very sensitive to city-specific factors. Population densities will affect the cost of the distribution networks of water pipes or bus services. Geographic features will also play a role. Even the incremental nature of infrastructural investment affects its unit costs: costs may differ depending upon whether services are added in a piecemeal fashion or all at once. Costs also will vary depending whether completely new production facilities (water, power) must be constructed. In sum, the unit cost issue is extremely complex, and any single optimizing rule is hardly adequate.[13] Instead, as Mills (1983) has noted:

> Service cost and per capita expenditures imply nothing as to whether infrastructure service levels are excessive or deficient in particular places. That can be done only by careful benefit-cost analysis. The more fundamental question is what system of infrastructure financing and decision-making leads to incentives that induce appropriate infrastructural investments and hence appropriate levels of urbanization.

A more sophisticated hypothesis about optimal city size is that there are economic benefits and costs of doing business associated with different city sizes. At some size (given a static environment where prices, technology, demand, and other such factors are frozen) net benefits will be maximized (see Henderson [1977] and Richardson [1977]). But identifying such a maximum and doing something about it are virtually insurmountable problems:

> First, data on all the relevant parameters are not available and statistical tools of measurement are sufficiently crude that we can only confidently specify wide estimated ranges of any particular parameter value that we have the data to estimate.
> Second, in even the simplest numerical examples, the calculated efficient size can be very sensitive to alterations in the hypothetical values of parameters. (Henderson [1980])

In fact, a small alteration in the assumed parameters can alter "efficient city size" by a factor of two or three.

Finally, whatever the optimal size of a city may be, it is dependent upon several factors that change over time: the location and size of other cities, the level of national development, and the functions performed by that center. This leads Richardson (1977) to conclude that

> It might be possible to dilute the concept of a unique optimum into the weaker proposition of an optimum size for an individual city at a specific location with specific functions at a particular phase of its development. Needless to say, this dilution generates so many optima that it can provide no guidelines to policymakers.

But while quantifying optimal sizes for African centers may be both quite difficult and of very limited policy relevance, it is clear that Africa's largest cities have benefited from infrastructural policies, pricing, and exchange rate policies that favor their growth relative both to smaller cities and to rural areas. Growth of government has propelled these cities too, while smaller towns have been hurt by stagnant agricultural and agro-industrial sectors. Stated differently, the best option for controlling growth of the largest cities is simply to avoid measures that favor them inappropriately.

3.1.3. Are African City Systems Too Primate?

Empirically, there seems to be limited but growing cause for alarm concerning primacy in Africa. As we document below, urban concentration does not seem to be exceptional in most of Africa. However, the relative growth of largest cities (until recently) implies that primacy has increased since Independence, and certainly since the midcentury (for striking documentation of Dar es Salaam's increased primacy, see Sawers [1989]). Furthermore, it is clear that the distributions of modern sector employment and earnings are far more concentrated than is the distribution of urban population.[14]

But if we define "large" cities to be those with over 500,000 inhabitants, Africa had only twenty-eight as of 1980, nine of which were in Nigeria. The percentage of the 1980 urban population living in these centers is low by international standards. For the low-income semiarid countries the proportion is zero, and for other low-income countries in sub-Saharan Africa it is approximately 32 percent.[15] The proportion of the urban population in large cities rises to 35 percent for middle-income oil importers, and 25 percent for middle-income oil exporters. Turning to the share of these large cities in the total population, some sixteen cities have total population shares above 10 percent: Abidjan, Accra, Bangui, Brazzaville, Conakry, Cotonou, Dakar, Freetown, Harare, Kinshasa, Lome, Luanda, Lusaka, Maputo, Mogadishu, and Nouakchott. However, only Brazzaville (30 percent), Dakar (23 percent), Cotonou (18 percent), and Conakry (16 percent) had more than 15 percent of the national population within their boundaries. Dar es Salaam, Nairobi, and N'Djamena had joined the "over 10 percent" group by 1987, so that nineteen of the twenty-nine countries for which data were reported had more than 10 percent of their national population living in a single city.

Another way of looking at this issue is to examine the size of the largest cities in each country. Only nine African cities had 1980 populations above one million; of these only Lagos, Kinshasa, Ibadan, Abidjan, and Khartoum had populations well over one million. By international standards, few cities in Africa would be considered very large.

This impressionistic evidence is supported by the statistical studies discussed in the following sections. Furthermore, as we find in section 3.5, a modest proportion of the variation in different countries' degrees of primacy (a measure of the importance of the largest cities in an urban system) is readily explicable by economic theory. Unusually primate countries include Congo, The Gambia, Uganda, Sudan, Tanzania, Mauritius, Ghana, Liberia, and Ethiopia.

O'Connor (1983: 42–47) is somewhat ambivalent about the welfare implications of excessive primacy, as his survey finds no evidence of a correlation between per capita income and the degree of primacy. He attributes what he regards as a fairly high degree of spatial concentration within countries to the continent's "Balkanization," and alleges that the degree of primacy is rising (p.267). Yet he provides little empirical evidence for that assertion. On the one hand, estimates of the proportion of urban populations in the largest cities have been rising over time; on the other, the economic crisis may have curbed growth quite dramatically in Africa's largest cities (see Chapter 6 for evidence on this score for Zambia).

The existing neoclassical urban economics literature on the evolution of the size distribution of cities over time suggests that, for any one country, there is a tendency to begin the process of development with a relatively dispersed urban structure anchored around poorly linked, economically autonomous subsystems. Development tends to bring selective improvements in interregional transport and communications, often based on efforts to promote primary product exports. As noted, large centers tend to get access to urban infrastructure first, thus creating economic "city-states" that can produce a varied mix of goods and services with far less total infrastructure than it would take if a large number of small centers were so equipped.[16] In early development stages, these same centers provide easy access to monetized markets and attract complementary inputs like specialized labor and business services.

Eventually, dispersion does take place, as regional centers begin to grow more rapidly than the largest cities. Many factors appear to be involved. National infrastructure development generates improved access to other parts of the country, while improved infrastructure in regional centers, income growth in the "periphery" due to exploitation of local resource endowments, and emigration of manufacturing originally located in large cities but later forced out due the relatively high costs of doing business there, all contribute to decentralization as well.[17] Rural development is especially critical, for agricultural commercialization provides demand for the growth of weight-losing (and hence decentralized) processing industries and simultaneously induces the decentralized growth of market towns to provide goods and services to rural areas.

In summary, economic theory predicts that urban concentration will be very high in countries with small populations, low per capita incomes, small agricultural surpluses, and which have only recently begun to develop their economies outside of the agricultural and traditional services sectors. As these characteristics apply to most African countries (Nigeria is a notable exception), it is not surprising that primacy indices are high. On the other hand, they can also be expected to fall in the coming decades, especially if agricultural production increases.

A somewhat different approach, consistent with the basic needs and "trickle-up" development viewpoints, has been advanced by Rondinelli (1983) and associates (for a critical assessment, see Gore [1984]; for a brief, compelling exposition of the argument, see Gaile [1988]). A stylized depiction of Rondinelli's theory is that large metropolitan areas have "backwash effects" that drain the hinterlands of human and natural resources.[18] Greater spatial diffusion thus enables market demand to mature, and hence spurs Hirschmanian forward linkages, while improved access to raw materials and more remote suppliers simultaneously enhance the development of backward linkages, in both cases to economic groups and regions previously left out of the development process. Consequently, spatial deconcentration should lead to relatively rapid, egalitarian growth. While Rondinelli does not decry urbanization per se (indeed, he too acknowledges that rural development may actually increase overall urbanization for standard neoclassical reasons), he does claim that there appears to be a relationship between economic development and the city-size distribution. Unfortunately, the preceding paragraph indicates that the direction of causality is unclear. A further argument in favor of small-town promotion is that small-town firms tend to generate much more employment per unit of output or capital than do large cities, and also are skilled-labor-saving. Again, however, the direction of causality is uncertain.

Rondinelli's arguments are strong, although they omit the scale and agglomeration forces that are almost certainly important in infrastructure- and capital-scarce Africa. Given the terribly weak marketing and transport infrastructure in most of Africa, it seems obvious that growth of secondary towns that generate improvements in these areas will be critically important for rural development. Furthermore, it is also clear (Chapter 6) that secondary cities are important centers for agricultural processing, the growth of which is also a necessary condition for rapid rural output growth in many countries. Finally, it is difficult not to notice the lack of interaction (other than remittances) between modern sector enclaves and the rest of the economy in all too many countries. While development of linkages may be an effective way of raising recorded per capita incomes, there may be only a weak connection in Africa between national income aggregates and actual economic modernization or, for that matter, incomes of the poor.

For these reasons, and in part for political arguments relating to equity and the reduced need to provide extremely costly services to urban dwellers in smaller cities, the Rondinelli view has attracted a diverse group of adherents. USAID pursued spatial strategies based on the thesis in a number of countries, including

Cameroon, Kenya, and Burkina Faso.[19] Among African governments, the two most determined advocates of decentralization ideology have been otherwise ideologically conflicting Kenya and Tanzania.

The answer to the question of excessive urban primacy remains unresolved. Our view is a fairly conservative one: spatial policy in many but not all cases represents a second-best solution to problems that are only partially spatial in origin. Spatial policy is obviously important in designing infrastructural strategies. But it alone will do little to convert enclave economies into more integrated economies.

3.2 Measures of Urban Concentration in Africa

Having described the debates surrounding urban structure, the remainder of this chapter turns to a more detailed examination of African patterns. In order to compare the urbanization experience of different countries, or even to examine the evolution of a given country's urban system over time, a set of descriptive statistics is needed. Particularly useful are measures that summarize the characteristics of an urban system in a single descriptive statistic. Four such urban concentration measures are examined in this section: two primacy indices and three measures based on statistical distributions.

The concept of primacy is a straightforward one that refers to the relative importance of the largest city or cities in an urban system. The first primacy measure is the sum of squares value, H, given by:

$$H = \sum_{i=1}^{n} \left(\frac{P_i}{P}\right)^2 \tag{3.1}$$

where P is total national population, P_i is the population in city i, and n is the number of cities in the nation. If the entire population lived in the same city, H = 1.0. If, on the other hand, the population were distributed evenly between the n cities, H approaches zero as n becomes large. Note that H attaches heavy weight to urban populations far from the mean. The sum of squares measure has the advantage of being simple to compute. As with all primacy measures, however, different H values have no normative significance.

A second primacy measure is the urban primacy index, UP, and is given by:

$$UP = \frac{P_1}{P_u} \tag{3.2}$$

where P_1 is the population of the largest city and P_u is total national urban population. The trouble with UP is that it effectively ignores the size distribution of cities below the largest (Wheaton and Shishido [1981:19]). Two nations could have quite different urban systems and still share the same urban primacy index score. Estimates of UP appear in Table 3.2.[20]

These simple measures suggest that African city systems are somewhat more primate than are systems in most developing countries (or, for that matter, the developed world), even when China and India are excluded from the comparison. Nigeria is a striking exception to this statement; so, though to a somewhat lesser

TABLE 3.2. Total Urban Population Shares of the Largest Cities, Sub-Saharan Africa, 1960 and 1980

Country	Share in total urban population of the		
	(1) largest city, 1980	(2) largest city, 1960	(3) largest four cities, 1980
(a) *Low-income countries*			
Benin	63		50
Burkina Faso	41		46
Burundi			85
Central African Republic	36	40	60
Chad	39		57
Ghana	35	25	50
Guinea	80	37	54
Guinea-Bissau			90
Ethiopia	37	30	52
Kenya	57	40	66
Lesotho			62
Liberia			61
Madagascar	36	44	61
Malawi	19		79
Mali	24	32	57
Mauritania	39		67
Mozambique	83	75	74
Namibia			52
Niger	31		65
Nigeria	17	13	22
Rwanda			84
Sierra Leone	47	37	76
Somalia	34		62
Sudan	31	30	37
Swaziland			100
Tanzania	50	34	58
Togo	60		61
Uganda	52	38	63
Zaire	28	14	52
Zambia	35		55
(b) *Middle-income countries*			
Angola	64	44	68
Botswana			34
Cameroon	21	26	46
Congo	56	77	83
Côte d'Ivoire	34	27	59
Djibouti			100
Gabon			72
Senegal	65	53	71
Zimbabwe	50	40	75

TABLE 3.2. (continued)

Country	Share in total urban population of the		
	(1) largest city, 1980	(2) largest city, 1960	(3) largest four cities, 1980
Africa			
Low-income countries	35		
excluding Nigeria	42		
Middle-income countries	45		
Sahelian countries	40		
Oil exporters	21		
World			
All low-income countries	13		
excluding China,			
India	29		
South Asia, excluding			
India	25		

Note: All aggregates are weighted averages. Categories follow World Bank designations.

Sources: Columns (1) and (2): World Bank (1989a); Column (3): Ledent (1990).

degree, are Botswana, Sudan, Mali, and Cameroon. Much of this apparently greater primacy simply reflects the tiny geographical sizes and economic bases of many African countries. It is hardly surprising to find that virtually the entire urban population of Djibouti, Guinea-Bissau, Rwanda, Burundi, or Malawi live in four or fewer cities. Indeed, had Ledent (1990) treated the greater Banjul region as one urban area, he would have found that The Gambia fell in this group as well.

In fifteen of twenty countries for which data are available, the proportion of the urban population living in the largest city increased between 1960 and 1980, suggesting that primacy may have indeed been increasing in most of the continent. But there is no obvious set of distinguishing factors between those with growing and those with decreasing concentration. War and a surging refugee population appear to have swelled the largest cities in Mozambique and Ethiopia, but not Uganda, the Central African Republic, or, to any significant degree, Sudan (if one is willing to place any credence in its population statistics). Economic decay saw growing centralization in Sierra Leone, but apparently diminishing primacy in Madagascar. Oil wealth was accompanied by slowly growing urban concentration in Nigeria, but not in Congo.[21] In short, the forces driving urban population concentration are not obvious, and must await more careful statistical analysis.

A second type of concentration measure is based explicitly on statistical distributions. Examples include the "near-neighbor" statistic and the Pareto exponent, based on the Poisson and Pareto distributions, respectively. In a Poisson distribution, the expected mean distance between each city and its nearest neighbor is equal to $(1/2) \pi^{-1/2}$, where π is the observed density of cities in the nation. The near-neighbor statistic is simply the ratio of the observed mean distance to the expected mean distance. The ratio is less than, equal to, or greater than one according to whether the distribution pattern of cities is more concentrated, the same as, or more uniform than would be expected in an infinitely large, random distribution of the same density.

Bohra (1979) uses the near-neighbor statistic to analyze the spatial distribution of cities in Somalia, examining fourteen regions of the country separately. He finds that the actual distribution for most regions is much more uniform than would be expected if cities were distributed according to the Poisson distribution, thus providing some counterevidence to urban concentration arguments. It must be emphasized, however, that only the distance between population centers—not their populations—is considered in the analysis, so that the refutation of urban concentration in Somalia is incomplete. Perhaps a divisia index of "urbanness" based on city size could be incorporated, thus resolving this problem.

The most famous urban concentration measure based on a statistical distribution is the Pareto exponent. Many geographers have long thought that city sizes within a nation follow the Pareto distribution. That is,

$$R_i = AP_i^{-\alpha} \tag{3.3}$$

where R_i is the ith city's rank in the urban hierarchy, P_i is the ith city's population, and A is a constant. In the special case when α equals 1, this distribution reduces to the rank-size rule. It is not uncommon for analysts to pass casual judgments on the city size distribution according to its deviation from the rank-size rule:

> The rank-size distribution for Nigeria . . . shows there are still gaps in the hierarchy of settlements in many areas. (Sada and Onokerhoraye [1984])

> The population of each city multiplied by its rank should be equal to the population of the largest city in the system. [Excess] primacy is present if there are fewer cities of intermediate size than would be expected from the rank-size rule . . . [Aside from Mombasa] the other intermediate towns [in Kenya] have a much smaller population compared to Nairobi than would be expected in a normal rank-size distribution. (McKim [1979])

The Pareto exponents for thirty-eight African nations are given in Table 3.3. Some very dissimilar countries have similar Pareto exponents; perhaps the most striking example is Nigeria and Lesotho. While $\alpha>1$ for both countries—indicating a dispersed urban hierarchy—the need for decentralization is much greater in Nigeria. Nigeria is a highly federated nation with a relatively large industrial base. It is also large and highly populated. In contrast, due to its tiny size and economic integration with neighboring South Africa, Lesotho probably does not need as full a range of city types, and hence sizes.

Overall, Mali's (1983) estimates in Table 3.3 indicate that African city systems are not particularly primate by international standards, in contrast to the UP measures presented in Table 3.2. The mean value for α is exactly 1.00. Given the rather small size of African urban systems (except for Nigeria's), and given the natural economies of scale to be realized from initially concentrating infrastructure investments in one or a few urban areas, this value of α seems fairly high. Indeed, it is only slightly below the mean value of 1.136 reported by Rosen and Resnick (1980) for forty-four countries. In general, subdivision into smaller regions tends to decrease the value of the Pareto coefficient.[22] Thus, the fact that even small African countries do not have particularly small Pareto coefficients supports the conclusion that African city systems are not exceptionally primate by world standards.

A comparison of Mali's and Ledent's (1990) findings is also instructive. First, it is important to note that their α estimates are only very weakly positively correlated; they are within 10 percent of each other only in nine of twenty-four cases. This divergence should suffice to discourage anyone from regarding any particular statistic describing African cities as being unquestionably reliable, especially those that summarize information from many cities. Indeed, as Ledent points out, the α measure is highly sensitive to the number of cities in the sample. In general, Ledent finds that the greater the number of cities and towns included, the less primate the urban system. This finding in part suggests that many African countries have a few (one or two) exceptionally large cities, and that the structure is less primate thereafter. But this finding is driven partly by the simple fact that very primate urban systems have fewer cities.

Secondly, when Ledent estimates Pareto coefficients using all the cities and towns available for each country, as reported in Table 3.4, the mean Pareto coefficient value is only 0.90, considerably less than Mali's. About half of this difference is due to the fact that the samples differ: Ledent included more small countries, so that his mean Pareto coefficient rises to 0.94 when the countries not in Mali's sample are excluded.

Sheppard (1982) and Sada and Onokerhoraye (see above quote) suggest that the Pareto exponent may be useful in identifying gaps in the urban hierarchy. While this may be true, it is also true that there is no direct relation between social welfare and the size distribution of cities. Despite the fact that several ad hoc theories have been concocted to explain the rank-size result, we agree with Sheppard's (1982:128) critique:

> [Theories which justify the rank-size relationship] . . . are themselves constructed in a manner that ignores the specifics of relationships between cities. In short, the level of abstraction matches that represented by the rank-size rule.

Finally, a third statistical distribution useful in analyzing urban concentration is the three parameter displaced lognormal. It is advocated by De Cola (1985), who finds that it fits actual distributions better than the Pareto distribution in most cases, and in particular provides a much better fit around the upper and lower bounds (i.e., the largest and smallest cities). In this case, one estimates the mean μ and variance σ^2 of the normal variate y, where $y = \ln(x - x^1)$, with x representing city population and x^1 the displacement parameter. The standard deviation σ then serves as a measure of urban concentration: the larger is σ, the further a city's population is from the mean of the log normal distribution, and hence the greater the degree of concentration of urban population. When De Cola examines the distribution of the largest cities by continent, he finds that the African city-size distribution is quite unconcentrated by world standards. Of his regions, only the USSR has a smaller degree of concentration. Unfortunately, though, these characteristics of Africa's largest cities are of quite limited relevance for urban distributions within a given country.

In summary, it appears that the current studies have yielded mixed results. The inconsistencies are due far more to underlying data quality than conflicting measures. But the concern of policymakers should not be lightly dismissed, since primacy does appear to have been increasing, and the economic crisis probably has hit large African cities as least as hard and perhaps harder than other regions.

TABLE 3.3. Estimates of African Pareto Coefficients from the 1970s, α_1 (based on the simple regression model, $\ln \text{Rank}_i = \alpha_0 + \alpha_1 \ln P_i$.

Country	I. Mali's estimates				II. Ledent's estimates	
	Number of Cities in Sample	α_0	$\alpha_1 = -PC$	R^2	Number of Cities in Sample	$\alpha_1 = -PC$
Botswana	10	26.0 (14.1)**	2.47 (13.25)**	0.96	8	0.80 (1.74)
Niger	15	31.6 (9.2)**	2.45 (8.62)**	0.85	40	1.03 (0.92)
Nigeria	16	20.9 (15.9)**	1.55 (14.48)**	0.94	22	1.60 (10.66)
Lesotho	9	18.9 (10.0)**	1.49 (9.22)**	0.92	10	1.01 (0.04)
Zambia	7	17.2 (13.1)**	1.30 (12.16)**	0.97	15	0.86 (2.13)
Ghana	15	16.6 (9.2)**	1.25 (8.23)**	0.84	135	1.25 (19.57)
Liberia					32	1.25 (5.87)
Sudan	7	14.3 (8.9)**	1.09 (8.12)**	0.93	84	0.94 (4.04)
Namibia					15	1.05 (0.72)
Central African Republic					25	1.04 (0.61)
Madagascar					36	1.02 (0.52)
Burkina Faso	4	11.9 (3.31)	0.97 (3.09)	0.83	19	0.97 (0.47)

Zaire	15	13.1 (21.0)**	0.93 (18.09)**	0.96	10	0.80 (2.40)
Mali	12	11.0 (11.8)**	0.91 (10.01)**	0.91	43	0.99 (0.46)
Tanzania	15	11.3 (14.3)**	0.91 (12.01)**	0.92	67	0.94 (3.08)
Chad	12	10.6 (16.3)**	0.89 (13.80)**	0.95	29	1.03 (0.74)
Somalia					8	0.85 (1.41)
Gabon					11	0.85 (2.36)
Benin					9	0.79 (2.60)
Ethiopia	15	10.3 (10.6)*	0.75 (8.76)*	0.86	157	1.15 (11.51)
Kenya	17	10.3 (37.6)**	0.76 (30.53)**	0.98	49	0.80 (17.55)
Mauritania	13	9.9 (5.7)**	0.72 (4.70)**	0.67	36	0.95 (1.52)
Togo	9	8.7 (9.5)**	0.72 (7.99)**	0.90	15	0.94 (0.51)
Uganda	11	9.0 (13.0)**	0.72 (10.75)**	0.93	20	0.84 (3.06)
Senegal	14	9.5 (18.8)**	0.72 (15.34)**	0.95	31	0.74 (7.95)
Rwanda					7	0.71 (2.62)
Mozambique					35	0.69 (8.52)

TABLE 3.3. (continued)

Country	I. Mali's estimates				II. Ledent's estimates	
	Number of Cities in Sample	α_0	$\alpha_1 = -PC$	R^2	Number of Cities in Sample	$\alpha_1 = -PC$
Swaziland					8	0.69 (2.57)
Cameroon	7	8.86 (7.5)**	0.67 (6.46)**	0.83	59	0.97 (1.36)
South Africa	16	10.2 (11.3)**	0.66 (9.19)**	0.86	45	0.73 (12.87)
Zimbabwe	12	8.7 (16.5)**	0.65 (13.40)**	0.95	19	0.70 (2.13)
Burundi					8	0.64 (2.84)
Guinea					7	0.59 (2.95)
Côte d'Ivoire	14	8.0 (13.1)**	0.55 (10.22)**	0.90	62	1.05 (1.59)
Congo					9	0.54 (7.08)
Malawi	4	10.3 (37.6)**	0.48 (6.00)*	0.98	14	0.61 (5.49)
Sierra Leone	5	6.0 (15.8)**	0.47 (13.37)**	0.98	20	0.78 (5.83)
Djibouti					8	0.44 (5.28)

	Mali	*Ledent*
Mean α_1	1.00	0.90
Standard Deviation α_1	0.52	0.27

Notes: Sample includes all cities with a population over ten thousand.

Numbers in parentheses are t-statistics.

PC = Pareto coefficient

* Significant at 5 percent significance level.

** Significant at 1 percent significance level.

Ledent estimates a constant term but does not report these estimates.

Sources: Mali (1983) and Ledent (1990).

TABLE 3.4. Annual Rates of National Population Growth

Region and Country or Area	1950–1955	1955–1960	1960–1965	1965–1970	1970–1975	1975–1980	1980–1985	1985–1990ᵖ	1990–1995ᵖ	1995–2000ᵖ
World Total	1.84	1.86	1.96	2.06	2.03	1.77	1.67	1.61	1.58	1.52
More Developed Regions	1.28	1.27	1.19	0.87	0.89	0.74	0.64	0.60	0.56	0.52
Less Developed Regions	2.11	2.14	2.30	2.55	2.46	2.14	2.02	1.92	1.87	1.79
Africa	2.11	2.32	2.44	2.61	2.74	3.00	3.01	3.08	3.09	3.05
Eastern Africa	2.22	2.48	2.77	2.85	2.94	3.14	3.23	3.33	3.39	3.39
Burundi	1.75	1.76	1.87	1.45	1.62	1.56	2.67	2.71	2.74	2.67
Comoros	2.31	2.04	2.25	2.43	3.40	3.97	3.04	3.07	3.04	2.84
Djibouti	1.87	2.19	2.31	2.42	5.79	7.41	3.23	3.32	3.39	3.39
Ethiopia	2.02	2.18	2.32	2.47	2.65	1.94	2.60	3.14	3.22	3.07
Kenya	2.90	3.21	3.48	3.66	3.87	4.03	4.12	4.20	4.21	4.11
Madagascar	1.81	2.02	2.18	2.32	2.48	2.70	2.80	2.90	2.94	2.97
Malawi	1.90	2.15	2.38	2.56	2.68	2.89	3.23	3.36	3.41	3.41
Mauritius	2.91	3.17	3.18	1.82	0.47	1.91	1.90	1.65	1.40	1.19
Mozambique	1.19	1.54	2.08	2.28	3.55	4.37	3.05	2.84	2.93	2.94
Rwanda	2.34	2.84	2.96	3.05	3.19	3.31	3.46	3.60	3.67	3.66
Somalia	1.65	1.83	1.98	2.13	2.27	7.78	3.71	1.17	1.15	2.54
Tanzania	2.20	2.60	2.89	3.08	3.25	3.42	3.52	3.65	3.71	3.71
Uganda	3.08	3.33	4.08	3.95	2.68	3.23	3.50	3.58	3.59	3.51
Zambia	2.41	2.63	2.80	2.96	2.89	3.08	3.31	3.43	3.49	3.52
Zimbabwe	4.04	3.97	4.13	3.61	3.17	3.37	3.50	3.61	3.65	3.65
Middle Africa	1.82	1.98	1.78	1.92	2.50	2.73	2.70	2.80	2.87	2.92
Angola	1.43	1.64	1.45	1.52	3.08	3.39	2.51	2.47	2.78	2.82
Cameroon	1.85	1.90	1.95	2.06	2.24	2.41	2.54	2.60	2.65	2.66
Central African Rep.	1.16	1.33	1.48	1.63	1.85	2.14	2.29	2.43	2.51	2.57
Chad	1.31	1.53	1.69	1.82	1.97	2.10	2.28	2.44	2.51	2.56
Congo	1.69	1.90	2.06	2.18	2.37	2.46	2.59	2.73	2.80	2.85

Equatorial Guinea	1.06	1.18	1.33	1.56	1.78	1.99	2.15	2.31	2.39	2.41
Gabon	0.56	0.75	0.87	0.97	1.08	1.37	1.64	1.89	2.14	2.42
Zaire	2.18	2.32	1.90	2.86	2.65	2.88	2.94	3.02	3.08	3.12
Northern Africa	2.23	2.35	2.36	2.49	2.44	2.85	2.88	2.81	2.67	2.45
Algeria	2.09	2.12	1.90	2.85	3.06	3.06	3.28	3.34	3.20	2.86
Egypt	2.38	2.49	2.50	2.26	1.95	2.56	2.52	2.38	2.23	2.02
Libya	1.80	3.61	3.70	4.04	4.04	4.04	3.84	3.65	3.50	3.27
Morocco	2.47	2.75	2.72	2.78	2.45	2.94	3.26	3.11	2.88	2.63
Sudan	1.99	1.91	2.03	2.29	2.89	3.08	2.86	2.89	2.85	2.75
Tunisia	1.79	1.79	1.85	2.04	1.81	2.61	2.40	2.28	1.99	1.73
Southern Africa	1.74	1.95	2.14	2.27	2.32	2.37	2.53	2.59	2.56	2.48
Botswana	2.15	2.10	2.63	2.54	3.77	3.75	3.45	3.61	3.65	3.68
Lesotho	1.57	1.83	2.01	2.01	2.18	2.41	2.53	2.60	2.62	2.63
Namibia	2.01	2.19	2.33	2.45	2.52	2.65	2.78	2.84	2.88	2.87
South Africa	1.73	1.94	2.12	2.27	2.27	2.30	2.48	2.53	2.49	2.39
Swaziland	1.47	2.12	2.31	2.30	2.52	2.87	3.03	3.12	3.17	3.16
Western Africa	2.12	2.38	2.56	2.84	2.98	3.10	3.11	3.25	3.30	3.31
Benin	0.71	1.20	1.64	2.06	2.33	2.65	2.86	3.03	3.12	3.14
Burkina Faso	1.42	1.75	1.65	1.76	1.85	2.07	2.34	2.72	2.80	2.84
Gambia	1.08	1.36	2.28	2.24	2.23	2.15	1.94	2.13	2.25	2.30
Ghana	4.85	4.51	2.79	2.02	2.58	3.12	3.25	3.29	3.28	3.16
Guinea	1.03	1.38	1.68	1.94	2.01	2.17	2.33	2.48	2.54	2.57
Guinea-Bissau	0.60	0.73	−0.56	0.06	3.55	5.04	1.91	2.08	2.25	2.32
Ivory Coast	1.23	1.58	3.80	4.15	3.95	3.96	3.44	3.20	3.00	3.01
Liberia	1.94	2.11	2.58	2.73	2.94	3.36	3.16	3.20	3.26	3.20
Mali	1.72	1.99	1.93	2.15	2.03	2.15	2.78	2.85	2.88	2.84
Mauritania	2.00	2.17	2.35	2.45	2.61	2.75	2.93	3.08	3.10	3.08
Niger	1.04	1.36	2.89	2.08	2.36	2.59	2.82	3.01	3.13	3.19
Nigeria	2.38	2.63	2.81	3.23	3.36	3.49	3.34	3.49	3.56	3.57
Senegal	1.89	2.03	2.64	2.89	3.48	3.59	2.66	2.80	2.89	2.94
Sierra Leone	1.13	1.25	1.33	1.38	1.43	1.59	1.77	1.93	2.00	2.09
Togo	1.23	1.37	1.44	4.33	2.17	2.36	2.86	2.90	3.03	3.05

TABLE 3.4. (continued)

	1950–1955	1955–1960	1960–1965	1965–1970	1970–1975	1975–1980	1980–1985	1985–1990ᴾ	1990–1995ᴾ	1995–2000ᴾ
Americas	2.27	2.28	2.18	1.93	1.87	1.83	1.73	1.68	1.58	1.46
Latin America	2.72	2.75	2.60	2.59	2.51	2.37	2.30	2.19	2.02	1.85
Northern America	1.80	1.78	1.49	1.14	1.05	1.07	0.89	0.88	0.83	0.74
Asia	2.00	1.97	2.14	2.46	2.35	1.89	1.72	1.59	1.53	1.43
East Asia	2.00	1.55	1.72	2.40	2.25	1.41	1.14	1.02	1.08	1.11
South Asia	2.00	2.36	2.51	2.50	2.44	2.30	2.20	2.03	1.86	1.65
Southeastern Asia	2.03	2.35	2.43	2.49	2.39	2.20	2.06	1.88	1.75	1.56
Southern Asia	1.92	2.32	2.52	2.49	2.41	2.29	2.19	2.01	1.80	1.59
Western Asia	2.70	2.79	2.76	2.77	2.91	2.76	2.85	2.82	2.70	2.48

Note: 1985–2000 growth rates are projections.
Source: United Nations (1988).

3.3 Determinants of African City Location

The summary measures of urban concentration discussed above provide a convenient but highly simplified summary of a nation's urban system. Most critically, though, they provide no explanation for why a nation's cities developed as they did. This section offers a set of likely explanations.

Loschian central place theory (CPT) predicts that a well-ordered system of cities will develop because of the interaction of agglomeration economies and transportation costs. CPT, however, is likely to have limited relevance in the African context. First, a central place hierarchy depends on a system of triangular trade. The largest cities, possessing the most industries, export to small cities. The smaller cities, in turn, export to agricultural areas, and agricultural areas export to the large cities. Balanced trade is the result. But much of Africa, especially before independence, had little industry in even the largest cities; moreover, rural areas have been fairly autarkic, largely providing for their own needs.

To be sure, industry has existed in Africa for many centuries, as evidenced by the medieval tailoring guilds in Timbuktu, brass and bronze guilds in Benin, and glass and bead guilds in Nupe (now northern Nigeria). Blacksmiths were important throughout the Sudan region (Austin [1987:46]) in the precolonial era, but faced limited demand, especially given the lack of draught animals and hence implements and animal shoes. Throughout Africa, mass production techniques were slow in developing or did not develop at all. While some trade took place between larger cities and villages, it was quite limited in scope (Rodney [1981:42–3]). Consequently, while many villages and small towns became centers of artisanal production, virtually no African cities arose in the precolonial era to be manufacturing centers based on nearby raw materials and the realization of scale economies. Nor were manufacturing centers developed in the colonial era, although mining towns did spring up in some regions. Since Independence, manufacturing towns have formed, usually at an already existing town. But there has been a strong political influence in choosing these sites. Many—in fact, probably most except for those with a clear market orientation (i.e., those located in the largest existing cities, producing goods aimed at the domestic market) or minerals orientation—had little solid production and transport cost minimizing motives for their selection.

CPT also hinges on a well-developed transportation network. Transportation infrastructure remains very weak in most African countries today; it was strong (judged by present standards) in virtually none when initial urban systems were formed. In short, traditional CPT hinges on assumptions with limited plausibility, excluding a few relatively advanced and densely populated parts of Africa.

Geographers have offered many plausible alternative location explanations in the African context. A major determinant of the location of African cities and towns undoubtedly is terrain and climate. Many areas, especially in the Sahelian region, did not attract permanent settlements because of low rainfall and infertile soils. Towns and cities that did spring up in inhospitable environments also were relatively susceptible to forces that would cause their decline. Other such arid areas include the Kalahari Desert in Botswana and the Namib Desert in Namibia. Areas in which serious diseases were (and in many cases still are) endemic are similarly not conducive to concentrated human settlements. Such areas include the

Volta River valleys (river blindness), and areas of the Central African Republic and Burkina Faso (leprosy).

Urban locations also were chosen historically for defensive reasons, and some cities' locations changed as defensive needs changed. Zaria (Nigeria), for example, was located successively at Kawar, Rikoci, Wuciciri, Turunku, and finally, Kufena. The last site was a stretch of level ground confined between two rocky outcrops—an ideal defensive position (Ajaegbu [1976:38–9]).

Perhaps the most important determinant of city location during the precolonial period was location along a trade route. Barter trade in which different societies exchanged goods, services, and gifts was widespread, and certain important points of contact between groups emerged along routes of communication. At first semisedentary, many settlements eventually became permanent fixtures along the trade routes. Examples of this type of city include Timbuktu, Bagamoyo, Pangani, and Tanga. With the coming of the age of exploration and the monetarization of exchange, the importance of marketing centers changed too. Those viable in the new international system—such as Casablanca, Lagos, Accra, and Mombasa—expanded rapidly, while other centers that did not serve as contact points between Africa and the foreign powers declined in importance (Ligale [1982:177–8]). Cities sited at mineral deposits also accompanied colonization, as did towns centered on the shipping and processing of agricultural exports.

Trade-based cities and towns were extremely sensitive to the cost of trade along their routes. Interior towns suffered crippling blows when European ocean navigation arose to compete with the trans-Saharan caravans. They were also sensitive to collapses of demand and supply when empires on either side of the Sahara fell.

Administrative control has been an important factor in town development prior to, during, and after the colonial period (Udo [1982: Ch.8]). Administrative sites usually have had military or commercial significance as well. But the determining factor in the development of such sites has been the importance attached by the ruling power, not society as a whole, and in particular, not indigenous commercial interests.

The enduring trade patterns, associated transport infrastructure, and administrative centers largely were established by the colonial powers. Not surprisingly, they were designed to assist in the extraction and export of goods of interest to Europeans. Tropical crops and minerals were paramount, and roads to the "labor reserves" also were important, especially where displacing less distant peasants from their land was insufficient to meet colonial labor requirements. What rarely drew initial attention from the colonists were areas suited to food but not cash crop production.

The nature of colonial rule may have had some impact on the location of colonial towns. The system of indirect rule preferred by the British in the nonsettler colonies *should* have led to less concentration, although until recently there has been no clear evidence that it did.[23] Colonies in which peasant rather than plantation cash crop agriculture was dominant were probably more likely to have only rudimentary trading centers outside the large towns, while those colonies that attracted significant European farmer populations (such as Kenya or Zimbabwe) would have had a more developed secondary town system. But the impact of these colonial differences seems to be limited today, in part because the growth of agriculturally based towns now depends mainly on the wealth of peasant farmers rather than on the wealth of expatriate farmers.

What does seem clear is that colonial settlement patterns were imposed with little thought to building on existing urban systems (O'Connor [1983:245]). Nor were they constructed with the objective of "developing" a region: European trade and military objectives were paramount. On the other hand, it certainly is the case that European objectives, once the slave trade had ended, were positively correlated with the development of at least portions of African economies. The problem with most colonial settlement and transport infrastructure was not that the locations were utterly inappropriate, but rather that many projects that would have been of equal or greater value to the indigenous populations were not pursued as well. Furthermore, the deliberate colonial construction of enclave economies in many colonies ensured that purchasing power did not rise (or was even depressed) in "native reserves," thereby stunting the development of towns and transport routes in much of the country.

3.4 Factors Contributing to City Growth and Changes in City Systems

Factors affecting city growth can be categorized according to a number of criteria. They can be grouped chronologically according to those prominent in precolonial, colonial, and postcolonial eras, or they can be divided into factors that affect all cities in an urban system as distinguished from those which affect only certain cities. The latter classification is not useful for addressing a nation's system or hierarchy of cities, though. For example, in considering Mali, we would focus in isolation on those factors which caused Bamako to grow, ignoring Kayes and Gao completely. But Bamako's growth affects the relative position—and hence the functions—of Kayes and Gao in the national urban hierarchy. Consequently, we distinguish urban growth forces according to the historical period in which they were most critical.

3.4.1 The Precolonial and Colonial Periods

The forces determining the locations of urban settlements were discussed in the preceding section. In general, neither in the traditional empires nor in the colonial era until near the end were there strong forces to encourage rapid town growth. Certainly, the precolonial cities grew with the growth of commercial ties, and with increased military power in the case of administrative centers. But the absence of a manufacturing base and high transport costs served as severe constraints to urban population growth. Even more binding was the absence of a marketed agricultural surplus to feed large cities in most parts of Africa, especially as nonmining centers did not produce a tradeable surplus that would have enabled food imports. Agricultural surpluses require a rudimentary transport network, the capacity for farmers to produce in excess of subsistence needs (an ability historically severely restricted by the scarcity of draught animals south of the Sahara), and a reasonably high rural population density. These conditions rarely existed simultaneously in precolonial Africa; where they did, especially in the Sudan region in what is now central and northern Nigeria, large cities grew at a pace and level comparable to those in Europe outside of the industrial revolution heartland.

Excepting a few military outposts and slave trading centers, the colonial powers rarely established cities, but they did stimulate growth in some existing cities while discouraging it in others. There was virtually no interest by any colonial power in encouraging urbanization, and most took active steps to curtail it. From the perspective of the colonial power (see Hansen [1979] and Becker [1989]), urbanization could only cause indigenous workers to shift away from occupations of direct use to the central country while increasing potential political unrest and demands for social services.

Colonists generally avoided arid and semiarid terrain, leading to the decline of existing cities in such regions (Ligale [1982:179]). While many (e.g., Franke [1980]) have criticized such neglect, it did have the unintended effect of keeping populations within the carrying capacity of economically marginal land. Designation as a colonial administrative center, whether on the national, regional, or district level, was a strong impetus to town or city growth. This is vividly illustrated by the case of Dakar, the former capital of French West Africa. After the West African nations gained their independence, Dakar lost some public sector employment, despite the fact that it remained the capital of Senegal (Cohen [1979:7]). This undoubtedly acted as a (temporary) brake on Dakar's growth.

The major European contribution to the development of African urban systems grew out of the colonial preoccupation with natural resources and export crops. To gain access to the interior where most croplands and mines were located necessitated the construction of roads and railways. Port facilities were improved at the terminal points of these transport links. Port cities as well as towns along transport routes grew rapidly as their economic bases expanded; traditional towns were left behind. Two examples serve to illustrate this point.

The geography of Namibia is striking because its major cities are situated along a north-south and an east-west axis centered at Windhoek. A rail system constructed by the Germans is largely responsible for this pattern. There were three original lines. In the north, the rails linked Swakopmund with the copper mines of Otavi and continued onward to Tsumeb, where copper was also discovered. The northern line split at Uskos, and the southern branch connected the capital of Windhoek (from there a spur went to the Matchless Mine in the Komas Highlands), the sheep raising area of Gibeon, and Keetmanshoop. A third line extended from Luderitz on the southern coast inland to join the north-south line south of Keetmanshoop. This line then continued southwestward, leaving Namibia at Ariamsvlei. The rail system provided the copper and sheep industry with inexpensive transport, in turn enabling them to produce for export. The railroad also spurred diamond prospecting, after railroad workers on the southern route discovered diamonds in Kolmanskop near Luderitz while improving the roadbed. A sizable diamond rush ensued, causing Luderitz and its environs to grow (Calvert [1969:9-10, 59-64]).

The second example is that of Zambia. The Zambia Railways line was built by Rhodesian Railways in the early 1900s, crossing the Zambezi at Victoria Falls and continuing to Lusaka, Kabwe, Kapiri Mposhi, and the Copper Belt. At Kapiri Mposhi it now joins the Tazara rail line, built in the mid-1970s and providing access to the Tanzanian port of Dar es Salaam. Commercial agriculture and industry are concentrated along the older rail line, though rapid growth has occurred in recent years in the towns along the Tazara line. Conversely, much of Zambia's potentially arable land goes un- or underutilized because of inaccessibility to transport lines. Indeed, Due (1983:13–20) argues that Zambia's geographic pattern of economic development may have been more influenced by railways than the pattern of any other African nation.[24]

Simultaneously, competition from European imports caused the collapse of African small-scale manufacturing and some towns, especially along the coasts (Austen [1987:99]). Textiles and some metalworking were most susceptible. At the same time, other African craftsmen producing more finished goods were able to expand because of the possibility of importing intermediate inputs, such as cloth, yarn, and iron and copper bars. But preference for cheaper Asian labor discouraged colonial industrialization in Africa; so too, of course, did colonial powers' view that their colonies were a natural outlet for their own manufactured exports. In summary, the climate for industrial towns, save for a few mining centers, was extremely inhospitable in both precolonial and colonial Africa. Together with low population densities, high transport costs, and limited agricultural surpluses, this climate limited urbanization to a relatively small number of slowly growing cities well into the twentieth century.

3.4.2 The Postcolonial Era

Many factors have contributed to the rapid growth of cities as a class and to individual cities in the postcolonial era. Most obvious is the rapid rate of total population growth. National population growth rates are given in Table 3.4 (for a detailed assessment and projections, see Zachariah and Vu [1987]). No other continent has had an estimated growth rate of over 3 percent for the past decade. Furthermore, growth rates are projected to continue to increase at least until 1995, although there are some indications of the beginning of a fertility transition in many countries. But Africa's cities are growing far more quickly than the overall rate of population increase.

Three explanations can be offered for this phenomenon. First, mortality rates are lower in most urban areas than in the surrounding countryside, largely because basic services are more readily available in urban areas, but also because urban dwellers have higher average real incomes than their rural counterparts. The second factor causing high growth rate of cities is rural-urban migration, which is analyzed in detail in Chapter 4.

Third, a factor having the reverse effect is that fertility rates may be lower in urban areas, although the evidence for this point is not conclusive. Aggregate rural and urban fertility rates for a limited number of African countries can be inferred from intercensal comparisons, which can be made using data provided in the U.N. *Demographic Yearbooks*. These comparisons suggest virtually no urban-rural differences in terms of total fertility, although more refined techniques are needed in order to provide stronger evidence. Fertility data from the 1983 Gambian census, however, do suggest that rural women have higher fertility rates (Becker [1990]). Furthermore, Cochrane and Farid (1989) in their comprehensive survey find from cohort-specific birth rates across Africa that urban women have clearly lower fertility rates. So do urban women in Kenya, though fertility rates are not substantially lower. In a large micro survey, Hyatt and Milne (1990) found that 22.5 percent of urban respondents had had a child in the past year, while 25.8 percent of rural respondents had given birth in the preceding year. For these findings to be consistent, it should be the case that the age distribution of urban African women is more concentrated in peak fertility age groups (the twenties) than is the distribution of rural women—which at least in some countries appears to be the case. More striking, though, is Hyatt and Milne's econometric finding that education, and especially secondary education in rural areas, significantly lowers lifetime fertility.

Several general factors may affect individual cities' populations, including regional income and distance from other major cities (see Mills and Becker [1986. Ch. 5]). *High regional wages and incomes* should attract migrants to an area. The *degree of isolation* has a more complex influence on an area's growth. On the one hand, great distance from other cities implies a large hinterland, and hence large multipliers from growth in rural demand for urban goods and services, and from the supply of agricultural products for processing. Multipliers based on the growth of demands for the urban area's products from other cities, however, will be smaller.

Within some radius of a major growth center, impulses generated by the growth pole city's development undoubtedly will exert a strong growth influence on nearby towns, but there may be some limit to the scope of growth due to the presence of the major urban center. Richardson (1980:111), for example, argues that central Kenyan towns such as Athi River would develop quickly without any special government policies because of their proximity to Nairobi. Towns close to rapidly growing cities become bedroom suburbs (especially if the major city's industrial area is not centrally located), usually housing part of the major city's working class in a lower-rent environment. Nearby towns themselves often become industrial satellites (e.g., Chitungwiza, south of Harare; the Kanefing-Serra Kunda area west of Banjul in The Gambia; or Athi River), especially when the primary city is mainly a service or administrative center. Nearby areas also typically experience intensive agricultural development, and often become marketing and distribution centers, as well as in some cases low-rent centers for artisans producing goods for the central city.

Presumably at some distance the growth center's developmental impulses disappear, yet this distance is unlikely to be large enough to support another major urban center. At a still farther distance, the net impact of the growth pole's development will cause emigration, since the central city's development and higher wages also attract people from the surrounding areas. In summary, growth of a central city is likely to cause growth in nearby areas and population decline at greater distances. Such a nonlinear structure is conjectural but has more appeal than the linear hypothesis, especially if one views cities as sources of technology diffusion and innovation.[25]

Technological progress is itself often viewed as a cause of city growth. If technological progress is not distributed evenly in a system of cities, innovation may be a causal factor in the creation of primate cities. While authors have confirmed this hypothesis for other regions (e.g., Pederson [1970] for Latin America), the African case is still unresolved. In an interesting but preliminary study, Abiodun [1981] finds little relation between the city size and technological innovation in Nigeria.[26] Further investigation of this relationship is needed. Researchers, however, must be cognizant that the direction of causality is by no means clear: does city size determine the pace of innovation or does innovation determine city size? Or, as seems most probable, is the system simultaneous?

Government policies, whether targeted at the urban system or designed to meet other objectives, in principle have a powerful effect on the size distribution of cities (for formal models, see Ruane [1981]). The urban bias thesis, which describes the advantages that producers and consumers in urban areas receive as a result of government policy, is described in detail in Chapter 4. *Government structure* also makes a difference. Federal governments are more likely to foster a decentralized city system than are centralized governments because federal systems are less able to discriminate against particular ethnic groups or regions (Henderson [1980: 33–34]). In addition, smaller regions and population centers are better able to capitalize on their emerging economic strength by taxing themselves and borrowing funds to improve their infrastructure if political power is decentralized.

The *level of development* is another powerful determinant of the degree of concentration in an urban system. If a nation is relatively underdeveloped, the transport system will likely be incomplete, imposing high costs on its users. This has two consequences: 1) markets of small-town firms will be protected, but at the same time, transport constraints will limit the dynamism exhibited by smaller, emerging centers and 2) firms will cluster close to each other to avoid incurring high transportation costs. Although theoretically uncertain, the city-size distribution in least developed countries is probably made more dispersed as a result of the first factor, but more concentrated due to the second effect. Wheaton and Shishido (1981), in their study of urban concentration in thirty-eight countries, find a U-shaped relationship between decentralization and level of development. An intuitive explanation for this finding is that poor countries have low levels of interregional interaction, and hence are highly decentralized. In contrast, richer countries with better developed communications will have a more concentrated urban system (Sheppard [1982:139]), while very high income countries have demand structures that can support many large cities. But Rosing (1966) and Sheppard find no empirical evidence for the U shape. The impacts of government policy, public sector growth, and general economic development on urban structure are analyzed empirically in the following section; their effects on city growth are addressed in Chapter 6.

A host of other factors also lead to high degrees of urban concentration in the most underdeveloped countries. *Market density* (which may be defined as yN, where y is per capita income and N equals population) will be lower in a poor city than in a developed country city with the same population. Thus, the market area of an African city must be large in order for the production of specialized goods or services to be economical. In addition, the *scarcity of skilled labor* necessitates the concentration of firms in order to develop a specialized labor force (Henderson [1980]).

What patterns have in fact been noted? While formal statistical analysis of the growth of individual cities is postponed to Chapter 6 (with labor market models and styled facts discussed in the intervening chapters), a few characteristics merit noting here. Anticipating Chapter 6, the distance effect and location of a town within a spatial structure is complicated, while rising wages and employment growth do seem to have strong "pull" effects. The growth of government certainly matters, and almost certainly has been a force for increased primacy. Indeed, this is Cohen's (1979:7–8) strong conclusion, as he cites evidence that government investments and recurrent expenditures are disproportionately urban, and are especially disproportionately devoted to capital cities.

O'Connor (1983:48) asserts that "indigenous" cities have grown and continue to grow more slowly than those of colonial origin. The evidence for this claim is weak, although the proposition is certainly plausible. Almost no African countries have truly restructured their economies away from the colonial pattern; many that have done so somewhat have simply experienced economic collapse (and by centralizing resources have concentrated growth in the capital cities, and virtually nowhere else). O'Connor also notes that the highest rates of urban growth appear in the most pristine economies that began their independence virtually without urban centers. The evidence here is much stronger, given the rapid growth of cities such as Nouakchott, Gaborone, and Kigali.

Quite dishearteningly, "push" effects occasioned by rural disasters and wars seem to be important as well (O'Connor [1983]; for econometric evidence, see Becker and Morrison [1988]). Both Cohen (1979) and Rondinelli (1983) stress the importance of interregional and, implicitly, interindustry linkages in determining the growth of cities, especially smaller ones (for an excellent summary, see Gore [1984: 153–54]). Preliminary evidence generally supports their argument that greater linkages imply relatively rapid secondary city growth, but much more work needs to be done. Actually, a sufficient number of input-output tables have been compiled for African countries that, given close ties between city size and industrial type in many nations, it should be possible to conduct a detailed study of the impact of different patterns of development on the growth of various types of urban areas.

Finally, the development of transport infrastructure has been critical in determining the growth of individual cities. The post-1945 era has seen dramatic improvements in human transport, effectively making it easier to migrate from the countryside to all towns. Urban areas particularly favored were those that received rail links, good paved roads, or improved rural road networks in reasonably nearby agricultural areas.

3.5 International Trade Theorems, Foreign Trade Regimes, and City Systems

International trade theory can be used to derive some strong predictions about the evolution of a nation's urban system over time, and also to compare city systems across nations.[27] Two of the central propositions of the economics of international trade are the Heckscher-Ohlin and Rybczynski theorems:

Heckscher-Ohlin: If two countries (or regions) are engaged in bilateral exchange of goods, the relatively capital-abundant economy will export the capital-intensive good and import the labor-intensive good.

Rybczynski: If an open economy faces fixed terms of trade, an increase in a country's (or region's) capital/labor ratio will increase its output of the capital-intensive traded good relative to the labor-intensive good.

Note that the Rybczynski theorem is framed in terms of capital-intensive *goods*, not high-capital-usage *cities*. In the case in which a country is not highly specialized in terms of commodity production, it is possible to make the connection between capital-intensive goods and high-capital-usage cities. In this incomplete specialization case, the country will produce both relatively capital-intensive and relatively labor-intensive goods. The Heckscher-Ohlin theorem can then be used to explain the domestic patterns of production: the capital-intensive good will be produced in the capital-intensive region (i.e., large cities), while the labor-intensive good will be produced elsewhere in the country.

Thus, the combination of the Heckscher-Ohlin and Rybczynski theorems allows for international comparisons of city systems. The larger the national capital/labor ratio, the more capital-intensive cities a country will have; these capital-intensive cities will also have relatively large populations:

> Compare any two economies trading freely in the world market that have technological and consumption conditions such that same types of cities are identical across the economies. Then the determinant of the relative size distribution of cities between the two economies is solely their relative factor endowments. *The relatively capital abundant economy will produce more of the capital intensive good and will have a relatively greater number of high capital usage cities.* (Henderson [1980:69]; his emphasis)

Incomplete specialization is crucial in making predictions based upon these two international trade theorems; nonspecialization and fixed terms of trade are required to assure that high-capital-usage cities produce capital-intensive goods. Furthermore, such incomplete specialization must emanate from "natural" causes, such as market size, population, or other market forces. Since neither the Rybczynski nor Heckscher-Ohlin theorems take account of trade restrictions, predictions based upon them implicitly assume free trade.

Such a pure, free-trade environment necessary to test the implications of these theorems for city systems does not exist anywhere in the world, and certainly not in Africa, where trade barriers are endemic.[28] Thus, it is necessary to consider how the introduction of trade barriers modifies the predictions of these theorems.

Imagine two hypothetical countries that produce with identical factor (capital, labor, and land) endowments. In the absence of trade barriers, we would expect the two countries to have identical city systems. Now let one country depart from this free-trade assumption. Country A, with free trade, has productivity-adjusted factor prices at world levels, and the factor price equalization theorem applies. Country B protects capital-intensive domestic manufacturing with high tariff barriers. Country B's manufacturing production thus expands behind the wall of tariff protection. Since capital-intensive manufacturing takes place in the largest cities, the degree of urban concentration in country B increases relative to that in country A. Thus, even though the two countries have identical factor endowments, they have different city systems.[29] Consequently, any empirical test that purports to test the power of the Heckscher-Ohlin and Rybczynski theorems to explain African city systems must also take into account departures from the free-trade assumptions of these theorems. Otherwise, powerful omitted variable bias would make the results undependable and uninterpretable.

With these caveats in mind, let us now turn to an empirical test of the implications of the Rybczynski and Heckscher-Ohlin theorems for African city systems.

Our tentative hypothesis is that the more capital intensive a country, the greater the percentage of its cities that are large—that is, the more primate its urban system will be. In the majority of African countries, large-scale, capital-intensive manufacturing takes place in only one or two large cities. Consequently, there will be little distortion of reality if several very simple measures of urban concentration are used. The first measure is the absolute size of the largest city; the second is the percentage of the national population living in the largest city. The Pareto coefficient and the proportion of the urban population living in the largest cities are also used as alternative urban concentration measures.

Choosing the independent variable to measure capital intensity is much more difficult. No estimates of capital stocks are available on a cross-country basis for Africa (or, for that matter, for any set of developing countries). Two logical proxies for capital intensity are:

1. government capital expenditures, and
2. the share of industry or manufacturing in GDP.

In earlier research analyzing African urbanization during the 1970s, Becker and Morrison (1988) used government capital expenditures as a proxy for capital stock. The reasoning behind this choice was that, regardless of national ideology, most African industrial sectors have been dominated by large parastatal enterprises. One of the key characteristics of the current structural adjustment period, though, is that governments are supposed to be ridding themselves of their most inefficient firms. Thus, the correlation between formal sector manufacturing and parastatal manufacturing can be expected to become weaker over time. Since the data used for the empirical investigation are for 1985 (when the process of structural adjustment had begun, albeit barely, but the process of government collapse was well underway in many countries), it seems prudent not to use government capital expenditure as a proxy for capital stock.

The second option is to use the share of manufacturing or industry in GDP as a proxy variable for the national capital stock. The justification for this choice is straightforward. Since production in these sectors tends to be relatively capital intensive in the African setting, the larger the GDP share of these sectors, the higher will be the national capital-labor ratio. The choice between using manufacturing or industrial production (as a percentage of GDP) as an independent variable is dictated by data availability. The World Bank (1988b) reports manufacturing to GDP ratios for twenty-two African nations and industry's share of GDP for twenty-seven nations. In order to preserve degrees of freedom in the estimation, the latter series is employed.

Regression results for the simple model (omitting consideration of the degree of protection afforded to domestic manufacturing) are reported column 1 of Table 3.5. The regression using the population of the largest city as the dependent variable gives results consistent with our a priori hypothesis: increasing capital intensity is associated with increasing city size. Unfortunately but unsurprisingly, a Goldfeld-Quandt test reveals that this regression suffers from heteroskedasticity.[30] Thus, while the ordinary least squares (OLS) estimators of the regression coefficients are unbiased and consistent, the estimated variances of the estimators are biased. Conventionally calculated confidence intervals are invalid, thus limiting the confidence that can be placed in the regression's results.

TABLE 3.5. The Determinants of the Concentration of African City Systems: Regressions Based on Neoclassical Economic Trade Theory

Dependent variable: population of the largest city (columns 1, 5)
: largest city as a proportion of total population (columns 2, 4)
: largest city as a proportion of total urban population (columns 3, 6)
: Pareto coefficient (column 7)

	(1)	(2)	(3)	(4)	(5)	(6)	(7)
explanatory variables							
C: constant	0.34	38.00**	0.06*	62.12*	12.76	0.76**	-0.57
	(1.01)	(4.13)	(2.40)	(2.26)	(0.58)	(1.74)	(-0.64)
INDGDP85: industry share of GDP, 1985	26.92**	3.09	1.60***	0.91	1.75**	0.026***	-0.04***
	(1.83)	(0.01)	(1.61)	(0.81)	(1.96)	(1.63)	(1.53)
ARP: average rate of protection[1]				0.53	-0.93	-1.842	
				(0.67)	(-1.50)	(-1.49)	
GNP80: 1980 per capita income, x 1000, US $							11.13**
							(1.80)
LANDAREA: land area, ln km^2							0.24**
							(1.95)
GOVGDP80: government share of GDP, 1980, divided by 100							0.45
							(0.30)
R^2				0.055	0.176	0.155	0.432
$-R^2$				-0.024	0.107	0.085	0.243
d.f.	24	24	24	24	24	24	12

[1] ARP: tariff receipts and other revenue from import duties as a share of total value of imports

t-statistics appear in parentheses

Note: columns 1-5 estimated coefficients multiplied by 1000

*: significant at the 95% level
**: significant at the 90% level
***: significant at the 80% level

Source: World Bank (1988b), Mali (1983).

Excluding regression 5, the other regressions reported in Table 3.5 successfully control for heteroskedasticity by taking urban population shares of national and urban populations, respectively, as the dependent variables, thereby restricting the dependent variable's range of values. Once heteroskedastic errors are eliminated, however, there is only a very weak relationship between capital intensivity and urban concentration (regressions 2 and 3). When urban concentration is measured by the ratio of the largest city's population to total urban population, the estimated coefficient is not significantly different from zero. When urban concentration is measured by the ratio of the largest city's population to national population, the estimated coefficient is significant only at the 80 percent level.

As mentioned above, the presence of tariff barriers can be expected to affect a country's city-size distribution. Ceteris paribus, protectionism and the accompanying import substitution industrialization (ISI) will divert an African country's resources away from sectors in which it has a true (static) comparative advantage to those that are more capital intensive. As these sectors tend to be concentrated in the largest cities, one would expect that countries most determinedly following ISI policies would have a few exceptionally large cities.

Regressions 4–6 in Table 3.5 consider the impact of trade barriers by including a measure of protectionism along with the industrial structure measure. Interestingly, the general effect is to increase the significance of the industrial structure term. Once again, we find that urban concentration does increase with a country's capital intensity, as trade theory predicts.

Surprisingly, however, protectionism appears to *reduce* the degree of urban concentration, although the protection measure never reaches highly statistically significant levels. Two explanations may account for this finding. First, the finding may merely reflect measurement error: our proxy for the degree of protection is the ratio of import duties to total imports. This measure will be monotonically related to the true degree of protectionism as long as 1) tariffs rather than quotas are used to protect industries, and 2) the elasticity of tariff revenue with respect to rate is positive for all countries. Less technically, a rise in the tariff rate must increase total tariff revenue; the relationship is reversed if a country is (foolishly, but quite frequently in reality) on the declining part of its "Laffer curve." Unfortunately, superior measures of the degree of protectionism are not available for African countries.

Another possibility is that general equilibrium effects dominate the partial equilibrium effects. Import-substitution policies are usually promoted by overvalued exchange rates, and restricting imports also naturally causes exchange rate appreciation. In most African countries, the consequence appears to be declining terms of trade for agricultural export goods and sharply reduced foreign exchange earnings. Large cities are not only capital intensive; they are also intensive in the use of imports. That is, the standard theory (Ruane [1981]) may need to be modified in the case of small, open African economies to recognize a third critical input (along with capital and labor) in the production process: imports. *Consequently, measures taken that apparently favor large cities may in reality choke their growth by limiting import availability.*

Looking at the residuals from regression 6 is not particularly helpful in suggesting omitted variables. The two countries with by far the largest positive residuals (indicating higher than predicted urban concentration) are The Gambia and

Uganda. The reasons for Uganda's primacy are not transparent. While it is difficult to imagine that the Gambia could support a major urban area beyond the Banjul-Kombo-St. Mary area (despite very halfhearted efforts by the government to promote other regional centers), there are several small African countries with negative residuals. On the other hand, the largest negative residual is Zambia, which has a mature mining industry strung out in several cities away from the capital region. But so does Zaire, which lies right on the regression line.

In addition to international trade theory, several other forces have been advanced as determinants of urban concentration. Both we and Ledent (1990) have tested many of the variables discussed earlier in this chapter. Briefly, the empirical findings are (which, other than Table 3.5, are not presented):

* As expected, per capita income tends to be associated (but only weakly) with greater urban decentralization (for example, see Table 3.5, col. 7). Ledent's measure of development, per capita energy consumption, however, is negatively associated with urban decentralization.
* Large countries tend to be more decentralized.
* Former British colonies tend to be more decentralized, although the statistical significance of this variable in our and Ledent's estimates is sporadic.
* Rapid urban and national population growth is associated with greater urban concentration (Ledent), although the theoretical basis for these variables is not clear.
* Urban concentration first increases and then decreases with total national population (Ledent).
* The share of government in GDP is associated with increasing concentration, but at some point (when the share reaches about 35 percent by our estimates) the effect reverses, and government share is associated with diminishing urban concentration in African countries.
* Large ratios of investment to GNP are associated with high degrees of urban concentration (Ledent), a finding consistent with the Rybczynski and Heckscher-Ohlin theorems.
* Countries in which the share of trade (imports plus exports) in GNP is large tend to have high degrees of urban concentration (Ledent)—a finding consistent with the signs in our empirical work on the average rate of protection.

Before one accepts these results as firm conclusions, however, four points need to be recognized. First, only a limited share of the variance in urban concentration measures is explained by the independent variables in our and Ledent's statistical estimates. This share ranges from virtually zero to about 60 percent, depending on the regression equation. Second, as Ledent notes, the statistical fit is very sensitive to the functional form chosen. Third, the explanatory power of the regressions is equally sensitive to the measure of concentration chosen. Finally, the fit is also quite sensitive to the sample employed. In short, the results are far from being highly robust, and therefore should be treated with considerable caution.

What conclusions can be drawn from our findings in this chapter? First, African urban systems appear to be somewhat but not exceptionally primate. Furthermore, there is some variability in primacy patterns across countries, some of which can be explained by simple economic and demographic factors. Third, Africa's major urban areas are located on sites that are generally quite rational, although the rationales were often provided by the interests of colonial rulers rather than Africans themselves. Finally, there seems to be little merit in pursuing policies directly aimed at altering African city systems (specifically, reducing the degree of concentration in the largest cities). It would be quite sufficient if policies that simply provide unwarranted protection to the largest cities were removed—although such removal would not inevitably reduce the largest cities' growth.

4

The Role of Migration in African Urbanization

4.1 Introduction

Zachariah and Conde (1981) provide net rural-urban migration data for eight West African nations for the 1960s and 1970s, replicated below in Table 4.1. Nearly 50 percent of these countries' urban growth came from rural-urban migration; similar results for the entire continent are derived by Kelley (1991). Note that the rate of urban population growth accounted for by migration varies significantly by country, ranging from 5.6 percent in Côte d'Ivoire to 1.2 percent in Ghana. This wide variation probably results almost entirely from differential economic performance, rather than an Ivoiran proclivity to migrate, especially since external migration is not excluded from these figures.

Superior economic performance (as in Côte d'Ivoire) can stimulate migration by raising incomes, but during the 1950s and 1960s the causality was thought to run the other way. Rural-urban migration was deemed a prerequisite for national economic development. This conception was based on the preeminent role given to industrialization in national development plans and on the low productivity and backwardness of Third World agriculture. The Lewis and Ranis-Fei models captured the essence of this position. In these two closely related models, surplus agricultural labor could be transferred to the cities without the loss of any agricultural output for some finite period. Not only was the transfer of labor costless to the agricultural sector, but the migrants also were immediately absorbed into urban, modern sector jobs so that no urban unemployment ensued. Since modern sector production was of higher productivity than the traditional agricultural sector, society as a whole benefited from the migration in these models.

But, as is now painfully clear (and as is documented in Chapter 5), urban unemployment did ensue. Harris and Todaro (1970) gave a theoretical base to the empirical phenomenon of widespread unemployment that economists and policymakers were witnessing. Furthermore, their model specifically targeted the African milieu. The model provided a rationale for continued rural-urban migration even in the face of massive urban unemployment—as long as the urban expected wage exceeds the wage available in the agricultural sector. No longer could

TABLE 4.1. Net Rural-Urban Migration, Intercensal Period, Circa 1965–76

Country	Period	Net Rural-Urban Migration[a]	Average Annual Percentage Increase in Urban Population from Migration	Migration as Percent of Total Urban Growth
Gambia	1963–73	44,000	3.8	65
Ghana	1960–70	226,000	1.2	28
Côte d'Ivoire	1965–75	715,000	5.6	59
Liberia	1962–74	144,000	3.8	60
Senegal	1960–70	278,000	3.3	40
Sierra Leone	1963–74	170,000	3.8	63[b]
Togo	1960–70	42,000	2.5	44
Burkina Faso[c]	1960–75	99,000	4.1	55
Total		1,718,000	3.2	48

[a]For all countries except Liberia and Côte d'Ivoire, migration estimates are made for the same set of towns so that reclassification of localities will not vitiate the estimate. External migration is not eliminated for any country.

[b]Adjusted for the 1973 boundary change for Freetown.

[c]Two principal towns.

Source: Zachariah and Conde (1981:82).

economists blithely assume that migration was compatible with economic efficiency in the face of deviations from perfect competition.

The Harris-Todaro (hereafter HT) model has been criticized severely, in large part for its "institutionally determined" urban wage rate. In many cases, living standards for unskilled workers differ little in urban and rural areas, and relatively high formal sector wages in urban activities can be accounted for in large part by standard human capital considerations. Nevertheless, as Chapter 5 discusses, urban/rural wage gaps appear to have been unusually high in Africa during the 1960s and 1970s, and it is difficult to believe that human capital and cost of living differences accounted for the entire gap. This skepticism is reinforced if one considers the broad role of the public sector in African modern sectors and typical public sector wage policies, which appear to be at best tenuously linked to labor market equilibrium considerations.

Nor must one rely exclusively on institutional arguments in order to generate an urban wage which exceeds the opportunity cost of urban labor. In fact, many neoclassical economic models can do just that. Perhaps the simplest is that unmeasured labor quality—factors such as motivation and innate ability—varies between sectors. Or perhaps firms pay workers above-market wages in order to give them an incentive not to shirk tasks on the job (Alchian and Demsetz [1972]; Shapiro and Stiglitz [1984]). Models of adverse selection (Stiglitz [1976]) suggest that employers are able to judge only imperfectly the abilities of workers either before or after they are hired. Thus, firms will pay above-market wages in order to attract high-ability workers. Finally, labor turnover models (Stiglitz [1974]) posit that modern sector employers pay this premium to avoid training costs associated with high turnover rates (assumed to decrease with the wage rate), despite the presence of open unemployment.

In summary, HT's institutional wage appears to have been a realistic, dependable assumption for most African formal sectors of the 1960s and 1970s. There is, however, clear evidence that formal sector wage premia over both rural earnings and urban informal sector earnings have diminished and perhaps disappeared in recent years (see Chapter 5 for a presentation of this evidence).

A central issue to be addressed is whether rural-urban migration rates are economically efficient. In general, migration represents a response to opportunity differentials, especially in labor markets, and thus plays a vital role in reducing economic inefficiencies. As workers migrate from region A to region B, labor becomes scarcer in A, thereby driving wages up, and labor becomes more plentiful in B, thereby driving wages down. A vivid example of this equilibrating mechanism is provided by the United States. For much of the twentieth century, poor southerners, both black and white, migrated to the industrial Midwest. The consequence has been a dramatic shift in income differentials: per capita income in the Southeast rose from 45 percent of the national average in 1900 to 97 percent of the U.S. average in 1985 (Mills and Hamilton [1989:43]).

But can this process be expected to take place in Africa? Will labor markets function as they appeared to have done in the United States? Or are there barriers to market competition that generate inefficient outcomes from migration?

Both in the HT framework and almost certainly in many African economies, the most important deviation from perfect competition is an urban wage artificially maintained at a level above that prevailing in the agricultural sector. Neoclassical economic theory tells us that surplus labor will drive down the wage until the market clears; a government-imposed minimum wage, however, circumvents this mechanism. Firm-set wages may also circumvent the clearing mechanism if their levels reflect desires to keep down training costs, if managers believe that effort is positively related to a worker's wage, or if workers are successful in capturing a portion of firms' rents.

A second factor causing social costs to exceed private costs is the educational selectivity of migration. There is convincing evidence that educated individuals are much more likely to migrate than are uneducated rural dwellers. This means that the migration stream can be thought of as a human capital transfer from rural to urban areas. The large number of unemployed school-leavers in urban areas represents a misallocation of valuable resources that could otherwise be used in the agricultural sector (Byerlee [1974:560]). Moreover, the high wage premia paid to educated labor in many African countries may reflect the absence of more efficient screening devices, and also may be based on institutional salary scales only slightly related to true productivity differentials.

Finally, rural-urban migration itself causes a host of externalities—some positive and some negative, some pecuniary and some real.[1] Since pecuniary externalities are changes in relative prices caused by shifts in demand, a distributionally neutral policymaker is unconcerned with pecuniary externalities. Most African policymakers, however, are not distributionally neutral, and any complete analysis must account for the changes in the relative prices caused by migration. Under reasonable conditions we might expect that rural-urban migration would turn the terms of trade against urban manufactured goods and services, thus acting as a natural brake on urbanization. Real (non-pecuniary) negative externalities include any possible increase in the per capita cost of providing public services to the migrant[2] as well as increases in pollution, congestion, and crime which are often associated with rapid urbanization. The theory of the second best also applies: Becker, Williamson, and Mills (1992) show that if other resources in which there are market distortions (namely, capital) follow labor, then rural-urban migration may reduce market inefficiencies elsewhere if rates of return to capital are higher in urban areas—or, as is more likely, will reduce overall efficiency if resources are drawn from the capital-starved countryside.[3]

With these comments to set the stage, we now turn to an examination of the determinants, standard models, and consequences of rural-urban migration in sub-Saharan Africa. We focus on migration's consequences for urban areas, but some mention of its rural consequences is made as well. Attention is then turned to government policy responses to massive rural-urban migration and rapid urbanization. In an era of International Monetary Fund (IMF) conditionality and World Bank structural adjustment lending, however, it is not only the attitude of domestic policymakers that is important. External financing comes at a price above that indicated by the interest rate alone; national policymaking autonomy is reduced, and international agencies play a larger role in the formation of policy. In an age of structural adjustment, therefore, it is important to look at the effect of such multinational agency policy prescriptions and urban growth.

4.2 The Proximate Determinants of Rural-Urban Migration: Hypotheses and Evidence

Rural-urban migration results from a complex set of economic and noneconomic forces. Many of these proximate forces have been present in Africa for a relatively long period; others have made a more recent appearance. These factors combine to determine the massive increase in rural-urban migration rates in the postwar era. Clearly, this increase resulted either from the impetus of new forces, a dramatic increase in the potency of traditional forces, or a combination of effects. In this section we briefly survey the main theories of rural-urban migration and then survey some of the many empirical studies of migration in Africa.

4.2.1. Social Factors

Gugler and Flanagan (1978) have proposed the following noneconomic factors in the migration decision: the desire for freedom from control of the older generation, the weak social position of childless women in traditional cultures, marital instability, and short-term cash needs, especially for brideswealth. Adepoju (1982a:125–27) lists other impulses to migrate, including the social status and psychological satisfaction of living in an urban, heterogeneous environment, the ease of adjusting to the urban milieu, the proximity of most urban areas to the homeplace, and the short distance between villages and medium-sized towns.

The first motivations on both Gugler and Flanagan's and Adepoju's lists seem little more than a restatement of the discredited "bright lights" theory of migration. Adepoju's second motivation is more credible—the support system provided by relatives or kinsmen of migrants is extensive in Africa and is well documented. This safety net allows the migrant to undertake job search for a longer time than would otherwise be possible; moreover, it makes the socialization of the migrant into the urban culture easier.

Adepoju's third proposition seems self-evident, but in fact it appears that the importance of proximity to home villages varies markedly across Africa. Both Peil (1981) and Gugler (1991) have found that the overwhelming majority of urban Nigerians interviewed (from very different regions) intend to return to their villages upon retirement—but Peil found that a slight majority of Gambians in the Banjul metro area did not expect to return to their rural "homes." Plausible reasons for this striking difference is that the differential between urban and rural living standards in The Gambia is probably greater in Nigeria, both because rural Gambia is poor and because the Banjul metro area maintains much more of a small-town atmosphere than do large Nigerian cities. Consequently, the expected gain in *relative* social position from returning to one's rural "home" will be greater in Nigeria than in The Gambia.

Another important finding from Gugler's study is that urban Nigerians' desire to return to their villages was greater in 1987 than it was in similar groups twenty-six years earlier. Gugler attributes much of the difference to the deteriorating economic fortunes of many urban dwellers. As his study was carried out in Igbo areas in Nigeria, the loss of the Nigerian civil war may well have added to urban insecurities.

Joshi et al. (1976), in their pioneering work on Abidjan, cite four noneconomic causes of migration. Like Adepoju, they cite the importance of prestige and the image of the big city, observing that individuals who remain in their village suffer a loss of status. Similarly, return migrants may exaggerate their success in order to gain status. Perceptions of the probability of success in the city are likely to be distorted, or the nation's capital may be overglorified as a matter of national pride.

The Migration of Women.

Most of the rural-urban migration literature focuses on labor market adjustments by full-time workers. By implication, these people are household heads who are the effective decision makers; other people either accompany primary workers as dependents or do not migrate.

Is this a realistic paradigm for Africa? In particular, do women migrate primarily as dependents or do they migrate independently? Fortunately, census information and a few excellent studies (notably Shields [1980], from which the following data are drawn, unless stated otherwise) enable us to examine this issue in some detail.

Joshi et al. (1976:34–37) note three incentives that spur the migration of women. If wives migrate, they escape their rural responsibilities for cultivation, but do not necessarily suffer a loss of personal autonomy, despite their smaller economic role. Secondly, educated rural women migrate to the city to escape the stifling social position imposed on them by men in the village. Finally, this study claims that spouse hunting is better in Abidjan than in rural areas.

Historically, rural-urban migration in Africa was largely a male phenomenon. As of 1962, the male/female population ratio in Kenya's towns typically ranged from 1.5 to 1.9. These ratios tend to be much lower now, even in the conservative Moslem regions in the Sahel. Kenya's male/female ratio fell from 1.52 in 1962 to

1.27 only seven years later. This reduction indicates that female migration rates have been rising more rapidly than male migration rates.

Indeed, the shift has been stunning. In Tanzania during the colonial era, 60–70 percent of rural-urban migrants were male; by 1971, 54 percent were female. But even in Tanzania, most women migrated to join their husbands or families; only one-third who migrated in 1971 were unmarried (a dramatic rise, though, from the 13 percent unmarried among those who migrated before 1952, but well below the 64 percent of male migrants who were unmarried). Thus, while 70 percent of Tanzanian male migrants stated that seeking employment was their cause of migration, only 9 percent of women migrated to seek employment, while 73 percent went to join their families. Still, this general result hides significant differences between women with differing levels of education. Only 5 percent of women with less than four years of education went to seek employment, while 29 percent of those with Form 1 or more schooling went to seek employment, and 11 percent went for additional schooling.

A brief glance at Table 4.2 suggests that different forces probably affect female and male migration, and that these forces vary in strength and/or importance over time. In general, male rural-urban migration is more concentrated in the fifteen to twenty-nine year-old age groups. But otherwise, the ratio of female/male migration for any age cohort appears to fluctuate considerably over time for both Zambia and Kenya.

There are several plausible explanations, but the most important probably has to do with urban employment. Women are far more likely to be unpaid family workers or informal sector workers than are men; their opportunities, therefore, do not coincide exactly with that of male migrants. Because women tend to look after rural farms, they have more regular rural links, and therefore may be more susceptible to rural "push" forces. Men, in contrast, are more vulnerable to downturns in the modern, wage-employment sector.

It seems plausible that in many African societies women, who do most daily farm work, are if anything more responsive to changes in relative urban/rural earnings opportunities than are men. On the other hand, they have to maintain urban households and watch children as well, contributing to a situation in which they typically earn lower incomes and have higher unemployment rates. These factors, along with their lower educational levels, ensures that women will be overrepresented in the informal sector and have relatively few formal sector jobs. With its relatively flexible hours, location, and working conditions, informal sector employment minimizes conflicts between labor and household duties. Shields also finds that women wage earners have distinctly fewer children (mean = 1.7) than those working in the nonwage sector (mean = 2.5), although these differences do not control for age.

If men leave their families in the countryside, it implies that many rural households must be headed by women. This appears to be true in Kenya, where over one-quarter of rural households are headed by women (Elkan [1976]). This pattern is also consistent with one in which urban dwellers continue to regard their rural origin a "home," mainly because much of the nuclear family continues to reside there. Even with rising female rural-urban migration rates, as recently as about 1970 only 34 percent of employed males in Nairobi had their wives living with them; 46 percent had wives outside Nairobi. And, finally, male-dominated migra-

TABLE 4.2. Age-Specific Rural Out-Migration Rates for Botswana, Zambia, and Kenya*

A. Men cohort	Zambia 1963–74	1974–80	Botswana 1971–81
10–14	1.84	0.60	0.10
15–19	3.50	1.69	1.54
20–24	5.14	1.86	6.51
25–29	4.99	0.55	5.05
30–34	3.27	−0.45	2.67
35–39	2.21	−0.30	1.26
40–44	1.77	−0.01	0.89
45–49	0.25	−0.44	0.35
50–54	−0.82	−0.58	0.14
55–59	1.61	−1.08	−0.07
60–64	0.61	−0.23	−0.10
65–69	0.03	0.09	−0.28
70–74	7.53	1.83	−0.24
75–79	4.38	17.51	−0.25
80–84	−0.12	−16.71	0.01
85+	−0.60	1.00	0.12

Women cohort	1963–74	1974–80	1971–81
10–14	2.20	1.21	0.38
15–19	3.86	0.97	1.73
20–24	3.84	0.86	2.40
25–29	3.21	0.28	1.64
30–34	1.29	−0.25	0.99
35–39	1.03	0.23	0.42
40–44	0.56	−0.26	0.28
45–49	0.07	−0.07	−0.01
50–54	−0.02	0.25	−0.05
55–59	0.17	0.86	−0.08
60–64	0.26	1.16	−0.03
65–69	0.40	1.15	−0.13
70–74	0.37	1.20	−0.13
75–79	0.40	1.41	−0.19
80–84	0.22	1.04	−0.00
85+	0.19	1.27	−0.04

*Net migration divided by origin at-risk population.

Source: United Nations, Demographic Yearbook, various years.

B. Migration to Nairobi, by Cohort (in thousands)

Age group	Males 1969–73	1973–77	1977–79	Females 1969–73	1973–77	1977–79
0–14	16.9	−4.2	−2.8	18.8	−4.7	−0.7
15–19	6.4	8.0	6.5	13.5	11.5	6.8
20–24	20.4	19.9	36.2	24.6	3.6	10.6
25–29	12.6	5.1	15.4	0.8	−11.2	1.6
30–39	5.0	−4.4	−7.0	−3.3	−6.4	−3.3
40–49	−0.7	−1.9	−7.1	−5.8	−3.0	−0.5
50+	−9.6	−1.9	−12.6	−2.3	−1.5	−0.7

Source: Collier and Lal (1986:244).

tion flows may leave agriculture vulnerable, since the clearing of new plots and other "investment" activities are often traditionally male tasks.

There is no doubt that noneconomic factors are of critical importance in rural-urban migration, especially for people who are not full-time labor force participants. Urban amenities—especially schooling—are critically important for many, not so much because adult migrants expect to benefit, but because they hope their children may do so. But most noneconomic factors are largely ongoing, and have either remained constant or, more likely, declined in importance over time. Where they have not, as in the desire to return to one's traditional home region, social forces do not appear to be responsible for accelerating urbanization. Thus, social forces have little obvious link to the massive increase in rural-urban migration in the postwar period, and consequently we turn our attention to changes in economic and demographic structure.

4.2.2. The Urban Bias Thesis

Neoclassical economists have focused almost exclusively on the role of differences between urban and rural expected incomes in triggering migration. Two approaches may be taken here. The first focuses on output markets (based on the identity that national income is the value of the flow of final products)[4], identifying forces that favor consumers in urban areas; the second identifies national income as the sum of factor returns. In a simple, stylized model of a closed economy, both approaches would yield identical estimates of gross national product (GNP). For regional analysis, however, there may be subtle or not-so-subtle differences. For example, just because the income on a factor is earned in a region does not mean that this income will remain in the region; absentee landowners and remittances from migrant workers are the prime examples. But the perspective remains a useful one: researchers can concentrate on forces that 1) encourage urban in-migration because they lead to an increase in the relative demand for urban production, which trickles down into increased urban incomes and labor demand, or that 2) directly raise relative urban incomes.

The urban bias thesis, originally advanced by Lipton (1976), mainly takes the first approach. Specifically, it focuses on the advantages that producers and consumers in urban areas (especially capital cities) receive through government policy, and the simultaneous bias against agricultural development.[5] According to this school of thought, national policies have been biased against agricultural development on three counts. First, macroeconomic decisions involving trade, tariff structure, exchange rates, and price controls led to distorted economic signals, and relative factor and product prices consequently do not reflect true scarcity values. In particular, these policies, as a group, tend to raise nonagricultural units value-added above what would prevail at international prices.[6] Second, the public sector deliberately has invested resources in urban areas to improve infrastructure and public services without regard for high rate of return opportunities elsewhere in the economy and without recovering costs from the beneficiaries. Third, the central government has compounded the effects of the first two transgressions by augmenting public employment and public directly productive investment in cities to a degree not justified by any conceivable efficiency criteria.

There is ample evidence of all three types of "bureaucratic failure" both in Africa and elsewhere. For example, a survey by Agarwala (1983), drawing on the experience of thirty-one countries, suggests that price distortions in foreign exchange, as well as in factor and product pricing, have been widespread—and that these distortions have caused lower growth rates in many countries. The mean growth rate of high distortion countries was a full 2 percent below that of the average growth rate in the sample; conversely, low distortion countries had a mean growth rate 2 percent above the sample mean. Of the African countries in the sample, Malawi, Cameroon, and Kenya are classified as low distortion. Ethiopia, Côte d'Ivoire, and Senegal are classified as having a medium level of distortions, while Tanzania, Nigeria, and Ghana are classified as having severe distortions.[7] These results underline three key points: 1) the macroeconomic policies of the region's countries are not uniform; 2) the presence of at least this type of "urban bias" has not, in the past, kept the World Bank and other donors from working in the urban sectors of Brazil, Mexico, Indonesia, India, and Pakistan—none of which are star performers on Agarwala's list; and 3) there is a fairly strong but imperfect link between absence of severe price distortions and growth performance. During the decades of the 1970s and 1980s the low distortion economies performed quite well, while the high distortion economies either performed poorly (the cases of Tanzania and Ghana) or realized per capita income growth only because of abundant oil reserves, despite distorted domestic prices (Nigeria).

Lipton's second type of bias involving public services has been well documented for Africa and elsewhere. The main biases are heavy subsidization of public services, inadequate attention to affordable standards, and the consequent restricted coverage of most public services. The World Bank has taken the lead in convincing African governments to scale down the standards of additional infrastructure and public services, and to employ user charges and local taxes to recover a large fraction of capital and recurrent expenses in urban areas.[8] This should free resources, over time, for new initiatives in rural areas.

Finally, the present process of structural adjustment is helping to raise rural foodstuff and export crop prices, reverse widespread overstaffing of public sector enterprises, and curtail inappropriate productive investments in parastatal ventures. Since most of these investments are located in urban areas, they have promoted particular cities to the detriment of other urban centers and rural areas. But structural adjustment is also associated with large foreign exchange inflows (that are used mainly for urban activities, and which help support exchange rates), restrictions on fertilizer and other agricultural input subsidies, and fees for clinics, schools, and other rural services. Consequently, while it seems likely that urban biases of public policies are diminishing, it is by no means certain.

This having been said, several caveats are in order. First, no one has yet established the impact of the various sources of urban bias on city growth in Africa or anywhere else in the developing world (Williamson [1988]). Second, note that the urban bias argument fails to distinguish between urban/rural and farm/nonfarm dichotomies; the two are treated as synonymous. Undoubtedly the distinction is purely an academic one for some countries of the world, but the existence of rural service and cottage industries in parts of Africa could make such imprecision misleading.[9] Third, strong pro-rural rhetoric in and of itself is not sufficient to overcome urban bias. The Tanzanian case illustrates this point dramatically; Ellis (1984:33) claims that—stated intentions notwithstanding—the Tanzanian experience of the 1970s fits the urban bias model well, with the terms of trade turning significantly against agriculture. Fourth, and perhaps most important, is the fact that even in the absence of these biases, one would still find disparities. *The very process of economic development involves per capita differences between rural areas, between urban centers, between regions, and even between rural and urban sectors, taken globally.*[10] These disequilibria are apparent at all stages of development except at the poles of development experience: either in a subsistence or fully developed economy. Thus, under most circumstances, there will be incentives to move between regions, between occupations, and between economic subsectors.

For this reason, it is incorrect to argue that per capita investments—be they in infrastructure or in directly productive activities—should be roughly equivalent between city and country, or even between different-sized centers or different regions. Departures from equal allocations per capita are the norm in an efficient economy. Getting rid of "urban bias" does not lead automatically to the adoption of misplaced egalitarianism, nor should it.

A final point needs to be made about urban policy biases. An urban bias raises returns to urban residents above the level that would prevail in a "neutral" policy environment (in which the government sought to maximize some general objective, such as per capita gross domestic product [GDP] in the absence of factor and product price distortions). But these biases may or may not attract in-migrants, and therefore may or may not be urbanizing. Policies that raise the profitability of urban activities, but that do so in a way that encourages firms to economize on labor and use more capital and imports may actually reduce urban growth, even in a general equilibrium setting. To repeat, then: urban bias is not identical to overurbanization.

4.2.3. Economic Factors I: The Labor Surplus Model

Thus far, we have concentrated on outlining social and policy forces that drive urban growth. But what do the economic models say? What economic forces appear to matter?

The point of departure for virtually all simple development paradigms is the model introduced by Lewis (1954). The model has two sectors. The first is a rural, low-productivity agricultural sector, in which the total output level X_A is invariant with respect to changes in employment N_A. There is also a high-productivity, modern, urban, industrial sector M for which output X_M varies both with employment N_M and capital K_M.

The development process involves capital accumulation in the modern sector, which in turn raises the value of the marginal product of labor (MPL) and increases the demand for labor until the MPL recedes to equal the urban wage. As long as average agricultural incomes are constant, and labor is drawn from the countryside, then wages will be constant for a prolonged period. This era will be characterized by high rates of capital accumulation, rapid modern sector growth, and the transfer of labor from rural to urban areas. Eventually, increased scarcities will drive up agricultural sector prices, as product demand grows; at a still more distant point, agricultural wages will be bid up, and real wages (in terms of agricultural goods) will begin to rise—and aggregate growth will slow down.

This story was written with a country more like India than Zambia in mind. For high population density countries such as Rwanda or Burundi, the paradigm seems reasonable, but it is hard to reconcile with the apparent presence of excess land and labor shortages in many African countries. As it turns out, however, the key to the constant wage, "surplus population" story was not rural labor abundance per se, but rather the presence of any abundant rural factor of production. Consequently, Hansen (1979) was able to retell the story in a more "African" setting, involving unlimited supplies of low-quality rural land, and in doing so, derived essentially the same qualitative results.

What were these results? First, urban labor demand (and hence population growth) is driven by the rate of urban capital accumulation, and, to a lesser degree, favorable changes in urban/rural terms of trade and urban technological progress. The model is similar in spirit to neoclassical growth models, for capital accumulation is driven by savings, which in turn is tied to capital incomes in the modern, urban sector. An interesting implication of this story is that unequal income distributions are essential for the growth process, since it is capitalists who save and provide the engine for development.

While not stressed in Lewis and the initial mathematical formulation by Ranis and Fei (1961), Hansen also emphasized the important role of rural earnings. Prosperity in "subsistence" agriculture means a high reservation wage for potential migrants to urban jobs, and hence a necessarily high urban wage. High urban wages, in turn, imply lower profits, lower rates of reinvestment, lower rates of urban output and employment growth, and lower rates of total GDP growth. Steps taken to encourage rural-urban migration, from the benign construction of rural roads to the oppressive levy of harsh taxes, will have the reverse effect.

The surplus labor model thus centers around migration as the core labor market event that enables national economic development. Migration in search of higher wages is both inevitable and desirable. Its role is to redistribute labor not only from a low labor-productivity rural sector to urban occupations with higher labor productivity, but also to enable growth in the dynamic urban sector that more rapidly accumulates capital.

As a depiction of the general development process, the fundamental notion of labor movement from relatively stagnant to dynamic sectors continues to have great appeal to development economists. But in its pure form, the Lewis-Ranis/Fei-Hansen model misses several stylized facts of contemporary Africa. To start with, it is not entirely obvious that urban rates of capital accumulation are actually greater than rural rates, if the latter were measured properly. Nor is the connection between urban and rural wages all that simple (the surplus labor models generally assume that migration either causes urban and rural wages to be equal, or to form a constant ratio, where an urban wage premium may reflect higher living costs, human capital differentials, and psychological costs of moving), as we see in the following chapter. Third, the models ignore the critical role of the rural sector as producer of foreign exchange in many countries, as well as African urban sectors' import dependency. Finally, and perhaps most critically, the surplus labor models ignore the fact that most labor in urban Africa is either employed in the informal sector or is unemployed, rather than working in the modern sector.[11]

As it turns out, urban unemployment can be incorporated readily into the two-sector framework of the surplus labor model. So, for that matter, can be an urban informal sector and balance of payments constraints (Becker and Morrison [1988]).

As these modifications begin with the work of Harris and Todaro, their model is presented in the following section; further refinements are discussed later in this chapter, and in Chapter 6.

4.2.4. Economic Factors II: The Harris-Todaro Model

The second approach used to analyze the relation between expected income differences and migration focuses on factor returns, specifically targeting the gap between urban and rural expected wages. Using the HT framework, the expected urban wage, $W_U{}^e$, is equal to the product of fixed urban wage (W_m) and the probability of obtaining employment (N_m/N_u), where N_m is urban employment and N_u is the urban labor force.

$$W_U{}^e = \frac{W_M N_M}{N_U} \tag{4.1}$$

Agricultural production (X_r) uses land (L), capital (K_r), and labor (N_r).

$$X_r = q(N_r, L, K_r) \tag{4.2}$$

Manufacturing production (X_m) uses only capital (K_m) and labor (N_m).

$$X_m = f(N_m, K_m) \tag{4.3}$$

Only labor is mobile between sectors, and

$$N_r + N_u = \tilde{N}_r + \tilde{N}_u = \overline{N} \tag{4.4}$$

where $\tilde{N}_r$ and $\tilde{N}_u$ are the initial endowments of labor in each sector. The equilibrium condition is that the urban expected wage equal the agricultural wage, W_r.

$$W_r = W_U{}^e \tag{4.5}$$

In competitive equilibrium, the rural wage will be equal to the value of its marginal product. That is, $W_r = Pq_1$, where q_1 denotes the partial derivative of q with respect to its first argument N_r, and P is the relative price of the agricultural good. In reality, of course, this efficiency condition may well not hold, but even under most simple alternative models of agricultural behavior earnings will be closely related to values of marginal products, so the simplification is not too critical.

Let us further assume that rural-urban migration at any instant (which can be expressed as the time derivative of the urban labor force, N) is a positive function of the difference between expected urban earnings and expected rural earnings. Then substituting in for W_r we obtain HT's fundamental equation of motion:

$$\dot{N}_u = \phi \left[\frac{W_m N_m}{N_u} - Pq_1 \right] \tag{4.6}$$

Note that the probability of obtaining urban employment is a function of the relative price of the agricultural good, the marginal product of labor in agriculture, and the urban wage. Thus, in equilibrium in which past migration has caused expected urban wages to exactly equal rural wages,

$$\frac{N_m}{N_u} = \frac{W_r}{W_m} = \frac{Pq_1}{W_m} = \frac{\theta\left(\frac{X_m}{X_r}\right)q_1}{W_m} \qquad (4.7)$$

In (4.7) the relative price term P has been replaced by $\theta(X_m/X_r)$—that is, prices depend on relative production in the two sectors, given exogenous demand structures. Given the fixed stock of agricultural land and capital, productivity and wages are determined by the amount of agricultural labor. Urban wages, on the other hand, are assumed to be set exogenously by institutional forces such as government policy or union behavior that divorce levels from productivity.

In the HT framework, urban capital accumulation matters once again, since firms will hire labor until $f_1 = W_m$. As growth in K_m will increase the f_m schedule, demand for labor (normally) will increase with urban capital stock. So, however, will unemployment, as can be seen from (4.7): if W_r/W_m is constant, any force that causes N_m to increase will result in an equiproportionate rise in the unemployed urban labor force. It is also apparent that urban unemployment (or underemployment) will rise with changes in relative urban/rural wages. Indeed, these were key policy points: 1) any effort to raise urban wages by governments would lead not only to a reduction in employment, but also to a rise in unemployment, and 2) even a rise in urban employment—occasioned, say, by a public works program—would also cause an *increase* in urban unemployment. Depending on the exact migration and labor market adjustment process specified, it is even possible that an urban jobs program actually could increase the unemployment rate.[12]

Thus, HT caused a switch in emphasis away from traditional factors of capital accumulation in explaining urban employment growth and urbanization. The role of public policy, especially in regard to wage policy and employment creation, instead rose to the fore. The model seemed to account successfully for the obvious presence of large numbers of unemployed and part-time workers who were not better off in cities than in rural areas—but who had hopes of landing favored high-wage jobs that would make them better off. And HT also disputed from the neoclassical implication that high wages would actually choke off urbanization: it is quite possible that high-wage policies will lead to increases in expected wages, thereby leading to dramatic growth in the urban unemployed and informal sectors by hopeful but thus far disappointed formal sector job seekers.

The HT paradigm continues to be an important and powerful one. But it too suffers from a number of clear limitations, thus giving rise to a growth industry in the publication of extensions. First, the model emphasizes urban policy and economic events—while evidence suggests that rural conditions in Africa were critically important. Second, the informal sector is ignored in the bare bones HT statement. So, too, is the well-known fact that urban wages have a fairly wide distribution, and, in fact, many informal sector workers have incomes that exceed average formal sector wages (for detailed evidence, see Livingstone [1991]). Fourth, the view that formal sector wages are exogenously set is an inherently unsatisfactory assumption, especially in the face of evidence that real wages have changed considerably in recent years. Fifth, the HT model does not explicitly take account of individuals' labor/leisure choice.

Of these matters, the first can be easily addressed with straightforward extensions to HT. The greater the rural population density, ceteris paribus, the smaller

TABLE 4.3.   Adjusted Rural Out-Migration Rates by Age and Education: Kenya
(all figures annualized rates, in percent)

cohort	Uneducated		Educated	
	1962–69	1969–79	1962–69	1972–79
0–9	−0.30	−0.30	−0.30	−1.93
10–14	0.34	0.21	2.17	1.34
15–19	0.81	0.56	5.24	3.62
20–24	2.03	1.59	13.16	10.29
25–29	0.37	0.26	2.42	1.68
30–39	−0.40	−0.32	−2.57	−2.10
40–49	−0.80	−0.84	−5.18	−5.43
50+	−0.79	−0.88	−5.13	−5.66

Sources: Barnum and Sabot (1982); Republic of Kenya Central Statistical Office (1979, 1982), World Bank (1981).
Note: Rates are combined for men and women. "Educated" people are those with eight or more years of schooling.

are the average and marginal products in agriculture. This suggests that population pressure in rural areas may be a potent factor in migration decisions. Economists think of population pressure simply as a factor depressing the rural wage; sociologists label it a "push factor" in the migration decision.[13] These sort of rural forces appear in many theoretical restatements of HT, and in virtually all empirical tests.

The HT model also has been modified in a straightforward manner to accommodate the presence of an urban informal sector (see Steel and Takagi [1983] and Cole and Sanders [1985]). Nor is the wage distribution problem major: the assumption of homogeneity must simply be modified to permit us to examine the effects of individual's characteristics on the migration decision. Relevant characteristics include sex, age, marital status, and education level. The consensus for Africa is that migrants tend to be male, young, single, and better educated than their nonmigrating peers. This result has been confirmed repeatedly for African countries (see Tables 4.2–4.4)

The most critical convenient simplification of the HT model is the assumption that an individual's reservation wage remains constant throughout his search for employment. But this is unlikely for two reasons: family charity and patience may diminish, while at the same time the migrant's own savings may become depleted if job search is prolonged (Collier [1979:209]). Family patience and ability to continue to support a migrant are crucially important; several studies indicate that there is a significant net cash flow from rural to urban areas during the migrant's first year. The presence of multiple reservation wages implies that plausible models must admit urban labor market choices other than modern sector employment or unemployment.

4.2.5. Economic Factors III: The Labor Turnover Model

Implicit in the HT model is an assumption of continuous job turnover, since job seekers' expected wage is equal to the prevailing wage multiplied by the fraction of the urban labor force that is employed. If, however, none of the presently

TABLE 4.4.   Sex Ratios of Migrants and Total Population of Working Age, Circa 1975.

| | | Males per 100 females | |
| | | | |
Difference Country	Immigrants (A)	Total population (B)	(A − B)
Gambia	181	104	77
Ghana	166	96	70
Côte d'Ivoire	177	110	67
Liberia	164	103	61
Senegal	119	84	35
Sierra Leone	187	97	90
Togo	88	105	−17
Burkina Faso	79	94	−15
All countries	156	97	59

Source: Zachariah and Conde (1981:46).

employed plan to leave their jobs, the likelihood of a new migrant earning the formal sector wage is very low, and the probability of formal sector employment is far less than N_m/N_u. In reality, urban formal sector jobs are difficult to obtain, so once a worker becomes employed there, he is reluctant to undertake job search. Blomqvist (1981) extends the HT model to allow for varying rates of job turnover and shows that Todaro paradox of increasing unemployment resulting from job creation is less likely when job turnover is less than instantaneous.

The basic idea in the labor turnover model, first advanced by Stiglitz (1974) (also see Bardhan [1979] and Stiglitz [1982]), is a very simple one. Firms are assumed to employ labor *and* set wages in order to maximize profits, which depend on both direct wage payments and on labor training costs. Training costs are assumed to rise with the labor turnover rate, r, so that total labor costs, aggregated for the entire urban sector, are:

$$TC_{L_U} = W_U L_U + r(W_U/EW_{U'}\ W_U/W_{R'}\ U_U) \cdot t \cdot L_U \qquad (4.8)$$

Here training costs per new employee are given by t. Secondly, the quit rate r is assumed to depend on 1) the difference between the actual wage and the wage that workers expect to prevail, 2) the ratio of the urban wage to the prevailing rural wage, and 3) the urban unemployment rate, U_U. The higher is W_U relative to expected and rural wages, the lower will be quit rates; quit rates are also lowered by higher urban unemployment rates.

If firms believe that they can reduce turnover by paying a slightly higher wage than the average firm (which, of course, they cannot actually do if the problem is symmetric for all firms), or by paying more than the rural reservation wage, then it will be in firms' interest to pay a wage above the "purely competitive" level that would prevail in the absence of turnover costs. Furthermore, labor market equality in the Harris-Todaro sense (where expected urban earnings equals expected rural earnings) cannot obtain without positive unemployment. To see this point, note that if $r = 0$ or $t = 0$, then firms would be unable to hire any labor at $W_U < W_{R'}$ and could hire an essentially infinite amount at wage W_R. But if $r > 0$ and $t > 0$, then a slightly higher wage will reduce costs by

$$\left\{ t \cdot \left[\frac{r_1}{EW_U} + \frac{r_2}{W_R} + r_3 U_{W_u} \right] - L_U \right\} \Delta W_U \qquad (4.9)$$

If this term is positive, then it will be in the firm's interest to pay a higher wage than W_R—the firm will continue to raise the wage rate it offers until the returns to doing so (the first two parts of equation [4.9]) just offset the costs of doing so.

The labor turnover model is highly appealing theoretically, since it generates a high formal sector wage and urban unemployment without assuming an institutional wage. It is also intuitively appealing, since real world firms clearly do face significant training costs, and should seek to avoid them. The model also generates the plausible hypothesis that modern sector wage premia will decline during periods of economic deterioration, since unemployment will be high, and workers will be reluctant to give up their jobs.

Relatively little is known about actual job turnover and training costs in Africa. Collier and Lal's (1980:42) survey of Kenyan labor markets during the relatively prosperous 1970s found turnover patterns similar to those in the U.S. labor market. Specifically, they found:

* mean and median lengths of formal sector job stay ranging from 3.5 to 5.0 years
* that about 12 percent of skilled workers and 17 percent of unskilled workers left their jobs in the preceding twelve months.

But these fairly high turnover rates may not have lasted; Knight and Sabot (1990:171) estimated the average turnover rate in Kenya to have fallen to once every 9.3 years by 1980, and to once every 16.8 years in Tanzania. The International Labour Organisation's (ILO) Labor Turnover Survey in Kenya (cited in Elkan [1976]) found an annual formal sector turnover rate of only 11.5 percent. The Kenya Turnover Survey and the Tanzanian data both indicate strong declines in labor mobility and labor turnover after the late 1960s (also see Knight and Sabot [1981]). These patterns are not surprising: in fairly tight labor markets, urban workers are relatively likely to quit, both to search for new jobs and to make sojourns back to the countryside, confident that they can obtain new jobs upon return. In a depressed environment, though, quitting one's job is to be avoided if at all possible.

The labor turnover framework represented a major improvement in the realism of labor market modeling. As an empirical proposition, it is fairly difficult to test, given the paucity and poor quality of unemployment data. But its focus on nonmechanistic labor market processes is critical, and it represented one of the first dual economy models to successfully endogenize wages while retaining the realism of unemployment and rural-urban wage gaps.

It is not the final word, however, and several competing—but often not mutually exclusive—hypotheses have been introduced as well. A few are discussed briefly in the following sections; our own models and empirical work is postponed until Chapter 6.

4.2.6. Economic Factors IV: The Role of Education and Other Factors

The simple HT and labor turnover paradigms posit that all migrants trek to the city in search of formal sector employment; moreover, they implicitly assume that

TABLE 4.5.   Rates of Rural-Urban Migration for Four Education Groups in Three Time Periods: Tanzanian Males (percentages).

Current Age	Arrival Age*	No Formal Education	Standard 1–4	Standard 5–8	Form 1 and Higher
35+	1955–61	0.012	0.030	0.106	0.180
25–34	1962–66	0.013	0.038	0.144	0.399
20–44	1967–70	0.014	0.067	0.277	0.318

*Period in which the majority of migrants in the age subgroup arrived in town.
Source: Sabot (1979:134).

all migrants possess identical human capital characteristics, since all migrants have an equal chance to obtain formal sector employment. Several interesting migration models, however, incorporate the role of education levels in the migration and job search process. Cole and Sanders (1985), for example, note that in parts of the Third World the average educational level of migrants is falling. Due to extensive information networks provided by kin and clan, prospective migrants must know that some formal education is generally prerequisite to formal sector employment. Yet the dramatic movement to urban areas continues. The only reasonable conclusion is that a large number of migrants come the cities knowing that formal sector employment is impossible; instead, they aim for the informal or service sector. Indeed, given the limited growth of formal sector employment, it may be wildly incorrect to focus exclusively on it as the leading force in attracting rural out-migrants.

A quite different model is proposed by Sabot (1979), motivated by the recent experience of Tanzania. Sabot observes that the migration rate for uneducated or low-education individuals has increased more slowly than that of more highly educated individuals in Tanzania (see Table 4.5). The explanation for this trend is ingenious. Sabot suggests that the supply of educated workers has expanded at a faster rate than demand for skilled labor. Consequently, educated workers "filter down" into low-skill jobs, displacing poorly educated workers.

Sabot's model predicts that the average education level of migrants will rise over time. Cole and Sanders, of course, suggest just the opposite. Which is most plausible for Africa? At this point, data on trends in the educational profiles of migrants are too sketchy to venture a generalization.[14]

Several other models of labor migration are worth mentioning briefly. The purpose here is not to be exhaustive—for that, see Williamson's (1988) chapter on the subject in the North-Holland *Handbook* series—but rather to mention the paradigms of greatest importance in African contexts.

Knight and Sabot (1988) provide a simple modification of the standard HT framework. In their model, government also seeks to provide urban employment in response to growing unemployment. The implication is that migration costs include not only outright urban unemployment, but also any hidden unemployment that occurs in the public sector. Low-productivity government employment adds further costs as well, since 1) it attracts still more in-migrants, 2) it may also absorb valuable capital, and 3) it necessitates taxes, which generate additional distortions.

Shukla and Stark (1989), on the other hand, take a more benign view of high turnover and urban wage gaps. They suggest that firms may view some turnover favorably, since it will reduce the pain of contraction during recessions. For that matter, it will also enable more internal promotions (which have positive morale effects), and will be especially valuable if different "vintages" of labor have different strengths. At the same time, urban workers with occasional rural obligations (and rural family) will prefer a system in which they can leave urban jobs and eventually get a new position at some point after they return. In this setting, then, institutional wage gaps actually can be beneficial to the economy as a whole. Firms will locate where there is a pool of unemployed, available labor (even at a higher wage); workers will prefer sporadic employment at high wages to continual employment at lower wages, and so will not bid down wage rates.

This position is a fairly extreme one, though. A bit more mainstream is the notion that information is costly, and that workers with scarce attributes will engage in a lengthy search to find firms that will take advantage of their scarce skills. These scarce skills then generate rents that will be distributed between the worker and the firm. Unemployment emerges because search is time consuming—especially if the underlying conditions are changing, so that expectations must frequently readjust (see Harris and Sabot [1982]).

At the same time, firms have incentives to offer higher wages, if this attracts more applicants, some of whom may have rare skills that the firm values; this is consistent with the adverse selection model described in section 4.1. At the same time, workers over time will acquire job-specific skills and will increasingly reveal their true ability. Exceptionally able workers cannot capture performance-based rents immediately, but can do so eventually if other firms are willing to compete for already-employed workers. Firms also eventually have to reward workers at least in part for the firm-specific and any general skills they acquire; the alternative is to risk losing employees (Collier and Lal [1986: Ch. 6]). These skill accumulation factors (also emphasized in Stark [1991]) will lead to average wages in urban enterprises above the rural wage (or other opportunity cost of migration).

In fact, an extreme statement of the neoclassical thesis attributes all of the wage gaps that occur to 1) general human capital—education, and personal characteristics and 2) firm-specific human capital—experience. Combined with a theory of optimal search, one can in principle obtain the paradigmatic African income and employment structures as the outcome of a perfectly competitive labor market process.

But while detailed assessment of studies of wage formation are postponed to Chapter 5, it should be noted that evidence of labor market segmentation is very strong in Africa, and migration theories based on perfect competition are still less plausible than those based on fairly random turnover. For example, Collier and Lal (1986: Ch. 6) find that wage rates for unskilled Kenyan workers (over a sample of thirty-three firms from 1974/75) are positively and significantly related both to firm size and a dummy variable that indicated multinational corporation status. Obviously, competitive wage theory suggests that workers should be paid the same regardless of firm size and ownership. Some modification of simple microeconomic theory is needed, since wage rates do not vary exclusively with human capital characteristics. Moreover, this finding also indicates that migration in search of a high-wage prize may not be irrational, and that a modified version of HT may be the best migration model.

Both Collier and Bigsten (1981) and Collier and Lal (1986) hypothesize that firms hire workers with limited information about a key unobservable variable, willingness to work (Z). Historically, Z depends in part on firm pay, a point recognized by many economists, and automatically leading to a wage premium in firms in which monitoring is unusually costly (namely in large firms, or in firms in which piecework is impractical). Z also depends on individuals' characteristics, and these are slowly revealed during the course of employment. Consequently, the pattern often observed in Third World (and First World) labor markets is for a large firm to have a pool of low-wage, casual workers alongside a pool of permanent, high-wage workers. The best casual workers are selected for permanent employment as positions open; during their casual "apprenticeship," the firm has a chance to observe each person's Z. The casual wage must be close to rural earnings in poor countries with imperfect capital markets, as people cannot borrow against the uncertain promise of higher future wages as permanent employees. Moreover, firms must eventually pay some sort of premium to high Z casual workers, as otherwise they risk losing them to another employer's pool.[15]

The extension of education has an important impact in this model. While the correlation is imperfect, high Z people are also likely to have earned high grades (G) in school.[16] Firms will therefore offer higher salaries (and possibly immediate semipermanent employment) to high G labor force entrants, as G is a proxy for Z. The implication for migration is straightforward. High G school-leavers and individuals with much schooling have enormous incentive to migrate to cities, as they should be able to obtain high-wage work with minimal job search unemployment. Low G school-leavers have less incentive to migrate, and, if they do, they will head for the informal sector. They should know that they have little chance of obtaining a high-wage job, and therefore should experience little unemployment. Unemployment, rather, will fall most cruelly on the middle G and middle L labor force entrants. This pattern, in fact, is exactly what Collier and Bigsten find to have been the case in Kenya.

One final strand of labor migration literature is worth mentioning. Migration may typically be sequential. The hypothesis that the urban informal sector is a point of entry to the formal sector has received limited confirmation (for a survey of findings, see Rempel [1981:123–25]). What is fairly clear is that a pattern of true "subsistence self-employment because of an inability to obtain regular wage employment" (Rempel [1981:124]) is rare, because migrants utilize family and kin ties in cities, temporary remittances from rural relatives, and their own savings. Moreover, some do move directly to formal sector jobs. Perhaps the lack of clarity is due to the fact that there are many rural-urban migration streams, and that many of the models described above have limited validity, varying in strength across groups and countries.

What Rempel (1981:166) does find is that there is something of a town hierarchy in the migration process. Migrants often head to nearby towns first, and only subsequently to large cities. The reverse is far less frequent.

4.2.7. Demographic Factors

Assuming homogeneity of migrants may lead to significant errors in predicting the size of future migration flows.[17] Disaggregation of migration flows by age cohort for Botswana and Zambia, for example, reveals huge differences between sex and age cohorts (see Table 4.2). The probability of a prime age male migrating from a rural area is approximately 33 to 171 percent higher than a prime age female (in Zambia and Botswana, respectively). The probability of a prime age male or female migrating is between five and ten times that of an individual aged sixty to sixty-nine in Zambia; in Botswana the net out-migration probability of this older cohort is negative. In sum, it is clear that the age and sex compositions of at-risk populations are important determinants of the size of migration flows. The flattening of the population pyramids characterizing sub-Saharan nations in recent decades has expanded the number of individuals in "migration-prone" cohorts and contributed to the vast rural-urban flows that were observed.

It should be emphasized that rural-urban migration is a phenomenon of the relatively young. In Kenya, net outmigration from Nairobi is typical for all age groups over thirty. In more recent years, this also appears to be true for Zambian men, although for women this pattern does not emerge. In more rapidly urbanizing Botswana, rural net outmigration becomes negative (and hence urban net outmigration becomes positive) for age groups above fifty. In short, census data unquestionably pick up a "retirement to the village" phenomenon, along with peak urban inmigration for cohorts around fifteen to thirty-five years old.

Similarly, migrant educational characteristics are an important determinant of migration flows, and implicit or explicit assumptions of migrant homogeneity with respect to educational characteristics may lead to misleading predictions of migration patterns. Using a unique data set from Kenya, it is possible to estimate populations (and hence migration rates) by educational status, rural or urban location, and age.[18] These migration rates are given in Table 4.3. These data show the vastly greater migration responsiveness of those with eight or more years of schooling. The young with schooling are vastly more likely to migrate to the cities than their less-educated rural counterparts, while they also may be more likely to return to their rural homes in their later years.[19] The pattern of higher rural outmigration by the relatively educated almost certainly reflects differential employment opportunities in Kenyan cities.

It has been Kenyan policy to promote the rapid growth of education, and the outcome has been a population with far greater mean education levels than in most of Africa. In consequence, few urban jobs that demand significant skills or that pay a significant differential above rural opportunities have gone to those without secondary schooling since 1970. On the other hand, Kenya has also managed to create modest real income growth in many rural areas even in the face of 3.5–4 percent annual population growth, thus reducing push factors for the rural unskilled.

Homogeneity similarly precludes the characteristics of households from being included in the analysis. In Lucas' study of Botswana (1982), household characteristics such as the number of cattle owned, the size of the household, presence or absence of the male head of household, and village or nonvillage location of the household were all included in the estimated migration equation. The assumption of homogeneity also precludes the analysis of the effects of ethnicity on migration. The phenomenon of networking within an ethnic group is quite common in Africa; employers are likely to give preference in hiring to workers who are of their ethnic background. The importance of ethnicity in the migration decision is confirmed for Kenya by Huntington (1977).[20]

In contrast with economic models, demographic models tend to focus on shifting cohort structures. As a rule (see Rogers [1982], Ledent [1982] and Ledent [1990]), demographic models either assume that economic forces do not matter, or that they work in a vaguely specified manner. In particular, urbanization may be posited to depend on per capita income, but this relationship is not derived from a structural model.

On the other hand, demographic models do take account of changes in fertility and mortality in a far more sophisticated way than economic models (which often ignore them: for a contrast of economic and demographic models, see Rogers and Williamson [1982]). More complex models also use (age, sex) cohort-specific migration rates, and, in addition, take into account shifting migration base weights by using gross rather than net migration rates (for the seminal work, see Rogers [1990]).

The main focus of these models of interest to us is their projections of urban population growth, and the share of that growth accounted for by rural-urban migration. Interestingly, demographic and economic models often tend to give very similar projections (for a comparison of Indian projections, see Becker, Williamson and Mills [1992]), although their foundations differ greatly. The demographic based estimates and projections from the United Nations for Africa, as of around 1980 (given in Rogers [1982]), however, should make one pause:

period	annual urban growth rate, Africa (percentage)
1950–60	4.4
1960–70	4.9
1970–80	5.0
1980–90	5.0
1990–2000	4.6

While these figures include the entire continent, and hence are not strictly comparable to the figures we have given, it seems unlikely that comparability is the main problem. Rather, the U.N. estimates' projected leveling out of urban growth in the 1970s and 1980s certainly did not happen for sub-Saharan Africa, and probably did not happen for the entire continent. Part of the problem is likely to stem from increasing overall migration propensities, and another part probably stems from overly optimistic assumptions about fertility decline.

4.2.8. Empirical Findings

A sampling of empirical migration studies are presented in Table 4.6. It should be stressed that the number of such studies is enormous, and we are confined to a (hopefully representative) subset. The findings may be summarized as follows:

(1) *The results are often highly sensitive to the equation specification, degree of data aggregation, time period, and country.* That is, the first generalization is that one should be cautious about making generalizations!

(2) *Distance appears to deter migration.* This is a standard finding everywhere.

TABLE 4.6. Migration Function Estimates

A. Barnum and Sabot (1977)—Tanzania; linear regression with average net propensity to migrate as dependent variable

Reg.	Const.	WU	WR	WU-WR	DIST	UP	D_1	D_2	D_3	Prob.	R^2
1	.15	.0040	-.0106		-.0085	.027					.48
	(.40)	(.0005)	(.0067)		(.0039)	(.004)					
2	-.14			.0039	-.0073	.027					.49
	(.26)			(.0005)	(.0037)	(.004)					
3	.43			.0030*	-.0074	.002					.55
	(.23)			(.0003)	(.0035)	(.004)					
4	.11	.0024	-.0077		-.0077	.023				.666	.55
	(.37)	(.0006)	(.0063)		(.0036)	(.004)				(.163)	
5	-.09			.0023	-.0069	.023				.676	.55
	(.24)			(.0006)	(.0035)	(.004)				(.162)	
6	1.19				.0075	.027	-.94	-.87	-.40		.51
	(.25)				(.0036)	(.004)	(.12)	(.12)	(.12)		
7	.57			.0022	-.0074	.027	-.64	-.58	-.22		.57
	(.28)			(.0006)	(.0034)	(.004)	(.14)	(.14)	(.14)		
8	.65			.0022*	-.0074	.023	-.33	.29	-.01		.56
	(.29)			(.0007)	(.0034)	(.004)	(.22)	(.21)	(.17)		

*P(WU) - WR used instead of WU-WR; standard errors in parentheses

WU = urban wage
WR = rural wage
DIST = distance covered by migration
UP = urban population
$D_{1,2,3}$ = dummy variables for educational groups
Prob = probability of urban employment.

B. Christiansen (1984)—Malawi; linear regression

Regression	Dep. Var.	AE	TE	DIST	PD	MIGR	PYM	R^2
1	Migr. 1966–77		−.03 (5.69)	−2.80 (3.84)	10.31 (4.64)		−26.59 (2.43)	.23
2	Migr. 1966–77	−.04 (4.92)		2.48 (3.34)	11.26 (4.86)		−21.40 (1.87)	.21
3	Migr. 1976–77			.21 (.17)	−.26 (.71)	.13 (2.84)	−8.19 (4.52)	.49

t-statistics in parentheses.
AE = agricultural employment
TE = total employment
DIST = distance
PD = population density in district
MIGR = 1966–1977 migration
PYM = part-year migration.

C. House and Rempel (1980)—Kenya; double log regression with average net propensity to migrate as dependent variable.

Reg.	Const.	W_j	W_i	E_j	E_i	W_jE_j	W_iE_i	D_{ij}	S_j	S_i	U_j	U_i	R^2
1	−2.92 (3.00)	.28[b] (2.23)	.12 (.98)	1.97[c] (1.63)	−.13[b] (1.79)			−1.65[a] (25.4)	−1.65 (1.38)	.21[b] (2.16)	.49[a] (12.7)	.52[a] (9.8)	.54[a]
2	−3.04 (3.13)	.30[a] (2.43)	.13 (1.00)	.32[a] (3.31)	−.14[b] (1.88)			−1.65[a] (25.3)		.22[b] (2.22)	.49[a] (12.6)	.52[a] (9.8)	.54[a]
3	−2.96 (3.04)	.31[a] (2.51)	.08 (.64)					1.63[a] (25.3)	.31[a] (3.24)	.22[b] (1.77)	.49[a] (12.5)	.45[a] (11.7)	.54[a]
4	−2.35 (2.79)					.31[a] (4.80)	.06 (1.08)	−1.64[a] (25.6)		.22[b] (2.28)	.48[a] (12.7)	.50[a] (9.68)	.54[a]

[a] = significant at 1 percent level.
[b] = significant at 5 percent level.
[c] = significant at 10 percent level.

t-statistics in parentheses.
i = district of origin
j = district of destination
w = unskilled modern sector wage
E = proportion of labor force in formal sector
D = distance between headquarters of two districts
S = proportion of population with at least one year of schooling
U = proportion of district's population in towns of five thousand or more residents

D. Byerlee, Tommy, and Fatoo (1976)—Sierra Leone: linear regressions with gross migration as dependent variable

Type of Migration Stream	Reg.	Intercept	$WAGE_i$	$WAGE_j$	$UNEMP_j$	EXP	POP_j	$DIST_{ij}$
Uneducated	Standard	-.3910 (0.264)	-.10406 (0.610)	.00666* (4.240)	-.00199 (0.225)		.00119* (3.565)	-.00166* (3.956)
	Expected Wage	-.05369 (0.379)	-.10413 (0.591)			.00718* (3.760)	.00127* (4.676)	.00164* (3.818)
Educated	Standard	3.2695 (1.229)	-.13638 (0.102)		-.10052 (0.747)		.00981* (4.900)	-.00986* (3.017)
	Urban Size	-5.6964 (1.502)	-.14372 (0.102)	.08919* (4.240)	.13370 (0.837)			-.00875* (2.565)
	Dropped							
	Expected Wage	-1.8343 (0.834)	-.13606 (0.819)			.07501* (1.682)	.00512 (1.404)	-.01004* (3.199)
Pooled	Standard	.04461 (0.797)	-.12306 (0.819)	.00659 (0.093)			.00114 (0.038)	-.00164 (0.048)
	Urban Sized	-.11995 (0.867)	-.12489 (0.839)	.00546 (0.095)	.01827 (0.199)			-.00120 (0.048)
	Dropped							
	Expected Wage	-.04473 (0.801)	-.1201 (0.806)			.00718 (0.100)	.00127 (0.038)	-.00164 (0.047)

WAGE, E

WR	ER	POP	PD	PDO/PD_j	R̄²
-.09801 (0.721)					.539
.11539 (0.963)					.494
					.449
					.386
		.00858* (2.286)	-.00821* (2.499)	3.2105 (0.787)	.478
			-.00754* (2.247)	-5.5857* (2.053)	.571
-.00568 (0.160)	.06783* (1.936)	.00385 (1.307)	-.0084* (2.660)	-1.7937 (1.154)	.521
.08372* (4.813)					.592

i = rural
j = urban
E = dummy for education, set equal to zero for an uneducated migrant

E. Barber and Milne (1986)—Kenya; log linear regression

Regression	Dep. Var.	WR	WRO/WR	ER	ERO/ER	POP	POPO/POP_j	PD	PDO/PD_j	D_ij	No. Obs.	R̄²
1	$\ln(OM_i)$	0.46 (1.93)	1.11 (0.64)	0.24 (2.24)	-1.40 (1.38)	0.69 (4.06)	0.80 (1.03)	0.067 (0.75)	0.42 (0.65)	—	41	.75
2	$\ln(M_{ij}/OM_i)$	0.53 (6.52)	0.74 (9.15)	0.15 (4.02)	0.61 (16.0)	-0.10 (1.69)	0.66 (11.5)	-0.12 (4.09)	-0.11 (3.79)	-1.26 (32.3)	1640	.59
3	$\ln(M_{ij}/OM_i)$	—	0.70 (8.41)	—	0.62 (15.6)	—	0.67 (11.4)	—	-0.10 (3.33)	-1.15 (30.1)	1640	.55

Notes: (a) absolute values of t-statistics are given in parentheses; (b) "other" variables are used inly in regression (1); destination variables are used in the allocation regressions (2) and (3) ; (c) unless denoted by a subscript j, all variables refer to origin region i; (d) intercept terms excluded.

M_{ij}: migration of persons from region i to region j
OM: region i total out-migration
WR: modern sector wage rate
POP: origin population
PD: population density
ER: modern sector employment/population

D_{ij}: distance between regions i and j
WRO: distance weighted average destination wage rate
POPO: distance weighted average population
PDO: distance weighted average population density
ERO: distance weighted average employment ratio

F. Rempel (1981)—Kenya 1969; males and females; linear regression

Regression	Dep. Var.	X_i	U_i	A_{ij}	G_{ij}	DA_{ij}	DB_{ij}	Y_i	X_i	$\tilde{X}_i$	T_i	F_i	E_i	No. Obs.	R^2
(1) Males	$(M_{ij}/M_{i.})$	1.13[b]	-0.12[a]	0.38[a]	0.46[a]	-.01	-.40[a]	.53[a]	-.12	-.06[a]	-.09	-.06	-.12[a]	256	.86
(1) Females	$(M_{ij}/M_{i.})$	0.64[b]	-0.08	0.33[a]	0.50[a]	-.02	-.37[a]	.31[a]	-.06	-.08[a]	-.06	-.12[a]	-.11[a]	256	.85

Regression		X_i	U_i	A_i	S_i	G_{ij}	K_{ij}	DA_{ij}	DB_{ij}	X_a	$\tilde{X}_a$	U_a	A_a	No. Obs.	R^2
(2) Males	(c)	2.99[a]	-0.41[a]	-.15	-.05	.12[a]	-.02	0.24	-0.64[a]	-4.33[a]	0.39[a]	0.10		256	.55
(2) Females	(c)	-0.24	-1.54[b]	-.10	.46[b]	.13[b]	-.01	0.31	-0.73[b]	2.00[b]	-0.01	-0.70[b]		256	.49

Notes: (a) significantly different from 0 at 1 percent level
(b) significantly different from 0 at 5 percent level

(c) $\left(\dfrac{M_{ij}}{\sum_k M_{kj}} \right) \cdot \left(\dfrac{\sum_k P_k}{P_j} \right)$ is dependent variable

constant term not reported

X_j:	urban income	U_j:	urban employment prospects	A_{ij}:	amenity index
G_{ij}:	urban-based kin	DA_{ij}:	cost of move	DB_{ij}:	extent of separation
Y_i:	rural aspiration level	X_i:	rural income level	$\tilde{X}_i$:	rural income distribution
T_i:	interaction with outside	F_i:	access to rural resources	E_i:	inheritance system
S_i:	urban informal sector prospects	U_a:	alternative employment	K_{ij}:	ethnic similarity
X_a:	alternative income			A_a:	alternative amenities'Z

(3) *Higher urban wages attract urban in-migrants—at least men.* By the same to-ken, *higher rural wages tend to deter rural-urban migration.* These findings are quite consistent with axioms of rational behavior.
(4) *Increased likelihood of urban employment also increases migration.*
(5) *Land pressure, as measured by population density, contributes to migration.* Whether this is true in low density areas, or whether a threshold is re-quired, is uncertain.
(6) *The possibility of part-time migration deters permanent migration.*
(7) *People tend to migrate from low formal sector employment to high formal sector employment regions.*
(8) *Migrants do not necessarily tend to head to areas of high schooling.* This result in part may reflect fear of greater labor market competition.
(9) The relationship between education and migration is complex. In general, though, *sensitivity to factors affecting returns to migration rises with level of education.*
(10) *Urban amenities* also matter, as does the presence of *urban kin;* surprisingly, *monetary costs* of migration are unimportant, at least in Kenya.
(11) *People appear drawn to high unemployment locations*—suggesting variable si-multaneity, rather than migrant irrationality.
(12) *Men and women appear to have very similar motives to migrate when they are compared with non-migrants* (Barnum's regression 1). But when empirical analysis shifts to an examination of a particular location for migrants (Bar-num's regression 2), *men and women appear to choose specific locations for dif-ferent reasons.* Women tend to be more heavily influenced by amenities and men by employment opportunities; at any rate, the modern sector wage rates used by Barnum appear to have little relevance for most women migrants.

A few other findings are worth mentioning as well. To start with, both Jamal and Weeks (1988) and Collier and Bigsten (1982) find ample evidence of wage flex-ibility in African formal sectors. Wage structures do not, however, always follow obvious shifts in relative scarcities. This topic receives more attention in the fol-lowing chapter.

Secondly, the urban informal sector is far from being monolithic. As House (1987:894) describes Juba, in southern Sudan: "Our data suggest a dispersed and flexible wage structure which is responsive to large numbers of migrant job-seekers, so that they are absorbed into the urban economy. The result is that open unemployment is negligible." Livingstone (1991:661) in his study of Kenya also finds urban informal sector earnings that "on average compare quite satisfactorily with minimum wages and with a good deal of employment in the formal sector." Earlier confirmation of this finding comes from Aboagye (1986).

A final empirical pattern of note, discussed more in Chapter 6, is that migra-tion to large cities is hardly uniform. Cities with natural constraints or in relative economic decline generally have not grown very rapidly. Indeed, in a geographi-cally constrained city like Banjul, Gambia, there has actually been net out-migration—mainly to the rapidly growing industrial towns and suburbs to the west, but still in the metro area (Becker [1991:130]).

4.3 The Consequences of Rural-Urban Migration

Standard neoclassical economic theory has a clear prediction for the effect of rural-urban migration on the nonmigrants remaining at the rural origin. Given the presence of a fixed factor in the production function—either land or capital—the marginal product of agricultural labor increases as workers are withdrawn from the agricultural areas. This, combined with the neoclassical assumption of productive factors being paid their marginal product, yields the result that real agricultural earnings rise because of the migration.

If there are vast pools of surplus labor, however, migration results in minimal wage changes in rural or urban area. As discussed above in section 4.2.3 (see also Hansen [1979]), a horizontal labor supply curve can be generated even without surplus labor. Since Hansen's model of dualistic development is essentially based on African stylized facts, including an unlimited supply of low-quality land, it may be the case that African migration results in minimal wage changes in rural or urban areas. Certainly, there is little evidence to suggest otherwise.

Yet it is not clear that Hansen's neoclassical model or other neoclassical assumptions are appropriate in the African context. Perhaps the strongest case against marginalism is that kinship groups other than the individual are the correct unit of analysis.[21] There may be variations in productivity between different members of a household; if the more productive members of a household decide to migrate, the average productivity of the household may actually fall (Hedlund and Lundahl [1983]).[22] The type of decision-making group relevant for migration choices is hardly of trivial importance. As Stiglitz (1969) shows, the rural reservation wage in the migration decision will depend upon the decision-making authority and on the institutional procedures for allocating property rights. Similarly, the attractiveness of urban jobs will depend on whose consumption is being maximized. Thus, both the importance of various determinants of migration and the welfare and efficiency consequences of migration will depend critically on the form of decision-making groups. Given the lack of consensus on the appropriate decision-making unit, further research along these lines is of particular importance for a better understanding of African migration.

If the impact of migration on the rural wage rate is unclear, nor is the effect of migrants' remittances on rural incomes. Remittances from urban to rural areas were discussed in detail in section 2.8 and were seen to be quite significant in the African milieu. Remittances may permit more rapid adoption of new technologies in rural areas, in addition to being supplements to rural incomes in times of crisis.

While migration's effect on source regions is crucially important, so too is the effect of migration on urban destination areas.[23] The HT model suggests that the main consequence of rural-urban migration will be an increase in the number of unemployed urban workers. This is undoubtedly at least partially true for Africa. Nonetheless, it is probably true as well that migrants have lower rates of unemployment than natives—perhaps because they accept jobs that natives refuse (Findley [1976:41]).

Zachariah and Conde (1981) report this result for Côte d'Ivoire and Ghana (Table 4.7), citing an employment ratio (employed as a percentage of total group population) for migrants of 65.8 percent versus 37.4 percent for the total population. This difference of over 28 percentage points overstates the case, because 80 percent of the migrants are of working age, while only 55 percent of the general population is over age 15. Once the difference is the composition of the two groups is corrected for, migrants have an employment ratio of 76.4, and the general population has a ratio of 69. Even if their unemployment rate as a group is lower than that of natives,

TABLE 4.7. Employment Ratios by Migration Status and Sex: Ghana and Côte d'Ivoire Combined, Circa 1975

Item	Total population	Immigrants	Difference
Male			
Employed	3,474,900	746,300	
Total	7,726,800	863,200	
Employment ratio			
All ages	45.0	86.5	−41.5
15 and over	83.1	97.5	−14.4
Female			
Employed	2,233,800	176,800	
Total	7,535,600	540,600	
Employment ratio			
All ages	29.6	32.7	−3.1
15 and over	54.5	40.2	14.3
Both sexes			
Employed	5,708,700	923,100	
Total	15,262,400	1,403,800	
Employment ratio			
All ages	37.4	65.8	−28.4
15 and over	69.0	76.4	−7.4

Source: Zachariah and Conde (1981:49).

the increase in the absolute number of urban unemployed deeply troubles government policymakers, largely because of the perceived potential for political instability. Moreover, to the extent that new migrants occupy jobs which otherwise would have been occupied by native urbanites, employment creation policies can have only a very limited impact.

Another consequence of rural-urban migration is a change in the structure of African cities. Many migrants live in squatter settlements, and since squatter settlements are often situated on land unsuitable for other urban development because of terrain (steep hills or low-lying wetlands), this location makes provision of water, sewerage, and drainage facilities quite difficult and expensive. Even if migrants are not located in squatter settlements, adequate service provision may not be forthcoming because of financial constraints.

City budgets in African cities are already tight, and revenue collection is difficult. Newly arrived migrants are especially difficult to tax, particularly those who find employment in the unregistered informal sector. But the short-run strain on public service provision capabilities is not incompatible with long-run efficiency gains in service provision if the financial bottlenecks can be overcome. While per unit costs may rise for the existing size of the providing governmental unit, a larger, more cost-efficient "plant" size may be constructed as more residents are served. This exploitation of economies of scale is one possible benefit of rural-urban migration.

Increased unemployment and the short-run strain on urban services do result from the rapid rise in urban population occasioned by migration. If migration were to have a "multiplier effect" on population growth rates—that is, if migration caused the rate of population growth to rise—its potential for exacerbating these problems would increase. There is lively debate on the effect of migration on migrant women's fertility. Proponents of the *socialization* hypothesis argue that the fertility behavior of migrants reflects the fertility preferences present in their childhood environment; thus, migration will not change their fertility levels. Proponents of the *disruption* hypothesis argue that migrants have low fertility in the period immediately following their move due to the disruptive effects of migration (principally the separation of husbands and wives); this lowering of fertility rates is only temporary, and individuals may subsequently have above-normal fertility rates to compensate for the period of disruption. The *adaptation* hypothesis states that migrants will gradually adapt to the fertility preferences in their new location; for rural-urban migration, this means that fertility of migrants will fall over time. Lastly, the *selectivity* hypothesis recognizes that migrants are not a random sample of the origin population. Only after age, education, marital status, and other factors have been controlled for are comparisons between migrants, stayers, and residents of destination regions meaningful (Hervitz [1985]).

Thus, even if studies confirm that women in rural areas in Africa have higher fertility than women in urban areas (and the evidence on this is somewhat mixed), this is not sufficient evidence to argue that rural-urban migration increases fertility rates in urban areas. If the selectivity hypothesis applies to African countries, the migrants arriving in large cities might be women who would have had low fertility even if they had remained in rural areas. Similarly, the disruption hypothesis suggests that the effect of rural-urban migration on urban fertility rates is ambiguous. On the other hand, if it is assumed that the adaptation and/or socialization hypotheses apply to Africa, then it is likely that rural-urban migration increases fertility rates in urban areas.

Some of the rural-urban fertility differential certainly is due to a difference in the benefits and costs of children in the two areas; children probably contribute less to family incomes in urban areas, while costing parents more to raise (Faruqee et al. [1980: 129]). A part of the fertility differential, however is due to the different education levels in rural and urban areas. Three observationally equivalent hypothesis can be advanced here: 1) urban women, by virtue of their superior education, may be better able to calculate the costs of children, and when correct calculations are made, women opt for smaller families; 2) education can be viewed as synonymous with Westernization, and education simply changes women's family size preferences; or 3) education, itself costly in labor time and money, changes the net benefit calculus. A test to disentangle these effects is needed. Hyatt and Milne (1990) find that education matters, and that being an urban resident does not have a separate fertility-reducing effect, except for women with jobs in urban areas or who live in Nairobi or Mombasa. Otherwise, the evidence is mixed: rural women reduce fertility more rapidly as education increases, but are less likely to reduce fertility as the number of previous births increases.

4.3.1. The Effect of Rural-Urban Migration on GDP

Static productivity gains from rural-urban migration cannot be ignored. It is a fact that most capital accumulation occurs not in rural areas but in the large cities. Imagine a spurt of capital accumulation that raises the marginal productivity of urban workers. In the HT model, a zero migration equilibrium is restored only after some rural workers migrate to the city, lowering urban marginal productivity so that

$$W_A = \frac{\partial f(N_M, K_M)}{\partial N_M} \frac{1}{P} \frac{N_M}{N_U} \qquad (4.10)$$

where the variables are as defined above. The difference between the migrants' productivity in rural areas (before migrating) and their higher productivity in urban areas—including the loss of productivity by those who are unemployed—is a gain to society.

How important are these productivity gains (where they exist)? Is migration an important contributing factor to the growth of per capita incomes in developing countries? Though many will be surprised at the answer, it is clearly affirmative. This is especially true in a purely statistical sense in countries that overvalue the prices of their urban goods (typically by protecting urban goods by imposing tariff walls). But in virtually all countries, migration represents citizens' attempts to improve their welfare by altering their work and living locations, and measures of welfare and productivity ought to increase unless migrants are systematically misguided.

To our knowledge, Morrison (1993) is the only author to have estimated GDP gains from internal migration. He estimates sectoral stochastic frontier production functions using data from Peruvian regions, and obtains estimates of the marginal product of labor in each of Peru's regions. Such an approach is extraordinarily data-intensive; data are needed on regional capital stocks, employment and output by economic sector, as well as on interregional migration flows and the origin and destination sectors of work of these migrants. In the Peruvian case, migration over the period 1976–81 increased GDP 2 percent vis-à-vis what it would have been in the absence of migration.

One obvious critique of this result is that it computes output gains at domestic prices, when in fact urban bias skews relative prices in favor of urban areas. Recalculating the gains to migration at world—rather than domestic—prices, however, does not change the result that much; Morrison still finds GDP gains of between 1.0 and 1.6 percent of GDP. Nor does inclusion of the potential negative externalities—primarily pollution and congestion—caused by migrants to urban areas significantly lower the positive output gains resulting from internal migration.

African data do not permit the estimation of regional stochastic frontier production function estimates by sector, and therefore the Peruvian study cannot be replicated here. But a much simpler set of figures can be derived. Let us assume a typical African economy in which the proportion of the population living in urban areas ranges from 10 percent to 40 percent. Let us further assume that the urban per capita income premium ranges from 50 percent to 300 percent (so that the urban/rural per capita income ratio, y_U/y_R, ranges from 1.5 to 4.0), and also that this premium is constant for all workers. That is, productivity and income of the typical migrant will rise between 50 percent and 300 percent: the gap reflects true productivity differences rather than skill selectivity of migrants.[24] Finally, let us assume that urban and rural fertility rates and age structures are roughly equal, so that the difference between the urban and national population growth rates roughly equals the urban in-migration rate.

TABLE 4.8.   Annual GDP Gains from Rural-Urban Migration and Implied Rural Out-Migration Rates (percentage growth rates)

A. *Urban Population Growth Rate: 9 percent*
   National Population Growth Rate: 4 percent
   Urban In-Migration Rate: 5 percent

Initial Level Of Urbanization	Rural-Out Migration Rate	GDP Gain from Migration: Urban/Rural per Capita Income Ratio		
		1.50	2.50	4.00
40	3.30	0.83	1.88	2.73
30	2.14	0.65	1.55	2.37
20	1.25	0.45	1.15	1.88
10	0.56	0.24	0.65	1.15

B. *Urban Population Growth Rate: 6 percent*
   National Population Growth Rate: 3 percent
   Urban In-Migration Rate: 3 percent

Initial Level of Urbanization	Rural Out- Migration Rate	GDP Gain from Migration: Urban/Rural per Capita Income Ratio		
		1.50	2.50	4.00
40	2.00	0.50	1.12	1.64
30	1.29	0.39	0.93	1.42
20	0.75	0.27	0.69	1.13
10	0.33	0.14	0.39	0.69

C. *Urban Population Growth Rate: 4 percent*
   National Population Growth Rate: 2 percent
   Urban In-Migration Rate: 2 percent

Initial Level of Urbanization	Rural Out- Migration Rate	GDP Gain from Migration: Urban/Rural per Capita Income Ratio		
		1.50	2.50	4.00
40	1.33	0.33	0.75	1.09
30	0.86	0.26	0.62	0.95
20	0.50	0.18	0.46	0.75
10	0.22	0.10	0.26	0.46

Given these extreme simplifying assumptions, we can estimate GDP gains from rural-urban migration for different in-migration rates, initial urbanization rates, and plausible productivity differentials. These estimates appear in Table 4.8.

The striking result from Table 4.8 is that GDP gains from migration range from the trivially small to the very large. In countries with high urban growth rates, high initial urbanization levels (implying that many people are moving from low to high productivity sectors), and high productivity gaps, the GDP gain can be as high as 2 to 3 percent annually. On the other hand, in overwhelmingly rural countries where productivity gaps are small, GDP gains are near zero.

In terms of the characteristics in Table 4.8, African countries are widely dispersed (figures cited below are taken from UNDP/World Bank [1992] and World

Bank [1991]). A country such as Botswana, with 9 percent urban population growth, 3.2 percent population growth, and a ratio of nonagricultural output per male worker to agricultural output per male worker of thirty-six (largely reflecting the capital intensity of the mining industry, but probably nonetheless implying a considerable urban wage premium), is likely to be realizing close to 3 percent annual GDP gains from rural-urban migration. Put differently, rural-urban migration under these circumstances virtually offsets the negative (in an accounting sense) impact of population growth on per capita income; it also adds another 3 percent to Botswana's already exceptionally high GDP growth (11 percent per annum in total).

At the other end of the scale, Uganda is only 10 percent urban, has an urban population growth rate of only about 5 percent but a total population growth rate of 3.4 percent, and has a nonagricultural/agricultural output per male worker ratio of only 2.1, implying wage differentials that are smaller still. In this environment, the annual increase in GDP from rural-urban migration is probably only about 0.10 percent—about one-thirtieth of that in Botswana.

In summary, there are several critical points to be grasped from this analysis. *First, the impact of rural-urban migration on African GDP growth varies enormously.* It will be highest in middle-income countries with thriving or reviving industrial sectors.

Second, the process of economic deterioration and structural adjustment has caused these gains to diminish over time in most countries. Productivity gaps appear to have fallen greatly, thereby reducing gains to migration. *Put differently, economic collapse not only lowers productivity gains of existing workers, but, when concentrated in high productivity sectors, it reduces the gains to be had by reallocating resources.* Much of total productivity growth in nascent, dualistic economies is to be had by such redistribution, and its diminution during the past fifteen years has made Africa's economic deterioration appear even greater than it otherwise would have been.

Third, to the extent that structural adjustment policies ease foreign exchange conditions and promote growth in industry, thereby raising urban labor productivity and permitting wage increases, they will automatically increase GDP gains due to migration even if they have no impact on rural poverty at all. What actually happens will, of course, depend on rural and urban labor markets, and on the allocation of foreign exchange. But one should not automatically associate GDP growth with welfare enhancement for the majority of African populations.

To reiterate, GDP gains from migration are likely to be important in many but not all African countries. They certainly are not to be dismissed in the present low-growth environment. These points should seriously temper hostility toward urbanization by policymakers; at the same time, they should create an awareness of the partially illusory aspect of GDP growth, especially when urban goods' remain overvalued, so that wage differentials partially reflect purchasing power gaps.

Dynamic gains from rural-urban migration are possible also, but unfortunately they are difficult to quantify. Increased activity in the informal sector may lead to the creation of entrepreneurship and entrepreneurial spirit,[25] and a greater variety of products and services may become available to society as the country's labor force is more productively employed. As Katz and Stark (1986) point out, agglomeration economies and increased savings rates also may be achieved.

4.4 Policy Responses to Rural-Urban Migration

The preceding section has emphasized that—contrary to accepted wisdom—rural-urban migration can have positive impacts on urban centers; hypertrophy and unemployment need not be the sole outcomes of migration. At the risk of stating the obvious, it must be emphasized that the policy response to migration depends on governmental perception of migration's desirability. The overwhelming majority of African nations are dissatisfied with their spatial population distributions, as evidenced by a recent U.N. survey. Not a single African nation's policymakers deemed its spatial distribution of population "appropriate," and only seventeen of fifty-one deemed their distribution even "partially appropriate." The remaining thirty-four deemed the existing population distribution "inappropriate" (U.N. [1988a]). It is interesting to note that this almost uniform discontent with the distribution of population and trends in internal migration bears no relation to the degree to which population is concentrated in a few large cities.

The discontent with the existing spatial distribution, not surprisingly, is mirrored by dissatisfaction with the direction and magnitudes of migration flows. Only two of fifty-one nations' policymakers thought that existing trends in internal migration should be speeded up, while thirty-two thought that internal migration should be decelerated. The remainder either thought that migration trends should be reversed (seven), or that no policy interventions were needed (ten). Of the ten "noninterventionist" nations, seven (Burundi, Comoros and Cape Verde islands, Rwanda, Lesotho, Benin, and Sierra Leone) are quite small geographically, while Guinea is medium-sized. Chad and Niger are the other two noninterventionist nations. Note that no geographically large, populous countries are in this category.

Given this high level of dissatisfaction, the large number of policy prescriptions to stem African rural-urban migration is hardly surprising. While many authors offer nothing more than an unorganized menu of possible policy choices, a few do provide frameworks for analysis. Adepoju (1983), for example, delineates three categories of policies: rural development, urban and industrial development, and measures directed at the migrants themselves. Todaro [1971] categorizes policies by the lag between policy implementation and effectiveness. These two types of categorizations—the former based on the geographical location of the policy impact and the latter on the policy effectiveness lag—are useful, but they do not adequately identify the groups that will be affected by the policies. Alternatively, we prefer a categorization based on policy toward the size of the migration pool and flow. Policies either aim to

(1) reduce the stock of potential migrants,
(2) decrease the flow of migrants to the city by inducing migrants to stay in their rural homes,
(3) create attractive alternate (nonprimate city) destinations for the migrants, or
(4) successfully absorb the flow of migrants into existing urban centers.

A policy based on employment creation in major urban centers (no. 4, above) can be thought of as optimistic or pessimistic. It is optimistic in the sense that it minimizes the importance of the unemployment that the HT model suggests will result from a policy of urban job creation.[26] It is pessimistic if migration is beyond the level deemed socially desirable, but government policies to slow or stop the migration flow are deemed futile. The Kenyan government pursued such a strategy between 1968 and 1978. As GDP expanded rapidly in this period, wage increases were limited to 75 percent of the inflation rate, and modern sector jobs expanded at a rate of about 4 percent per year (Faruqee and Gulhati [1983:35]).[27]

If migrants are absorbed into the existing large cities in Africa, a centralized development strategy is being pursued by default. One rationale for such a strategy is that economic development requires a "substantial concentration of economic and social resources" (Findley [1976:103]). Resources are so scarce that a "substantial concentration" can be gathered at only a very few locations. Henderson [1988:34–35] buttresses this argument by suggesting that agglomeration economies may be more important for less developed country firms than for enterprises in industrialized countries. Africa's large, sparsely populated countries with numerous distinct ethnic groups have found, however, that truly centralized urban development schemes are politically impractical. Nearly all countries stress, at least at an official level, the need for decentralized regional development.

Nevertheless, the practical effects of policies aimed at high rates of capital formation have been to promote population growth in a highly limited number of cities. Many different measures are implemented to induce the desired capital investment. They include capital investment allowances (such as tax credits and subsidized interest rates), concentration of loanable funds in the largest cities, tax systems which favor the employment of capital rather than labor, and subsidized prices of basic inputs such as electricity and water. They also include tariff barriers that raise the profitability of new investments—and also cause exchange rate overvaluation, thereby making imported capital goods cheap, so that a given savings pool purchases more capital assets.

Artificially lowering the price of capital while at the same time maintaining urban modern sector wages at above market-clearing levels may well have been an important contributor to severe urban unemployment and underemployment in many African countries. But Findley (1976:52) finds a silver lining:

> Migrants have shown a widespread aptitude and potential for labor intensive technologies in the urban environment. This, together with their pressure for more jobs, may have resulted in the current deemphasis of highly capital-intensive, Western-type industries.

Cole and Sanders (1985:493) are less apologetic in their support of the centralized development paradigm. Noting the strong links between urban formal and informal sectors (as posited by export base theory), they believe that growth in the former fuels growth in the latter. Educated migrants obtain employment in the formal sector and contribute to economic growth, and uneducated migrants make a similar contribution in the informal (subsistence) sector. So both sets of migrants produce more in the urban setting than they would have produced in rural areas.

If the short-run maximization of national product is the planner's goal, centralized development may be an appropriate policy selection. Some other policy options—convincing migrants to return to their rural origins and creating growth poles—either do not change national product or have a longer gestation period than centralized development.[28] In any event, modern sector employment growth in Africa's leading cities has been painfully slow, particularly in recent years.

Another policy option (no.3, above) is to make destinations other than primate cities attractive to migrants. Migrants will be steered away from the primate city by making smaller, intermediate-size cities the focus of development efforts. Such a policy is particularly desirable if high unemployment rates and institutional wage rigidity are more prevalent in primate cities than in other urban or rural areas. While documentation of these patterns remains weak, both are likely events.

A decentralization strategy is also attractive to adherents of "growth pole" models. The growth pole strategy stresses that the city is the most important dynamic force in the growth process, but that linkages to the countryside are necessary if development is to be a truly national occurrence. Furthermore, a hierarchy of cities is required to create such linkages from the primate city to the countryside. Cities stimulate the surrounding rural areas by increasing the demand for raw materials and food, providing employment for labor attracted to the cities, as well as supplying needed services such as grain processing and agricultural extension (Adalemo [1977]).

Many African nations have chosen a growth center strategy as a means of altering their spatial structures. Kenya is chosen as a fairly representative and quite well-planned example. As early as 1970 Kenyan planners included growth centers in their second national plan. Seven growth centers were selected; their major purpose was to improve rural conditions so that rural-urban migration would be slowed. Subsequent plans (1974 and 1979) retained the growth center concept, simply adding two and three more centers, respectively (Obudho 1983:97). Kenyan planners are cognizant of the economic efficiency argument for primacy, because they have not attempted to space the growth centers uniformly.[29] Through its Rural Trade and Production Centers program, the Kenyan government also has been careful to emphasize the development of small towns, and in particular of spatial concentrations that provide small-town functions in rural areas, rather than assuming urban population dispersal automatically would provide the desired functions (see Gaile [1988a], [1988b], and [1990]).

Cohen (1979:67) succinctly summarizes this approach to growth center selection:

> The projected sizes, functions, activities, and locations of these towns should be based on a national spatial development strategy which focuses investment in geographical area with the highest economic potential.

Financing growth pole strategies will be difficult, because basic services and infrastructure will need to be provided in many small- and medium-sized towns. Some authors, daunted by the scale of the effort required, have concluded that the programs are not feasible. Whitney (1983) speaks for this group:

> It is doubtful that building a network of small- or medium-sized urban places, scattered over wide areas and integrated with surrounding rural territory, is feasible in most LEACs [least economically advanced countries], particularly on a scale sufficient to reduce the flow of migrants to the larger cities.

Whitney instead advocates the concentration of available resources in existing metropolitan centers. While growth poles may create more balanced development than a centralized industrialization strategy, there are dangers inherent in the growth pole concept. One danger is that the growth poles will serve as just so many more "steps" in the step-wise migration process to the primate city (Riddell [1978:255]). Probably more important in sparsely populated African countries are the high fixed costs of infrastructure provision, which may make decentralization impractical for financially strapped African governments. Decentralization will occur to a limited degree if reasonably good roads are built to reasonably populated areas, and if government takes steps to ensure that rural marketing functions develop; beyond that, there is little that government can do directly that is cost effective.

Other policies besides the creation of growth poles are available to redirect migrants away from primate cities. Colonization and land grant schemes are an example, in which governments seek to attract migrants to sparsely settled land by providing basic infrastructure and title to the land, low-cost credit, or other incentives. Land settlement schemes face the same obstacle as growth poles: lack of financial resources to construct the requisite infrastructure. Moreover, the per settler cost is often surprisingly high. In the Somali resettlement program (1975), cost were estimated at US $5,800–8,300 per settler, while the Nigerian resettlement of 1970 had even higher costs, averaging US $9,000 per settler (Adepoju [1982a:62]).

Some resettlement schemes in Africa have been compulsory. A few, such as Nigeria's Kainji Lake Resettlement (1963) and Ghana's Volta Dam Resettlement (1964), have been occasioned by the construction of dams and the resulting man-made lakes. Others aim at a more complete restructuring of the national spatial system. The most notable resettlement scheme was Tanzania's *ujamaa* villagization. Originally begun in 1967 as a voluntary resettlement effort in which people were urged by President Nyerere and other government officials to "return to the land," financial and technical assistance were added in 1970 as rewards for moving to *ujamaa* villages. After witnessing a rise in the percentage of the population living in villages of only 9 percent between 1970 and the end of 1973 (Yeager [1982:500]), the government initiated a policy of forced resettlement. "Operation Tanzania," as the forced resettlement was called, was remarkably successful in redistributing population. Although only 14 percent of the mainland population was living in villages in 1974, this percentage had risen to 79 percent by 1978. As rural development policy, however, it proved to be a disaster, and was formally concluded in 1977 (and, indeed, many *ujamaa* villages were never truly functioning entities).

Another policy option available is the relocation of the capital city or the redrawing of internal political boundaries. Of course, there may be political reasons for these changes as well. The old capital may be deemed unacceptable because it is identified with a particular ethnic group or because it is evidence of the European subjugation of Africa rather than a symbol of national pride. More self-serving motives for the relocation of a capital include an autocratic ruler's desire for a source of prestige or his need to locate the national capital near the core of his ethnic group (Potts [1985:42–44]).[30]

Table 4.9 lists the countries that have changed their national capitals. Two points should be noted. First, Botswana and Mauritania had no capital to change upon independence, because the colonial capitals were located outside their borders. In a sense, then, these two nations established capitals rather than changed them. Second, Nigeria has yet to begin the move to the newly designated capital of Abuja. As in the creation of growth centers, fixed costs are high and there may be losses of economies of scale and agglomeration. High fixed costs have certainly

TABLE 4.9.　Capital Relocations of African Nations.

Country Year decision made	Old Capital	New Capital
Mauritania 1957	St. Louis (Senegal)	Nouakchott
Botswana 1961	Mafeking (South Africa)	Gaberone
Malawi 1965	Zomba	Lilongwe
Tanzania 1973	Dar-es-Salaam	Dodoma
Nigeria 1976	Lagos	Abuja

plagued the proposed move of the Nigerian capital, although corruption has raised fixed costs beyond the level they otherwise would have been.

Nigeria is a good example of an African country that has redrawn internal political boundaries. Nigeria has twice increased the number of states to make its government more federal in character. In 1967 the number of states was increased from four to twelve, and in 1976 the number was further increased to nineteen. Few would dispute that the primary purpose of the state creation was political and not economic; above all, it was an attempt to diffuse the dangerous north-south confrontation that had resulted in a solidification of two hostile political coalitions (Odetola [1978:182–83]). Yet the move has stimulated development in some hitherto peripheral areas such as Gongola, Bauchi, and Niger states (Abiodun [1981:123]).

The third category of policy response (no. 2, above) open to governments is to induce migrants to remain in their rural homeplaces. "Induce" may be a misnomer for one type of government policy: coercive return of migrants to their homeplace. Tanzania and Ethiopia are two countries in Africa that have pursued this option. Individuals in urban areas in Tanzania at least until recently had to carry identification cards which proved they were gainfully employed. Persons unable to produce a card could be returned to their homeplace (or to some other rural area if they did not own land). Forced repatriation to rural areas is a radical step and trods on individual liberty; yet, if urban unemployment and poverty are severe enough, governments may opt for forced resettlement programs. Not only are forced resettlement schemes distasteful politically, they also fail to address the causes of rural-urban migration, focusing instead only on the visible symptoms of the underlying process. Migration, we stress once again, is not inherently undesirable.

A narrowing of urban-rural wage gaps certainly would reduce migration to urban areas, but attempts to reduce urban workers' real incomes have contributed to political instability throughout the developing world. Freezes in public sector wages and increases in food prices also affect the welfare of the armed forces as well as of urban workers; hence, few civilian or military governments are willing to invite a coup by pursuing policies that antagonize two powerful groups. Indeed, perhaps the only feasible way to pursue these unpopular policies is to convince the affected groups that international lenders and agencies have dictated the terms—consequently, it is in this light that structural adjustment policies are usually presented.

The more politically palatable option is to raise rural incomes. The previously mentioned growth poles may keep migrants near their rural homes if regional growth center has sufficiently strong linkages to the region's agricultural sector. A multitude of other policies have been suggested to raise rural incomes, including 1) provision of amenities, 2) delivery of agricultural extension services, including supervised credit for small farmers, 3) location of industries in rural areas, 4) shifting of tax incidence to the urban sector, 5) initiation of labor-intensive rural works, and 6) decontrol of food prices.

Riddell refers to amenity provision as an "opportunity to overcome the colonial legacy" (Riddell [1978:259]). Africa's colonial rulers provided amenities (basic infrastructure) only in capitals and major port cities, and these two sites often coincide. Increasing the amount of available amenities would increase rural real incomes, broadly defined.

Agricultural extension services aim to increase rural incomes by increasing productivity. The problem is that extension services often have unattractive distributional effects, widening the gap between rich and poor farmers. This occurs because large farmers are better able to bear the risks associated with adopting new seed varieties and have easier access to credit facilities, which enables them to use the full package of complementary inputs. At the same time, extension agents tend to seek out the relatively rich and powerful.

An increase in the incomes of the richest farmers in a district may allow them to send more of their sons and daughters to urban areas for education or may allow more children to attend school in rural areas. Given education's causal role in the migration decision, we might expect migration to increase. A counteracting force would be the trickle-down increases in poor farmer income. This income increase would likely induce more people to remain in rural areas. Some have suggested redesigning the curriculum in rural schools, but as Gugler and Flanagan [1978:60] sensibly observe, "when urban opportunities are perceived to be significantly better than those in rural areas . . . no change in school syllabi will inculcate a commitment to agriculture." In addition, the per unit cost of education (and other amenities) will be quite high because of low rural population densities and the impermanence of many settlement sites.

Another policy response attempts to stem migration by providing nonagricultural employment opportunities in rural areas (see Haggblade and Brown [1989] and Livingstone [1991]). Policies of industrial decentralization in developing countries, however, often have merely shifted capital-intensive plants from urban to rural locations; due to their highly capital-intensive technology, little rural employment is generated. Locating manufacturing firms in rural areas is not enough; the firms must employ technology appropriate to labor or land surplus economies. In addition, many rational economic factors deter firms from locating in rural areas, including lack of infrastructure, shortage of skilled labor, and high transportation costs (Findley [1976:78]). Africa is sadly overendowed with industrial projects located in remote towns that experience astoundingly high transport, electricity, and infrastructure costs. The authors are unaware of a decentralization program other than in Kenya that has not encountered these problems. In fact, in Zambia and probably in many other countries, regional investment decisions are made with virtually no consideration of implied infrastructure needs or costs.

Will rural development stem migration? Many analysts seem to take an affirmative answer for granted, but the actual result is unclear. Productivity gains in agriculture will lead to proportionately greater output expansion (and hence increases in labor and other factor use) if the demand for its products is relatively elastic. But if the agricultural sector's gains come in food production, and sufficiently low price and income elasticities ("Engels effects") prevail, then the sector actually releases labor. The issue is an empirical one. While productivity gains in rural nonagricultural activities are likely to be met with higher price elasticities of demand than food production, some of these products also may be inferior goods at rather low levels of per capita income.

If rural production growth is associated with increases in the marketed food supply, and if governments compensate for this increase by reducing food imports, then food prices will remain constant and rural agricultural employment will expand. Governments will now be able to increase urban production as well since the import constraint is eased. Urban labor demand also may increase, pulling workers from rural nonagricultural activities. Once again, the issue is an empirical one, and a priori theorizing serves only to emphasize the needed focus of future empirical research.

Tax burdens could be redistributed so that African governments collect a larger share of their tax revenues in urban areas, thus narrowing the difference in real incomes between rural and urban areas (Riddell [1978]). Many governments collect a significant percentage of their tax revenue through export taxes on cash crops like cocoa or groundnuts. But transferring this burden to urban consumers or producers may not be politically feasible, and government expenditures are already inadequate to meet basic needs.

Another policy that would increase agricultural incomes is to decontrol food prices. Again, political feasibility is the crux of the matter, as food riots in the late 1980s and early 1990s in Tunisia and Sudan have demonstrated. Urban workers' support for the government is conditional upon the affordability of basic foodstuffs.

A frequently heard proposal for increasing rural incomes is a program of labor-intensive public works. It is especially attractive because it could be run during nonpeak periods in agriculture, thus allowing individuals to sacrifice less agricultural income by accepting public works employment than by migrating to urban areas (Todaro [1980:405–6]). Public works should be attractive to government planners for the same reason. Rather than paying each individual a salary so as to make him indifferent between migrating or staying, the government need only pay the equivalent variation, that is, an amount that will compensate him for the difference between urban and rural utility levels, rather than an amount which would allow the individual to purchase goods and services that yield the urban utility level.

The final type of policy (no. 1, above) available to African governments to reduce the migration flow is to decrease the stock of potential migrants, that is, to reduce the rate of population increase. This brief survey is not the place to chronicle the steps taken (or not taken) by various African governments to control fertility. Two observations will suffice. First, the rate of population growth in Africa is the highest in the world. Although not faced with the severe population pressures of some Asian nations, the high rate of population growth is a major contributor to uncontrolled urban growth, both directly and indirectly via an increase in the stock of potential migrants. Second, Africa's demographic profile is very young. Population policies enacted today will affect migration streams in the year 2000 and beyond. There is no "quick fix" to be had here.

4.5 International Agency Policies and Urban Growth

This section undertakes a digression to ask a major question: have the macro, micro, and sectoral policies promoted by international agencies had an urbanizing impact, or have they reduced urban population growth in Africa? The assessment offered is both brief and purely qualitative.[31]

At the risk of oversimplification, we can divide international agencies' loans and grants into three types. First, most individual nations, plus the World Bank and U.N. agencies, engage mainly in project-oriented assistance. The funding tends to be long term, and is accompanied in some cases by compliance with prescribed policies with regard to specific sectors, as well as macroeconomic practices. Second, the IMF and debtor clubs tend to make short-term loans to enable countries to weather short-term balance of payments difficulties. In recent practice, these groups have become increasingly involved in making longer-term loans to assist in structural adjustment, while organizations like the World Bank have also given more general macroeconomic assistance loans. Finally, both individual countries and international organizations have given relief aid in response to civil strife and agricultural disasters. All together, these different forms of assistance have been accompanied by intervention (or "interference") in domestic policies at virtually every level.

Let us turn first to relief assistance and, in particular, food aid. In a recent set of Granger causality tests, Tabi et al. (1991) found that urbanization caused increased food imports in thirteen of twenty-four countries, while food imports caused increased urbanization in sixteen of twenty-four nations. That urbanization should cause increased food imports is unsurprising, both because it implies a reallocation of domestic resources away from agriculture, and because African urban dwellers often acquire tastes for (imported) rice and wheat. On the other hand, growing food imports, often donated by the West, effectively undercut local supplies, and reduce the return to domestic farming.

At the macroeconomic level, much concern has been with *reviving economic growth*. As international assistance tends to be oriented toward modern sector growth, loans will almost inevitably be disproportionately aimed at urban activities, and this is not necessarily undesirable. Foreign exchange inflows enabled by international loans and grants also breathe life into import-intensive cities. On the other hand, the push to contract government is extremely de-urbanizing, since it appears that government expenditures (both on goods and civil servants) are extremely urban-intensive—as are civil servants' consumption patterns (see Becker, Wiliamson, and Mills [1992]).

The World Bank also has played an important role in redirecting African governments' from small, high-quality housing programs to schemes aimed at the poor with far lower unit costs. These sorts of *"sites and services" schemes* were introduced in the early 1970s by the World Bank; among the first were projects in Nairobi and Dakar.[32] These projects typically involve land consolidation, simple housing design, infrastructure upgrading, and loans for construction. They also typically require substantial investments by the affected households, both in terms of labor inputs for construction, and repayments for the local infrastructure and equipment.

These schemes unquestionably have been vastly more socially productive than the high-quality housing projects promoted by most governments. Many also have been quite large: the First Lusaka Upgrading Sites and Services Project, for example, involved the construction of 11,500 new units, and infrastructural and physical improvements to about 20,000 housing units. Thus some 150–200,000 Lusakans benefited from the project—roughly one-third to one-half of the city's 1974 population. The Senegal and Tanzania programs were of comparable size.

What has been the consequence of these large projects for Africa's urban growth? Migration theory suggests that by raising the standard of living in urban areas they should attract people. Furthermore, because these investments are overwhelmingly located in the largest cities (Nairobi, Mombasa, and Kisumu in Kenya; Dakar and Thies in Senegal; and Lusaka in Zambia), they should spur growth of the largest cities.

More important is the counterfactual impact: were these loans more urbanizing than standard Bank loans or high-quality housing construction schemes? Results from a large sites-and-services scheme in a computable general equilibrium model of India (Becker, Williamson, and Mills [1992]) indicate that the general equilibrium urbanization effects of such a diversion of funds are practically nil. However, commitment of new loanable funds from abroad is highly urbanizing.

There has also been a heavy emphasis on loans for *transport sector investments*, perhaps in part because they represent an extremely visible aid commitment. Moreover, it is apparent that many African governments have responded to prolonged economic crisis by neglecting replacement investment in transportation and other infrastructure. Consequently, the international community has responded with many "rehabilitation" loans. To the extent that these are for intraurban transport, they clearly lower urban production costs, leading to expanded city growth. On the other hand, removal of port and city transport gridlocks alone will not expand modern sector output and employment, so the effects are unlikely to have been large.

Improvements in highways and rail links may well be more important. Vast areas of Africa remain remote and inaccessible, thus isolating their populations from marketed production. Greater ease of transport leads to increased incomes in these areas (deterring migration), lower migration costs (increasing migration), and growth of agricultural processing and consumer goods' industries in towns (promoting urban growth). These latter effects probably dominate.

Energy, water, and telecommunications' infrastructure loans are also likely to be urbanizing. The main reason for this is that urban economic activities use these inputs far more intensively than do rural sectors, so that infrastructural development will raise urban labor productivity and hence demand.

Education loans that enable the *expansion of secondary and university education* are highly urbanizing. Urban economic activities are far more skill intensive than are rural activities; growth in supply of skilled labor will therefore further urban growth. In addition, increasing numbers of high skilled urban workers will bring in the less skilled, through demand expansion by the former for low-skill goods and services.[33]

The effect on an *expansion of primary schooling* is less obvious. It is likely to raise agricultural productivity sharply if dovetailed with growth in extension services, thus increasing marketed surpluses. Such growth will give rise mainly to the development of medium-sized marketing and processing centers. To the extent that World Bank and other agencies emphasize cost recovery, though, schooling ratios may decline, especially in rural Africa. It should also be noted that World Bank education loans (as of the late 1970s/early 1980s) have been heavily urban: 48 percent of the value of Bank education projects in Côte d'Ivoire, 57 percent in Mali, and 63 percent in Cameroon were located in urban areas (Mathieu [1982]). Even more striking, 42 percent of all education sector loans by the World Bank to Mali were in Bamako alone and 29 percent of those to Cameroon went to Yaoundé, although only 5 percent of those to Côte d'Ivoire went to Abidjan.

Of particular interest, given the large amount of funds dispersed, are World Bank urban sector projects. In order to accurately gauge the policy content of these projects, we examined a random sample of 50 percent of all Bank urban sector projects undertaken between 1987 and 1992.[34]

The projects examined include:

(1) Ivory Coast Côte d'Ivoire Third Urban Project (1987);
(2) Burundi Second Urban Project (1988);
(3) Mozambique Urban Rehabilitation Project (1988);
(4) Zimbabwe Urban Sectoral and Regional Development Project (1989);
(5) Guinea Second Urban Project (1990);
(6) Nigeria Ogo State Urban Project (1990);
(7) Ghana Urban II Project (1990);
(8) Uganda First Urban Project (1990); and
(9) Benin Urban Rehabilitation and Management Project (1992).

These projects were evaluated across a number of dimensions. *All* projects included components dealing with the following issues:

(1) promotion of urban sector and local government financial self-sufficiency, through reduction in subsidies and promotion of cost recovery and mobilization of resources;
(2) strengthening of urban management institutions at the central and local levels, consistent with the devolution of authority;
(3) rehabilitation of infrastructure networks and restoration of services, with modest extensions of such facilities; and
(4) strengthening of urban land management procedures, including such aspects as land registration and titling, taxation cadasters, and promotion of appropriate standards of land development.

The similarity in policy content across countries is impressive; and these projects target major problem areas such as government deficits, infrastructure deficiencies, and imperfect factor markets.

In specific cases, projects advance the development of microenterprises by such measures as improving access to capital markets. Thus, in the Côte d'Ivoire project, a pilot program is helping to stimulate access by microenterprises to commercial bank credit, using nongovernmental organizations as facilitators. The Burundi project promotes such enterprises by providing assistance in the form of workshops and market facilities, as well as technical and financial aid. The

Mozambique project provides lines of credit and technical assistance to small businesses. Smaller components are found in other projects as well.

The projects are generally identified with macroeconomic reform initiatives, some of which are linked to "structural adjustment" plans and some to more general national development programs. The Côte d'Ivoire project has a housing finance component that helps to remove subsidized government involvement in the shelter sector, and thus promotes a key structural adjustment objective, namely reduced central government expenditures and the substitution of those resources with private ones. In a few cases, however, the projects are closely tied to advancing very specific national objectives. An example of this is the Mozambique project, designed to promote the transit of foreign exchange-producing goods through specific urban areas.

Many donors have sponsored programs to promote *fertility control* and *mortality declines*. Obviously, declining birth rates reduce population growth and, eventually, city growth; declining mortality rates have the opposite effect. While this is not the place for a comprehensive review of these programs, it seems safe to say that mortality programs have had a greater impact thus far. The consequence has been increased population growth rates and, hence, urban population growth. The impact on urbanization (the proportion of the national population living in urban areas) is less clear, as both urban and rural populations increase. Indeed, the factor proportions result from the Rybczynski Theorem (see section 3.5) suggests that rural production (which is relatively labor intensive) should grow more rapidly. In this case, the proportion of African populations in urban areas would decline.

In the medium run, though, the impact is still less obvious. Mortality declines have not been neutral with respect to cohort; rather, there have been gains mainly in reducing infant and child mortality. Since younger people have more to gain from migration, and if anything bear lower moving costs, the consequence (lagged roughly ten years) has been a dramatic push to the cities.

The core of structural adjustment programs seems unlikely to be urbanizing in the short and medium runs. *Shrinking public sector and parastatal employment, reduced tariff protection, exchange rate devaluation,* and *deemphasis of import-substitution industrialization* all seem certain to favor rural areas. The alternative industrial strategy, focusing on the promotion of small-scale enterprises and modern processing industries with substantial backward linkages, is likely to generate population shifts away from the largest cities to smaller towns, in part because weight-losing processing industries are inherently tied to their raw material bases. Furthermore, the World Bank and USAID have been explicit in their support for secondary city growth at various times (see Rondinelli [1983] and Richardson [1977]).

General equilibrium effects, however, may reverse many of these conclusions in the long run. Structural adjustment programs (SAPs) may not favor big cities directly, but they seek to restructure in such a way that export growth resumes (and also provide immediate debt relief and new loans). Improved access to foreign exchange is extremely urbanizing, as Africa's modern industrial sector is extremely dependent on intermediate and capital good imports (and the urban elite has import-dependent consumption patterns). Consequently, SAPs may ultimately remove a major impediment to urban growth at the same time as they reduce urban growth incentives in the short run by reducing urban "biases."

4.6 The Urban Sector After Structural Adjustment: A New Beginning

The standard discussion of "urban bias" in sub-Saharan Africa needs to be updated to take into account the effect of SAPs. By the late 1980s, major reform programs were in place in nineteen countries, accounting for 59 percent of sub-Saharan Africa's population and 52 percent of the region's GDP.[35] The very foundations of "urban bias" are thus being destroyed. Urban real wages have fallen, both in absolute terms and relative to rural earnings (see Chapter 5 for details), but the restructuring of relative wages is only part of a larger reform, affecting relative prices. An excellent example of the impact of this wider effort has been documented for Zaire (see Arnaud [1985]), often a major offender in terms of inappropriate macroeconomic policies. Between 1972 and 1982, real national output stagnated as modest gains in agricultural output were offset by declines in the secondary and tertiary sectors. The 20 percent increase in real agricultural output was accompanied by a fifty-nine-fold increase in agricultural prices, a rate which far outdistanced the sixteen-fold increase in industrial prices, and the twenty-four-fold increase in service prices. As a result, the ratio of current nonagricultural to agricultural value added fell from 4.8 to 1.8. Since the nonagricultural population also rose much more rapidly than the agricultural population, the ratio cited, when adjusted to reflect per capita value-added, fell from 17.7 in 1972 to 3.5 in 1982. This provides a graphic illustration that future urban economic growth will be based on very different price signals than in the past.

Other efforts are worth highlighting as well. Beginning in April 1983, Ghana imposed an economic recovery program (see World Bank [1987]) which:

(1) markedly depreciated the exchange rate;
(2) more than doubled the real returns to cocoa production;
(3) radically restructured the price of gasoline and public services;
(4) abolished export licenses;
(5) simplified and substantially lowered tariffs;
(6) virtually dismantled price controls;
(7) reintroduced positive real rates of interest;
(8) fired eighty-thousand civil servants with plans to dismiss fifteen thousand more each year through 1991; and
(9) progressively introduced management autonomy and performance plans for state-owned enterprises, while planning to sell, liquidate, or transform into joint ventures roughly 40 percent of government-owned firms.

Nigeria, in a similar effort (see World Bank [1988b]), has:

(1) abolished all agricultural commodity boards;
(2) devalued its exchange rate to 30 percent of its original value;
(3) abolished virtually all price controls;
(4) eliminated virtually all import licensing regulations, while drastically reducing the size of its import prohibition list; and
(5) reduced the level of import duties to a relatively low average level, while sharply curtailing the dispersion of rates.

Guinea began its reform program in late 1985, shortly after the death of Sékou Touré. The Economic and Financial Reform Program (EFRP) was an attempt to "radically restructure the Guinean economy by a drastic reduction of the interventionist role of the state, in order to allow the private sector to become the engine of growth" (World Bank [1990a: 10]). The EFRP can be divided into two phases. In the first phase, from 1985 to the end of 1988, the economy was subjected to radical shock treatment that involved:

(1) massive devaluation of the syli,
(2) liberalization of pricing and marketing,
(3) extensive privatization, including the entire banking system,
(4) fundamental trade reform and liberalization, and
(5) large-scale layoffs of public employees.

The second phase, dating from the end of 1988 and continuing until the present, has involved "a much more complex and difficult process of reforming institutions and changing attitudes both within the administration and in the private sector" (World Bank [1990a: 10–29]). One of the most important achievements of Guinea's SAP has been the dismantling of price controls on food that favored urban areas at the expense of farmers:

> As a result of the various reform measures, trade in agricultural products now takes place in a relatively competitive environment. The private sector is permitted to engage in all levels of internal and external marketing- . . . . Public enterprises purchase some agricultural exports, but producers are free to market their output as they like, and exports by public parastatals now represent only a small percentage of the total. (World Bank [1990a: 19 (volume 2)]

Madagascar has also been pursuing vigorous, market-oriented policies during the 1985–89 period. Sector by sector, they are:

(1) *agriculture:* the removal of state monopolies, administrative barriers, and price controls has been virtually complete.
(2) *industry:* controls on prices and profit margins have been scuttled.
(3) *external sector:* tariff reform, foreign exchange management, and elimination of export restrictions have proceeded as programmed in the reform package, although more liberalization and infrastructure improvements are needed. (World Bank [1991a: 9])

An initial assessment by the World Bank and the United Nations Development Program suggests that the reform programs have been accompanied by a noticeable improvement in economic performance across the region. Unweighted average growth rates of real GDP approximately doubled between 1980–84 and 1985–87, reaching almost 3 percent per year. A comparison between countries with strong reform programs and countries with weak or no reform programs suggests that the reformers are now growing three times more rapidly than in 1980–84 and are experiencing real increases in per capita consumption, reversing the annual declines registered earlier.[36] Nonreformers, while experiencing faster growth than before, are growing too slowly to reverse declines in per capita real consumption growth. GDP growth rates among this subset of reformer countries now approach 4 percent per annum in real terms, while the subset of nonreformers is growing at 1.5 percent per year. Agricultural expansion and expanding exports appear to be significant contributors to changing performance.[37]

Our own assessment is that the evidence is less clear. For reasons we have enumerated above, GDP gains from the reforms may have little connection to welfare gains. This point emerges even more clearly from an analysis of individual countries (see, for example, Radelet's [1990] study of The Gambia). Nor is it clear how much of the recovery in a country like Ghana is due to structural reform, and how much is due to international capital inflows following acceptance of Bank and Fund policy formulae. But we also believe that other policy alternatives typically would have generated continued economic deterioration, against which stabilization or slow growth is definitely preferable.

What is the likely future of the urban sector in the emerging age of agriculture-led development strategies? With the restructuring of production, there will be a shift toward labor-intensive, urban agroprocessing activities, and a shift away from import-intensive and capital-intensive outputs. This should encourage the growth of jobs in secondary urban centers, whose links with agriculture will increase. A redistribution of incomes, away from "formal" sector employees in and out of government, and toward farmers and the "informal" urban worker, should generate new demand for "basic" urban goods and services that rely relatively heavily on domestic inputs and labor-intensive technologies. Finally, the urban sector will share the benefits of a rise in domestic savings, due to the removal of subsidies and price controls. This will help boost economic expansion and that, inevitably, will increase the demand for urban products.

It is thus possible to foresee an economic basis for the demographic projections which forecast a continuing growth of the urban sector at rates that exceed natural population growth, despite the decline in real wages experienced by urban workers. In fact, some analysts would argue that even under more pessimistic scenarios about urban economic expansion, rural-to-urban migration will continue to be significant because the rural decision-making unit is not an individual comparing average incomes in rural and urban areas, but a household seeking net additions to cash income. The changing macroeconomic environment, they believe, will not be sufficient to reverse the decisions of would-be migrants (see, for example, Jamal and Weeks [1988]). Though evidence to date is sketchy, it is not inconsistent with this viewpoint.[38]

It is important to recognize as well that migration is a response by individuals and households to a disequilibrium in their opportunity sets. If the opportunities they face are determined by factor and product prices that reflect true scarcities, then their interest is identical to that of the social planner, and there is no need to interfere with their migration decision. In other words, the flow of migration and the speed of urbanization will be socially efficient if prices faced by private agents reflect social opportunity costs.

Furthermore, to the extent that private prices diverge from social ones, the appropriate response is to correct the distortion rather than interfere with labor flows. The sorts of externalities which obviate this statement (congestion in urban areas, loss of rural critical mass, urban or rural agglomeration economies) are likely to be relatively minor. Congestion costs may be substantial in many large African cities (though in part they will be offset by agglomeration economies), but it is difficult to believe that their lack of internalization, rather than labor market distortions, are responsible for the vast majority of any excessive migration that occurs.

In summary, the distortions in labor and product markets that make urban activities relatively profitable, and the uneven provision of social services that make urban life relatively attractive, are likely to be the main cause of excessive migration. The structural adjustment process lays the foundations for growth relatively free of the problems generated by "urban bias." That growth, however, can only be fully exploited if urban institutions are made to function more effectively. The high political visibility of the urban sector, especially the largest cities, provides an excellent arena for dramatic demonstrations of the benefits of continued structural adjustment measures. Policies that have promoted inappropriate investments, inequitable subsidies, and unrealistic standards in cities can be modified, thus freeing up scarce resources for priority spending. The city can become a laboratory where more private initiative—in business ventures, shelter construction, or public services—can be harnessed and public initiative can be redirected. To refuse this opportunity to tackle the urban agenda, out of fear of residual "urban bias," is irresponsible.

5

Employment Growth and the Wage Structure in Urban Africa

The migration models surveyed in Chapter 4 often explained urbanization by recourse to simple two- or three-sector models. In the case of the Harris-Todaro model, migrants left agricultural pursuits in search of employment in the urban formal sector. If unsuccessful in this quest, they resorted to working in the urban informal sector. These three sectors are stylized theoretical constructs. This chapter puts meat on these theoretical bones, providing descriptive statistics of African formal and informal sectors and examining the evolution of both employment and wages in more detail than in Chapter 4. This chapter also discusses several of the main econometric studies of urban wage determination in sub-Saharan Africa, and thus sets the stage for our own empirical work in Chapter 6.

In particular, the following pages challenge some of the time-worn "stylized facts" of the economic development literature. Are wages in African formal sectors many times above labor's opportunity cost? Are there virtually no links between urban formal and informal production? Do wage differentials between sectors mirror the skill differentials of their workers, or are individuals with similar human capital endowments receiving different wages solely because they work in different sectors? Has the rural-urban divide grown smaller or wider in recent years? Finally, the impact of the AIDS pandemic on African labor forces and economic welfare is analyzed.

Before embarking on an overview of the stylized facts, a key point of departure bears mentioning. *Wage and employment levels and trends, and intraurban and urban-rural distributions of earnings vary enormously from country to country.* While trends do exist, there are almost always exceptions. Furthermore, the most salient trends—nearly stagnant formal sector employment growth and declining real formal sector wages—vary considerably in degree across countries. We also would assert (alas, without formal evidence) that countries' departures from common trends depend

135

more on their internal policies than on external forces or the particular region in which they are located.

5.1. The Urban Formal Sector

The logical starting point is the purported engine of growth for modern economies, the formal sector. The formal sector has been defined many different ways in order to distinguish it from informal production. Formal sector firms tend to be larger (both in terms of employment and value of output), more capital-intensive, and more intensive in their use of imported capital and intermediate goods than their informal counterparts. Formal sector firms are covered by government labor legislation such as minimum wage requirements and collective bargaining codes. Clearly, any definition based on the value of one or a subset of these measures will be arbitrary, but the distinction between formal and informal firms is crucial because the two types of firms may face different economic environments and consequently behave quite differently.

5.1.1. Output and Employment Trends, and Formal Sector Structure

Table 5.1 provides index numbers of manufacturing employment for twenty-four African countries over the 1970–85 period, using 1980 as the base year. Since these data only include employment in firms of five or more workers, the majority of small-scale, informal production will not be captured here, and these figures consequently provide a reasonable but somewhat exaggerated approximation to formal sector employment.

The first thing to note from Table 5.1 is that most countries experienced rapid employment growth in the 1970–75 period. Mali, Nigeria, and Somalia all had manufacturing employment growth rates of over 10 percent per year; many nations had annual growth rates of 7 percent, and only two countries (Cameroon and Ethiopia) had growth rates below 6 percent per year. Clearly some of these impressive growth numbers are statistical artifacts produced by very small initial period levels of manufacturing employment, but many nations did have rapid employment growth.

All countries (for which initial period data are available) reported slower growth in employment during 1975–80, with the sole exception of Ethiopia. In large part this is due to the effects of the oil shock. The rise in the price of oil imports meant that increasing amounts of foreign exchange were allocated to oil and lesser amounts were available for other intermediate inputs or capital goods. Five nations (Cameroon, Central African Republic, The Gambia, Ghana, and Madagascar) reported negative employment growth for 1975–80, and many nations had extremely modest annual growth rates of 1 percent or less.[1] Even modest growth, of course, implies declining modern sector shares both of the population and the labor force.

The 1980–85 period saw renewed or accelerated manufacturing employment growth in some countries, but continued stagnation in others. It is telling that the most rapid growth rates in this period are for countries with initially small man-

TABLE 5.1. Manufacturing Employment in Establishments Employing More Than Five Workers, 1970–85. (1980 = 100)

Country	1970	1975	1985 or most recent
Benin	—	95.2	123.8
Botswana	—	70.3	182.5
Burkina Faso	—	93.1	107.0
Burundi	60.0	85.4	138.9[a]
Cameroon	80.5	103.7	111.2
Central Afr. Rep.	—	159.0	176.0
Côte d'Ivoire	49.7	73.5	80.7[a]
Ethiopia	65.1	78.7	117.8
The Gambia	—	164.0	108.4
Ghana	71.9	110.9	73.6[a]
Kenya	48.0	74.2	123.2
Lesotho	—	96.6	105.2
Liberia	—	—	149.6
Madagascar	88.6	104.7	121.9[b]
Malawi	47.4	71.0	91.9[a]
Mali	36.3	68.4	—
Nigeria	29.8	55.9	75.3[a]
Senegal	—	73.7	114.2
Somalia	45.3	79.1	150.0
Swaziland	51.6	72.9[d]	104.6
Tanzania	47.8	69.3[e]	107.2
Togo	67.7	97.4	—
Zambia	69.1	94.7	106.9
Zimbabwe	67.3	94.6	103.1

a = 1983
b = 1984
c = 1985
d = 1976
e = 1974

Source: World Bank (1989c).

ufacturing sectors (Botswana, Central African Republic, Liberia, and Somalia). The index number problem again may be responsible for creating such impressive gains in that manufacturing sectors in these countries employed very small numbers of people even after a period of rapid growth. Countries with larger manufacturing sectors, on the other hand, had mediocre to poor employment growth in this period. Côte d'Ivoire, Ghana, and Nigeria reported annual manufacturing growth rates of -7, -10, and -9 percent, respectively. Kenya, Senegal, and Zambia had annual employment growth rates of only 4, 3, and 1 percent, respectively.

These patterns also appear repeatedly in a set of internal World Bank in-depth studies of poverty and social conditions in the wake of Africa's economic deterioration and adoption of structural adjustment programs (SAPs) (see World Bank [1989d–k]). Census data from Cameroon (World Bank [1989d:71]) indicate that the employment growth rate halved after 1976, falling from 2.89 percent annual growth in 1965–76 to 1.47 percent growth in 1976–87. In Côte d'Ivoire, an employment growth rate of 3.4 percent between 1975 and 1980 declined to 2.1 percent between

1980 and 1985. Shockingly, though, for one of Africa's strongest economies, the *formal sector employment growth rate* in Côte d'Ivoire fell from a 6.6 percent during 1975–80 annual growth rate to an annual rate of *decline* of 2.9 percent during 1980–85 (World Bank [1989f]).

The experience of economically weaker countries was not always as bad, largely because they had less room for decline in the first place. The annual modern sector employment growth rate in Madagascar was 1.6 percent—less than the population growth rate, but growth nonetheless (Pryor [1988] and World Bank [1989g]). On the other hand, total modern sector employment in Togo fell 4 percent between 1981 and 1985 after rising 30 percent during 1977–80. Moreover, private, mixed public-private, and parastatal employment declined by 19 percent, 6 percent, and 23 percent, respectively, during the 1981–85 period—only (nonproductive) government employment grew (by 16 percent: World Bank [1989h:23]). In contrast, The Gambia's formal sector labor force rose at an annual rate of only 0.4 percent between 1983 and 1988, mainly because the public sector *contracted* at a rate of 8.4 percent (Becker [1991]). Private formal sector employment, initially a tiny fraction of the total, actually grew at 21.2 percent, and by late 1988 had surpassed the public sector in total employment.

Overall, the picture is of rapid employment gains in the early 1970s, followed by far slower growth in the late 1970s. While few countries with large manufacturing sectors reported employment declines in this period, employment growth did slow in almost all countries. When the full impact of the second oil shock hit in the early 1980s, and African nations found international creditors unwilling to continue lending, manufacturing employment growth became negligible in many countries, and several of the region's most important manufacturing sectors suffered absolute declines in employment.

What other aspects of African formal sectors are worth noting, with an eye to gleaning variables of importance in the determination of formal and informal sector wages? One could well start with *foreign ownership* and *parastatal dominance*. Surprisingly, while the latter is well-demonstrated (see the carefully constructed table in UNDP/World Bank [1992]), the former is not. But Karmiloff (1990), for example, reports that 64 percent of capital in Cameroon's metal industry is French-owned, as of 1984, and foreign ownership shares overall have an unweighted average by sector of 45 percent. State-owned enterprises accounted for 39 percent of capital, on average; the remaining 16 percent was owned by private Cameroonians. A similar unweighted average for Côte d'Ivoire in the late 1980s reveals that 61 percent is foreign-owned (Roger Riddell [1990a]). To put it simply, African manufacturing differs from that in other developing countries not only because of a large parastatal presence in its formal sectors, but also because of a large foreign ownership share in the modern sector, and especially in manufacturing.

There is considerable variation in the importance of parastatals in African economies. Swanson and Wolde-Semait (1989) estimate that, for the period 1980–86, parastatals accounted for 15 percent of African gross domestic product (GDP), 25–30 percent of formal sector employment, and 25 percent of gross domestic investment. Parastatal shares in investment, employment, and output tended to be far greater than the same figures in comparable Asian countries. But it is unquestionably clear from a comparison of parastatal and public investment shares in total investment during the 1970s and 1980s that parastatals' importance is diminishing (see UNDP/World Bank [1992] and Gulhati and Datta [1983]). Given that parastatals already accounted for much—and in many cases a majority—of modern sector capital and output, however, it is apparent that it will be a decade or two before modern sector structures have really changed unless public divestment plans are carried out.[2] At present, the fate of the divestment components of structural adjustment programs is unclear, but we should note that many firms will be worthless without continued high tariff protection, and should be closed rather than sold.

The decay of African parastatals has, of course, been an important part of the modern sector's decline. Parastatal employment growth has been slow, erratic, or negative in all but a few countries for which data are available (for an excellent compilation of available data, see Swanson and Wolde-Semait [1989]). It is not clear that public ownership of much of the modern sector made matters worse than they otherwise would have been, but it may well have done so. Parastatals are particularly effective in garnering protectionist measures when threatened by competition; they also are particularly susceptible to political pressures to modify pricing, production, location, and employment behavior.

Another common feature of African formal sectors is *low-capacity utilization*. While measurement of capacity is arbitrary and somewhat tricky, low utilization is patently obvious in many cases. Insofar as statistics are available, they consistently point to low utilization rates, especially in agricultural processing (such as Zambia's cotton ginning parastatal, Lintco) or in alcohol or tobacco manufacturing. Gulhati and Datta (1983) find that in Tanzania during 1978 and 1979, only the alcohol, tobacco, and cement sectors had 80 percent or higher capacity utilization rates. Electrical machinery, footwear, and spinning and weaving had 60–70 percent utilization rates; the worst were motorcycles and bicycles (12 percent, 1979), glass (15 percent, 1979), plastic (24 percent, 1979), and motor vehicles (33 percent, 1979). Gulhati and Datta's data for Somalia are similarly dismal, with utilization rates ranging from 22 percent (ITOP Fruit Cannery, 1978) to SOMALTEX (75 percent, 1978). They also found that only five of twenty-seven Sudanese parastatals in 1975 (but seven of eleven in 1973) had utilization rates above 65 percent; ten in 1975 (and apparently two in 1973) had rates below 35 percent. The highest rates appeared in sugar processing, beer brewing, vegetable processing, and tanning. Zambia's INDECO parastatal holding company for nonmining manufacturing had seventeen of fifty-seven plants with utilization rates below 30 percent in 1981/82; oils and fats, batteries, auto assembly (which, by our private estimates, generated negative value added at world prices; it would have been cheaper in terms of foreign exchange costs to import fully assembled vehicles), fertilizer, and tires were among those with the lowest rates. Three plants, all in textiles or explosives, had utilization rates above 90 percent. Finally, between 1982 and 1987, only 4 percent to 14 percent of those Zimbabwean firms responding to opinion surveys listed plant capacity as a factor constraining industrial expansion; in 1987, import quotas were given as a constraining factor by 83 percent and raw material shortages by 73 percent (Roger Riddell [1990b]).

This last point is highly revealing. Low-capacity utilization does not generally reflect incompetence. Rather, it reflects adverse demand shifts, or constraints externally imposed. Foreign exchange shortages rank high among these; transport, electricity, water supply, and other infrastructural deficiencies are also problematic. The Zimbabwe survey also indicated that absence of sources of finance (or high costs of borrowing) were secondary problems; lack of skilled manpower was listed by about 11 percent. Since Zimbabwe has a relatively skilled labor force, managerial and skilled labor force limitations may be more important elsewhere.

To some extent, these problems are self-imposed. With their parastatal and foreign domination, it would be unsurprising if African modern sector firms were *more capital intensive* than comparable firms in India, China, or other developing countries. Evidence is sparse; the only data of which we are aware (Pack [1972]) confirm this hunch, however. It is also likely that African modern sectors are highly *import intensive;* in part, small sizes make this inevitable. Detailed evidence on import intensity can be found in Roger Riddell (1990c). Briefly, the most import-intensive industries are usually involved in final assembly processing. In 1980, the Côte d'Ivoire chemicals and rubber industry purchased 65 percent of capital and intermediate goods (excluding final factor expenses) from abroad (Roger Riddell [1990a]). Other import-intensive sectors included leather/shoes (69 percent) and transport equipment (70 percent). The 1980 Zambia input-output tables indicate that import shares of intermediates are highest in basic metals (77 percent), chemicals (72 percent), and rubber products (58 percent); they are lowest in nonmetallic minerals (5 percent), food processing (6 percent), and beverages and tobacco (6 percent), (Karmiloff [1990a]).

Furthermore, it is clear that Africa's formal sector is *highly protected by tariff and quota barriers.* The typical pattern is one of cascading protection: capital goods face low tariffs, while producers of consumer goods face both high tariffs and relatively cheap imported capital goods and intermediates (made cheaper by the fact that protection raises the equilibrium exchange rate). Since tariff rates usually apply to the price of a good (rather than to the value-added component), a given tariff is much more effective when the domestic producers are engaged largely in the final assembly of unprotected kits or components.

An example of this cascading structure is Nigeria (see Stevens [1990]). The average *net effective rate of protection* (ERP) to intermediate and capital goods industries that use mainly domestic raw materials is 16 percent (for 1979–80); for those that are dependent on imported components, the rate rises to 66 percent. For consumer goods that use mainly domestic intermediates, the ERP is 82 percent, while for those that mainly assemble imported goods, the ERP is a very high 147 percent. With this sort of structure of protection, it is far from surprising that African industry has been very import intensive, and that it has been concentrated in *consumer goods industries.* Naturally, producers will tend to concentrate in high tariff sectors, so the average ERP facing African formal sector firms will be far higher than the unweighted mean. Low tariffs on capital good imports and exchange rate overvaluation also lead to excessive capital intensity of modern sector enterprises with access to imports and credit.

The other effect of extremely high protection is to make value added at domestic prices greatly exceed value added of manufacturing at world prices. Since manufacturing is generally urban, this also implies that the urban GDP shares would be far lower at world prices. A fascinating example of the structural implications of this protection is given by Sharpley and Lewis (1990). For the period 1970–84, they found that, while manufacturing production in Kenya increased by Ksh. 142 million in constant *domestic* prices, it rose by only Ksh. 50 million in constant *world* prices. The difference, of course, is a subsidy to manufacturing—worth 33 percent of the increment in agricultural production or 40 percent of additional imports.

The World Bank and others have, in fact, calculated the protective structure by industry for several countries. One often views this from a slightly different perspective, asking how costly it would be to produce a given good in terms of the value of its inputs relative to the cost of the good, all computed at world prices. This measure is known as the *domestic resource cost (DRC)* Firms with high DRCs of production are also firms with high degrees of effective protection—otherwise they could not exist. The DRC measure for a set of industries also offers a convenient (if static and somewhat mechanistic) ranking of comparative advantage: those with lowest DRCs use fewer domestic resources to produce a dollar's worth of foreign exchange (save a dollar's worth of imports) than those with higher DRCs.

Karmiloff (1990) found very low DRCs for Cameroon in beverages, cement, agricultural tools, and food processing as of mid-1970s. Negative value added at world prices (and hence negative DRCs) occurred in wheat processing, radio and appliance assembling, steel rods, and fertilizers. Textiles either had high or negative DRCs. Estimated DRCs of new industrial projects being planned tended to have much lower DRCs—typically below 1.0, a general efficiency criterion. Taking these figures at face value, it appears that Cameroon has a comparative advantage in agricultural processing, petrochemical industries, wood processing, and some basic machinery. Even regarding these projected DRCs as optimistic (*ex ante* projections typically miss some costs), it is clear that a middle-income country such as Cameroon has a wide array of industrial goods in which it has a comparative advantage. Thus, the problem, at least for larger and wealthier African countries, is not an absence of viable manufacturing industries, but rather industrial strategies that have been inappropriate. Import-intensive firms with sophisticated technologies that face small markets and high transportation costs are poor choices—but there are many good ones.

The Cameroonian example also hints at another issue. Many industrial enterprises with high DRCs are in sectors that are not obviously inappropriate. But bad management, absence of incentives to be efficient (for example, the likely removal of protective tariffs), overstaffing, and poor location choice all can make a potentially low DRC industry into an inefficient one. In Zambia, for example, the decision to place a bicycle assembly plant in Chipata, distant both from sources of imported components and the market, and with weak infrastructural support, virtually ensured a high DRC for bicycle assembly. But the proper conclusion to draw is not that Zambia does not have a comparative advantage in bicycle assembly (though it may well not), but rather that Chipata in 1985 did not have a comparative advantage in bicycle assembly.

Other DRC estimates for Africa include Zambia (Karmiloff [1990a]), Côte d'Ivoire (Roger Riddell [1990a]), and Zimbabwe (Roger Riddell [1990b]). Recent studies for Côte d'Ivoire also find high DRCs in textiles and coffee processing. The high DRC in textiles in particular is a counterintuitive result for a middle-income country, suggestive of parastatal inefficiency rather than an inherent lack of comparative advantage. Low DRCs occurred in chemicals, plastics, and cocoa processing. Zambian estimates for the early 1980s found a very low DRC for food products, but high DRCs elsewhere, which, in ascending order, were capital goods (1.45), nonfood consumer nondurables (1.53), light intermediates (1.60), consumer durables (2.38), and heavy intermediates (3.02). Roger Riddell (1990b) presents two important results for Zimbabwe. First, within any given industrial category, there are typically vast ranges in DRCs—usually from well below 1.0 to well above 2.0! Secondly, the implications are that 1) comparative advantage must be defined well below the "sectoral" level except in countries with particular natural resources, and 2) firm management and environment is, as noted above, a critical determinant of efficiency.

5.1.2. Wage Trends

Accompanying these employment declines has been a sustained fall in real manufacturing wages in most African countries. To our knowledge, evidence for this secular decline was first pointed out in two seminal and still underappreciated pieces by Weeks (1986) and Jamal and Weeks (1988). Weeks provides evidence of secular declines in average urban real wages in several Anglophone countries:

	Percentage Decline from Peak to Trough	Peak	Trough
Ghana	88	1971–72	1983
Kenya	32	1970	1983
Nigeria	57	1985	1984
Sierra Leone	48	1974	1981
Swaziland	37	1979	1980
Tanzania	68	1974	1983[3]
Uganda	95	1965	1981

These are huge declines, and certainly do not suggest a fixed wage formal sector![3] At the same time, Weeks finds evidence for the period 1978–83 of more moderate declines in Mauritius and Cameroon, stagnation in Burundi and Malawi (but see below: real wages in Malawi declined by 38 percent during the period 1969–77), and a 22 percent rise in Zimbabwe (where wages appear to have since stagnated). Sharpley and Lewis (1990) confirm Jamal and Weeks' findings for Kenya, and make another important point (also noted by Radelet [1990] in the Gambian context): *the choice of deflator used in estimating real wage trends greatly affects one's results.* Taking 1976 as 100, average real earnings in manufacturing relative to the manufacturing GDP deflator peaked at about 135 in 1970, declined to 100 in the late 1970s, and recovered to 112 by 1984. But using the lower income cost of living index as the deflator, real wages peaked at 122 in 1970, and then underwent a fairly secular decline to 75 in 1984.[4]

Bevan et al. (1988) confirm Jamal and Weeks' finding for Tanzania. Their painstaking estimates find that real urban incomes declined by 61 percent between 1969 and 1984. They also report that 1974 urban incomes were not a peak, but rather were 17 percent below the 1969 level (measured in 1981/2 prices), apparently because of declining informal sector incomes.

In any event, there is growing evidence from many sources that the decline in real wages has been precipitous:

(1) **Sudan:** [Civil service] salaries had already decreased by 50 percent in real terms during the early 1970s; and lost another 30 percentage points since 1978. (World Bank [1985d])

(2) **Zaire:** One of the stark consequences of Zaire's economic and financial crisis has been the continuous decline in the real purchasing power of income for both public and private sector employees. Although in 1983 public service salaries were seven times higher in nominal terms than in 1975 . . . , in real terms, they . . . represented less than one-fifth of the 1975 level. A similar erosion in the level of income has affected employees of the private sector. . . .

   As of June 1984, the implementation of the [ongoing administration] reform had led to the firing of around 5,000 civil servants, the retirement of about 17,000, and an annual reduction of roughly 25,000 staff since 1980. Such actions have reduced total civil employment . . . to about 200,000 employees in 1983. (World Bank [1985e])

(3) **Tanzania:** Real wages of urban workers have declined by 50 percent to 65 percent since the mid-1970s. (World Bank [1983f])

(4) **Sierra Leone:** Most civil servants experienced a 30–50 percent drop in real wages during the 1970s. Urban wages for unskilled works fell by a third from the mid-1970s through 1983. (World Bank [1983g])

Table 5.2 presents additional data for 20 African countries. Real wages either remained constant or fell during the 1970s in ten of the twelve countries for which data are available. Nor have the 1980s been much kinder to manufacturing workers: real wages have fallen in 10 of the 14 countries for which data are available (and the Zimbabwean case is unclear). This wage flexibility contradicts one of the basic hypotheses of the simpler probabilistic migration models, that is that there is a fixed minimum wage in urban formal sector employment. As Fallon (1985) observes, "The movement in real wages and real incomes seems broadly consistent with what one would expect from a changeover from a fixed formal sector wage Todaro type regime to one in which supply prices were equated across the rural, urban informal and formal sectors."

Again, more detailed country analyses support the aggregate World Bank data. Incomes per family were estimated to have declined at an annual rate of 2.0 percent in Nouakchott between 1977 and 1986, and between 1 and 6 percent annually in other Mauritanian towns (World Bank [1989e]). In Togo, the deflated minimum wage grew modestly (by 4.4 percent) between 1966 and 1976; it then declined at an *annual* rate of 4.6 percent through 1987 (World Bank [1989h]). In Madagascar, the deterioration was steadier: from 1974 through 1980, the real industrial minimum wage declined at an annual rate of 5.2 percent; for 1980 through 1988 the rate of decline was 3.8 percent. The average decline in all industrial wages for the period 1966–84 was 2.3 percent per annum—a stunning prolonged deterioration (Pryor [1988] and World Bank [1989g]). For the period 1979–89, the deflated minimum wage fell at an annual rate of 5.3 percent in the Central African Republic (World Bank [1989i]). But private sector average wages rose significantly during at least part of this period, and average salaries appear to have been roughly constant in real terms during the 1980s. In The Gambia, both real minimum wages and mean formal sector incomes experienced prolonged declines between the mid-1970s and late 1980s (the latter fell from 1,323 constant 1989 U.S. dollars in 1974/5 to

$991 in 1987/8, an annual rate of decline of 2.2 percent), though they appear to have since stabilized (Becker [1991]).

In some countries, declines in the real wage were accompanied by employment growth; this is the case in the 1980–85 period for Madagascar, Tanzania, Somalia, Botswana, Kenya, Ethiopia, and Senegal. But a wage decline is not a necessary condition for employment growth, since Burkina Faso and Zimbabwe recorded both increasing manufacturing wages and employment. In other words, it would be a mistake to focus exclusively on the supply side of the labor market, since demand conditions matter too.

Overall, it appears likely that real wages declined more slowly in the CFA-zone (Communauté Financière Africaine: African Financial Community) countries (nearly all of Francophone Africa) than in other African countries during the late 1970s and 1980s. The CFA franc (CFAF) is tied to the French franc at 50:1, and therefore inflation in CFA zone countries is tied closely to the French inflation rate. Since many formal sector nominal wages and prices are sticky downward, real wage adjustment tends to accelerate in high inflation environments. Formal labor market arrangements in many Francophone countries also may have impeded rapid real wage adjustments.

There is also some evidence that, at least in some countries, real earnings began to fall well before the continent-wide crisis that began in the mid-1970s. In Malawi, for example, real mean formal sector earnings in both the public and private sectors exhibited continual deterioration between 1969 and 1977, with stagnation then setting in during the late 1970s (World Bank [1982b]). Furthermore, the largest declines took place at the start of the reported series (6.8 percent decline in 1969 and 7.0 percent decline in 1970), excluding the OPEC-shock induced decline of 12.7 percent in 1974.

Three other points regarding formal sector earnings and urban income distributions are worth mentioning. First, poverty levels vary significantly from city to city within a given country—and usually are much lower in the capital and other large cities. In one of the most extreme examples, grande pauvrete' incidences in Mauritania in 1986 ranged from 10 percent in Nouadhibou and 22 percent in Nouakchott to 66 percent in Kaedi and 74 percent in Kiffa (World Bank [1989e]). Second, the income distribution in African cities can be highly unequal, even when the formal sector is dominant. For example, the Gini coefficient for income in Dakar in 1975 was 0.39—higher than in many other countries (World Bank [1989j]).

A third point is that unemployment may be much higher than is commonly recognized, especially in countries where the formal sector dominates and the informal sector is relatively small. One indication of this problem comes from Cameroon's 1987 census, which found that 11.6 percent of urban residents (and 3.2 percent of rural dwellers) were unemployed (World Bank [1989d]). From Madagascar, we find that registered urban unemployment in 1984 was 9.5 percent of the labor force (Pryor [1988]). This figure actually represented a sharp decrease from 15.7 percent in 1979, as employment grew by 4.4 percent during the intervening period. Much of the decline also may have reflected discouragement, especially as real wages fell sharply. But it is also possible that the decline in Madagascar does reflect movement toward an equilibrium. This, indeed, is Collier and Lal's (1986:232) and Collier and Bigsten's (1981) thesis about the Kenyan labor market: those most likely to get jobs (labor market entrants with good school records) and those least likely to land "good" formal sector jobs (those with failing exam marks) suffer the lowest unemployment rates. Rather, those for whom opportunities are uncertain are most likely to experience prolonged unemployment spells. Ishumi's [1984] study of Tanzanian urban unemployment is consistent with this thesis. The typical unemployed Tanzanian is fairly young, and is a primary or secondary school leaver. Only 23 percent of the unemployed had fewer than four years of schooling, suggesting that the very unskilled are not actively unemployed (though, as Shields' study indicates, there are many passively unemployed, especially women).

It also should be noted that migrants, while initially suffering high unemployment rates, do not necessarily experience permanently higher rates. In Nairobi in the early 1970s it was found that 27 percent of migrants were unemployed during their first quarter following migration, but that only 14 percent were unemployed after eight quarters, as against 10 percent of the entire Nairobi labor force (Rempel [1981:107]).

5.1.3. Wage structures, Education, and Income

There is a vast descriptive literature on African urban formal sector wage structures, and we will provide only a brief overview here. Generally speaking, the salient characteristics are as follows:

(1) *Wages rise with skill requirements and supervisory responsibility.* The extent to which they rise, however, depends in part on public wage policies (for example, there is more apparent "wage-stretching" in capitalist Kenya than in socialist Tanzania) (Knight and Sabot [1990]).

(2) *Temporary, or casual workers, are important in many formal sector economies. Their wage rates are generally considerably less than those of regular workers.*

(3) *Wages and incomes tend to be markedly higher in capitals and the larger cities.* At least in Côte d'Ivoire (but almost certainly elsewhere, too), measures of income inequality are greater in the largest cities as well (see Kozel [1990]).

(4) *Measures of urban inequality are often extremely high by developed country standards.* They also tend to be greater than rural inequality measures. Some examples: the Gini coefficient for per capita household income is 0.52 for Abidjan, 0.51 for other Ivoiran urban areas, and 0.48 for rural Côte d'Ivoire (Kozel [1990]). For 1980 Madagascar, the rural Gini coefficient for per family income was 0.44; for secondary urban centers it was 0.49 (Pryor [1988]). For Malawi, the Gini coefficient for per family income in the four major towns in 1984/5 was 0.621; for smallholder households it was 0.45 (Pryor [1988a]).

(5) *The urban poor are typically self-employed.* Some do work for government, however, usually as casual workers (Glewwe and de Tray [1988]).

(6) *Migrants, at least initially, earn less than average urban wages* (for a revealing table, see Rempel [1981:108]). Overall, Rempel found that Kenyan migrants earned 52 percent of the average urban wage in the first quarter after they migrated, and 59 percent after eight quarters. For Mombasa and Nairobi, these percentages were (taking unweighted averages) 48 percent and 52 percent, respectively. For secondary Kenyan cities, the means were 72 percent and 81 percent, respectively (and 76 percent and 94 percent, respectively, if one excludes Nakuru, an extreme outlier). If one can generalize from these Kenyan figures, then it would appear that migrants

catch up more rapidly in smaller towns than in the largest cities. The difference also appears to vanish as education level rises (Sabot et al. [1981:Table 2.15]).

(7) *Public sector wages are higher than comparable private sector wages in some, but not all, countries.* Kenyan data from 1972, for both professional workers and skilled craftsmen, show consistently higher private formal sector wages (Collier and Lal [1986:170]). In Tanzania during the mid-1970s, a very clear pattern emerged: parastatal wages were uniformly higher in skilled and unskilled blue collar occupations, for given educational levels, followed by the private sector and government. In nonmanual occupations, private sector wages were highest, followed by parastatal and then government wages (Sabot et al. [1981: Table 5.24]).[5] It is unlikely that this pattern is replicated in nonsocialist countries, though. In Kenya, average public sector earnings are higher, but they are not systematically higher across categories (see Rempel [1981:38]). Controlling for characteristics is important, though, since *general government is skill-intensive relative to both parastatals and the private formal sector* (Knight and Sabot [1990:150]). Finally, in Malawi, while private sector wages in a given industrial sector are typically higher than government wages, average public sector earnings are higher because of the different compositional mix (see World Bank [1985h] and Pryor [1988a:45]).

(8) *In effecting short-run structural adjustment, public sector real wages appear to move more rapidly than private sector wages* (which, of course, may merely indicate that the former were more in disequilibrium to start with). Direct evidence for this assertion is hard to establish; indications appear, for example, in van der Gaag et al. (1989:19).

(9) *Wages rise strongly with level of education.* Typical gaps between no education and Forms 1–4 are 1–200 percent premia (or more). Looking at it from a different angle, in 1979/80 Malawi the heads of the top 10 percent of urban families (ranked by income) had 12.6 years of schooling on average; the mean for the bottom 28 percent was 4.8 years (Pryor [1988a:63]). In Côte d'Ivoire, while only 2.4 percent of household heads had any university education, 11 percent of the top income quintile did (Glewwe [1988]).

(10) *There is some indication that education/skill premia have diminished in countries with rapid skills' supply growth.* The evidence comes mainly from Kenya. Collier and Bigsten (1981), for example, find that the mean salary of those with Form 6 education relative to those who had only completed primary school fell from 2.8 in 1968 to 2.3 a decade later, while the university education premium declined from 6.1 to 3.9. Nor is the source of the narrowing mysterious: Collier and Lal's (1986:199) estimates of the stock of Kenyans with Form 6 education grew at an annual rate of 14.4 percent between 1965 and 1980, and the stock of Kenyan Form 4 graduates grew at 22.2 percent annually during 1965–79. This pace almost certainly exceeded demand growth. Indeed, even rural migrants in Kenya are fairly skilled. In the mid-1960s, 34 percent had some secondary schooling, and by the late 1970s, the majority (51 percent) had some secondary schooling (Collier and Lal [1986:245]). It is also the case that wage premia appear to have diminished in Tanzania between 1970 and 1980, even though skilled labor supply did not grow rapidly. Here, it appears that public policy worked to forced wage compression (Sabot et al. [1981a]; Valentine [1982]).

(11) *Earnings rise with academic performance,* at least in Kenya (see Sabot et al. [1981:Table 2.21]; Collier and Lal [1986]; Collier and Bigsten [1981]). Those

with top grades in Form 4 mathematics exams had mean earnings more than five times as high as those who failed; rewards for academic performance in English and sciences were comparably great.

(12) *Controlling for level of education, women earn less than men at lower levels of education.* At higher levels in Kenya, however, the gap is not always present, though it does appear at all Tanzanian occupational levels and nearly all educational levels (see Sabot et al. [1981: Tables 2.1, 5.4, 5.11]).

(13) *Women are far less likely than men to be employed in the formal sector.* This is nearly universal, and in part reflects women's time constraints, child rearing, and household management responsibilities. It also reflects men's superior access to human capital—and may reflect discrimination beyond that causing differential levels of human capital. Female headed households tend to be poorer than average (for Côte d'Ivoire, see Glewwe [1988]).

(14) *While education is an important determinant of earnings, social class and gender are important determinants of access to education* (Knight and Sabot [1990] and Appleton, Collier, and Horsnell [1990]). In consequence, ideologically conservative countries such as Kenya that rapidly extended secondary education to girls, and into rural areas, in practice have often followed a much more egalitarian development strategy than those nations that preached socialism but did not extend education rapidly.

Finally, it is crucial to note that supplies of skilled labor have varied greatly across Africa. In Kenya, for example, secondary school enrollment has mushroomed—from 30,000 students in 1963, to 410,000 in 1980. In contrast, Tanzanian secondary school enrollment grew much more slowly, from 17,000 in 1963 to 67,000 in 1980. As of 1988, national secondary school gross enrollment ratios (SSGER) exhibited the following range (UNDP/World Bank [1992]):

High SSGER		Low SSGER	
Mauritius	53%	Malawi	4%
Zimbabwe	51	Tanzania	4
Swaziland	44	Burundi	4 (1985)
Ghana	39	Mozambique	5
Botswana	33	Burkina Faso	6
Cameroon	27	Chad	6
Lesotho	25	Guinea-Bissau	6
Togo	24	Rwanda	6
Kenya	23	Niger	7
Zaire	22	Uganda	8

With differences in supply conditions of this magnitude, we would expect to find that markedly different wage structures exist. Specifically, one would expect to find smaller skill premia in countries with rapidly growing skilled labor forces—unless the supply itself reflected existing gaps, or unless international investors altered their investments and the skill intensity of those investments to match each country's skill structure. Large groups of skilled workers may also affect the ability of the industrial sector to favor particular groups, as the scope for competition is greater.

Size of a country's economy, the presence of rents from natural resources, ownership, and macroeconomic policies all may affect wage structures as well. The next step is to examine the formal evidence, and see if any clear patterns of wage differentials emerge.

5.1.4. Econometric Studies of Wage Determinants

A surprisingly large number of studies at the micro level have been undertaken on the determinants of wages and other labor market variables. The econometric specifications differ from model to model, in part because the issues (dependent variables) differ, and in part because the theoretical framework varies from researcher to researcher, but most importantly because data constraints vary. So does underlying econometric sophistication, and, as one would expect, more recent studies exhibit more advanced statistical techniques.

Virtually all studies begin with the hypothesis that wages are positively related to formal skills, true ability, or both. These points suggest that an individual's wage (or the mean for a group, if aggregated data are used) should rise with level of education, efforts to acquire technical skills, experience, and indications of true ability. We refer to these hypotheses collectively as the *human capital (HC) theory of wages*. Like the other theories discussed, HC theory does not regard African settings as unique, and the model has been employed successfully in countless non-African developing countries, as well as in developed nations.

Evidence for HC theory tends to be strong in Africa and elsewhere. The really interesting questions actually involve its limitations. Does HC theory hold for particular sectors and not for others? Are workers able to enforce some profit sharing—or does management find it desirable to adjust wages procyclically? Do multinationals pay more, and, if so, why? Do unions matter? Are labor markets segmented by gender? Do firms find that productivity rises with wages? Are turnover costs an important consideration to firms? Are there positive returns to education 1) because it improves basic cognitive skills, 2) because educational attainment is a signal of underlying worker ability, 3) because educational attainment affects one's place in the queue, and institutionally determined wages rise with job prestige, 4) because education involves acquiring specific technical skills, or 5) two or more of the above? Do shifts in cohort size and the supply side—skill structure of the labor force—greatly affect wages? The answers to these questions shed light on the way African labor markets function, and hence on the scope for public policy to affect income growth, wage and income distribution, unemployment, and urbanization.

So what are the findings? The following paragraphs will focus on conclusions, without belaboring differences in model construction and statistical technique. The reader interested in technical details should consult the original sources—and pay particular attention to differences in sample coverage, underlying economic structure, and, of course, model design and econometric formulation.

Two main sets of studies dominate the empirical findings and serve as the basis for our discussion. The first are a set of studies on the Kenyan and Tanzanian economies undertaken by a group of researchers associated with the World Bank. The senior authors involved are Paul Collier, John Knight, Dipak Lal, Richard Sabot, and Albert Berry. The second set was also Bank-sponsored, but as part of its

Living Standards Measurement Study. It involved several detailed surveys, most importantly from Côte d'Ivoire (with Jacques van der Gaag and Wim Vijverberg the main authors). House and Rempel's studies of Kenya and Svejnar and Terrell's studies of Senegal are the other primary micro studies. The findings are:

1. *Returns to experience are positive*—about 4 percent per annum in Kenya, 5 percent in Tanzania (Knight and Sabot [1990:64–65]), and 1.6 percent in Senegal (Terrell and Svejnar [1989]). They also appear to interact positively with educational attainment and cognitive skill.

2. *Returns to education are also strongly positive, although public policy affects returns.* For example, the return to completing secondary education in Kenya (as opposed to completing primary education) is 61 percent; in Tanzania it is only 32 percent. Secondary school educated workers earn more even though they have less job experience. House (1987) also finds that schooling matters in the informal sector: each additional year increases proprietors' incomes by about 2 percent, and employees' incomes by nearly 4 percent. Terrell and Svejnar (1989) estimate the annual return to an additional year of education in Senegal to be 11.1 percent, while those who have received some training earn about 10 percent more than those who have not. Van der Gaag and Vijverberg (1988) estimate returns to higher education in Côte d'Ivoire of 20 percent per annum, far higher than other estimates produced for other countries. Returns to primary schooling are about 8 percent.

3. *Measures of ability do not appear to greatly influence wages; measures of achievement do* (Knight and Sabot [1990:65]). The main caveat is that measurement error could be important here. In any event, in the only careful study of which we are aware, Knight and Sabot find that the returns to reasoning ability are low, while returns to specific skills (literacy and numeracy) are high, for both manual and nonmanual workers. Van der Gaag and Vijverberg (1988) also find that cognitive skills do not affect wages in a study of Côte d'Ivoire. Svejnar's (1984) study of Senegalese earnings found standard positive returns to skill level/occupational attainment. Occupation in high-skill areas is the main determinant of earnings; for less skilled workers, industrial sector is as or more important. The high returns to skills are taken as strong support for HC theory; the additional returns to education are consistent with HC theory, but also with *credentialist* or *screening* views of the labor market (though subsequent work by Knight and Sabot [1990: Ch. 4] casts both views into doubt). That is, firms may pay for workers' credentials. They may also value education not for itself, but rather because academic ability is correlated with otherwise unobservable (and desirable) attributes of workers. This last view is also supported by the work of Collier and Bigsten (1981) and Collier and Lal (1986). But Knight and Sabot (1990:Ch.12) estimate that four years of secondary schooling in Kenya raises lifetime earnings exclusively via its impact on cognitive skills by 33 percent (but the costs depress the return by 7 percent).

4. Determining whether there are returns to being in a high-prestige *occupation* is tricky, since occupational choice is at least partially endogenous. As one would expect, Knight and Sabot (1990:Ch.5) find that education, experience, race, gender, and family background are good—but hardly perfect—predictors of occupational attainment. Academic performance is an important determinant both of occupation and wage given occupation, and in both Kenya and Tanzania, suggesting that employers are seeking more than mere credentials. But the East African surveys also indicated 1) social position affected occupation, and 2) that occupational change was infre-

quent, indicating that *labor market discrimination and segmentation do matter.* In any event, *occupation does strongly influence wages,* and HC variables influence earnings both directly and indirectly through their effect on occupation.

5. A corollary of point 4: *social returns to education are likely to be less than private returns,* since upward occupational mobility afforded by education is privately beneficial, but has no obvious productivity effect.[6] Knight and Sabot (1990) also provide evidence of *job filtering or queuing.* That is, as the numbers of people with secondary education increase, they gradually fill positions that used to be filled by those with only primary educations; the primary educated then move down the ladder, displacing those with still less education. These filtering effects make the marginal return to education less than the average return—but the differences are not necessarily great. Marginal returns to primary education are estimated to be 12 percent and 10 percent in Kenya and Tanzania, respectively, while marginal returns to secondary schooling are 13 percent and 12 percent, respectively.

6. *Supply policies matter greatly.* One of Knight and Sabot's (1990: Ch. 8) important exercises was to estimate the consequence of Kenya and Tanzania following each other's education supply strategies. They find:

When relative supply in Tanzania is raised to Kenya's level, the premium in Tanzania falls from 0.640 to 0.545, whereas the Kenyan premium is 0.510. . . . when relative supply in Kenya is lowered to Tanzania's level, the Kenyan premium rises from, 0.510 to 0.669, whereas the Tanzanian premium is 0.640. (pp.171–72)

7. As noted in preceding chapters, *labor mobility is limited.* Knight and Sabot (1981a) estimate that voluntary job changes in Tanzania occurred only once every 12.3 years. Their econometric work indicated further that employment experience *reduced* mobility, as did a measure of regular employment status (that is, and unsurprisingly, casual workers change jobs more frequently). More surprisingly, men are actually more mobile than women, especially in manual occupations. As expected, the educated are more mobile. Finally, Knight and Sabot find that wages rise with voluntary mobility and fall with involuntary job changes.

8. The positive interaction between returns to education and experience is natural, but also troubling. This interaction could reflect greater innate ability by the relatively educated, in which case returns to experience might be higher. It could also reflect a positive correlation between schooling and postschool training, or the possible effect that schooling has on lifetime ability to learn on the job. But it could also reflect cohort effects: the highly educated in early cohorts (who are more experienced in cross-sectional samples) may receive higher pay than later cohorts. If this is true, then *cohort effects will cause cross-sectional estimates of returns to schooling to be upwardly biased*—possibly by as much as one-third (Knight and Sabot [1981b]).

9. In a study of Tanzanian earnings, Knight and Sabot (1981) found that employees of multinational corporations (MNCs) did in fact earn about 15 percent more than those in domestic firms. MNCs also were larger and more capital intensive, more unionized, and more skill intensive. Of course, these characteristics cannot be attributed to foreign ownership, since it may merely reflect subsectoral composition. But when earnings functions are estimated, it appears that *MNCs pay higher returns to education, previous employment experience, and permanent employment status, and less for sheer age and social status.* Terrell and Svejnar (1989) find that parastatals,

Syro-Lebanese owned, and other privately owned Senegalese firms have comparable wage structures for base pay, but that French firms pay more.[7] MNCs in partnership with the Tanzanian government paid particularly high premia—but this is interpreted by Knight and Sabot as reflecting government's tendency to nationalize high-wage, capital-intensive firms. Wholly private MNC-owned status did not affect mean earnings.

10. *Once one controls for other personal attributes, gender does not seem to have a great impact on earnings.* This finding should not be taken to indicate an absence of sex discrimination. Rather, the most important elements of discrimination occur in access to 1) education and skills, 2) favored sectors, and 3) favored occupations. This conclusion is Shields' (1980) central finding in a study on Tanzania, although illiterate women do appear to be at a disadvantage relative to their male counterparts (in regressions that do not, however, control for occupation or sector). Appleton, Collier, and Horsnell (1990) obtain a similar result for Côte d'Ivoire, showing that while returns to education are as high for women as for men, women receive less education and hence lower total returns. Women have lower labor force participation rates and are less likely to work for wages than men, even after controlling for education. This suggests that 1) there is discrimination against women at the time of recruitment, and/or 2) women have lower labor market aspirations (and higher domestic commitments).

    But the finding of no male/female wage gap is not universal. After controlling for other variables, Svejnar (1984) finds that males earn 19 percent more in a sample of seventeen Senegalese firms in the early 1980s, and van der Gaag and Vijverberg (1988) find evidence of male/female wage gaps for Côte d'Ivoire.

11. Increased industry profitability may or may not lead to higher labor earnings. Svejnar (1984) finds that, in Senegal, increased industry profitability resulted in increased earnings for expatriates, but not Senegalese workers. Increased capital intensity within a sector does have a positive effect on Senegalese workers' earnings, confirming a prediction of simple neoclassical economic theory. The need to expand, as measured by investment/value added, adversely affects wages, while labor cost/value added (seen as a measure of union strength) is positive. Svejnar and Terrell (1989) find that in Senegal effective rate of protection, export orientation, and per worker profitability do not appear to affect wages. *Sales growth, however, is strongly associated with higher pay:* a 1 percent increase in annual sales growth is associated with a 1.02 percent increase in total compensation.

12. In an econometrically elegant piece, Vijverberg and van der Gaag (1991) simultaneously estimate the wage functions along with the choice of degree of formality of one's sector for Côte d'Ivoire. Formality is associated with education, technical training, and experience. *Once entered in the wage equation, degree of formality does appear to influence wages positively.* This is consistent with a *labor market segmentation view,* but it is not necessarily inconsistent with neoclassical models (especially if firms use education as a screening device). But regardless of theory, the Vijverberg–van der Gaag study clearly points to the dual sector hypothesis as being a theoretical abstraction rather than reflecting an empirical gulf. That is, "rather than two segments with a chasm between them, there exist many little segments separated by little gaps" (p. 418).

Collier and Lal (1986) emphasize the importance of having simultaneous casual and permanent work forces in the formal sector, with recruiting to permanent status an important market event. Public policy to regulate casual employment thus could reduce the ability of firms to observe workers' abilities, and therefore could adversely affect both selection efficiency and workers' effort incentives. Collier and Lal also find that wages rise with firm size, capital intensity, and foreign ownership, but note that the need to promote from within will be greater in large firms, so that they need to recruit higher quality low- and middle-level employees. In short, *while empirical findings are consistent with labor market segmentation, there are competing neoclassical stories that generate similar implications.*

What do these varied bits of information imply? First, a warning is in order. While there are many studies of high caliber, the number relative to the cultural and political diversity of Africa is tiny. One must be very cautious about generalizing from these results.

Second, the HC paradigm does fairly well, for both formal and informal sectors. But segmentation may well occur, as may credentialism, especially in modern sectors in which governments are powerful. Our hunch, however, is that factors not driven directly by competitive forces, including filtering, gender discrimination, ability to pay, willingness to pay, and sheer returns to age all will diminish as structural adjustment policies take hold. The surprising finding here is that they are not more important now, and have not been in the 1970s and 1980s.

Third, the discrimination that does occur is largely framed in terms of access to human capital variables (what economists might term "premarket discrimination"). Here discrimination, by gender, social class, and ethnic group does exist and in fact is very strong.

Finally, earnings structures are shaped by public policy. This occurs unwittingly in a country such as Tanzania, where educational policy has given rise to (long suppressed) large skill gaps. And it probably occurs more consciously in Senegal, Côte d'Ivoire, and some other Francophone countries, where public sector credentialism greatly affects equilibrium wage structures.

For our purposes, these studies, along with indisputable evidence of large real urban mean wage movements, indicate that fixed wage models are inappropriate. They also indicate that the labor market regime may well differ from country to country—suggesting that future studies of African wage movements and rural-urban migration should either be 1) based on a time series model within a country that explicitly allows for changes in regime, or 2) based on a cross-sectional model that has sufficient flexibility to incorporate the different regimes characterizing different countries in the sample.

5.1.5. Public-Private Sector Distinctions and
the Effect of Public Policy on Wages

It is important to point out that African manufacturing sectors are not just developed country manufacturing sectors in miniature. One key difference is the important role played by parastatal firms in African manufacturing sectors, in terms of both employment and output shares. *There is some dispute as to whether public sector workers earn more or less than private sector workers.* Some of this dispute may be due to the fact that the wage gap has begun to shrink with the advent of structural adjustment policies. Collier and Lal (1986) find little impact of public sector employment on wages in Kenya, regarding government as a follower rather than a wage setter. A recent World Bank report (1990b: v) goes even further, arguing that public sector salaries—especially for more skilled positions—are not competitive with those offered by the private sector. Van der Gaag and Vijverberg (1988) estimate different government and private sector earnings functions for Côte d'Ivoire, together with a switching equation to determine sectoral choice. They find that individuals with little education earn higher wages in the private sector, while the reverse is true for those with higher levels of education. Van de Gaag and Vijverberg's results are especially important, since they demonstrate that ordinary least squares (OLS) estimates or earnings equations are severely biased, as they do not account for selectivity in sectoral choice. The OLS estimates appear to show that women receive lower public sector wages than men, but this disappears once the selection process is taken into account.[8] So to does the apparently universally higher wage paid by the public sector. Other, more impressionistic evidence from Togo (World Bank [1989h:17]) and The Gambia (on the basis of one author's conversations with government officials) point to private sector wages above public sector wages, at least at relatively senior levels.

Earlier studies tended to find wage differentials in favor of the public sector. Sabot et al. (1982), for example, found that public sector employees in Tanzania in 1980 earned 29 percent higher wages than their private sector counterparts. One could argue, of course, that human capital characteristics of workers differ between the two sectors. Even after standardizing for educational levels, however, Sabot et al. found that most education cohorts earned higher incomes in the public sector; the highest premium was received by those who completed five or six standards, who earned 105 percent higher wages than their counterparts in the private sector. Interestingly, individuals with high educational credentials earn lower wages in the public sector—exactly opposite the result reported by van der Gaag and Vijverberg for Côte d'Ivoire. Sabot et al. find a very similar pattern in Kenya in 1980. Overall, public sector workers earned 13 percent higher wages. In fact, the only educational cohort to earn higher wages in the private sector was the cohort composed of individuals with post-Form 4 education.

On the basis of the evidence described above, one can rather confidently claim that African governments currently do not distort urban wage structures to the degree that they once did. It is important to qualify this claim, though. In some countries, it seems that private sector workers even earn higher wages than comparable public sector workers. This situation may be quite different, however, in small countries where governments employ a higher proportion of the formal sector. Second, government's absorption of skilled labor also alters wage structures—and greater government is associated with greater skilled labor demand, and hence greater inequality. Third, educational policies, as noted above, matter via their effect on skill supplies. So does industrial policy, as government industrial development policy may greatly affect the structure of skill demand. In short, then, most African governments do not appear to directly determine urban wage structures, either within the formal sector, or with regard to informal/formal sector gaps. But their indirect influence is vast, and to some degree has exacerbated inequalities.

5.1.6. The Roots of Decline in Formal Sector Manufacturing

Despite the differences between public and private sector firms, they share one common characteristic: slow or even declining employment growth since 1980.

TABLE 5.2. Annual Growth Rates of Manufacturing Wages (Earnings Per Employee) for 20 African Nations, 1970–86.

	(1) 1970–80	(2) 1980–86	(3) 1975–80	(4) 1980–85	(5) 1986–88
Botswana	10.4	−4.2	−1.9	−18.2	—
Burkina Faso	—	2.6	15.5	—	—
Burundi	−7.8	—	−12.0	—	—
Cameroon	—	—	3.5	—	—
Côte d'Ivoire	−0.9	—	−0.2	—	—
Ethiopia	−4.6	−3.1	—	−2.2	2.8
Kenya	−3.4	−3.7	−5.5	−16.0	−0.2
Liberia	—	1.6	—	—	—
Madagascar	−0.9	−12.9	1.9	−29.0	—
Malawi	—	—	—	−12.7	—
Mali	−8.4	—	—	—	—
Nigeria	0.0	—	—	—	—
Senegal	−4.8	−0.2	−4.1	—	—
Seychelles	—	—	—	4.1	—
Somalia	−6.4	−8.6	−23.5	—	—
Swaziland	—	—	—	−22.7	—
Tanzania	—	−11.4	—	−26.0	—
Togo	—	—	8.6	—	—
Zambia	−3.3	0.2	−11.3	—	—
Zimbabwe	1.6	6.1	−5.4	−17.6	−3.7

Source: Columns 1 and 2: World Bank (1989c).
Columns 3, 4, and 5: UNDP/World Bank (1992), constant 1987 U.S. dollars.

For those African countries reporting parastatal employment, about half show declining employment since 1980 (for these data, see U.N. [1989:167]). Thus, although Tables 5.1 and 5.2 point out some exceptions to the generalization that African formal sectors have had only mediocre employment growth performances and falling real wages since the late 1970s by and large the characterization escapes intact. After the halcyon days of the early 1970s, African formal sectors have provided neither increasing employment opportunities nor rising standards of living for those who are employed there. What has caused this depressing state of affairs?

Formal sector firms (both private and parastatal) often were created as a result of import substitution policies; high tariff barriers and other trade restrictions limited the access of foreign-produced goods to the domestic market, and domestic production was encouraged to replace goods formerly imported. The Kenyan experience with import substitution industrialization is typical of many African countries. Kenyan import-substituting industries often produced items that could not compete on world markets. Eglin (1978) ranked a number of Kenyan import-substituting manufacturing industries by the level of effective protection from foreign competition received and by international competitiveness. Not surprisingly, those industries receiving the most protection (nylon dyeing, margarine, pork products, sugar, and rayon cloth) were the five industries that ranked lowest out of twenty-three in terms of international competitiveness.

In Kenya and other African countries, world demand for African-produced manufactures has been quite modest and played little role in the early expansion of African manufacturing sectors. Gulhati and Sekhar (1982) estimate that only 13 percent of the growth in Kenyan manufactures from 1963 to 1971 can be accounted for by export demand. Even this modest share dwarfs the estimated contribution of manufactured exports in Tanzania (1965–72) and Zambia (1965–72), where export demand accounted for only 5 and 1 percent of the growth in manufacturing output, respectively.

Given the small role played by foreign demand, there were only two ways in which domestic manufacturing production could expand. The first possibility would be for domestic demand to increase. Yet African domestic markets are small, and per capita income growth has not been rapid; consequently, efficient scale economies rarely have been reached.

The second possibility would be to deepen import substitution beyond the easy consumer goods stage into intermediate and capital goods. The evidence is clear that this has not happened. Table 5.3, taken from Steel and Evans (1984), shows the changes in the distribution of manufacturing production between consumer, intermediate, and capital goods industries for seven African countries. In fact, three of the seven countries show a smaller percentage of manufacturing production coming from capital goods in the late 1970s than in the early 1960s. Even the countries showing relative increases in the production of capital goods do not show impressive gains, with the exception of Nigeria, which almost doubled the share of manufactured capital goods.

This failure to deepen the import-substitution process is due to several factors. First, consumer goods–producing industries received significantly higher rates of effective protection than those industries producing intermediate or capital goods in all African countries. This cascading tariff structure made it more profitable for entrepreneurs to invest in final goods production, rather than capital goods production. Second, the market size required to produce most capital goods at lowest cost is larger than that required for consumer goods. Most African nations do not possess such market size.

Had import substitution been deepened, dependence on imported products would have been reduced. The necessity of importing intermediate and capital goods, however, simply shifted import dependence from final goods to intermediate and capital goods. Consumer goods imports fell from 48 to 18 percent of all import spending in Ghana from 1962 to 1979, from 49 to 20 percent in Tanzania (1963–79), from 61 to 28 percent in Nigeria (1960–78), and from 56 to 26 percent in Côte d'Ivoire (1960–79). At the same time, the percentage spent on intermediate and capital goods was rising rapidly, from 52 to 82 percent in Ghana, from 51 to 80 percent in Tanzania, from 39 to 72 percent in Nigeria, and from 44 to 74 percent in Côte d'Ivoire (Steel and Evans [1984:46]). For the continent as a whole, the share of machinery, transport equipment, and fuels rose from 36 percent of imports in 1965 to 42 percent in 1987, while imports of other manufactures declined in share from 45 percent to 41 percent (World Bank [1989a]).

Imports of capital goods were promoted by cascading tariff structures, as well as by subsidized credit programs to finance capital good purchase, and preferential tax treatment often available for expansions in a firms' capital stocks. The net result was a formal sector which, according to many development economists, was overly

TABLE 5.3. Changes in Distribution of Manufacturing Production in Selected Countries, early 1960s to 1980 (as a percentage of total production).

Country (years)	Early/mid-1960s			Mid-/late 1970s or 1980		
	consumer goods	intermediates	capital goods	consumer goods	intermediates	capital goods
A. *Value Added*						
Ghana	50.0	42.5	7.5	53.0	41.2	5.8
(1962, 1979)						
Zambia	43.9	34.0	22.2	40.8	35.5	23.7
(1965, 1980)						
Tanzania	74.0	23.0	3.0	57.0	35.0	8.0
(1961, 1978)						
Nigeria	54.5	36.3	9.4	42.6	34.4	18.1
(1964, 1977/78)						
Côte d'Ivoire	50.0	25.1	25.0	63.1	18.2	18.9
(1960, 1974)						
Kenya	55.2	30.6	14.2	51.1	29.9	18.9
(1960, 1980)						
Zaire	67.5	20.6	11.9	70.4	19.6	10.0
(1966, 1976)						
B. *Gross Output*						
Zimbabwe	49.1	26.0	24.8	54.0	21.7	24.0
(1965, 1978)						
Ethiopia	79.4	19.5	1.1	67.7	30.0	2.3
(1967, 1978/79)						

Source: Steel and Evans (1984).

capital intensive, given the factor endowments of labor and capital characterizing African nations.[9] This capital intensivity was viewed as a prime reason why African formal sectors were unable to absorb the surplus labor in these countries. Indeed, there is substantial evidence that capital intensivity varies positively with firm size in Africa, thus indicating the formal sector's capital-intensivity. Table 5.4 reports the value of fixed capital per worker for different size firms in three African countries. Large firms with more than fifty employees have between four and five times the capital intensivity of smaller firms in Ghana, Kenya, and Sierra Leone. Larger, formal sector firms are more capital intensive than their smaller, informal sector counterparts.

Other explanations have been offered to explain why African countries' formal sectors have remained relatively small, both in terms of output and employment. They include (initially) proworker labor legislation, extensive unionization, and the imposition of above-market-clearing minimum wages. We conclude this section by examining each of these in turn.

The labor codes initially promulgated by African governments were often patterned on those implanted by the colonial powers. In Francophone West Africa, this means the French Overseas Labor Code of 1952. This code severely limits employers' discretion over hiring, layoffs, contractual forms, and working conditions. The Senegalese case is typical of most West African nations. Senegal's 1961 labor code stipulates that the Tripartite Commission—composed of representatives of

TABLE 5.4.   Capital Intensity (Measured by Value of Fixed Capital Per Worker) by Firm Size for Three African Countries, 1960–70.

Country (year)	Size of Firm*		
Kenya (1960)	$772	$986	$3108
	[1–10]	[11–49]	[50+]
Sierra Leone (1974)	158	225	1175
	[1–10]	[15–19]	[100+]
Ghana (1970)	1372	3742	6468
	[1–10]	[10–29]	[100 +]

*Numbers in brackets refer to the size distribution for the figures immediately above; categories are not identical across countries.

Source: Liedholm and Mead (1987).

the government, the national labor confederation, and employers associations—is responsible for setting the minimum industrial wage. This wage is crucial because it is the benchmark to which wages of more highly skilled workers are tied (see Terrell and Svejnar [1989:13]).

Such institutional determination of formal sector wages is the rule rather than the exception in Africa. In Tanzania, wages in the parastatal sector are determined by the Presidential Standing Committee on Parastatal Organizations, and private sector wages are fixed by the Permanent Labour Tribunal (Jackson [1979]). In Kenya, all collective bargaining agreements must be approved by the Industrial Court, which is charged with rejecting any agreements that do not conform to the wage guidelines set out by the Kenyan government (Sabot [1981:6]).

Not only wages were determined in such an administrative, nonmarket fashion. In Senegal, for example, the hiring process was strictly controlled by the Senegalese government until 1987. All persons seeking employment were required to register with the Labor Office, and the Labor Office would supply a firm that wished to hire a worker with three or four possible candidates. If a firm did not wish to hire any of the first round of candidates, it could request additional candidates from the Labor Office. Terrell and Svejnar (1989:16–17) report that this process was very cumbersome and time-consuming. Nor can firms easily lay off workers. Dismissal of permanent workers requires a review by an inspector from the Labor Office; only if the inspector concludes that the economic difficulties of the firm are serious enough to warrant a layoff of personnel is the layoff permitted. This review can take as long as forty-five days, and rulings can be appealed, in principle, all the way to the Supreme Court.

While it is generally acknowledged that such proworker labor laws limited the expansion of both employment and output in African formal sectors, there is less agreement on the effect of unionization in African countries. It is clear that many African formal sectors are highly unionized. In Senegal 83 percent of all workers belong to a union (Terrell and Svejnar [1989:49]). Trade unions are also very visible in Kenya's formal sector (Fallon [1985]), and the same is true for many other nations. Most researchers believe, however, that unions have had very little impact on the wage level. House and Rempel (1976), analyzing contracts negotiated between individual firm or trade associations and sixteen trade unions between 1967 and 1972 in Kenya, find that the degree of unionization in an industrial sector (at the three-digit [Standard Industrial Classification] [SIC] level) does not affect the wage rate paid by firms in this sector. In Senegal, unions have generally been "aligned with powerful political groups and somewhat divorced from the workers' interests" (Terrell and Svejnar [1989:50]). Empirical work analyzing panel data from 1980–85 by Terrell and Svejnar confirmed that union membership does not affect individuals' wages. Knight and Sabot (1981) found that unionization actually reduced mean earnings in Tanzania. But it is not clear that this result can be generalized from Tanzania, where the labor movement was under firm government control by the 1970s. Still, unions tend to be weak in Africa, given elastic labor supply conditions and frequent government manipulation.[10] It is also possible that the causality is reversed, and unions are more successful in low-wage firms and industries. Given the negligible impact of unions on wages, one must ask why workers would bother to join a union at all. Terrell and Svejnar (1989) offer the hypothesis that union membership is chosen because of low union dues and a sense of protection against potentially extreme actions by employers.

What, then, have we learned from the now abundant literature on African labor markets? The central point is clear: *African urban labor market disequilibrium is not to blame for formal sector declines.* Wage gaps do exist, but they appear to exist for plausible economic reasons. They are also diminishing. Furthermore, public policy also must take much of the responsibility for the size of existing gaps, for they reflect government pay scales and, indirectly, public policy toward education. The skilled labor scarcity that persists in many (but not all) African countries, and that both helps maintain wage gaps and the scarcity of qualified public sector managers needed to implement structural adjustment policies, is the responsibility of governments—as well as of the international organizations that have downplayed secondary and university education.

5.2 The Urban Informal Sector

The inability of the formal sector to provide employment for Africa's rapidly expanding population has led to explosive growth in the continent's informal sectors. Before proceeding further, it is useful to specify what we mean by the term "informal." It is sometimes asserted that characteristics which form the basis of the formal/informal dichotomy are, in fact, continuous, and that therefore the simple dichotomy is misleading. Mazumdar (1976:656) has offered two responses to this criticism, with which we concur:

(1) the view that the formal sector is separated sharply in some ways from the rest of the urban market is more valid than the contrary one for many Less Developed Country (LDC) urban markets, and

(2) even if the difference between two types of employment is one of degree, rather than of kind, so long as it is of marked degree the methodology of economics can be applied successfully by operating with models which assume that the labor market is split into two different sectors.

Nonetheless, in order to dispel confusion about what types of firms are included in the informal sector, we present Page and Steel's (1984) categorization which provides more detail on firm characteristics. Their scheme is:

Dualistic Terminology	Description	Criterion
formal	large scale	more than fifty workers
	intermediate sector	some investment in fixed or human capital; less than fifty workers:
formal	medium scale	thirty to forty-nine workers
formal	small scale	ten to twenty-nine workers
informal	small scale	six to nine workers and some degree of specialization
informal	artisanal	one to five workers
informal	residual or casual	no fixed investment or full-time employees
informal	home production	nonagricultural production done in the home and not sold or traded.

As a practical matter, Page and Steel's "intermediate sector" should be regarded as being fairly dissimilar from both the large-scale formal sector and the informal sector. The intermediate sector firm is much larger in scale, has better access to capital, is likely to be much stronger economically, and is more likely to keep written records than informal sector enterprises. But it is not nearly as well connected as the (usually government or foreign-owned) large enterprise: the intermediate sector firm is much more likely to be run by an indigenous owner.

In much of Africa, though, the choice of where to draw the line is not a particularly important one, mainly because the intermediate sector is so small. Indeed, this observation has given rise to a recent literature about the "missing middle" (see Palmer [1991], Livingstone [1991], and World Bank [1991]). To some degree, however, the missing middle phenomenon merely reflects the colonial and neocolonial traditions of stifling African entrepreneurs.

In any event, for our purposes the important distinction in understanding labor markets and migration focuses on different wage and hiring practices. Unfortunately, there is virtually no empirical evidence on the behavior of the intermediate (or "small-scale enterprise"—SSE) sector. What we do know, though, is that wages of both informal sector and, especially, formal sector firms tend to rise with firm size (see section 5.1.4). *For our analytical purposes, then, it seems appropriate to lump the intermediate sector together with the true informal (microenterprise) sector, and to recognize that for much of Africa they form together the overwhelming majority of the indigenous private sector (IPS).* But we are fairly casual in the following pages, and report different studies' results without discussing whether the authors are using consistent definitions of the informal sector. Since sectoral distinctions emerge gradually with firm size and other characteristics, and since what is "small" in the context of Zimbabwe or Côte d'Ivoire may not be small in The Gambia or Guinea, strict definitions seem of little value.

5.2.1. What is the African Urban Informal Sector?

Despite this vagueness, the African informal sector can be fairly carefully defined. In the last twenty years, urban small-scale, artisanal, residual/casual, and home production have expanded considerably in African nations. Their relative importance varies considerably across countries, in accordance with economic structure and public policy. Nonetheless, the main informal activities include carpentry and furniture production, tailoring, trade, vehicle and other repairs, metal goods' fabrication, restaurants, construction, transport, textiles and apparel manufacturing, footwear, and miscellaneous services (for reports of extensive surveys, see House [1984] and Livingstone [1991] for Kenya, Fowler [1981] for Sierra Leone, Fapohunda [1981] for Lagos, Mabogunje and Filani [1981] for Kano, Haan [1982] for Zambia, Steel [1979] for Ghana and Cameroon, and Aryee [1981] for Ghana). As Page and Steel (1984) note, while SSEs tend to overlap at an aggregate level with formal sector firms, within industries they are disproportionately concentrated in light, relatively labor-intensive activities.

It appears that firm size rises sharply with capital requirements (for example, it is clear from Aryee (1981) that mean enterprise size in footwear/leatherware is far smaller than motor repair and maintenance or carpentry). This point leads to another that several studies have indicated: *entry into the informal sector is easy in some, but hardly all, occupations.* As a rough approximation, it also appears that activities with significant capital or skill requirements for entry also have considerably higher mean earnings.

Clearly, individuals will need to work at such a job for some time in order to successfully "amortize" the costs of entry. Thus, one of the stylized "facts" about the informal sector, namely that it serves as a temporary way station en route to formal sector jobs, clearly is misleading. Rather, the informal sector tends to attract people for long stretches, and many of its enterprises are long-standing ones. House (1984:282), for example, in his study of Nairobi's informal sector found that only 6 percent of enterprises were founded in the year preceding the interview; 40 percent were at least five years old, and 20 percent were more than ten years old. Fowler, in a study of Freetown, found that only 22 percent of all informal sector owners were migrants, although this figure almost certainly would be higher in more rapidly growing economies—casting further doubt on the way station hypothesis.

It is also clear that the informal sector is a critically important component of Africa's urban and rural economies, though this importance varies considerably across countries. In small economies with nascent industrial sectors, SSEs contribute half or more of industrial output; they typically provide one-quarter or less in larger countries with more established industrial sectors. Page and Steel (1984:15) cite Burundi and Botswana as examples of the first group, and Ghana, Kenya, and Tanzania as examples from the second. They also conjecture—on the basis of highly fragmentary evidence—that SSE shares in manufacturing are likely to fall during periods of rapid industrialization, but are likely to grow rapidly during periods of economic stagnation. Livingtsone (1991), though, hypothesizes that the entire informal sector, including services, may grow with economic development over a considerable range of the development process, mainly because many informal services are luxury goods (in the sense that their income elasticities exceed unity) for the poor and middle classes in very low-income economies, but eventually become necessities, and ultimately inferior goods.

Informal sector employment shares typically will exceed output shares, since the sector is relatively labor intensive. For Kenya in 1985, the informal/small-scale nonagricultural sector accounted for 40.3 percent of total urban employment (and 33.9 percent of the urban labor force), urban agriculture accounted for another 12.7 percent (10.7 percent of the labor force), and 47.0 percent (39.5 percent of the labor force) were employed in the modern sector (Livingstone [1991]); 15.8 percent of the urban labor force was unemployed. Page and Steel's (1984) survey finds that the employment shares in manufacturing of intermediate (fifty or fewer workers) and small-scale enterprises around 1970 ranged from 59 percent in Kenya and 63 percent in Tanzania to 83 percent in Ethiopia, 85 percent in Ghana and Nigeria, and 96 percent in Sierra Leone.

What are the critical characteristics of informal sector workers? Again, they vary from country to country: women, for example, dominate petty commerce in some (especially West African) but not all countries; they are relatively absent from the market economic scene in more conservative Moslem countries. Women were estimated to account for 36 percent of workers in Kenya's SSE sector in 1988 (Livingstone [1991]). But one should be *very* cautious about interpreting statistics, as gender intensity varies from subsector to subsector, and many surveys are not intended to be complete (and many undoubtedly miss many informal enterprises, especially those that are illegal, or that have no fixed location). In the Kenya survey, women are relatively uncommon in informal manufacturing except textiles, and account for 47 percent of all traders and 40 percent of restaurant workers. Apprenticeships are standard among artisans, at least in West Africa (see Fowler [1981:55], as well as Aryee [1976] on Kumasi). But in Haan's (1982) study of Zambia, there were only 0.3 apprentices per informal enterprise. A virtually universal finding for Africa is that informal sector workers tend to be less well educated on average than formal sector workers, but have higher average educational attainment than rural workers.

Turning to informal sector sales and linkages, numerous studies have shown that only a small proportion of goods and services are sold to formal sector firms. Virtually all authors have then made the inappropriate inference that formal and informal sector linkages are minimal, save for the (often considerable) extent to which the informal sector purchases formal sector intermediates. In fact, the linkages are important, but occur indirectly, through demand by formal sector workers. In particular, "SSEs provide much of the consumer goods demanded by the lower-income population" (Page and Steel [1984:25]). Backward linkages to the formal sector tend to be important, especially as much of the petty retail sector trades formal sector consumer goods. In addition, repair services and many other services depend on formal sector inputs—in Fowler's (1981:64) words, "only enterprises in food and leather manufacturing and non-mechanized transport escape the grip of the formal sector." Forward linkages are less common: informal sector enterprises sell overwhelmingly to individuals and households (81 percent of sales in Freetown; 87 percent in Fapohunda's [1981] study of Lagos) or other informal enterprises. In Freetown, only 1.1 percent of informal sector sales were to modern sector enterprises; even in Kumasi, with its relatively developed informal sector, the figure was only 5 percent (Aryee [1981:98]).

An important point noted by Livingstone (1991:666) is that the informal sector purchases many agricultural inputs, but supplies very little to the agricultural sector. The lack of strong linkages here (and if it is weak in Kenya, it surely is weak in most of the continent) act as a natural brake on the informal sector's growth—and is a barrier that will have to be overcome if African informal sectors are going to prosper and grow in output and firm size along the lines of informal sectors in south and east Asian countries.

TABLE 5.5.   Wages in Formal and Informal Sectors, Various African Cities.

City	Date	W_{fs}/W_{is}	W_{fu}/W_{iu}	W_f/W_i
Addis Ababa	1968–69	1.31	1.07	
Ibadan	1959–62	—	2.50	
Kenya (many cities)	early 1970s	3.75	3.21	
Nairobi	mid 1960s	0.80	0.85	
Niger (all urban)	1970			2.08
North Central State (Nigeria)	1972	1.59	2.43	
Tanzania (all urban)	1971	1.99	3.02	

Key:
W_{fs} = formal skilled wage
W_{fu} = formal unskilled wage
W_{is} = informal skilled wage
W_{iu} = informal unskilled wage
W_f = formal sector wage
W_i = informal sector wage
Sources: Kannappan (1983:155) and Cohen (1979:53).

5.2.2. Informal sector earnings

The traditional view of informal sector wages is that they were some small fraction of wages in the formal sector. Evidence from the 1960s and 1970s is plentiful to confirm this view. Table 5.5 culls information from various sources on formal/informal sector wage gaps for African cities. With the exception of the peculiar result from Nairobi in the mid-1960s, formal sector wages exceed informal wages by a significant margin in all cities or countries represented. In some countries the wage gap is greater for skilled workers, and in others for unskilled workers, but the apparent moral is clear: formal sector workers in the 1960s and 1970s enjoyed a wage premium over informal sector workers. Nor has this gap entirely vanished. In Cap Vert region (including Dakar), Senegal, 1980 data indicate that the average informal sector earning was 63 percent of the average salaried worker's pay (World Bank [1989j]). World Bank (1989d) estimates for Cameroon are that informal sector earnings in the late 1980s were only about half of average formal sector salaries. A 1982 survey of six thousand informal sector enterprises in Bangui, Central African Republic (see World Bank [1989i]), found that three-quarters of all small traders (the main informal sector group) earned less than the minimum wage.

House (1984) delineated the presence of multiple groups within the informal sector. There is a substantial group, heavily composed of proprietors and skilled employees working in furniture making, metal goods, restaurants, and vehicle repairs, with incomes above national per capita income (adjusted for household size, and implying earnings of about Ksh. 200 per week). Some 31 percent of the 1977 Nairobi sample fell into this group. On the other end, 42 percent earned below the minimum wage (Ksh. 350 per month), and were termed the *community of the poor*.

This latter group has far fewer assets than the higher end of the informal sector spectrum (which House terms the intermediate sector); its proprietors engage in easy-entry occupations, such as shoe and clothing repairs, tailoring, barbering, and shoe shining. Furthermore, while House's study is based on attributes of proprietors, it is also apparent that informal sector employees are disproportionately represented among the poor.

Several possible explanations can be offered for the existence of large wage gaps between formal and informal sectors. First, one could argue that the average human capital characteristics of workers in the two sectors differ dramatically. If formal sector workers have larger endowments of human capital (principally experience, training, and education), the wage gap is a market-driven result. Even if marginal returns to human capital in the two sectors were identical, workers in the formal sector would earn higher wages because they possess larger stocks of human capital. A second explanation is that wages in the two sectors differ because of labor market segmentation. In other words, even after subtracting out the wage gap caused by differences in average human capital endowments, workers in the informal sector still earn lower wages—the returns to human capital are simply lower in the informal sector.

The information contained in Table 5.5 is far too simple to allow us to distinguish conclusively between these two explanations. The comparison of wages within skill categories is a crude attempt to include some measure of human capital characteristics, and quite clearly it is better than no human capital correction. Even so, one cannot claim on the basis of Table 5.5 that the formal/informal sector wage gaps are a market-driven result. The ubiquitous presence of minimum wage legislation and public and private set wage scales, one of the prime causes of labor market segmentation, suggests otherwise.

So too do recent trends in these wage gaps. Real wages of most urban workers have fallen in the past ten years, but formal sector wages have declined more rapidly than informal wages. As noted earlier in this section and in Chapter 4, the empirical evidence for declining urban wages is quite strong. To the extent that manufacturing takes place in urban areas, Table 5.2 (showing growth rates of real manufacturing wages) shows declines in urban formal sector wages.

More explicit proof is also available. In Nigeria real unskilled average wages fell by 32 percent between 1973 and 1985, but real minimum wages—a benchmark for unskilled wages in the formal sector—fell an even more remarkable 42 percent over this period. The real minimum wage in Uganda fell by an incredible 92 percent over the 1974–84 period, and the percentage of the minimum wage earnings required to purchase family food requirements rose from under 50 percent to 450 percent (Jamal and Weeks [1988]). While informal sector earnings undoubtedly collapsed as well (though data are not available), it is most unlikely that the fall was so meteoric.

The case for narrowing formal/informal sector wage gaps is less clear for Tanzania, where the real minimum wage fell by 80 percent over the 1974–86 period. While data for all nonagricultural wages are not available for this entire period, they fell 68 percent between 1974 and 1983 (Jamal and Weeks [1988:285]).

Impressionistic evidence suggests 1) that public policy toward the informal sector has a considerable impact on relative earnings, as does 2) the demographic composition of the informal sector. Where the informal sector consists mainly of part-time secondary workers, average earnings are, of course, much lower than in formal sector occupations. Earnings are also depressed by government activities that, in effect, tax informal sector entrepreneurs by constraining their growth and production decisions, restricting access to credit and inputs, and restricting sources of demand.

Studies comparing informal sector incomes to formal sector minimum wages also typically find that *means* exceed the minimum wages, but *medians* do not. Even in the early 1970s, Gerry (1974) found that casual formal sector wages averaged 92 percent of the minimum wage in Senegal; comparable workers in regular informal sector employment surely did at least as well. Similarly, Fapohunda (1981) found that Lagos heads' of informal enterprises mean earnings were 65 percent more than the minimum wage—but the median was 17 percent less. Informal sector employees, especially women, earned far less on average than the minimum wage— but many were unpaid apprentices or part-time workers, and many received partial payment in kind. These results suggest a high variance in informal earnings, with a relatively small number of informal entrepreneurs doing quite well vis-à-vis the minimum wage. Survey evidence bears this out. A 1982 survey (World Bank [1989i]) of informal enterprises in Bangui found that mean earnings for "entrepreneurs" were 29 percent higher than the minimum wage; of these, those in "production" had mean incomes 244 percent higher than the minimum wage, those in services had mean incomes 102 percent above the minimum wage, and those in construction had mean earnings 67 percent above the minimum wage.

In Kenya, both urban median and, in many places, rural mean (and almost certainly median) incomes exceeded the minimum wage (for regions outside Nairobi and Mombasa: Livingstone [1991]). Indeed, in some rural districts, mean informal sector earnings were substantially greater than informal sector mean incomes in the major cities, while in other rural areas, mean informal sector incomes fell far below urban informal sector incomes. On the whole, though, there seems to be little prima facie evidence of labor market misfunctioning in Kenya in the sense of the existence of gaps between either the rural and urban informal sectors or, at the margin, between the urban formal and informal sectors.

5.2.3. Female-Headed Households in the Informal Sector

We have noted that after controlling for differences in human capital endowments, women earn wages comparable to men, at least in the formal sector. Differences in human capital levels, however, impose barriers that hinder women from entering the formal sector, and, once there, find many options further restricted. By implication, women will be overrepresented in the informal sector and urban agriculture relative to their share in the urban labor force.[11] And also by implication, women will have inferior access to credit and possibly earnings because of their sectoral restrictions.

Within the informal sector, though, women are further disadvantaged. One of the main reasons that women are overrepresented in the informal sector is that hours, conditions, and location are relatively flexible, so that employment conflicts less with child care and other traditionally female responsibilities. These advantages, plus inferior power bases within households, also restrict women to less remunerative occupations within the informal sector. As noted above, women tend to be located in unskilled services and commerce in the informal sector, and are only infrequently in manufacturing other than textiles and beer making (Palmer [1991]). Women also tend to work in smaller, more labor-intensive enterprises within the informal sector. Detailed and dramatic evidence of these differences is provided by Shields (1980), who had access to a detailed 1971 Tanzanian urban labor market survey. Relative to their overall share in the nonformal labor market (about one-third), women were overrepresented in urban farming ("shamba"—once again important, and the main occupation of 24 percent of nonformal sector workers), street trading, hotel and bar workers, house renting, transport, and craft manufacturing; they were underrepresented as shopkeepers, in fishing, portering, and (construction) contracting. Women also had vastly higher unemployment rates than men. Including passive search, women's unemployment rates ranged from 11 percent to 43 percent for those with education at or below Form 4 level, while men's unemployment rates ranged from 5 percent to 11 percent. And, revealingly, self-employed men used five times as much capital as women in starting up businesses.

Female-headed households typically are associated with a greater likelihood of being very poor. The pattern of men and women keeping linked but separate economic units in many African households adds both to women's economic independence and to their burdens. This partial separation has been exacerbated in many regions by the development of temporary (but often very lengthy) migration for the purpose of earning cash. This migration was historically male, and took root during the colonial period. But it has hardly disappeared, and today serves to reinforce the independence of adults within a given household. The consequence of these social patterns is that female-headed households are neither a rare aberration in much of (especially non-Moslem) Africa, nor are they necessarily strongly tied in economic terms to wealthier, male-headed households.

The importance of female-headed households is emphasized by Clark (1985), who reports that 29 percent of Kenya's 1.7 million households in the late 1970s were headed by women; across Africa, the proportion headed by women is reported to range from 5 percent to 31 percent. If anything, these percentages are growing: Livingstone (1991) reports that the Kenyan 1981–82 budget survey found that more than half of the thirty districts covered had female–headed household proportions of 29–49 percent. But these averages fail to capture the full importance of female-headed households in 1) urban squatter settlements, and 2) rural areas of high population density and labor out-migration. In the case of low-income urban settlements, female household heads range from being very rare (especially when the settlement consists mainly of male migrants from rural "labor reserves") to being extremely common in areas with longer-term residents. In Nairobi, Clark's figures indicate that the proportion of households in low-income areas headed by women range from 6 to 60 (and possibly 80) percent.

The next question to be raised concerns just how large gender earning gaps are within the informal sector. There are a small number of studies of determinants of informal sector earnings. Aryee (1976) finds that standard human capital values (education and training) contribute strongly to gross earnings and value added; so, of course, does the level of capital employed and raw materials used. Informal sector employees' incomes also rise strongly with length of employment and worker's age, and firm size (see House's [1987] study of Juba, southern Sudan). Proprietors' incomes rise with education, length of operation of business (but interpretability problems arise here, since unsuccessful businesses are less likely to survive), the capital/labor ratio, local birth (migrant proprietors are less successful, although migrant employees do not earn lower wages), and location in industries with greater barriers to entry. After controlling for these factors, gender does not seem to influence earnings. But as in the formal sector earnings equations, we suspect that premarket discrimination exists; that is, women find it more difficult to accumulate the human and physical capital necessary to achieve higher earnings.

5.2.4. Is the Formal/Informal Distinction Still Valid?

It is not only wages in the formal and informal sectors that have become more similar in recent years. The security and stability of formal sector employment has declined, as labor legislation has become less effective and the region's economic crisis has deepened. In many cases employment stability regulations are now simply ignored (Weeks [1986]), and formal sector employees have no more job security than those employed in the informal sector. In situations where labor legislation is still binding, many formal sector firms subcontract part of their production process to informal sector workers in order to avoid hiring more workers protected by labor legislation. As Jamal and Weeks (1988) have noted:

> The distinction between the formal and informal sectors is becoming blurred, even breaking down. The difference in incomes that can earned in two sectors is decreasing, as is the difference in the lifestyles and living standards.

Still, some relevant differences remain between the two sectors. Perhaps no example is more telling than the estimates of the importance of agricultural activities in urban Africa (which virtually all lie outside the modern sector). In the Central African Republic (for 1975, shown in World Bank [1989i]) it is estimated that 22 percent of households in Bangui and 45 percent in other cities and towns earned *cash income* from raising food crops. For that matter, outside Bangui, 31 percent of urban households earned cash from raising cotton, 18 percent earned income from growing coffee, and 6 percent raised tobacco for cash. Comparable rural figures for households earning cash from agricultural sales are 47 percent (food), 56 percent (cotton), 18 percent (coffee), and 13 percent (tobacco/roselle). Most strikingly, 60 percent of urban households in the mining zone raised food crops for sale. While urban surpluses per household may not be large, these figures indicate the extraordinary extent of extraformal sector activities in some African urban settings. Nor is this figure unique to the Central African Republic. As noted above, 13 percent of employed workers in urban Kenya work in agriculture. From Gerry's (1974) study of Dakar, we find that 36 percent of casual workers had incomes from farming (mainly groundnut cultivation, but also rice, millet, and vegetables). And in 1985 Côte d'Ivoire, 10 percent of all income earned in urban areas outside Abidjan was from farming (only 1.5 percent of incomes in Abidjan come from farming: see Kozel [1990:24]). For the bottom and second quintiles, moreover, 23 percent and 24 percent, respectively, come from farming—slightly more than the 23 percent and 22 percent that come from wage income! Indeed, only in the top two quintiles outside Abidjan does wage income exceed nonfarm family enterprise income.

In short, there is abundant evidence that Jamal and Weeks' startling claim (1988:289), "An urban wage earner in Africa today is most likely to be simultaneously a part-time farmer and/or a petty trader in the informal sector," is true, as the overwhelming incidence of mainly agricultural workers in rural areas surely indicates that there are many part-time farmers. What they fail to mention, however, is that this pattern is hardly a new one, and probably well antedated Africa's economic crisis.

TABLE 5.6. Sources of Finance (Percentage by Source) for Initial Investment by Informal Entrepreneurs in Three African Countries.

Source	Nigeria[1]	Sierra Leone[2]	Tanzania[3]
Own savings	94	60	78
Relatives	4	20	15
Banks	1	1	1
Government	—	—	1
Money lenders	—	1	—
Other[4]	—	18	6

Key:
1. for three states, 1980
2. entire country, 1976
3. rural towns, 1968
4. includes non-responses
—less than 1 percent

Source: Liedholm and Mead (1987).

The difference in capital intensivities between firms of different sizes already has been mentioned above. Since informal sector firms are smaller (see the Page and Steel typology), they are generally less capital intensive. One reason for this is that informal sector firms rarely have access to special, subsidized lines of credit that are available to formal sector firms. As a consequence, informal firms must rely on informal sources of credit (so-called curb markets) and pay much higher interest rates (Liedholm and Mead [1987:93]). It is not surprising, then, to find that informal sector entrepreneurs rely on their own savings and relatives much more than on banks or government credit programs to obtain the funds for their initial investment. And it is equally clear that access to credit has become a critical determinant of informal sector firm success.

Table 5.6 reports the origin of initial investment funds used by informal entrepreneurs in three African countries. In none of the three countries does more than two percent of initial investment funds come from government credit programs or banks. The vast majority of funds comes from personal savings. In Tanzania, and especially in Sierra Leone, relatives contribute an important share of initial capital.

The difference in formal and informal sector capital intensity in Africa is extremely large. House (1984) finds that, given capital and labor intensities of the late 1970s in Kenya, an investment of Ksh. 200,000 in the informal sector would result in fifty-five new jobs; in the formal sector it would create only five new positions. Part of this difference is due to the larger shares of capital-intensive industries within the modern sector, but an important component also appears to reflect greater capital intensity of comparable activities. Page and Steel (1984) make these points as well, and also note that formal sector firms tend to be far more infrastructure intensive than informal sector enterprises. It is also a virtually universal stylized fact that formal sector enterprises are more skilled-labor intensive, and, being large, require more formal managerial inputs per unit of output.

The differences in capital intensities were measured in a series of International Labor Organization (ILO) studies from the mid and late 1970s (see Fowler [1981],

Fapohunda [1981], Mabogunje and Filani [1981], and Aryee [1981]). These firm-level surveys emphasized the importance of capital constraints, which were repeatedly given as a key reason for lack of expansion. Capital per informal enterprises was only $78 in Freetown, a very low mean value. It was far higher in Lagos—the mean value was about $720, and the median $400—leading one to wonder if comparable measurements were made. Still, it is easy to imagine that significant differences would emerge between informal sectors in Nigeria during an oil boom and those in the least developed countries. In Kano, the median value of capital per firm was $80, but the mean was $450; in Kumasi the mean was about $675. But even in Kumasi the capital/annual value added ratio was only 0.17, and in no subsector did it exceed one-third. These are, in general, tiny figures, especially as the studies concentrated on artisans rather than commercial enterprises and petty services.

Another important distinction between formal and informal sector firms is the ease with which they can sell their output to governments. Evidence from other regions of the world indicates that informal firms typically sell less than 1 percent of the value of their output to government; the percentage for formal sector firms is much higher. Informal entrepreneurs often complain that formal bidding procedures and other formalities associated with government purchases are unnecessarily difficult and time-consuming, and that governments are notoriously late in settling their accounts (Liedholm and Mead [1987:48, 58]).

But perhaps the most important *potential* difference between formal and informal firms is one that has received insufficient attention to date: differences in productivity between the two sectors. Clearly one must be careful which productivity measure one uses; partial productivity measures (such as the marginal productivity of capital or labor, or the value added per worker or per dollar of capital) can be quite uninformative. For example, various studies have shown that capital productivity is highest in small firms and declines with increasing firm size.[12] No one familiar with the basic tenets of neoclassical economics will be surprised by these results, given that small firms are more labor-intensive than large firms; moreover, if policy-induced distortions cause the factor proportions to differ between small and large firms, the capital productivity "gap" is driven by government policy. It does not imply that informal sector firms use capital "better" than larger firms.[13]

The most analytically correct way to examine potential productivity gaps between formal and informal firms is to employ some comprehensive measure of economic efficiency. The two main types of comprehensive measures are 1) total factor productivity and 2) economic return. Total factor productivity measures are based on a ratio of a firm's value added to a weighted average of all its scarce factor inputs, where the weights should reflect these inputs' shadow prices. Economic return measures compute the net economic return (taking into account the shadow prices of other inputs); this net return is then compared with the input's shadow price to determine whether the activity in question is more or less efficient than other potential uses of a society's resources.[14]

Several studies of this type have been done for African economies.[15] Liedholm and Mead (1987:73), for example, calculate social benefit-cost ratios (a type of total factor productivity analysis) for different industries in Sierra Leone for 1974–75. They find that the social benefit-cost ratios for informal firms (defined in this study as having less than fifty persons) exceed that for formal sector firms. The largest gap was in the wearing apparel industry, where informal firms had a ratio 264 percent larger than formal sector firms. The smallest advantage for informal firms was in the metal products industry, where their social benefit-cost ratio exceeded that of formal firms by only 9 percent. More studies of this type could indicate whether—as seems likely—informal sector firms are more efficient than formal sector firms when comprehensive efficiency measures are employed.

5.3 Rural-Urban Wage Gaps and Structural Adjustment Programs

The preceding two sections have described the heterogeneous conditions extant in African urban labor markets. Wages and employment conditions differed markedly in urban formal and informal sectors in the 1960s and early 1970s, but wage gaps have become smaller and conditions of employment more similar since then. This section will investigate what has happened to rural-urban wage gaps over the past twenty years. These trends, together with the analysis presented in the previous two sections, will allow the formulation of some tentative predictions about trends in rural-urban migration flows.

Major policy reforms currently are underway in many African countries that will further narrow or eliminate wage differentials between urban and rural areas. Macroeconomic policies are being redirected and now increasingly support an agriculture-led development strategy. In addition, financial constraints, now and over the foreseeable future, will make subsidization of urban infrastructure, urban public services, and urban-based parastatals less and less attractive.

There is copious evidence of a narrowing of rural-urban wage gaps over much of Africa:

1. *Nigeria:* Unskilled wages in 1973 were about 80 percent higher in non-agricultural occupations than in agricultural ones. Over 1973–81 real agricultural wages rose 50 percent and in other sectors fell by 15 percent. As a result by the early 1980s earnings differentials were much less pronounced so that labor should have been willing to relocate into agriculture in the event of an alteration in employment opportunities. (Collier [1985])

2. *Nigeria:* . . . living standards for the average rural household are now probably somewhat higher than for urban households in general. (World Bank [1988b])

3. *Côte d'Ivoire:* Between 1980 and 1984 there was a 25 percent decline in per capita real income. The drop in per capita income mainly affected the urban population while agricultural producer price increases helped maintain rural real incomes. The lowest 40 percent of the urban population is now worse off than its rural counterparts. (World Bank [1985f])

4. *Ghana:* In 1970, the average urban unskilled wage rate in the formal sector was twice the rate for casual farm labor. By 1984, the rural wage rate was three times higher than the official minimum wage. (World Bank [1985g])

Table 5.7 presents estimates of rural urban wage gaps culled from various sources. Despite severe problems of measuring comparable incomes (or, equivalently, determining the "natural gap" that would occur in equilibrium because of differences in demographic composition, human capital, regional prices, and amenities in urban and rural areas), two obvious characteristics stand out.[16] First, the size of the rural-urban wage gap varies dramatically over countries. The fact that some countries report wage gaps and others report income gaps is unlikely to be responsible for this variation. The two countries (Sierra Leone and Tanzania) that report income gaps have two of the largest rural-urban gaps. But since non-wage income is likely a larger percentage of total income in rural—rather than urban—areas, these gaps are more likely to be underestimated rather than over-estimated for these two countries. If widely differing rural-urban wage (and income) gaps are not a statistical artifice, then they must be due to differing government policy or divergent labor market conditions or structures.

What may be responsible for the large differences across countries? One answer is that different samples and definitions are important—whether or not the urban sample is restricted to formal sector employment and whether or not rural wages refer only to plantation or cash crop sectors are critical. The data for Senegal are particularly telling in this regard. Beyond that, mining enclave economies (e.g., Niger) appear to have high wage gaps, while countries with developed small-holder, cash crop agricultural sectors and/or declining urban formal sectors (such as Ghana in both cases) have lower gaps.

Differences in the skill composition of migrants and labor forces also may be important. The "gap" appears large in Kenya, but it is a country with one of the most skilled migration flows in the Third World. When Rempel (1981:95) compares actual income gains from migration, he finds an average gain of 122 percent for those with primary education, and a gain of 51 percent for those with secondary education. These gains are far from trivial, but are smaller than would be suggested by the unadjusted gap estimates.

The second salient characteristic of Table 5.7 is that for nearly all of the countries for which there is time series evidence, the rural-urban wage gap in the 1980s is far lower than in the late 1960s or early 1970s. A more recent narrowing of wage gaps also appears to be taking place in Côte d'Ivoire, and the World Bank study of Togo (1989h) reports a similar recent narrowing. Thus, it seems that the fears expressed by some development economists and policymakers or ever-widening rural-urban gaps were misplaced. Rural-urban gaps have narrowed, and the evidence presented in Table 5.7 suggests that they have narrowed considerably. Over one-third of the gap was closed in Tanzania from 1969 to 1983/84, while Sierra Leone eliminated almost 40 percent of the gap in the 1970s. Malawi closed the entire urban-rural wage gap between 1969 and 1977; in the latter year, average agricultural wages actually exceeded urban minimum wages.

An important point not apparent from Table 5.7 is that rural-urban gaps gloss over an important dispersion in rural incomes as well as urban ones. There is little doubt that earnings in prosperous farming districts in many (and probably most) African countries are currently close to urban averages for unskilled and semi-skilled labor. That is, many regions do not have large gaps, and such migration that takes place presumably reflects normal flows in a labor market reasonably characterized by neoclassical equilibrium models.

But virtually all countries also have rural areas with extreme poverty, with mean wages and incomes far below the urban mean wage. For these regions, often fairly far from urban centers, huge gaps continue to exist despite the narrowing forces due to urban deterioration and the subsequent structural adjustment policies.

A few examples will illustrate this point. In Ghana, for example, the incidence of "poverty" in urban areas in 1975 was 53 percent (World Bank [1989k]). Rural poverty incidence, on the other hand, ranged from 47 percent near Accra and 66 percent in Western Region to 94 percent in Volta Region and 96 percent in Upper Region. In Togo in 1980, per capita income in rural Plateaux Region was 2.3 times that of rural Kara Region—though this gap had narrowed from 3.7 in 1969 (World Bank [1989h]). In Côte d'Ivoire (1984), rural per capita incomes in the south were 65 percent greater than in the northern part of the country; thus, per capita earnings in the Forest Region were 16 percent higher than average urban unskilled earnings, while in the Savanna Region average earnings were 29 percent lower. In Senegal, rural GDP per labor force participant in Cap Vert is 7.14 times that of Senegal Oriental and 7.20 times that of rural Casamance; for rural Thies the ratios relative to the poorer regions are 2.31 and 2.33, respectively.

What these figures indicate is that the "gap" is not merely an urban/rural one. Rather, rural areas near large cities often become part of the "enclave" and participate in the enclave labor market. These areas have the best infrastructure and produce locally consumed food crops. Further infrastructural investments in these rural areas may have quite neoclassical effects—that is, they may raise the opportunity costs of migrating, and hence will slow urban growth. In contrast, extension of roads and schooling to remote rural areas may improve the accessibility of towns but are unlikely to close the huge gaps that exist, and therefore may well accelerate rural-urban migration.

5.4 The AIDS Pandemic, African Labor Markets, and Economic Growth

The optimistic scenario charted above—structural adjustment policies leading to sustained economic growth free of urban bias—is certainly a possibility for African nations. At the same time as countries undergo structural adjustment, however, they are under attack from a most serious epidemic. The pandemic is presently surging with very limited control, especially though eastern and central Africa. Will the AIDS pandemic counteract the gains just beginning to be seen from structural adjustment programs? This section examines the consequences of the AIDS epidemic on the African countries' populations, labor forces, and economic growth prospects. We argue that while the human costs of AIDS will be staggering, the economic costs—narrowly defined—may not be that large.[17]

The first step in any effort to gauge the impact of the AIDS pandemic must be to gauge the magnitude of HIV infection rates and the incidence of AIDS in African countries. The World Health Organization (1988) estimates that there were roughly twelve thousand cases of AIDS throughout Africa as of June 1988—a number that doubled from the October 1977 level. This figure almost certainly represents a considerable underestimate, both because of poor coverage and because of reporting lags.

It is clear, however, that AIDS is a highly concentrated disease in Africa. Some 91 percent of the recorded cases occur in a ten-country belt that proceeds from

TABLE 5.7. Estimates of Rural Urban Wage Gaps for Selected African Countries, 1967–1984

West Africa	1967	1970/71	1974/77	1980/81	1984	1985
Burkina Faso[1,3]	7.3(1960)[25]		1.40	6.8[25]		
Côte d'Ivoire				3.6[15]	2.5[15]	
Abidjan				1.03[16]		2.8; 3.3[23]
Other urban areas						1.9; 2.2[23]
Gambia[18]					2.8	4.5
Ghana[1,4]	1.33			0.5[18]		
Mali[25]	12.8 (1960)					
Niger[1,3]			2.94		3.7	
Nigeria	4.6 (1969-70)[24]	3.4 (1973-4)[20] 1.1 (1973-4)[21]		1.9[18] 6.6[24] 3.8 (1975-6)[20] 1.5 (1975-6)[21]	4.6(1982-3)[24] 4.7 (1978-9)[20] 1.0 (1978-9)[21]	
Senegal[1,3]	16.6(1960)[25]		1.07 4.0[11]/3.4[12]/1.6[13]/0.6[14]	7.7[25]		
Sierra Leone[2,5]		6.07 6.0[24] 1.3[22]	4.05	2.0[18] 4.1[24] 0.7[22]	3.5 (1982-3)[24] 0.6 (1982-3)[22]	
Cameroon[9,10]				4.5[18]	3.0–4.4	
Togo[25]	3.3 (1960)				5.8	

East and Southern Africa	1962	1969	1972	1976/77	1977	1980	1983/84	1985
Burundi[18]						6.7	12.3	11.5
Kenya[1,6]	2.5–3.3[17]	7.4[24]	2.5	5.4(1973-4)[24]		4.8[18]	4.1(1982-3)[24]	4.9[18]
Madagascar						1.8–2.4[17]		
Malawi[1,7]		1.40			0.94	5.0[18]	3.6[18]	
		10.5[19]						
		3.91						
Tanzania[2,8]				2.46		3.7[18]	2.90	7.5[19]
Zambia[18]						6.8	4.8	

Notes:

1 wage income
2 total individual income
3 from Cohen (1979); rural-urban wage ratio defined as manufacturing wage divided by agricultural wage
4 from Kannapan (1983:143).
5 from Jamal and Weeks (1988).
6 from Rempel and House (1978).
7 from Ghai and Radwan (1983a); rural urban wage ratio defined as minimum urban wage divided by average agricultural wages.
8 from Bevan et al. (1988).
9 average annual expenditure per household
10 from World Bank (1989d)
11 modern sector unskilled workers and apprentices, divided by average income per rural worker, 1975; World Bank (1989j)
12 informal sector self employed, divided by average income per rural worker, 1975; World Bank (1989j)
13 informal sector laborers and journeymen earnings divided by average income per rural worker, 1975; World Bank (1989j)
14 earnings of informal sector apprentices divided by average income per rural worker, 1975; World Bank (1989j)
15 per capita disposable income, all urban vs. rural; World Bank (1989f)
16 unskilled urban vs. all rural per cap. disp. income; World Bank (1989f)
17 ratios of per family incomes for secondary urban centers and largest 6 towns, respectively, to rural family incomes. Pryor (1988)
18 average manufacturing wage as a multiple of average agricultural income; UNDP/World Bank (1992)
19 Pryor (1988a:52); average family income in big towns vs smallholders.
20 Jamal and Weeks (1988:278); average family income, urban vs. rural.
21 Jamal and weeks (1988:278); average urban unskilled wage / average rural family income ...
22 Jamal and Weeks (1988:280); average urban unskilled wage income / average agricultural income, per capita
23 Kozel (1990); urban/rural (1) per household and (2) adjusted per capita incomes
24 Weeks (1986); per capita family income in rural and urban areas; urban unskilled households
25 Jamal (1984); average urban and rural incomes

Kenya and Tanzania on the Indian Ocean to Congo and Zaire on the South Atlantic. It is also clear that the incidence of the HIV virus is quite high, and eventually will lead to a vastly greater number of AIDS victims. As Becker's (1990) survey details, *urban* incidence rates vary between roughly 2.5 percent and 20 percent or even 25 percent of the population aged 15–44. Rural HIV incidence in the AIDS belt is on average much lower than the rates recorded in the cities, although rural infection rates in the core area of Rwanda, Burundi, southern Uganda, and the Kagera Region of Tanzania may rival or even exceed those of major cities.

While it is possible to estimate current HIV incidence levels, projecting growth rates is quite difficult. Simple extrapolation of initial growth rates over time clearly is inappropriate, since the virus first will spread rapidly among those with high-risk behavior, leaving an uninfected population with decreasingly risky behavior. Consequently, the rate of growth of transmission must decline as high-risk groups become saturated.

Current projections suggest that without major behavioral changes with regard to numbers of sexual partners or condom use, and without effective sexually transmitted disease (STD) control, HIV incidence within the general population is likely to rise to 10–15 percent in the next fifteen to twenty years, and then level out. This estimate is consistent with a "back of the envelope" calculation: roughly half of the population is outside of the prime infection age group (zero to one and fifteen to forty). Within the most susceptible age group, probably 60–75 percent of the population does not display high-risk behavior and/or lives in areas with few linkages to vectors of infection. Consequently, near saturation of the at-risk group would imply a national infection rate of 10–20 percent.

The next step in estimating the future incidence of AIDS is to gauge what percentage of HIV-positive individuals will contract AIDS in any given year. Haq (1988a) estimates that 2–5 percent of HIV-infected persons in Africa develop AIDS annually. This figure, however, is computed for populations that have yet to reach steady-state infection rates. Because the infection rate is growing, there will be a relatively large number who contracted the infection recently. It is therefore reasonable to expect that conversion rates will rise, possibly to 5–8 percent by the early twenty-first century.

Table 5.8 combines HIV infection possibilities with a plausible conversion rate range. The implied 1990 AIDS mortality for a country like Uganda, with a population of roughly sixteen million, a present seropositive incidence of perhaps 1.5 percent and a conversion rate of possibly 2 percent, is 4,800—roughly twice the number reported in 1987. If HIV incidence rises to 10 percent by 2008 and the conversion rate rises to 5 percent, the number of AIDS deaths per 100,000 people will rise from perhaps 30 to 500. These, unfortunately, are not implausible numbers, although effective intervention may prevent full realization of the disaster. The most tragic numbers, however, come from the cohort-specific projections. For women, AIDS is a disease of the young—often of young mothers. For men, it is an older disease, but strikes at the group with the highest labor force participation rates.

But even a "worst-case scenario" (which is somewhat arbitrarily taken to be an infection rate of 15 percent and a conversion rate of 8 percent, implying that 1.25 percent of the population will die from AIDS annually) itself will not give rise to depopulation.[18] On the contrary, with regional crude birth rates near fifty and non-

AIDS death rates of about sixteen, the World Bank (1989a) projects population growth rates for East and central Africa ranging from 2.3 percent (Botswana) to 3.9 percent (Kenya) for the period 1987–2000. A scenario of 500 deaths per 100,000 would lower the unweighted mean regional population growth rate from 3.3 percent to 2.8 percent, still among the highest in the world.

Despite the small impact of AIDS on population growth rates, the pandemic will impose economic costs on African economies. Two types of direct costs can be readily quantified: direct medical costs and losses in labor productivity entailed by the disease.

Direct medical costs are rather small, mainly because health care systems in East and central Africa are poor. Poor health care facilities reflect the region's underlying poverty; per capita public expenditures on health care are tiny, and households generally are too poor to pay for expensive private treatment.[19] Over et al.'s (1988) estimate of total direct costs of the HIV infection per symptomatic *adult* were:

	Direct Cost		Direct Cost/ GNP per capita	
	Low	High	Low	High
Tanzania	$104	$631	0.36	2.18
Zaire	132	1,585	0.78	9.32
USA	27,571	50,380	1.65	3.02

(all values are in 1985 U.S. dollars)

In these estimates, Over et al. assumed that all symptomatic, HIV-infected adults would seek at least some modern sector treatment. The low cost estimates correspond to what can be obtained without direct charge; the high cost estimates are based on the costs of the best available private treatment.

A much larger cost from the pandemic will be lost productive labor. In Africa and elsewhere, AIDS is most prevalent among prime age persons. It is also concentrated in urban areas, where labor productivity (computed at domestic prices) is considerably above that of rural areas.[20] Over et al. calculate the number future years of healthy life lost by an average HIV-infected person (incorporating a year lost to disability as a portion of a year lost to death). They then assign productivity weights for different age ranges to obtain an estimate of productive healthy life years lost per case. By multiplying these estimates by average adult (full productivity) incomes for different groups and discounting future incomes to present value, they obtain a dollar value of the average future healthy life years lost to AIDS in Zaire and Tanzania. These values range from $144 for a rural resident in Zaire, to $5,093 for a high-school educated, urban resident of Tanzania (Over et al. [1988:Table 3]). But in terms of the discounted value of productivity-weighted healthy life years saved per case prevented, AIDS ranks behind (in order of importance) sickle cell anemia, neonatal tetanus, birth injuries, and severe malnutrition; it ranks ahead of cerebrovascular disease, child pneumonia, tuberculosis, measles, accidents, malaria, adult pneumonia, prematurity, and gastroenteritis.

The ultimate impact on (gross national product) GNP will depend on the yearly productivity costs per AIDS case and the weights of different socioeconomic

TABLE 5.8. AIDS Mortality Forecasts for Central Africa

(a) AIDS incidence, per hundred thousand

HIV infection rate	HIV-AIDS conversion rate, percent per annum				
	2%	4%	5%	7%	8%
1.0%	20	40	50		
2.0	30	60	75		
4.0		160	200	280	
6.0		240	300	420	
8.0			400	560	640
10.0			500	700	800

(b) AIDS mortality by cohort, assuming a national infection rate of 8%

Cohort	Group-Specific Infection Rate		Mortality Probability from AIDS, Percent		Percentage Increase in Cohort Mortality due to AIDS	
	Male	Female	Male	Female	Male	Female
<1	14.80	14.16	2.68	2.54	22.2	20.1
1–4	1.60	2.56	0.91	0.99	6.0	5.7
5–9	1.68	2.48	0.92	1.28	47.7	56.9
10–14	1.76	14.48	0.82	2.30	113.9	310.8
15–19	7.52	15.44	1.44	6.82	221.5	483.7
20–24	11.60	18.40	4.66	8.33	480.4	433.9
25–29	11.36	10.80	5.23	7.56	458.8	350.0
30–34	16.80	11.28	5.56	5.17	386.1	195.8
35–39	16.32	13.44	7.59	5.20	358.0	168.8
40–44	10.00	12.64	6.01	6.70	210.9	210.0
45–49	10.72	3.76	5.08	5.87	122.1	160.4
50–54	9.60	3.76	4.56	1.79	74.3	39.4
55–59	11.76	0.00	5.71	1.72	63.6	28.3
60–64	7.44	0.00	3.73	0.00	25.9	0.0
65+	4.40	0.00	4.10	0.00	20.0	0.0

Source: Taken from Becker [1990]. Infection rate distribution based on Quinn's [1986] estimates for Kinshasa, and is assumed to remain stable regardless of infection rate. Population distribution needed to obtain infection rates is taken from Zambia (Zairan data are unavailable): United Nations [1984: Table 2]. Infection-AIDS and AIDS-mortality conversion rates are taken from Bulatao's [1987] medium run assumptions. Cohort mortality rates are taken from Table 13, Hypothetical West African Model Life Tables, in United Nations [1982b].

classes among those infected. The total effect on GNP is likely to be quite small; even if all AIDS victims were in the labor force and had mean incomes equal to urban workers with a primary school education, an AIDS incidence of 500/100,000 would mean a permanent GNP reduction of 0.8 percent in Tanzania and 1.0 percent in Zaire. If victims were assumed to earn incomes equal to the mean for urban workers with secondary education, AIDS would result in direct labor productivity losses of at most 1.5–2.0 percent of GNP. Counting in medical costs and withdrawals from the labor market by others to help take care of the ill might possibly double these figures, but an estimate of 3–4 percent surely is an upper bound.[21] These figures are unfortunate, but are not nearly as large as the fluctuations caused by export and import price trends, or by fluctuations in the effectiveness of government policy.

While these costs will be difficult to bear for nations as poor as those in East and central Africa, they would not be unbearable in a rapidly growing country. Thus, one further crucial question must be addressed: does the AIDS pandemic unleash forces that are likely to cause long-run *growth rates* to decline in addition to those that will certainly depress income *levels*? While the answer can be offered only qualitatively, it appears that such forces do exist.

Given sub-Saharan Africa's very low rates of domestic capital formation and savings since the mid-1970s, the effect of AIDS on saving rates is crucial.[22] While foreign capital inflows can substitute for domestic savings, many East and central African nations have exhausted commercial credit facilities and are attracting few private investors. There can be little doubt that the AIDS crisis will act as yet another deterrent to direct private foreign investment in the region.

If the pandemic is likely to tighten the already limited inflow of nonaid capital, maintenance of domestic capital formation requires additional domestic savings. Unfortunately, the AIDS pandemic may depress these as well. The immediate impact of the pandemic will be on government savings, which almost certainly will be reduced. The public sector will be pressured to allocate more of its budget to health care services and associated capital expenditures. These added spending demands could be offset by higher taxation, but the scope for obtaining additional tax revenue often is not great. Consequently, diversion is likely to come from capital investments or infrastructure maintenance. Another alternative involves running a larger deficit, that is, using private savings to finance health care needs. Whether this is done by formal borrowing or inflationary finance, government savings will still decline.

Corporate savings also are likely to decline. In many affected countries, parastatals dominate the corporate economy, and even the private corporate sector is subject to much government intervention. While parastatals currently are under great pressure to increase retained earnings, and hence savings, they undoubtedly will face extraordinary pressure to cover the AIDS-related medical costs of their employees. They may also face strong pressure to retain ill employees on the payroll.

The impact of the pandemic on private savings is less clear. Since individuals (even those who are not currently seropositive) rationally expect to live shorter lives, there is less incentive to save for future needs. That is, it is no longer rational to defer consumption, since the likelihood of being alive to enjoy the consumption stream is diminished. On the other hand, reduced life expectancies imply that income earners must save at a higher rate in order to meet expected bequest targets, and for consumption during a possible period of prolonged illness. Especially given the emphasis on intergenerational continuity in many African societies, government programs that encourage private savings might generate a surprisingly large response. A precondition for this success, however, is confidence in government's ability to handle both the AIDS crisis and the ongoing economic crisis.

In sum, then, the AIDS pandemic is likely to lower gross domestic savings, principally through its affect on government and corporate saving. Combined with the disincentive to private foreign investment, the AIDS pandemic has the potential to affect future growth rates above and beyond the magnitudes suggested by the calculation of static medical and labor productivity costs. As a primarily urban disease, it will further retard the recovery of Africa's urban economies. It will also have some impact (but probably a modest one in all but a few countries) on urban population growth rates, both because of the direct impact of increasing urban mortality and because of the indirect effect of reducing urban economic growth and labor demand.

6

Neoclassical Models of Urbanization and Competing Paradigms

6.1 Modeling Migration: Four Theoretical Models[1]

The challenge for economists and demographers has been to devise theoretical models that accurately describe Africa's rapid urbanization. This chapter briefly presents the assumptions and theoretical underpinnings of several models, and then provides empirical tests of their applicability to Africa. Yet a crucially important cautionary note must be sounded at the outset: extreme care must be used when empirical tests of these models are undertaken. Many authors have conducted tests of one of these hypotheses, confident that they were testing *only* its appropriateness.

As we saw in Chapter 4, there are numerous economic models of migration and labor market behavior that can be applied in African settings. Here, we will focus on four key models that represent generally competing philosophic approaches. The set includes a geographic spatial interaction framework, a modified neoclassical economic model, a non-neoclassical economic model based on rent-seeking behavior in the urban formal sector, and a demographic cohort shift model. As we show later in this chapter and in the appendices, however, the estimating equations for these different models are quite similar. Thus, results which "confirm" the validity of one model may equally well confirm the validity of a competing model. We refer to this problem as one of *observational equivalence* of competing hypotheses. By carefully examining the estimating equations or other implications of the various types of models, we will derive estimating equations that do allow the competing paradigms to be distinguished from one another. Before turning to this issue, however, we briefly describe the competing migration models.

The salient characteristic of neoclassical migration models is that production and demand conditions are carefully specified. While individuals migrate in search of higher wages in destination areas, the conditions that generate observed employment and wages are carefully laid out. These models can be adapted to include informal and service sector employment in urban areas, various assumptions about worker and job characteristics, and even foreign trade issues (for a detailed modeling discussion and mathematical statement, see Becker and Morrison [1988]). An econometric statement of a labor surplus model would be virtually identical to the neoclassical model, except that it would emphasize urban formal sector characteristics more heavily than rural forces. The Harris-Todaro model presented in Chapter 4 builds on a neoclassical framework, but adds an institutionally determined wage rate in modern sector production.

A second type of model, known by geographers as the spatial interaction or gravity model, is based upon an analogy to Newtonian physics. Factors affecting the migration decision typically are separated into origin, destination, and linking factors. Many empirical tests of the gravity model have been performed. Although the simplest version of the gravity model includes only origin and destination populations and the distance separating the origin from the destination, extended gravity models contain other factors as well. A typical empirical test includes measures of origin and destination income levels, unemployment rates, educational levels, urbanization levels, distance separating origin and destination levels, and contacts that migrants may have in destination regions. Yap (1977) provides a concise summary of the results of this type of empirical investigation.

Spatial interaction models are the source of the time-worn discussion of the relative importance of push and pull factors in the migration decision. Economists have criticized these models as lacking a sound theoretical base, but it is possible, as Niedercorn and Bechdolt (1969) show, to derive a simple gravity model from a utility-maximizing framework. Moreover, recent gravity models (such as Foot and Milne [1984]) are more sophisticated than their early predecessors, and generally include the same variables that are found in a reduced form equation derived from a neoclassical migration model. Perhaps a more justified criticism of spatial interaction models is that they suggest that origin and destination factors can be studied in isolation—a demonstrably false assumption. Events in urban labor markets, for example, certainly affect wages in rural labor markets, and vice versa. This remains the key distinction between spatial interaction and neoclassical models; neoclassical models begin with multi-sector labor market equilibrium behavior derived from demand and production functions, while spatial interaction models, in their most rigorous formulations, begin with a more general utility-maximizing postulate, but tend to be more partial equilibrium in practice.[2]

A third type of migration model describes rent-seeking behavior by workers. It is based in the neoclassical tradition in the sense that migration is assumed to be a market equilibrating response to differential opportunities, but the rent-seeking approach models labor markets quite differently. As in the Harris-Todaro model, formal sector workers are assumed to be paid a wage above the opportunity cost of labor in rural areas. This model diverges from the Harris-Todaro model in that the formal sector wage is not an institutionally fixed minimum wage, but rather varies with labor's ability to capture firms' economic rents. The type of labor behavior predicted by this model is clear: because workers are being paid more than their marginal product (certainly at world prices and probably even at artificially inflated domestic prices), they fiercely oppose any efforts to reduce employment and prefer to accept wage declines when firm profitability falls.

The fourth type of migration model that will be surveyed in this chapter is a demographic cohort shift (DCS) model. This model is constructed to highlight the key role that increasing education levels and declining mortality rates have played in Africa's urban explosion. Indeed, it is a stylized fact of the migration literature that younger and more highly educated individuals are more likely to migrate than older and less well educated individuals. The effect of a broadening in the base of the age pyramid and increasing education levels, then, has been to swell the number of individuals who are prime candidates to migrate to urban areas. The use of a demographic cohort shift model will allow us to estimate the effects on urbanization of the expansion in primary and secondary education in Africa during the 1960s and 1970s. Equally importantly, it will allow us to predict the effects of economic crisis—as reflected in falling educational levels and rising mortality rates[3]—on urbanization in coming years.

Beyond distinguishing among models, it is important to recognize differences in dimension and aggregation. First, because of the paucity of plausible time series or panel data, virtually all empirical studies to date have examined the sources of variation in migration behavior across a sample drawn at a given instant. Results from these cross-sectional studies are then used to infer, implicitly or explicitly, likely migration patterns over time. (Similar assumptions are made in inferring likely demographic trends). While this approach is fairly reasonable—especially given an absence of alternatives—for medium-run behavior, the practice of extrapolating from cross-sectional results is highly questionable for very long-run behavior.

Secondly, the migration functions reported in Chapter 4 came either from true micro—household—surveys, or were based on district level observations. The empirical work provided below examines migration at two different levels of aggregation. At the most aggregated level, we look at the determinants of growth of entire urban populations, using a cross-country data set in the spirit of most of the aggregate urbanization models. In addition, we examine determinants of the growth of individual towns and cities in a particular country, Zambia.

We now turn to a presentation of these different migration and urbanization models which we have estimated for the sub-Saharan African countries. After presenting the models and results in more detail, we will return to the issue of observational equivalence and suggest modeling and estimation strategies that will avoid this pitfall.

6.2 A Neoclassical Model of Urbanization[4]

The neoclassical model of urbanization presented in this section integrates the "push" and "pull" factors that spatial interaction models treat as separable. Only by examining many factors simultaneously can one determine whether economic variables exert systematic impacts on urban growth in African countries, and, if so, the size, sign, and importance of these impacts. In developing the neoclassical model we will pay particular attention to identifying variables that can be controlled or at least influenced by government policy, since these indicate the extent to which public policy can alter the rate of urban growth. Indeed, since African economies have not demonstrated the sort of growth pole factors normally associated with rapid urbanization, it is conceivable that government policies or rural "push" factors have accounted for a large share of urban growth.

The formal model is tested against a cross-country sample of African nations for the period 1970–80. The assumption implicit in this approach is that a single model is applicable to the entire continent; while such a strong assumption certainly is not ideal, there are no feasible alternatives. If one scorns the strong assumptions inherent in cross-sectional modeling, one must then opt either for time series analysis of an individual country's urbanization experience (impossible, given the infrequency with which urbanization data are collected—usually only in census years), or for cross-sectional analysis of an individual country's interprovincial migration flows. Moreover, techniques are available to allow for regional variation in economic structure. The simplest, of course, is to create dummy variables representing a region within which countries share certain economic or social characteristics. Even if some variations in structure are accounted for, however, the limitations of this approach must be acknowledged. Clearly, a cross-sectional neoclassical model—or any cross-sectional model, for that matter, that analyzes the determinants of variation in urban growth experiences—will only enable us to identify factors responsible for urbanization that are common to all African nations, and that actually vary in importance across countries.

As emphasized above, perhaps the key feature of neoclassical migration models is their focus on labor markets as the key to understanding migration behavior. African cities, however, are not just composed of laborers: young children, elderly or retired individuals, and many others may not participate in the labor force. To go from a discussion of labor markets to a discussion of urban population, one needs to bridge the gap between labor force participants and urban population. This bridge is provided by the labor force participation rate. For a given number of migrants entering the urban labor force, the increment to urban population will be larger the smaller is the labor force participation rate. In other words, the more dependents that accompany a migrant, the larger will be the contribution to urban growth of an individual's decision to migrate to the city.

Unfortunately, data detailing African urban labor force participation rates are not available. Since the ideal bridge is missing, we are forced to use national labor force participation rates rather than rates specifically for urban areas.[5] Even national labor force participation rate data suffer from severe comparability problems between countries. This data shortcoming is a major problem in our analysis. Even if our model tracks labor force growth very well, it may track urban population growth much less well if the link between labor force growth and population growth is attenuated due to weak or noncomparable data.

The neoclassical model we employ builds on Harris and Todaro's (1970) model that incorporates unemployment in urban areas, but our model is richer in certain respects. Specifically, like Cole and Sanders (1985) and Steel and Takagi (1983), our labor force model contains three productive sectors: an urban modern/formal sector, an urban traditional/informal sector, and a rural sector. The urban formal sector produces import-substituting goods, infrastructure, public services, services consumed by government, and other modern services. This sector reflects the presence in African cities of a small (in terms of national employment share), but important (in terms of contribution to gross domestic product [GDP]) modern sector that produces either nontradable goods (principally services) or tradable goods with the aid of tariffs and quantitative restrictions that limit the competitiveness of imported goods. The urban informal sector is composed of small firms, generally using labor-intensive methods, that produce consumer goods and services, as well as a few inputs that are used by formal sector firms. Although we alternately label the sector "traditional," we recognize that it contains many dynamic enterprises and serves as a fertile training ground for workers (see Chapter 5 and Steel and Takagi [1983]). The links between modern/formal and traditional/informal production are not limited to supply relations, though. The incomes generated in the two sectors will in part determine the demand for the two outputs in a general equilibrium framework.

The last group of workers in urban areas are those who are openly unemployed. The size of this group will depend on the level of per capita income in an economy, since the ability to finance job search while unemployed hinges on the amount of accumulated resources. Since workers do not migrate to urban areas with unemployment as their goal, these individuals can be thought of as (generally temporary) losers in the Harris-Todaro (HT) gamble. Thus, we incorporate the presence of the urban unemployed in the neoclassical migration model by including HT modern sector wage and migration equations. Note that the presence of open unemployment may be consistent with the presence of an urban informal sector with costless job entry. Some individuals will choose unemployment over employment in the urban informal sector because full-time employment in the informal sector either is incompatible with job search or lowers the effectiveness of such search activity in the formal sector.

The rural sector produces exports, food, and locally consumed nonagricultural items. Our specification of rural production and labor markets is a simple one, largely because data scarcity renders more sophisticated specifications irrelevant. This simplicity should not obscure the crucial importance of this sector in the migration model, since the urban wage structure will depend on the opportunity cost of labor in rural areas.

The model is not a fully consistent general equilibrium model, but it does capture most of the essential interactions. The number of sectors incorporated reflects the need to keep the model analytically tractable and to ensure that the resulting urban growth equations are empirically estimable. In the formal sector there are certainly major differences in labor intensities and capital vintages of different industries, so treating formal sector employment and capital as homogeneous entities suppresses relevant distinctions. But excessive detail leads to the loss of precious degrees of freedom in estimation, both directly and through the loss of observations by imposing more stringent data requirements. In short, while it would be desirable to divide the formal sector into labor-intensive and skill-/capital-intensive components, data and estimation considerations prevent us from making this division.

Let us turn now as a heuristic description of the workings of a neoclassical urbanization model is presented. A more complete, mathematical statement of the model appears in Appendix 6A.

The urban labor force is simply the sum of individuals working in the urban formal and informal sectors, plus the urban unemployed. Any change in the labor force will increase urban population by some multiple, with the exact multiple determined by the dependency ratio, or its inverse, the labor force participation rate.

The first step in developing a neoclassical model of urbanization is to describe how the number of workers in the urban formal and urban informal sectors is determined. Urban modern employment is determined by the sum of labor demands of all firms in the formal sector, given that labor supply is infinitely elastic at the (high) formal sector wage. Factor demands, in turn, are determined by the type of production function that is specified for this sector and by demand conditions for formal sector output. Urban modern production uses labor, inputs from the urban informal sector, capital, and imported inputs. Labor demand in the urban modern sector consequently is a function of the formal sector wage, the prices of the other inputs used in modern sector, the formal sector capital stock, as well as the factors that determine the demand for urban modern output.

Special care must be taken in the formulation of demand conditions for output. Since urban modern/formal sector production often substitutes for imports, demand for domestically produced output will rise as the price of imported goods rises. The price of imports, of course, must reflect any tariff or quota protection offered to domestic firms. Demand for formal sector goods typically also will depend on the amount of government spending, given governments' high propensity to consume these types of goods and services. Finally, since formal sector products generally are not inferior goods, urban modern output will depend on the level of national income or GDP. Specifically, since the weighted income elasticity of demand for formal sector goods is likely to exceed unity, urban formal (and, indirectly, informal) sector labor demand will grow more rapidly than rural labor demand as GDP rises.

Finally, the "stylized fact" is that African formal sectors are almost always subject to minimum wage legislation, and we follow HT and consequently impose the constraint of an institutionally imposed modern sector wage. As we have seen in Chapter 4, it is unclear that minimum wages or government wage policies ever determined the overall formal sector wage structure in many African countries, but the assumption may be a reasonable one for the 1970s (in any event, it turns out that reliable wage data cannot be obtained for a sufficient sample of countries, so that wage terms are omitted from the regressions reported below). Taken as a general, simplified statement, though, the model's formulation of formal sector labor demand captures some of the most important characteristics of modern sector production in Africa: linkages between the modern and traditional sectors, dependence upon imported inputs for production, and ubiquitous minimum wage legislation.

The informal sector model statement is simpler than its modern counterpart. It uses only capital and labor in production, and both the quantity and price of its labor inputs are determined competitively. Hence, labor demand in this sector is a function of informal sector wages, capital stocks, and the prices of traditional output. For a variety of reasons a demand equation for informal sector output is not specified. Most critically, neither informal sector output price nor most of its determinants are observable, and those observable determinants that could be used as instruments generally would appear in the reduced form estimating equations in any case (without any change in predicted sign).

When the labor force engaged in urban formal and informal sectors are summed, this total depends upon the following factors:

1) urban formal sector (minimum) wage
2) price of imported inputs into formal sector production
3) urban informal sector capital stock
4) urban formal sector capital stock
5) government spending
6) gross domestic product
7) price of imported goods that compete with formal sector products
8) urban informal sector wage

A change in any of these factors will change the number of individuals involved in urban production, and consequently change urban employment and population.

The one urban group yet to be discussed is the urban unemployed. As described in Chapter 4, open urban unemployment discourages migration to urban areas by lowering the probability of obtaining employment in the urban formal sector. Another way of expressing this is that urban unemployment depends upon the probability of obtaining a formal sector job and on the size of the urban formal sector labor force. Since the equilibrium condition of the Harris-Todaro model requires that expected wages in rural and urban areas be equal, the probability of getting a job is exactly equal to the ratio of the urban formal sector wage to the rural wage (assuming infinite rates of labor turnover; otherwise, the probability will differ, but generally will be related to the wage ratio: see Blomqvist [1981]). Thus, it is possible to express urban unemployment as a function of the size of the urban formal sector labor force and the ratio of the formal sector wage to the rural wage. If no new formal sector jobs are created and the urban formal sector labor force increases, the probability of obtaining a modern sector job falls. In other words, an increase in the urban labor force, with all other factors held constant, reduces migration since the number of unemployed individuals rises.

Once the expression for the determinants of the number of urban unemployed is derived, the expression for the urban labor force is complete. Workers in both traditional and modern urban sectors have been accounted for, as have unemployed individuals. It is straightforward to estimate a reduced form equation containing the determinants of these sectors' sizes to discover which factors (and which sectors) have been responsible for Africa's rapid urbanization.[6] This is the basic neoclassical model of urbanization. The model contains strong simplifying assumptions, but has the advantage of being reducible to a single estimating equation. This is an important consideration when confronting sparse African data, since complex models make demanding data requirements.

6.2.1 Variants of the Standard Neoclassical Model

The reduced form equation derived in the preceding section rests upon some rather strong assumptions. One of these, discussed more fully in Appendix 6A, is that the average product of labor in agriculture is constant, no matter what level of output is produced. One condition that can generate such an outcome is an infinite supply of marginal land, which as a simplifying assumption is appropriate for many though hardly all African countries, and which is formally modeled by Hansen (1979). If the assumption of an unlimited supply of rural land is removed, the estimating equation remains a single equation, reduced form expression, with one additional explanatory variable (a rural output elasticity) added. However, as can be seen from equation (6.A.10), the resulting estimating equation will be even more complicated than (6.A.12).

The removal of other assumptions introduces more serious complications into the neoclassical model. One assumption implicit in the model is that while import-substituting industries use imported inputs to produce their output, foreign exchange is always available for domestic producers to purchase these imported inputs. Periodic foreign exchange crises in African countries are of course quite common. Thus, it is reasonable to introduce a foreign exchange constraint into the model. Foreign exchange can be obtained by rural exports, other exports (typically urban modern industries that process raw materials for export), or by foreign capital inflows (foreign aid, short-term loans, private investments). Foreign exchange is spent on inputs into urban formal sector production and other imports (principally consumer goods and food).

The introduction of a foreign exchange constraint makes the exchange rate endogenous in the neoclassical urbanization model. Changes in the distribution of population between rural and urban areas affect both the supply of rural exports and the demand for imported inputs, and thus, indirectly, the equilibrium exchange rate. The exchange rate, in turn, affects the amount of foreign capital inflow and exports, as well as the domestic price of imported inputs. To the extent that imported inputs are unimportant in urban formal sector production and that exports and foreign capital inflows are insensitive to movements in the exchange rate, the error caused by treating the exchange rate as exogenous is minor. But these assumptions are clearly inappropriate for many African nations. If the exchange rate is endogenously determined, single equation estimation is no longer appropriate; a simultaneous equations system must be estimated with one equation describing the determinants of rural population and the other describing the determinants of urban population.[7]

Other assumptions made to enable single equation estimation can be relaxed as well. Rural intermediate goods can be incorporated into urban modern sector production—a desirable feature in economies in which agricultural or minerals' processing are important industries. It is also possible to close the demand side by adding an equilibrium condition equating the supply and demand for rural output. Given Walras' Law (an accounting identity which reminds us that if $n - 1$ markets clear, the nth must clear as well), rural demand specification also implies urban demand specification in aggregate, as long as one can safely ignore imports of consumer goods. But either of these steps precludes single equation estimation.

The mathematical treatment of these issues is presented in Appendix 6A; the point to be made here is that the neoclassical model of urbanization is sufficiently flexible to incorporate many of the salient features of African economies. If some stringent assumptions are imposed, single equation estimation is possible. The single equation approach has its simplicity, easily estimable form, and readily interpretable coefficients to recommend it. Additional verisimilitude can be purchased at the cost of modest econometric complication.

The real reason for building a single equation neoclassical model has little to do with econometric ease, however. Rather, data that would support more complex structural or quasi-reduced form estimates cannot be obtained, making formal estimation impossible. Consequently, what *will be estimated* in the name of neoclassical economics in a cross-country study of African urbanization *must be* a variant of the single equation statement (6.A.12). To repeat, this equation does not represent the pinnacle of neoclassical economic formalism—it instead represents a feasible estimating equation consistent with a neoclassical model that has imposed a great number of undesirably strong assumptions.

6.3 Empirical Tests of the Neoclassical Urbanization Model

"African economic data are largely unreliable and incomplete"—any empirical investigation of African economies must be prefaced by such a cautionary statement. Indeed, several important variables were omitted from the estimating equation because they were not available for a sufficiently wide cross section of countries. Economic theory dictates that the urban modern sector wage and the price of rural output should be in the estimating equation, yet consistent data simply are unavailable. Two options confront a researcher: 1) to estimate the equation anyway, cognizant of the fact that the omitted variables may bias the coefficients of those variables which remain, or 2) to refrain from estimating the equation until such time as a complete cross-sectional data set can be generated.

The second option carries with it an extremely unattractive policy implication. Economic policy, in the absence of empirical investigations, must be based entirely upon theoretical constructs, the validity of which have not been empirically validated. Underlying both formal mathematical theories and unmodeled assertions (which are themselves based on implicit theories) are further untested assumptions about parameter values. Put differently, most policy decisions cannot await satisfactory data collection, and using available information usually is preferable to using none at all. Thus, we have estimated the neoclassical urbanization equation, despite the absence of data for some variables.

Cautionary notes aside, the empirical results appear to be quite strong. Table 6.1 presents a summary of the effects of key variables on urbanization in the model. Factors determining the demand for urban formal sector output are consistently found to be important determinants of urbanization (defined as the proportion of total population living in urban areas). Gross domestic product (GDP) contributes strongly to urbanization, supporting the hypothesis of an "urbanizing bias" in the demand structure. As incomes increase, a larger share of income is spent on formal sector goods; estimates suggest that a doubling of GDP growth rates would elicit between a 14 percent and 21 percent increase in the urbanization rate.

Government expenditures, while not as important as GDP, do play a role in urbanization. The small estimated coefficients—a doubling in the growth rate of government expenditures would cause the urban growth rate to increase by only between 2.7 percent and 4.5 percent—indicate that government spending has not been a direct, major cause of Africa's rapid urbanization. It is important to note that this result refers to the average impact of all government spending, and particular types of spending may have far more potent impacts. Expenditures on urban social services and infrastructure, for example, may have strong urbanizing impacts. More generally, it would be desirable to include a (presently unavailable) measure of urban bias in the public expenditure term. It should also be noted that the government expenditures effect is *net* of taxes—that is, government growth is urbanizing despite the fact that urban goods and incomes tend to be taxed more heavily than their rural counterparts.

The price of imported products is the only demand argument that is not found to be a net determinant of urbanization. This is not surprising, given that an increase in the price of imported products has two conflicting effects. The first is to raise the demand for competing domestic products made relatively less expensive as import prices rise. At the same time, however, the increase in the price of imports raises the cost of production to urban firms that use imported inputs. The first force encourages urbanization; the second deters urban growth.

Increases in the rate of capital accumulation in the urban formal sector also spur urbanization by increasing the productivity of labor and hence stimulating labor demand. The size of this effect is quite small, perhaps due to empirical problems in the construction of this variable. Capital accumulation in the urban informal sector is not found to increase urbanization rates, but this finding may reflect measurement problems. Better data would allow a more accurate test of whether the informal sector plays an important role in absorbing migrants and providing goods and services to the modern/formal sector and the general populace.

The most potent determination of African urbanization in the neoclassical model is per capita caloric intake, the rural real wage variable. The estimates suggest that a 1 percent increase in the rate of caloric intake growth will lead to a 0.5 percent decrease in the urbanization rate. Thus, if a country such as Chad experienced a rise in caloric intake, to take an extreme example, to the Congo's level (roughly a 53 percent increase in 1986), Chad's urban population growth rate would be predicted to decline by over 25 percent. Thus, the neoclassical urbanization model supports the policy prescription of rural development to stem rural-urban migration. In a separate regression employing a the growth rate of a nation's largest city as the dependent variable, the retarding effect on urbanization of improvements in caloric intake was even stronger, almost reaching 1:1.

The seven regressions in Table 6.1 explain between 44 percent and 56 percent of the variation in urban population growth rates across Africa during the 1970s. While not exceptional, this level of explanatory power is encouraging. It must be stressed, though, that these regressions are but a start. Key variables are omitted because of an absence of reliable data; in the case of wage and earnings figures, this omission is particularly problematic. Simultaneous equations models using two stage least squares performed poorly—mainly, we suspect, because the urban modern sector employment (L_{UM}) series we generated was inconsistent across countries.

6.4 Neoclassical Theory and African Reality

The neoclassical model described above does a reasonably good job of identifying probable causes of Africa's recent urbanization experience. For those who believe the proof of an economic model resides in its power of prediction (or in this case, replication), the neoclassical model is quite acceptable. Yet we have increasingly come to believe that parts of the neoclassical model do not accurately describe Af-

TABLE 6.1. OLS Estimates of Urban Population Growth Rates

Independent Variable	(1)[a]	(2)[a]	(3)[a]	(4)[a]	(5)[a]	(6)[a]	(7)[b]
				Equation			
Constant	.0225	.0168	.0085	.0231***	.0153	.0204	.0014
	(1.134)	(1.058)	(.560)	(1.432)	(1.018)	.850	(−.064)
%ΔGDP	.1662***	.1854**	.2155*	.1388***	.1814***	.1831***	.2143***
	(1.582)	(1.877)	(2.173)	(1.399)	(1.852)	(1.562)	(1.562)
%ΔGOVEXP	.0223	.0273***	.0387*	.0362**	.0451*	.0240	−.0012
	(1.058)	(1.486)	(2.269)	(1.965)	(2.638)	(.896)	(−.054)
%ΔK_{um}	.0061***	.0058***	.0053***	—	—	.0061***	.0058
	(1.718)	(1.661)	(1.494)			(1.442)	(.980)
%ΔLFPR	.3728***	.3393***	—	.3026	—	.3433	—
	(1.485)	(1.421)	(1.215)	(.889)			
URBL	−.0123	—	—	—	—	−.0079	—
	(−.303)					(−.158)	
%ΔCAL	−.4729***	−.6018*	−.5305*	−.4869**	−.4561**	−.5683***	−.9026*
	(−1.373)	(−2.789)	(−1.899)	(−1.737)	(−1.606)	(−1.354)	(−2.183)
%ΔK_t	—	—	—	—	—	.0065	—

%ΔP*_m	—	—	—	—	—	(.224) −.0003 (−.01)	—
SIZE	.0030** (2.007)	.0033* (2.364)	.0038* (−2.178)	.0033* (2.27)	.0037* (2.60)	.0030*** (1.711)	.0056* (2.614)
F	2.957*	3.573*	3.675*	3.403*	3.662	1.984	3.164*
R²	.564	.558	.505	.486	.435	.561	.513
−R²	.373	.402	.368	.343	.316	.278	.351
SEE	.0107	.0104	.0107	.0109	.0112	.0115	.0141
No. obs.	24	24	24	24	24	24	21

Note: %ΔGDP = annual growth rate of GDP; %ΔGOVEXP = annual growth rate of government expenditures; %ΔK_um = annual growth rate of urban modern sector capital stock; %ΔLFPR = annual growth rate of labor force participation rate; URBL = percentage of population living in urban areas (1970); %ΔCAL = annual growth rate of percentage of minimum caloric intake received; %ΔK_t = annual growth rate of urban intermediate sector capital stock; %ΔP*_m = annual growth rate of "full price" of imports; SIZE = natural logarithm of habitable land area. T-statistics are in parentheses.

a. Dependent variable: annual urban population growth rates, 1970–80.

b. Dependent variable: annual growth rate of nation's largest city, 1970–80.

  * Statistically significant at 95 percent level.
 ** Statistically significant at 90 percent level.
*** Statistically significant at 80 percent level.

Table 6.1 will be broadside across 2 pages.

rican reality. If a model of urbanization is required not only to predict well, but also to accurately describe economic and social structures, alternative models may need to be devised. This section will examine how well the neoclassical urbanization model describes African economic and social institutions.

One criticism of the neoclassical urbanization model used in cross-country analysis (but not of migration studies based on household data sets that use neoclassical frameworks) is that it suffers from aggregation bias. In other words, labor is treated as completely homogeneous, and distinctions among laborers of different age, skill, and education classes are ignored. Yet a vast body of migration literature (see Mazumdar [1988] and Chapter 4) documents that migrants tend to be younger and better educated than nonmigrants. In African countries, at least until recently, migrants also were more likely to be male than female. Thus, any change in the composition of the population at risk to migrate with respect to these characteristics can change the magnitude of migration flows. Similarly, the proportion of the national population at risk to migrate out of cities to rural areas by definition rises with urbanization, so that constant *net* migration rates imply rising *gross* migration rates (Rogers [1990]). The neoclassical migration model, by focusing on a "typical" individual, misses these important effects. These shortcomings are the motivation for presenting a demographic cohort shift model of migration below in section 6.7.

Perhaps the most fundamental criticisms of the neoclassical model are that its assumptions of capitalistic rural labor markets (in which wages are determined by competitive forces) and cost-minimizing behavior by firms in urban areas are inaccurate portrayals of African economies. The neoclassical urbanization model sets the rural wage equal to the marginal revenue product of agricultural labor. The first obvious question relates to the degree to which wage labor is employed in African agriculture and what percentage of farms enjoy limited goods' market interactions and use only family members as workers. On subsistence farms a model of output sharing among workers (i.e., workers being paid their average product instead of their marginal product) is probably more appropriate. Clearly, subsistence farming is important in Africa—though decreasingly so; the exact distribution of farms between capitalist and subsistence types varies widely by country. As an econometric modeling point, however, this criticism is fairly unimportant, since alternative models of rural economies yield predictive equations very similar to those derived from the neoclassical paradigm, especially when data limitations are considered.

Since the marginal revenue product of labor is defined to be the marginal product of labor times the price of output (in competitive markets), government price controls on agricultural output complicate the analysis further. Resource allocation decisions *should* be made on the basis of market prices that reflect economic scarcity of resources, not on the basis of artificially controlled prices. Yet these price distortions are severe for some products in some African countries. The official prices for sorghum and rice in Mali (1986 data), for example, were 45 percent and 42 percent lower than the farmgate (market) prices, respectively. For Nigeria (1986 data), official prices for cocoa, groundnuts, and maize were 30 percent, 27 percent, and 44 percent below farmgate prices, respectively (UNDP [1989:135–45]). Price distortions typically have decreased in recent years as structural adjustment programs have been forced upon African governments. Even so, some distortions do persist, and so marginal revenue products computed at artificially controlled prices will understate the true (or shadow) marginal revenue products of rural workers. More critically from an econometric modeling standpoint, though, these distortions typically will not be constant across countries or over time.

While the neoclassical urbanization model may correctly capture the effects of rural wages in the presence of price distortions (after all, the real wage and not the shadow wage drives migration decisions), it is clear that much of this migration is socially inefficient. More importantly from a modeling perspective, rural-urban migration will surge or ebb according to changes in government pricing policies. Structural adjustment price reforms in general have worked to reduce rural-urban migration incentives, though the elimination of fertilizer subsidies in many countries and, in some cases, cash crop subsidies (such as those for groundnut production in The Gambia) have the opposite effect.

A key tenet of neoclassical theory is that entrepreneurs minimize costs. Indeed, the labor demand equations discussed above are derived under the assumption of cost-minimizing behavior. If entrepreneurs pursue some goal other than cost minimization, then neoclassical factor demand functions simply do not exist. There has been ample debate in the economic development literature about whether the private sector in Third World countries attempts to maximize profits (and hence minimize costs). The consensus has been that, especially in manufacturing sectors, tariff protection has fostered a legacy of high-cost, low-quality production. If entrepreneurs (in effect a misnomer, since the term implies a willingness to take risks, and producers protected by high tariff barriers may be content to "satisfice" profits rather than assume risk) can sell their output at cost without fear of price competition from foreign producers, there may be precious little incentive to minimize costs. This is especially true if improved economic performance is likely to lead to loss of protection and subsidies. If costs are not minimized, profit clearly cannot be maximized.

There is ample evidence of severe protectionism in Africa. While comparable cross-country estimates of effective rates of protection are not available for the sub-Saharan countries (though several detailed sets of net effective rates of production [ERPs] or domestic resource cost [DRCs] are reported in Roger Riddell [1990c]), indirect evidence of protectionism is provided by the large share of government revenues that is generated by import duties. The average share for all sub-Saharan countries was over 26 percent in 1986. The Gambia, Lesotho, Sudan, and Swaziland all raised over 50 percent of government revenues through import taxation. Large countries tend to have lower percentages, but a significant number of countries obtain over 40 percent of revenues from import duties (see UNDP [1989:113]). Demonstrating that high tariff barriers exist is far from conclusive evidence that entrepreneurs do not minimize costs, but such data are suggestive.

If private firms do not minimize costs, what then of publically owned firms? Clearly this in an important issue given the large contribution of public enterprises to gross domestic product (GDP). Although data are not available for a complete cross section of African countries, partial data highlight the key role public enterprises play. For the countries reporting such data, the smallest share of GDP generated by public enterprises in 1986 was 4.5 percent in the Central African Republic; even this percentage is significant. Almost 15 percent of Nigeria's GDP was produced by public enterprises. The highest percentage reported for 1986 was Somalia, where public enterprises accounted for over 47 percent of GDP (UNDP

[1989:164]). While these percentages have fallen with the implementation of structural adjustment programs (SAPs), the contribution of parastatals to output remains significant in many countries.

Formally determining whether these enterprises minimize costs is difficult, given existing data. Impressionistic evidence and case studies both strongly suggest that parastatals do not. For parastatal sectors as a whole, cost minimization is impossible in most countries, as 1) employment restrictions for public enterprises abound, and 2) bankrupt enterprises typically are supported rather than being permitted to dissolve. If capital costs will be forgiven under adverse circumstances, surely parastatal managers have little incentive to fully cost capital purchases.

If one excludes short-run adverse supply or demand shocks, persistent losses are evidence that public enterprises are pursuing some objective other than cost minimization. For the 1985–86 period, the public enterprises of six of eleven reporting countries posted losses for both years.[8] These countries were The Gambia, Malawi, Senegal, Côte d'Ivoire, and Mauritius. While in some cases—most notably Senegal—structural adjustment programs contracted aggregate demand and the consequent reduced demand for public enterprises' output can be blamed for their financial losses, Senegalese public enterprises have reported losses for all years (1982–86) for which data are available. Short-term adjustments cannot be the entire or even a significant explanation. Another legitimate excuse for short-run losses is a fall in the international price or export volume of an important export marketed by a public enterprise. This could be the case, for example, in The Gambia, where the volume of groundnut exports fell an average of 3 percent a year during the 1980–85 period, before rising 5.2 percent in 1986 (UNDP [1989:61]). Real farmgate groundnut prices fell in both 1985 and 1986 (UNDP [1989:138]). Yet public sector enterprises in The Gambia have reported losses for every year from 1981 to 1986, and this period contains years of increasing and decreasing export volumes, as well as increasing and decreasing farmgate prices.

While consistent financial losses cast doubt on the cost-minimizing hypothesis, financial profits do not necessarily confirm it. Public enterprises in Sierra Leone, Somalia, Zaire, Congo, and Nigeria reported profits during the 1985–86 period. Enterprises in these countries may be making profits in spite of not minimizing costs, due to a privileged position in the domestic market or control of an export for which world demand is relatively price inelastic. To put it bluntly, many African parastatals enjoy monopoly positions in the disposition of their goods, and often also enjoy monopsony positions with regard to raw material input purchases.

Non-cost-minimizing behavior may have important implications for labor market behavior and, consequently, for the migration modeling. If public enterprises do not face a hard budget constraint and are permitted to run recurrent deficits, workers' wage demands are unlikely to meet stiff resistance from management. Workers may be quite successful in obtaining a share of public sector rents, and the possibility of obtaining rents in the urban modern sector may be a powerful lure to potential migrants. This possibility motivates the development of a rent-seeking model of migration, which is presented in the following section.

The most troublesome point for the HT based neoclassical model, however, has to do with formal sector wages. As we have detailed in Chapter 5, many countries have experienced precipitous declines in real formal sector earnings per worker. This point alone obviates one of the central assumptions of the HT model:

institutionally set, high wages. But even endogenous-wage neoclassical statements would not normally predict such dramatic falls, as we discuss below.

6.5 A Rent-Seeking Urbanization Model for Africa

Any model purporting to describe Africa's modern sectors must explain why employment has remained remarkably stable (and typically grown slightly) in the face of continuing economic decline. Labor productivity (measured as output per worker) and real wages in the modern sector have fallen in many African countries between the mid 1970s and the mid 1980s, yet employment grew in most countries (see Table 2.7) during this period, albeit slowly. Of the twenty-four countries for which data are available, nine have declining manufacturing labor productivity during the period. The largest declines are registered in Ghana, Somalia, and Botswana, where worker productivity fell at the astounding annual rates of 9.4, 7.8, and 6.8 percent, respectively.[9] Impressive productivity gains of 13.2, 12.1, and 9.6 percent per year are recorded in Togo, Cameroon, and Lesotho, respectively. The employment growth rates for the countries with considerable productivity growth (annual employment growth rates of 1.4, 2.6, and 0.7 percent) differ significantly from those from countries with productivity declines (annual employment growth rates of −2.4, 7.0, and 11.4 percent), but in perhaps an unexpected direction.

Generally speaking, and with significant exceptions, countries with rapid productivity improvement had slower employment growth. Why did employment not expand if workers were becoming more productive? The simple answer is that this question has the causality reversed. These countries had more rapid productivity growth because they were shedding redundant labor more quickly than other African nations.[10]

A neoclassical model would suggest that employment and productivity should be positively related *if* expansions in employment are the result of increasing labor demand. Since labor demand is a derived demand (i.e., it depends on the level of output) and modern sector output was largely stagnant during this period, the negative relationship between employment and productivity need not be surprising, even within a neoclassical framework. The obvious neoclassical hypothesis is that the negative relationship between productivity and employment is caused by supply shifts. In other words, the arrival of more workers to urban areas increased the supply of labor to the urban modern sector, simultaneously increasing employment and (if the marginal product of labor diminishes, as is conventionally assumed) lowering productivity.

If this neoclassical scenario is accurate, wages in the urban modern sector should be depressed by the increased labor supply, and wages and productivity should fall in tandem. Indeed, the countries with the three largest productivity declines all had falling wages during the period (Table 2.7). Overall, of the nine countries with productivity declines, seven had falling wages. But six countries (Burundi, Côte d'Ivoire, Ethiopia, Kenya, Mali, and Nigeria) had falling wages *without* productivity declines. This could be explained by a decrease in labor demand, *were it not for the fact that employment increased all these countries.* The neoclassical paradigm is simply unable to explain the observed movements in wages, productivity, and employment in many African countries. An alternative model is needed.

Furthermore, the magnitudes of the wage declines are problematic even in those countries with productivity declines. Wage declines in the manufacturing sectors exceed any plausible declines in rural sector wages for some of the countries. Agricultural output was falling by 0.25 percent a year during this period in Ghana and 1.55 percent in Somalia (with per capita declines obviously larger; data are taken from UNDP [1989]). In a neoclassical world, agricultural earnings anchor the supply price of labor to the urban formal sector, and these per capita agricultural output declines clearly cannot account for the size of the fall in modern sector earnings. In other cases (such as Botswana and possibly Zambia), the agricultural output declines *can* account for the lion's share of urban formal wage declines.

One interpretation of these data is that unskilled and semiskilled modern sector labor is able to obtain a wage above its opportunity cost. This wage is obviously not institutionally fixed (note the declines in wages in Table 2.7; also see Chapter 5), but rather varies with labor's ability to capture rents. This paradigm is known as the *rent-seeking model*. Because it receives a noncompetitive wage, labor fiercely combats efforts to reduce employment and prefers to accept wage cuts. Consequently, modern sector managers face something closer to a quantity rather than a wage constraint, so that there is little employment fluctuation even in severe economic downturns. This lack of fluctuation in employment is known as "labor hoarding."

Another class of models—besides rent-seeking models—predicts little change in employment in recessions. They are known as labor turnover models, and are described in section 4.2.5. In a labor turnover model, the existence of hiring, training, and firing costs induces firms to at least partially maintain employment levels even when production declines, because reducing the level of employment is costly, as is returning employment to its prior level after workers have been dismissed. Labor productivity in these models behaves pro-cyclically, but wages are less volatile. If a firm were to cut wages and its workers were to perceive that wages had not been reduced elsewhere, workers would leave to search for employment elsewhere. Since this is costly to firms, labor turnover models predict that firms will not lower wages significantly during recessions. The dramatic wage declines in the manufacturing sectors of many African countries during 1975–85 suggest that the labor turnover model may not be highly appropriate for the entire cross section of African countries.

Thus, the focus in this section is on the development of a rent-seeking model of migration and urbanization. The mathematical derivation of this model is provided in Appendix 6C. As in the neoclassical model of urbanization, production in the urban modern/formal sector uses labor, capital, informal sector inputs, and imported intermediates. In the neoclassical model, labor is paid whatever share of total cost is not accounted for by other inputs (i.e., total revenue minus the returns to capital and the cost of imported intermediates and informal inputs). In the rent-seeking model, labor "negotiates" with (state) capitalists over its share of the available rents, once imported and informal sector inputs have been paid for. Thus, for example, if world prices of imports soar, import duties fall, or the value of gross formal sector output declines, then the wage bill will decline.

Labor cannot determine both the wage and the employment level, but it is usually able to prevent firms from dismissing or laying off workers. Thus, formal sector employment is likely to remain stable or grow, even in periods of economic stress. Indeed, data show that manufacturing employment increased during 1975–85 in all countries for which data are available, with the exception of the Central African Republic, The Gambia, and Ghana (see Table 2.7). As suggested above, in the rent-seeking paradigm labor negotiates with formal sector firms over the rent share *after* securing stable employment.

Labor's share in formal sector value added does not appear to be constant between different countries or within countries over time. A logical initial hypothesis is that labor's ability to raise its share of formal sector value added depends upon:

(1) government's capacity to pay higher wages in public enterprises;
(2) government's capacity to import food and other key consumption goods— or key intermediates to produce these goods domestically—that are consumed by the urban working class;
(3) the urban unemployment rate;
(4) the existence of true rents to be captured;
(5) the ability of firms to pass on higher labor costs in the form of higher prices, which in turn depends on the degree of competition (usually a simple function of the degree of protectionism) in the economy;
(6) the political position of the planning and labor ministries; and
(7) the share of public sector employment in total employment.

These factors can be easily embedded in a formal model of rent-seeking behavior, which then can be empirically tested. The structure of such a model is relatively simple and builds on the neoclassical model presented in section 6.2. If the rent-seeking parameter is equal to the total wage bill (employment multiplied by the wage) divided by total available rents, it is possible to derive an expression for urban formal sector employment that contains the rent-seeking parameter. The urban labor force is determined in the same way as in the neoclassical model, by summing the three urban portions of the labor force: urban formal and informal sectors, and unemployed individuals. The bridge between the urban labor force and urban population is the same as previously: the labor force participation rate. Once the determinants of the rent-seeking parameter (1–7 above) are embedded into an expression for urban labor force, a single reduced form equation is available to test the rent-seeking model. As with the neoclassical model, this estimating equation makes extremely strong assumptions to avoid simultaneity. On the other hand, the absence of wage data is no longer as critical in the rent-seeking model's reduced form, since the labor share terms in effect serve as instruments for the now endogenous wage.

It is apparent from Appendices 6A and 6C that the rent-seeking model contains all the terms present in the reduced form of the neoclassical model, and has the same signs or indeterminacies. One difference between the estimating equations is that the coefficients of the shared variables in the rent-seeking model are expected to be smaller. Neoclassical-type adjustments still take place, but they are tempered by the costs to firms of quick adjustments to changing demand conditions. But the differences in the predicted magnitudes of these shared coefficients are not sufficient to allow us to distinguish between the two models.

The main difference between the two reduced forms is that the rent-seeking reduced form contains a set of terms that determines labor's share. In attempting to distinguish between neoclassical and rent-seeking models of urban labor markets, then, our first approach is to examine a reduced form model with the factors thought to determine labor's share of modern sector rents. If these terms are statistically significant, this will confirm (actually, not reject) the relevance of the rent-seeking model.

Before turning to the estimates, it should also be mentioned that time series data on labor's share in manufacturing value added and on manufacturing employment has recently become available for a limited number of African countries (see UNDP/World Bank [1992:252]). While data presently are available only for a small sample of countries, in the not-too-distant future it may be possible to conduct some simple, direct tests of the relationship between labor's income share, employment, and economic cycles. The rent-seeking model predicts that labor's share of value added will move pro-cyclically, while manufacturing employment will have only modest cyclical variation. Informal sector employment, on the other hand, may exhibit much stronger responses to the short-run macroeconomic fluctuations; this may be the key explanation for why neoclassical urbanization models—which do not account for labor-hoarding—are able to replicate Africa's urbanization experience so well. In general, though, neoclassical models do not usually predict large shifts in factor shares.

For the seven countries with five or more years of labor share data in the manufacturing sector, the trends are broadly consistent with the rent-sharing hypothesis. Labor's share underwent a precipitous decline in Cameroon between 1980 and 1984 and in Niger between 1980 and 1988. It declined as well in Botswana during the early and mid-1980s, but Botswana's minerals orientation and rapid structural change make these shifts difficult to interpret. Labor shares were very stable in the generally stable Seychelles, and fluctuated without trend in Congo. The share rose in Ghana between 1980 and 1982, and then declined precipitously. A similar increase between 1980 and 1983 took place in Senegal, followed by a smaller decline. In summary, five of the seven cases seem to be consistent with pro-cyclical share movements, while the secular decline in Botswana and the rise followed by limited decline in Senegal are prima facie inconsistent.

6.6 Empirical Tests of the Rent-Seeking Urbanization Model

In contrast, the cross-country empirical support for the rent-seeking model of urbanization appears to be much weaker than that for the neoclassical model. In large part this may result from a smaller sample size. The sample size for the rent-seeking model was twenty-two, while the neoclassical model was tested with a sample size of twenty-seven.[11] The smaller sample size occurs because data on wages as a share of manufacturing value added are not available for five countries (Chad, Liberia, Mauritania, Uganda, and Zaire) included in the neoclassical analysis. The loss in degrees of freedom in estimation may cause the insignificance of some coefficients, while other coefficients may be insignificant because the smaller sample has significantly different characteristics than the larger sample. The rent-seeking results are reported in Table 6.2.

TABLE 6.2. OLS Estimates of Urban Population and Manufacturing Sector Growth Rates for Twenty-two African Nations, 1970–80.

Independent Variable	Equation[a]					
	(1)[b]	(2)[b]	(3)[b]	(4)[c]	(5)[c]	(6)[c]
constant	-0.01 (0.13)	-0.06 (0.70)	0.06* (11.46)	0.07 (1.10)	0.04 (0.56)	0.05 (10.9)*
GNP	0.0 (0.46)	0.55*** (1.52)		0.01 (0.80)	-0.07 (0.23)	
government current expenditures	0.01 (0.06)	-0.15 (0.82)		-0.09 (0.69)	-0.06 (0.35)	
government capital expenditures	0.34*** (1.73)	0.33** (2.03)		-0.26** (1.79)	-0.11 (0.74)	
average rate of protection	-0.12 (0.80)	-0.15 (1.06)		-0.23** (2.07)	-0.23** (1.85)	
import price	0.54 (0.69)	1.01 (1.25)		-0.16 (0.29)	-0.02 (0.03)	
per capita caloric intake	-0.29 (0.35)	0.09 (0.11)		0.30 (0.47)	-0.10 (0.15)	
labor's share in MVA	0.09 (0.69)		-0.07 (0.72)	-0.21** (2.08)		-0.13** (1.51)
labor's average share in MVA (level)		-0.01 (1.17)			0.01 (0.66)	
F	0.66	0.99	0.49	2.08	1.13	1.78
R^2	.25	.33	.03	.51	.36	.10
$\overline{R}^2$	-.13	.0	-.02	.26	.04	.06

a All variables are annual growth rates except where indicated.

b Dependent variable is annual growth rate of urban population.

c Dependent variable is annual growth rate of manufacturing employment.

* Statistically significant at 5 percent level.

** Statistically significant at 10 percent level.

*** Statistically significant at 20 percent level

T-statistics are in parentheses.

Unlike in the neoclassical model, demand-side variables are not very significant. GDP is a statistically significant determinant of urbanization in only one of the specifications (and only marginally significant at that), and government spending is never an important factor. An increase in tariffs does not on net stimulate demand for domestically produced import substitutes; rather, demand for modern sector output is reduced because of the increased cost of production resulting from more expensive imported intermediate goods. Overall, the rent-seeking equations explain at best 33 percent of the variation in urban population growth rate differences and 51 percent of the variation in manufacturing employment growth rate differences across African nations.

The only consistently significant determinant of urbanization is modern sector capital stock, and even it is significant at relatively low levels of statistical confidence. The rural wage (or opportunity cost of migration), measured by per capita caloric intake, is not an important determinant of urbanization. This contrasts sharply with the result in the neoclassical estimates, where the rural wage was the most potent determinant of urbanization rates. In sum, the neoclassical "portion" of the rent-seeking model performs very poorly.

The variables of particular interest in this section, however, are those measuring the ability of workers to extract rent from parastatals and capitalists. In either case, we expect higher shares to deter formal sector employment growth, and hence urbanization. Two different labor share variables were used:

(1) the annual rate of change of the share of wages in manufacturing value added between 1970 and 1980, and
(2) the average share of wages in manufacturing value added for the 1970–80 period.

The first variant reflects an equilibrium view of the world; in some initial period, a certain growth rate of urban population is consistent with a certain level of labor's share in value added, but a *change* in labor's share causes a *change* in urbanization rates. The second variant reflects a disequilibrium view of the world; no steady state equilibrium in an initial period is implied. As evidenced by equations (1) and (2) of Table 6.2, neither version of the variable explains urban growth rates.[12]

Some support is given to the equilibrium formulation when growth in manufacturing employment is used as the dependent variable. An increase in the ability of labor to appropriate the economic rents produced by manufacturing does lead to a decrease in manufacturing employment growth; if the share of manufacturing value added paid to labor increases by 10 percent, employment falls by about 2 percent.

The difference in results between regressions containing urban population and those containing manufacturing employment as the dependent variable suggests that while the rent-seeking model may explain formal sector behavior, the link between the formal sector and urban growth may be weak. Once again, the importance of the urban informal sector is emphasized. Unfortunately, the standard response must be repeated: data are simply unavailable to empirically validate the importance of this sector in the urban growth process.

Of course, even the most careful specification of the rent-seeking model still presents problems for empirical estimation. It must be acknowledged that some questions are not particularly amenable to cross-sectional analysis. Using annual growth rates of variables computed over a ten year period imposes an equilibrium structure that may obscure important disequilibrium phenomena. This cross-sectional analysis should be complemented with time series work on individual African countries that examines the relationship between urban modern sector growth, urbanization, macroeconomic performance, and labor's share in manufacturing value added. Ideally, quarterly or even monthly data should be used to capture adjustments over the business cycle, but income share data are not available with such frequency. Thus, even using time series data, only an imperfect test of the rent-seeking model could be conducted.

6.7 A Demographic Cohort Shift Model of African Urbanization

The neoclassical and rent-seeking economic models presented above are highly aggregated models of individual behavior. As with any simplified, aggregate explanation, important detail may be overlooked. The strength of these economic models lies in their derivation of estimating equations from formal, consistent statements of human behavior. Their weakness is the high degree of aggregation assumed. In contrast, demographers generally do not create models based on the assumption of optimizing behavior for all agents, but they do carefully disaggregate to capture relevant distinctions across groups.

Two such relevant details are the age and education characteristics of migrants. Since it is well known that migrants tend to be younger and better educated than nonmigrants, any increase in the share of young or well-educated people in the total population at greatest risk of migrating will serve to increase migration rates. Thus, in describing migration and urbanization trends it is important to track the age and education composition of at-risk populations. The DCS model is able to do so, departing from the assumption of a homogeneous labor force that characterizes neoclassical and rent-seeking models, and focusing instead on shifting population structure. In particular, the DCS model hypothesizes that these cohort shifts are the primary forces driving differential urban growth rates across countries, as well as acceleration or deceleration in urban growth rates within a country over time.

It should be noted as well that the sorts of factors causing declining mortality and expansion in educational availability—growth of government and social service provision, foreign capital inflows (aid, not physical capital), and generalized GDP growth—are very similar to the variables that are included in the neoclassical urbanization model. This provides another plausible reason for the good fit of the neoclassical urbanization model. Put differently, the demographic explanation offered here still implies that economic effects matter, but that they operate through quite different paths than is usually assumed.

Although African economies in general have performed poorly over the past thirty years, African societies have made major social gains. These gains include declines in mortality—especially infant and child mortality—that were especially great in the 1960s and 1970s. The patterns are reported in Table 6.3.[13] Furthermore, for many countries these declines have been at least as rapid, and probably slightly faster, than the declines in developing countries as a whole. The consequences

TABLE 6.3. Average Annual Decline in Total Death Rates, Africa and Other Regions, 1960–85.

	1960–75	1965–80	1975–85
Africa	0.93	1.08	0
–Western	0.79	2.34	0.54
–Eastern	0	0.67	0.54
–Northern	1.15	0.89	1.54
–Central	0	0.93	1.05
–Southern	0.40	2.50	−2.41
Northern America	0	0	0
Latin America	2.45	0	1.18
Asia	1.68	—	—
–East	4.29	2.38	0
–South	0.38	0.83	2.23
Europe	0	−0.64	0
–Western	0.64	−1.22	0.87
–Southern	0	0	−1.05
–Eastern	−0.70	0	−0.95
–Northern	0	−0.58	0
Oceania	0.64	0.70	1.18
USSR	−0.89	−0.79	0

Source: United Nations *Demographic Yearbook*, various years.

have been 1) a rise in overall population growth rates, and 2) a widening of the age pyramid in African nations, resulting from a concentration of mortality declines in young age cohorts.

An even more dramatic gain has been recorded in the expansion of education (see Table 6.4). In 1960 only 36 percent of the relevant age group was enrolled in primary school in Africa; by 1965 the figure had risen to 46 percent. It reached 63 percent in 1978 and 71 percent in 1982. For Less Developed Countries (LDCs) as a whole the rate of increase was much more modest, going from 76 percent in 1960 to 83 percent in 1978. For Kenya the increase was from 47 percent in 1960 to 99 percent in 1978, and to 104 percent in 1982. The secondary school enrollment ratio for sub-Saharan Africa went from 3 percent in 1960 and 13 percent in 1978 and 15 percent in 1982. Comparable figures for all LDCs are 14 percent in 1960 and 36 percent in 1978. For Kenya, the rise has been from 2 percent in 1960 to 18 percent in 1978 and 20 percent in 1982. Thus, the growth rate of the skilled labor force appears to have been much greater in Africa than elsewhere.

Given these impressive numbers, it is likely that a DCS model will contribute to our understanding of African urbanization. The problem—as usual in the African context—is data availability to test a model that has such severe data requirements. Specifically, the ideal data set would include gross migration rates by age, gender, and education for a broad set of African nations. While such data are not available for a large number of African countries, age and education breakdowns of the population are available for some countries for census years.[14] This section focuses primarily on the Kenyan case, using census data to derive age and education breakdowns for the population for each census year (1962, 1969, and 1979). *Net* mi-

TABLE 6.4. Average Annual Growth Rates in Secondary School Enrollment Ratio, Africa and Other Regions, 1960–85.

	1960–65	1965–70	1970–75	1975–80	1980–85
Africa	8.62	6.73	6.63	7.85	4.48
Asia	1.86	3.04	6.30	1.76	−0.10
Europe (including USSR)	4.67	1.77	2.22	0.74	1.21
Oceania	2.97	2.01	1.20	−0.56	2.36
Developing Countries	2.95	4.94	6.75	2.62	0.87
Latin America and the Caribbean	6.24	4.99	7.04	4.12	3.10
Northern America	1.54	−0.25	−1.38	−2.31	1.27

Source: United Nations (1989a).

gration rates are then obtained based on World Bank estimates,[15] and these rates are then stratified by education using estimates from Tanzania.[16]

The procedure used is thus to simulate base populations forward through time assuming constant age/education net migration rates. These hypothetical populations—hypothetical in the sense that presumably age and education-specific migration rates did not remain constant—are then "survived" by applying mortality and fertility rates taken from standard sources.[17] Individuals are divided into two educational categories: the "educated" with more than five years of schooling, and the "uneducated" with four or fewer years of schooling.[18]

The results from the DCS model are reproduced in Table 6.5, which gives urban population growth rates by age and education for 1962, 1969, 1979, and "1989"; the last year results from a simulation in which educational expansion is assumed to have halted in the early 1980s.[19] The "1989" figures do not specifically reflect Kenya's slowdown, but rather consider what would have happened should Kenya have experienced the general stagnation in social gains characteristic of most of the continent during the 1980s. In fact, Kenya continued to experience rapidly declining infant and child mortality rates in the 1980s, but secondary school enrollment ratios rose only from 20 percent (1980) to 23 percent (1988: see UNDP/World Bank [1992]).

The DCS model predicts Kenyan urban growth to be 4.86 percent per year in the mid-1960s. The predicted growth rate rises to 6.29 percent in the early 1970s, and continues to climb to 6.41 percent in the early 1980s. The stagnation in social gains in the early 1980s causes predicted urban growth rates for the 1990s to fall to 4.01 percent. These predicted results faithfully mimic historical trends: urban growth rates of 6.4 percent, 6.8 percent, and 8.6 percent in the 1960s, 1970s, and early 1980s, respectively (according to World Bank estimates). But perhaps most astonishing is its consistency with the newly released 1989 Kenyan census (Republic of Kenya [1991]), which reports an intercensal urban population growth rate of only 4.8 percent. While the World Bank estimates may well have been accurate for at least the initial years of "1980–87" (see World Bank [1989a]), presumably the latter part of the decade saw a dramatic decline of the sort forecast here.

Clearly some elements of urban growth are not explained by the DCS model, since the predicted urbanization rates are uniformly below historical rates; changes in age and educational structure do not tell the whole story. At the same time, however, the DCS model does accurately predict the accelerating urban growth

TABLE 6.5. Projected Kenyan Urban Population Growth 1962–94, Assuming
Constant Age and Education Specific Net Migration Rates (in tens of thousands)

	Base Population, 1962			Simulated Population, 1967	
Age Group	Educated	Uneducated	Age Group	Educated	Uneducated
0–9 years	0	190	0–4	0	107
10–19	17	126	5–14	0	127
20–29	28	163	15–24	63	182
30–39	12	114	25–34	126	234
40–49	6	59	35–44	1	95
50+	1	40	45–54	−10	36
			55+	−4	7
Total	64	692		177	787
1962–67 percent change in total urban population				27.53	
annual urban growth rate				4.86 percent	

	Base Population, 1969			Simulated Population, 1974	
Age Group	Educated	Uneducated	Age Group	Educated	Uneducated
0–9 years	0	251	0–4	0	144
10–19	84	90	5–14	0	178
20–29	134	89	15–24	183	135
30–39	61	76	25–34	313	143
40–49	25	46	35–44	46	61
50+	12	43	45–54	10	26
			55+	2	8
Total	316	595		554	694
1969–74 percent change in total urban population				36.97	
annual urban growth rate				6.29 percent	

	Base Population, 1979			Simulated Population, 1984	
Age Group	Educated	Uneducated	Age Group	Educated	Uneducated
0–9 years	1	418	0–4	1	222
10–19	205	96	5–14	1	329
20–29	298	74	15–24	409	130
30–39	173	43	25–34	558	112
40–49	75	43	35–44	153	31
50+	33	51	45–54	63	25
			55+	28	20
Total	785	725		1212	869
1979–84 percent change in total urban population				37.83	
annual urban growth rate				6.41 percent	

rates that Kenya and other African nations actually experienced in the 1960s and
1970s. The model also predicts a substantial momentum effect in the 1980s, when
the entrance into the labor force of youths educated in the 1970s and early 1980s
will still generate rapid city growth. Subsequently, the dismal economic experience
of the 1980s, resulting in diminished gains in mortality declines and educational
expansion, is predicted to have a large impact in the late 1980s and 1990s.

TABLE 6.5. Continued

	Base Population,1989			Simulated Population, 1994	
Age Group	Educated	Uneducated	Age Group	Educated	Uneducated
0–9 years	2	692	0–4	1	331
0–19	340	159	5–14	2	576
20–29	493	123	15–24	515	191
30–39	286	71	25–34	660	158
40–49	124	71	35–44	279	60
50+	55	84	45–54	123	54
			55+	53	53
Total	1300	1200		1632	1423
1989–94 percent change in total urban population				22.19	
annual urban growth rate				4.01 percent	

Several other important features of demographic change also can be determined by comparing different censuses for particular countries. This is possible for a limited number of African countries that have two or more comparable censuses; most such countries are in Anglophone southern or eastern Africa. Table 6.6 provides estimates of aggregate gross and net migration rates for persons aged ten and above for four such countries: Kenya, Tanzania, Zambia, and Botswana.

The technique used to derive these estimates is straightforward. First, we take estimates of gender-, age-, and location-specific mortality and "survive" the populations estimated in the base censuses, taking care to move the population into different cohorts as it ages. By examining aggregate migration of the population only alive in the base year, we are able to avoid problems of inferring urban and rural location-specific fertility rates. Second, this "survived" population gives us an estimate of urban and rural populations that would exist if no interregional migration had taken place, if no international migration had occurred, and if the mortality data were accurate. Third, to compensate for mortality rate errors and inconsistent census procedures (but, alas, also assuming away net international migration), we scale the "survived" urban and rural populations for each age and gender cohort so that they sum to the observed terminal year census total population. Fourth, the differences in recorded terminal year urban populations by cohort and "survived" cohort populations gives us an estimate of *net* rural-urban migration; dividing by urban population then gives the ith cohort's urban *net migration rate* ($NMR_U[i]$); dividing by rural population gives a cohort-specific rural net migration rate, $NMR_R(i)$. Finally, aggregate net migration rates (by gender) are taken as the population-weighted averages of the cohort-specific NMRs. It is a trivial identity that net urban in-migration must equal net rural out-migration, given our scaling procedure, but the net migration *rates* will differ, both because the denominator (urban versus rural population) will differ, and because the weights used in determining an aggregate will differ. Two aggregate NMRs are reported for each gender and region: the "base" runs calculate NMRs for each cohort by dividing estimated net migrants by an average of the original census population for the given cohort plus the terminal census population for the same (but now older) cohort. The estimate then weights the cohort-specific NMRs by the base year popu-

TABLE 6.6. Net and Gross Urban In-Migration and Rural Out-Migration Rates (Kenya, Botswana: for people aged 10+ years; Zambia: for people 17+ years; Tanzania: for people 11+ years; all rates are annual percentage changes)

country	gender	year	base year net in-migration rate	terminal year net in-migration rate	base year net out-migration rate	terminal year net out-migration rate	net in-migration rate assuming constant gross migration rate	net out-migration rate assuming constant gross migration rate	constant gross migration rate urban	constant gross migration rate rural
Kenya	M	1969	4.29		0.55					
	M	1979		4.40		0.57	2.28	0.47	1.57	1.45
	F	1969	3.86		0.45					
	F	1979		3.98		0.46	2.58	0.42	0.95	0.97
Botswana	M	1971	3.97		0.56					
	M	1981		5.18		0.60	1.88	0.40	2.20	1.66
	F	1971	3.60		0.50					
	F	1981		4.26		0.51	2.51	0.43	1.17	1.09
Zambia	M	1963	2.68		1.64					
	M	1980		2.03		1.56	0.85	0.60	5.37	5.15
	F	1963	2.35		1.48					
	F	1980		2.31		1.49	1.57	0.98	2.07	3.10
Tanzania	M	1967	7.12		1.06					
	M	1978		7.00		0.65	3.43	0.56	1.40	2.08
	F	1967	6.98		0.92					
	F	1978		7.02		0.56	3.58	0.51	1.12	1.67

Notes: (a) Base (terminal) year net migration rates are calculated by estimating the number of net migrants, calculated by taking the difference between actual and survived populations, after scaling to ensure total urban and rural survived population from the initial census equals the numbers recorded in the subsequent census, and dividing by base (terminal) population for each cohort. Aggregate NMRs reported here are then taken as a weighted average of cohort-specific NMRs.

(b) In-migration (out-migration) net migration rates are found by dividing estimated cohort net migration by urban (rural) cohort population.

(c) Gross migration rates by cohort are determined by assuming that gross urban-rural and rural-urban rates are equal, and solving the equation

$$NMR_R = \frac{NM}{POP_R} = \frac{POP_{RY} - POP_{UY}}{POP_R} \rightarrow \gamma = \frac{POP_R NMR_R}{POP_R - POP_U}$$

for γ, the constant gross migration rate, as a function of the base year net rural out-migration rate NMR_R (a similar and consistent expression can define gamma in terms of the net urban in-migration rate, base urban population POP_U, and rural population POP_R. Thus defined, the estimated gross migration rate will automatically replicate base year urban and rural $NMRs$, but not terminal year $NMRs$.

(d) Aggregate gross migration rates differ because cohort weights differ.

Source: United Nations, *Demographic Yearbook*, various years.

lation. The second "terminal" year run takes the same cohort-specific NMRs, but calculates a weighted average using terminal year populations. Since migration takes place over the intercensal period, the standard way of reporting the figures would be to take an average of the two rates, but in our case, we present both figures in order to discuss reasons for their differences.

In general, rural out-migration rates will be (much) smaller than urban in-migration rates. This point can be seen readily from Table 6.6. In the case of Kenya, for example, in-migration causes urban populations to grow by roughly 4 percent per annum—while rural out-migration rates are only about 0.5 percent per annum, implying rural population growth of roughly 3 percent, and urban population growth of nearly 8 percent. A more surprising finding from Table 6.6 is that while Zambia has the smallest NMR_Us (the average of the base and terminal year rates is 2.52 percent for men and 2.17 percent for women), it actually had by far the *highest* rural out-migration rates (an average of 1.56 percent for men and 1.52 percent for women).[20] Zambia's urban population growth rate in the 1960s and 1980s was about 5.4 percent, not particularly high by African standards, but more than three times as high as its rural rate of about 1.5 percent.

The reason for Zambia's distinctive patterns is also straightforward. The proportion of Zambians living in urban areas rose from roughly 23 percent to 43 percent between the period 1963–80. In contrast, Kenya was only about 14–15 percent urban by the date of the latter census reported in Table 6.6; Tanzania was only 12–13 percent urban, and Botswana only 21–22 percent urban (and only about 10 percent urban in the base year). Consequently, a given number of migrants would cause a much smaller percentage increase in Zambia's urban population than in any of the other countries. *Since rural out-migration rates are unlikely to exceed 1.5–2.0 percent—very high rates by any standard—except in times of crisis, the lesson from Zambia is that urbanization itself will ultimately force declines in urban population growth rates.*

Let us now turn to a comparison of the base and terminal year net migration rates. Because the cohort-specific NMRs are equal, and because the weights used in each case must sum to unity, the fact that the surviving population will be smaller than the base population will not affect the estimated aggregate NMR. But the weighted averages will differ because the population weights differ. As discussed above, shifting population structure toward high-migration propensity cohorts can be expected to cause increases in aggregate NMR_Us and NMR_Rs during the period 1965–85 for most African countries; thereafter, the reverse trend should set in for those countries with poor economic performances.

In fact, the population shift effect seems to be very strong in Botswana, as it was earlier in Kenya (Table 6.5). In Kenya and Tanzania, the cohort shifts do not have strong effects by the 1970s, suggesting that the urban surge due to cohort shifts should be having a reverse effect by now (a finding again consistent with Table 6.5, which suggests that the cohort shifts were strongest in Kenya between 1965 and 1975). In the more mature and slower-growing Zambian economy, cohort shift effects are negative, so that terminal year NMRs are smaller than those in the base year.

What do the gender differences tell us? In Kenya and Tanzania, urban in-migration rates differ little by gender, but men have much higher rural out-migration rates. This difference reflects the fact that male/female sex ratios are considerably above 1.0 in east African towns and cities. Men have slightly higher NMR_Us and NMR_Rs in Botswana and Zambia, but the differences are not dramatic.

Thus far, we have concentrated on *net* migration rates. In reality, of course, people move both from rural to urban areas, and from cities to the countryside. The census data, alas, do not permit us to determine both of these flows, but it seems likely that urban out-migration rates are far from trivial. Rogers (1985:92–3) finds that Indian urban out-migration rates to rural areas are higher than rural out-migration rates to cities for all age groups, and are about 47 percent higher on average. The figures reported in Becker (1991) suggest that urban out-migration is at least as high as rural out-migration in The Gambia as well. Here we take a fairly conservative view, and ask what would happen if gross urban and rural outmigration rates (γ) were equal.

The first step is to use the base period net migration rates to find cohort-specific $\gamma(i)$. The mathematical identity used to solve for $\gamma(i)$ is presented in note (c) of Table 6.6. It indicates that $\gamma(i)$ will rise with NMR_R and POP_U, but fall with POP_R. Note that while $\gamma_R(i)$ equals $\gamma_U(i)$ by assumption, the aggregate γ_R will not generally equal γ_U because the weights used in constructing the average will differ. The urban and rural aggregate γ's are reported in the last two columns of Table 6.6.

By construction, the estimated γ values will replicate the "observed" base year net migration rates. The question of interest, then, is this: Had gross migration rates remained constant across the intercensal period, how much would estimated *net* migration rates change? To estimate this, we simply determine for the terminal year

$$NMR_R = \frac{POP_R\gamma - POP_U\gamma}{POP_R} = \gamma \left(1 - \frac{POP_U}{POP_R}\right) \qquad (6.1)$$

for each cohort, and a similar equation holds for NMR_U, and where POP_R and POP_U are rural and urban cohort populations, respectively.

Comparing these constant-γ *NMR*s and comparing them with base year *NMR*s then gives the answer we seek. Constant-γ terminal year *NMR*s are far smaller than base year *NMR*s, especially for urban in-migration rates. For males in all four countries, urban net in-migration rates are virtually halved, and in Zambia decline 68 percent. The decline for female NMR_Us is smaller, though still nearly 50 percent in Tanzania, and large everywhere. A similar pattern of decline for rural net out-migration rates is observed in Zambia and Tanzania; in Botswana and Kenya, the declines are somewhat more moderate.

These declines reiterate a finding listed above: urbanization itself will cause lower net migration rates and slower rates of city growth. As national populations become increasingly urban, urban-rural migration's weight in total migration will increase in importance, and net rural-urban migration will decline, *unless rural gross migration rates rise relative to urban weights, or if cohort shares shift.* These changes in relative gross migration rates and shifts in cohort shares almost certainly did take place in the 1960s and 1970s (the period of the migration rate estimates in Table 6.6), since in-migration declines of the sort projected by the decline in the constant $\gamma(i)$ case imply far lower urban growth rates than were in fact observed. But the rising impact of urban return migration did have and will continue to have the effect of decreasing net urban in-migration. Furthermore, in an era of slack economic growth and social transformation, where economic variables cause smaller shifts in gross migration rates, this demographic accounting effect is likely to become increasingly important.

Which forces, then, appear to be the most important? The halving of Kenya's urban population growth rate suggests that Africa's urbanization pattern is indeed changing. It appears that this decline is inconsistent with Kenya's apparently declining per capita caloric intake, but that a fair amount can be explained by declines in the growth rates of real GDP and government expenditures. Roughly speaking, based on Table 6.1, perhaps 20 percent (at the outside, 25 percent) of the decline in the urban growth rate can be attributed to reduced urban demand forces—slowdowns in GDP growth, government expenditure growth, and capital formation. If the 8 percent decline in caloric intake reported in UNDP/World Bank (1992; 332) is accurate, it alone would more than offset the declines predicted due to deteriorating urban conditions. Thus, a very preliminary assessment is that the demographic cohort shift model—but not the neoclassical economic model—would predict the large, observed declines in Kenya's urban growth rate.

Yet another advantage of the DCS model vis-à-vis the other models presented above is its ability to explain why African cities grew more rapidly than cities in any other Third World region. The lackluster performance of Africa's industrial sector casts doubt upon the explanatory power of models that view urbanization almost exclusively as a response to events in the urban formal sector, that is, the neoclassical and, especially, rent-seeking models. The differences between Africa and the rest of the world, however, can be neatly explained by the cohort shifts described in the DCS model. In fact, in the absence of educational expansion, Kenya's forecasted city growth rates look very much like those experienced in other developing countries.

Africa's extraordinarily rapid urbanization will slow in the 1990s, largely because of declines in the expansion of education and increasing mortality rates. Such a conclusion should bring precious little comfort to urban planners, since ignorance and death are far from the ideal policy instruments to curb urban growth. Nor should the methodological conclusions of this study be of comfort to economists, since it is clear that the failure to account for demographic shifts within economic models has given rise to several complex models which, because they overlook elementary demographic forces, have only limited predictive power.

We must close this section by again raising the issue of observational equivalence. Thus far, the criterion of predictive accuracy does not really permit us to favor any of the models presented; indeed, as they are not entirely mutually exclusive, perhaps there is something to be said for (and against) all three. As we have seen above, the reduced form equations for the neoclassical and rent-seeking models are very similar. Furthermore, the economic transformation variables used in the economic models also strongly affect the education and population structural shifts that drive the abehavioral DCS model.[21]

In the next few years, enough censuses from the 1990s will become available so that it will be possible to estimate economic models for cross-country data sets using cohort-specific migration rates. Only then will it be possible to tell whether cohort migration rate shifts offset population structure shifts (implying that the demographers' disaggregation is not merely unnecessary, but also misleading), whether cohort-specific migration rates respond little to economic variables (implying that economic models fit well only because their explanatory variables have demographic consequences, and that these matter), or whether cohort-specific migration rates, at least for some age groups, are more sensitive than total migration rates to economic variables (implying that demographic and economic models reinforce each other).

In advance of a complete cohort-specific data base, censuses from the early 1990s will also help researchers to examine the predictive power of demographic and economic models: presumably, some countries will not have dramatic slowdowns predicted by both sets of models, as in Kenya's case. Improved data on urban labor markets also should make it possible to begin to disentangle neoclassical and non-neoclassical economic models. In the meanwhile, though, the important lesson from the numbers to date is that, given present data restrictions, the regression equations are consistent with very different paradigms, and hence hardly represent a strong "test" of competing hypotheses.

6.8. Determinants of Individual Cities' Growth: Evidence from Zambia

Chapter 6 thus far has discussed the broad patterns of city growth in sub-Saharan Africa. Sections 6.2–6.7 find that variation in national urban population growth could be explained by a wide range of variables. This section now considers what sort of factors influence migration to and hence growth of particular cities *within* a country.

Many of the variables that matter across countries will not affect differential growth rates of cities within a country, since several terms reflect national policy, and hence do not vary in their impact at the subnational level. Rather, what should matter most are those factors that distinguish one city from another.

Nor are expected signs always the same. In the case of total urban population growth, rapid rural development may either spur urbanization (reflecting Engels effects, labor-saving productivity gains in some cases, growth in demand for urban-produced intermediate inputs into agricultural production, relaxed foreign exchange constraints, and falling costs for urban-based processing industries) or impede it (reflecting increases in urban labor costs and diversion of investment away from urban areas). No similar ambiguity exists concerning the development of a particular city's rural hinterland: such growth should promote the city's population growth as well. As a city's hinterland develops, the supply of agricultural goods to the city's processing industries grows, while rural demand for both consumer goods and intermediates also increases. Naturally, these linkages should be most critical for smaller cities with close ties to the surrounding countryside. Such a pattern has been observed elsewhere: for the central Indian state of Madhya Pradesh, Mills and Becker (1986:90) find that the presence of a buoyant agricultural hinterland makes an important contribution to city growth.

What other forces should matter? The migration literature suggests that a city's relative attractiveness depends on the prevailing wage rate, availability of modern sector employment, quality of education and other public services, and distance from a migrant's current location. These variables appear to be critical for Africa and elsewhere.

Similar variables are suggested by economic base models stemming from the urban economics literature. In such models (*e.g.*, Mills and Becker [1986, Ch. 5]), migration is determined by the requirement that a household's equilibrium utility level, dependent upon income and public services, be equal at all locations. Production within each sector within a city depends on labor, capital, and public infrastructure (as well as on intermediate inputs in the case of processing industries). Demand is perfectly elastic for the "base" manufacturing and processing sectors, while it depends on local workers' incomes in the service sectors. As in theories of urban growth across countries, it is necessary in base models to link employment to total population growth. A standard assumption is that dependents' migration follows labor force migration, but with a lag. It can then be shown that a city's equilibrium growth rate will be a positive function of sectoral investments, of increases in the city's public services and industrial infrastructure, of the rate of growth of the city's "exported" or base goods, of the share of nonprimary workers in the adult population, and of supply shocks involving cost reductions or improvements in the availability of raw materials produced in surrounding agricultural areas.

In moving from theory to estimation, as usual, severe data problems arise when one tries to estimate a city growth equation for African cities. Very few countries have any systematic regional or city data related to city growth. From the limited set that do, some (such as Zimbabwe) must be discarded because the number of cities for which data are available is insufficient. We initially attempted to design a multicountry data set, but were unable to define or derive many comparable terms. Consequently, we have been limited to running city growth regressions for Zambia, and even here the variables used are at best modest proxies for ideal terms.[22] Key characteristics of different Zambian cities and their growth rates during three intercensal periods are presented in Table 6.7, while regression results appear in Table 6.8.

The Zambian results are striking, largely due to the diverse nature of the Zambian economy and the government's strong regional policies. Furthermore, and particularly fortuitously for our purposes, Zambian census years are 1963, 1969, 1974, and 1980; changes between 1969 and 1974 thus reflect the pressures of a copper boom era, while 1974–80 changes reflect the consequences of a collapse in copper prices (and, of course, soaring import prices). We hypothesize that the developed copperbelt cities should have grown rapidly prior to 1974, but stagnated thereafter. Since the Zambian government's revenue depends critically on mineral royalties, and since much of it is spent in the capital, Lusaka, one would expect decelerating growth there as well after 1974. Furthermore, the southern towns near the Zimbabwean border appear to have been hurt by Rhodesia's "Unilateral Declaration of Independence" (UDI) (1965–79). This period was marked by a closing of the border, increased militarization of the area, and reluctance by the Zambian government to make new investments in a potentially vulnerable region. Slow but steady migration from the Southern province by the private component of the nation's textile industry undoubtedly compounded these effects. In short, it seems likely that Southern towns received relatively small investments and experienced slow demand growth: base theory then suggests that they should have grown more slowly than average.

On the other hand, several Zambian towns experienced extraordinary investment booms. While investment figures by city are unavailable, for the smaller

TABLE 6.7. Patterns of Zambian City and Town Growth, 1963–80

	City Population (000) and Annual Growth Rate (per annum)			
	1980	I 1963–69	II 1969–74	III 1974–80	Major Economic Events; Era
Lusaka	538	13.4	9.9	4.2	
Kitwe	315	8.4	4.6	3.8	*
Ndola	285	9.5	7.4	3.6	*
Mufulira	150	5.0	4.7	1.6	*
Chingola	146	9.6	5.3	1.4	*
Kabwe	144	8.9	8.4	6.4	Industrial Fabrics: II Zambia RR.HQ:I-II-III Mulungushi Textiles: III
Luanshya	132	4.2	4.6	1.5	*
Livingstone	72	5.4	5.0	3.7	declining textile center: II,III
Chililabombwe	62	4.6	4.7	1.7	*
Kalulushi	59	7.2	4.9	6.3	*
Kasama	38	4.9	13.6	14.5	Tazara RR Line: II
Mansa	35	5.5	−1.2	28.0	Mansa Batteries: III
Chipata	32	9.0	4.3	11.7	Longwe Inds. (Bicycle Assembly): III
Kafue	30	31.7	11.3	7.2	Kafue Textiles: II,III Nit. Chem-Zambia: III
Mazabuka	30	3.5	11.6	18.2	Nakambala Sugar Estates: III
Mpika	26	8.8	47.1	24.7	Tazara RR Line: II
Mongu	25	11.5	4.3	13.2	
Choma	18	9.8	−2.7	9.5	Choma Milling: III
Solwezi	15	12.2	14.0	11.8	Tazara RR Line: II
Kapiri Mposhi	14	±12.8	31.7	25.1	Kapiri Glass: II
Monze	13	4.3	5.0	17.0	
Samfya/Mwanfuli	11	12.2	−1.0	11.9	
Mbala	11	6.1	8.4	5.9	
Mining towns, average		6.9	5.2	2.8	
Tazara line towns, average		8.8	30.8	21.4	
Other towns with a major (positive) economic event				13.5	
Towns with a positive economic event				9.7	

*mining town; Copper boom occurred during 1969–74; Copper bust occurred 1974–80.

Data Sources: Wood (1982), Republic of Zambia, Central Statistical Office (various issues); Becker (1985).

towns a good proxy for a high investment rate is whether or not a major parastatal investment project occurred during the period in question. The other major economic event that touched many previously isolated towns was the construction of the Tanzania-Zambia Railway (Tazara line), along with an accompanying highway link and oil pipeline, in the early 1970s. This increased accessibility both opened

TABLE 6.8. Determinants of Zambian City Growth
Twenty-three Cities; 1963–69, 1969–74, and 1974–80.
(absolute values of t-statistics are given in parentheses)

Independent Variable	Dependent Variables: Annual City Growth Rate, %			Residuals from regression (2)		
				1974–80 Observ.	1969–74 Observ.	1963–69 Observ.
	(1)	(2)	(3)	(4)	(5)	(6)
Constant	9.065	9.065	10.569	−0.76	−3.902	−1.385
	(5.15)	(5.76)	(6.89)	(0.62)	(1.68)	(0.59)
DZ4-80: Period 3 (1974–80) dummy	1.061	−0.391	−1.463			
	(0.43)	(0.14)	(0.53)			
D69-74: Period 2 (1969–74) dummy	−0.113	−1.656	−3.16			
	(0.05)	(0.59)	(1.20)			
DT: Tanzara line dummy		4.952	9.709			
		(1.77)	(3.26)			
DCOPPER 69-74: Copperbelt Location dummy × Period 2 dummy		−2.238	−2.238			
		(0.61)	(0.66)			
DCOPPER 74-80: Copperbelt Location dummy × Period 3 dummy		−5.832	−6.264			
		(1.55)	(1.79)			
DIND: Industrial Project location dummy		5.765	4.035			
		(1.71)	(1.27)			
DS: Southern region Location dummy			−8.649			
			(3.28)			
1972–77 Provincial Employment growth rate				−12.503		
				(2.15)		
1963–69 City Employment growth rate					6.434	2.533
					(1.19)	(0.46)
R^2	.00	.25	.36	.18	.17	.03
Number of Observations	69	69	69	23	9	9
F	0.14	3.48	4.99	4.62	1.42	0.22
Mean of dependent variables	9.38	9.38	9.38	0.00	−1.40	−0.40

markets and made import supplies more readily available to several small towns along the route, and should have served as an impetus to their growth.

Even without regression analysis, the impact of these events is obvious. From Table 6.7, it is clear that 1974–80 was a period of urban growth deceleration for the northern copperbelt cities and Lusaka. During this period, the most rapid growth occurred in Tazara line towns, and in other towns that enjoyed relatively large parastatal investments. Notable too is the more than tripling of Tazara line towns (excluding cities above 100,000 on the route) during 1969–74 over 1963–69.

The regressions in Table 6.8 also pick up these forces. Note from regression (1) that there is no general time trend: the coefficients on specific period dummies are insignificant when the growth rates for twenty-three towns and cities are pooled over three growth intervals. Individual cities appear to be neither accelerating nor decelerating: overall urban population growth has decelerated since 1974 because the largest cities (Lusaka and the main copperbelt cities) have decelerated, while several smaller cities have accelerated. Nor are the period dummies significantly different from zero when other explanatory variables are included.

The industrial location dummy is significant at the 90 percent level in regression (2), but only at about the 80 percent level in (3).[23] This decline in significance reflects its strong collinearity with the dummy for the Southern province, which received few new projects. The coefficient on *DIND* the industrial project location dummy variable, suggests that smaller cities can expect an increase of 4 to 6 percentage points in their *annual* population growth rates during a period of growing parastatal investment. Southern towns, on the other hand, grew nearly 9 percentage points more slowly than the others: the consequences of Rhodesia's UDI on southern Zambia were strong indeed.

The Tazara line dummy (*DT*) is quite strong, and during the early 1970s contributed 5 to 10 percentage points to growth rates of towns located along it. The copperbelt term (*DCOPPER*) is insignificant during the 1969–74 period, probably reflecting the industry's maturity by that period, and hence only a modest response to high world prices. But the collapse of world copper prices did have a marked impact, reducing copperbelt cities' growth rates by nearly 6 percent per annum between 1974 and 1980.

Regressions (4)–(6) attempt to link the residuals from regression (2) to provincial and city (formal sector) employment growth rates.[24] Obviously, simultaneity should be present, but one would expect the terms to be positively correlated in a base model. As it turns out, however, the residuals appear to be uncorrelated either with current (regression [6]) or lagged (regression [5]) city population growth rates, while 1974–80 residuals are inversely correlated with contemporaneous provincial formal sector employment growth. This latter pattern is somewhat surprising, and may reflect the Zambian government's efforts to promote industrial projects in generally stagnant regions. The absence of an apparent link between formal sector employment growth and population growth across cities is unsettling, but consistent with our cross-country empirical findings.

Overall, however, the regressions in Table 6.8 are encouraging. They suggest that migrants respond rapidly to changes in economic opportunities. In particular, the average mining town's growth rate was virtually halved in the late 1970s in comparison with earlier periods. The extremely large coefficients in Table 6.8 do not indicate that Zambians respond only slowly to market signals, or that city growth is uncontrollable. Decentralization can be achieved, although the inefficiency costs of pursuing regional industrialization (and possibly even infrastructure development) strategies do not make it necessarily desirable. Finally, the post-1974 recession has had a dramatic impact on the growth of the government-dependent capital as well as on the copper-dependent cities. There are no signs of "runaway cities" in Zambia. In summary, standard base models seem to fit Zambia reasonably well, and it seems safe to conclude that, given the further decline in public sector investment since 1980, further declines in city growth rates are likely to be recorded for the 1980s and 1990s.

6.9. Concluding Remarks

While microeconomic studies of the determinants of migration are abundant for Africa, the impact of macroeconomic variables on national migration flows and urbanization has gone largely uninvestigated. Yet there is a compelling need to understand those forces driving Africa's dramatic urbanization—particularly those forces subject to the influence of public policy.

The results here represent still tentative work. Further data improvements are highly desirable: longer series and more precise variable measures are particularly important; removal of omitted variables is equally desirable. We used several alternative proxies for important variables for which coefficient estimates were insignificant in the cross-country estimates (most critically, for the urban/modern manufacturing sector employment growth rate), but the estimates were not sensitive to the proxy employed. Nonetheless, qualitatively superior data might reverse this conclusion.

Several findings stand out. First, only a small portion (6 percent to 8 percent in unreported regressions) of the variation in African urban population growth rates can be explained by modern manufacturing employment growth rates, a surprisingly weak link. This finding, reinforced by the city growth estimates, casts doubt both on the unmodified Harris-Todaro (1970) model of rural-urban migration and on simple economic base models of aggregate urban growth in an African context.

On the other hand, public investment does appear to strongly influence population growth in the smaller cities of Zambia. Given the absence of a modern sector employment link, it would seem that the new infrastructure and expanded market surrounding a new project, rather than expectations of formal sector employment, are the main attractions for potential migrants.

The second finding is that governments do matter: the results presented above indicate that public policy has been an important contributor to urban growth. They also indicate that the continent's poor agricultural record (itself due largely to poor public policies) has been both a net contributor to overall urbanization, and is especially associated with extremely rapid growth of the capital cities (Table 6.1). Policies designed to promote rural growth presumably divert resources away from the largest cities, thereby restricting their growth both directly and due to rising opportunity costs for potential migrants. On the other hand, a pro-rural policy does generate some urban growth, but in smaller towns with closer economic links to the countryside. In short, not only is agricultural growth desirable for its direct welfare effects, it also redirects population movements in a manner desired by most governments.

Third, government spending patterns also strongly promote urbanization, especially with regard to investment projects. While such a "bias" to government policy is not necessarily inefficient, it is important that policymakers recognize the demographic consequences of their actions.

Fourth, the severe dependence of Africa's fledgling modern sectors on foreign exchange availability, critical for importing intermediate inputs and capital goods for import-substitution based urban industries, is reflected in the absence of a significantly positive sign on the world price of imported manufactured goods in Table 6.1. There can be little doubt that much of this foreign exchange dependence reflects inappropriate industrial choices, and is terribly unhealthy during a period of extreme foreign exchange scarcity in much of the continent. In better times, this dependence is also partially responsible for the continent's rapid urbanization.

Fifth, the appropriate economic paradigm for Africa remains unresolved. The neoclassical reduced form migration equation fits well in the cross-country regressions, but observational equivalence and small sample problems make it difficult to reject either the DCS or rent-seeking models. The rent-seeking regressions fit poorly, but the dramatic wage declines are far more consistent with rent-seeking than neoclassical theory. Meanwhile, demographic shifts seem to be important, but far more careful analysis is needed to bolster this claim.

All of the models, though, clearly suggest that the current era of structural adjustment should have a strong decelerating impact on the growth of African cities, especially capitals. In the short run, there appear to be continuing modern sector contractions that will reduce urban labor demand. There is also strong pressure from the major lending institutions to reduce the size of the public sector in most African nations, and to let at least the most inefficient parastatals fail. Once again, urban employment is likely to suffer. Reducing the urban-rural terms of trade will cut the purchasing power, and hence demand for consumer goods and services, even of those who do not lose their jobs. If the structural adjustment programs are sustained, and if they do generate better growth performances, urban growth will be likely to rebound. But it would be surprising if the 1980s and 1990s did not witness a strong continent-wide decline in the accelerating urbanization of the 1960s and 1970s.

Appendix 6A: A Mathematical Derivation of the Neoclassical Model

6.A.1. A Single Equation Model

Let urban modern/formal sector output UM be characterized by the production function

$$Q_{UM} = A_{UM}L_{UM}^{\alpha_1}M_{UM}^{\alpha_2}T_{UM}^{\alpha_3}K_{UM}^{\alpha_4} \qquad (6.A.1)$$

where A represents the level of technology, L is labor, M is imported intermediate goods, T is intermediate inputs produced by the urban traditional sector, and K is the urban modern capital stock.

Demand for urban modern output is given by:

$$P_{UM} = Q_{UM}^{\eta^1}\rho\,(P_M^*, GDP, GOV); \quad \eta^1<0 \qquad (6.A.2)$$

This demand function reflects the fact that urban modern (UM) output is import-substituting; demand for UM output thus depends upon the domestic price of imported goods P_M^*. P_M^*, in turn, is a function of the world price P_M^W and the degree of protection afforded domestic industry.

Solving the first-order conditions for profit maximization yields an equation for labor demand in the urban modern sector. After substituting the equilibrium demands for traditional sector output and imports, the labor demand equation is:

$$L_{UM} = \rho^{\beta_1} \left[\frac{\alpha_1}{W_{UM}}\right]^{\beta_1\beta_2} \left[\frac{\alpha_2}{P_M^*}\right]^{\beta_1\alpha_2\eta} \left[\frac{\alpha_3}{P_T}\right]^{\beta_3} [K_{UM}^{\alpha_4}A_{UM}]^{\beta_1\eta} \qquad (6.A.3)$$

where

$$\beta_1 = \frac{1}{\beta_2 - \alpha_1\eta}; \ \beta_2 = [1 - \alpha_2\eta][1 - \alpha_3\eta] - \alpha_2[\eta]^2;$$
$$\beta_3 = \beta_1\eta[\alpha_2\eta + \alpha_3 - \alpha_2\alpha_3\eta] \qquad (6.A.4)$$
$$\eta = 1 + \eta^1 > 0 \Rightarrow \eta^1 > -1.$$

Since η^1 is the inverse of the price elasticity of demand, $\eta > 0$ implies that the long-run demand for UM goods is price elastic. This is not obvious, but neither is it too unreasonable given the competition from imports and small-scale producers.

If urban traditional sector production is Cobb-Douglas, labor demand can be described as:

$$L_T = \left[\frac{\gamma_1 A_T K_T^{\gamma_4}}{W_T}\right]^{\frac{1}{1-\gamma_1}} \qquad (6.A.5)$$

where W_T is the traditional sector wage, γ_1 is labor's output elasticity, and γ_4 is capital's output elasticity. Labor demand is decreasing in the wage and increasing in technological efficiency (A_T) and capital stock (K_T).

The model's rural economy is quite simple, largely due to data restrictions. Our specification follows Hansen's (1979) stylized model for an African economy characterized by scarce high-quality but copious "marginal" land. If this is the case, the marginal product of peasant land is zero, and labor's average and marginal products are identical. In principle, rural output will depend on several factor inputs, including capital, labor, and intermediate goods such as fertilizers and pesticides. Since data for nonlabor inputs are unavailable, these factors are lumped into the technology term. Assuming a strictly concave production function, marginal returns to labor are diminishing, and average product declines with employment:

$$W_R = \frac{P_R Q_R}{L_R} = P_R q_R (L_R) \qquad (6.A.6)$$

where W_R = rural wage, or average rural earnings, L_R = rural employment, and Q_R = rural output.

If free entry is assumed into the urban traditional sector, there will be no unemployment in this sector. Further, zero migration equilibrium requires that $W_T = W_R$. If π is defined to be the probability of obtaining a UM sector job, labor market equilibrium requires $\pi W_{UM} = W_R$. We follow Harris and Todaro (1970) in assuming that π is a function of the ratio of currently unemployed to currently employed workers:

$$\pi = \left[\frac{U_{UM}}{L_{UM}}\right]^\phi; \ \phi < 0 \qquad (6.A.7)$$

To solve the model and reduce it to an estimable form, the labor force "adding-up" constraint is needed:

$$\bar{L} = L_{UM} + U_{UM} + L_T + L_R \tag{6.A.8}$$

where $\bar{L}$, the national labor force, is assumed to be exogenously given. Finally, we assume the average product of rural labor $q(L_R)$ takes the form:

$$q(L_R) = A_R L_R^{\delta}; \; \delta < 0 \tag{6.A.9}$$

Collecting terms yields a single equation solution for L_R:

$$L_R = \bar{L} - \left\{ \rho^{\beta_1} \left[\frac{\alpha_1}{W_{UM}} \right]^{\beta_1 \beta_2} \left[\frac{\alpha_2}{P_M^*} \right]^{\beta_1 \alpha_2 \eta} \left[\frac{\alpha_3}{P_T} \right]^{\beta_3} [K_{UM}^{\alpha_4} A_{UM}]^{\beta_1 \eta} \right\}$$
$$\left\{ 1 + \left[\frac{P_R A_R L_R^{\delta}}{W_{UM}} \right]^{\frac{1}{\phi}} \right\} + \left[\left[\frac{P_R A_R L_R^{\delta} K_T^{-\gamma_4}}{\gamma_1 A_T} \right] \right]^{\frac{1}{\gamma_1 - 1}} \tag{6.A.10}$$

Although (6.A.10) cannot be solved analytically for L_R, it can be differentiated to solve for dL_R. Urban labor force growth is then obtained residually:

$$dL_{URBAN} = d\bar{L} - dL_R \tag{6.A.11}$$

Hansen's assumption of abundant marginal land ($\delta = 0$) allows a single equation solution for (6.A.10). Letting primes denote percentage changes and defining ε_{ij} to be the elasticity of i with respect to j and λ_R to be the share of group k in the urban labor force:

$$L_U' = \left[-\beta_1 (\lambda_{UM} + \lambda_U) - \frac{\lambda_U}{\phi} \right] \overline{W'_{UM}} + [\varepsilon_{\rho, P_M^*} - \alpha_2 \eta] \beta_1 (\lambda_{UM} + \lambda_U) P_M^{*'}$$
$$+ \beta_1 \varepsilon_{\rho, GDP} (\lambda_{UM} + \lambda_U) GDP' + \beta_1 \varepsilon_{\rho, GOV} (\lambda_{UM} + \lambda_U) GOV' + \left[\frac{\gamma_4}{1 - \gamma_1} \right] \lambda_T K_T'$$
$$+ \beta_1 \alpha_4 \eta (\lambda_{UM} + \lambda_U) K_{UM}' + \left[\frac{\lambda_U}{\phi} + \frac{\lambda_T}{\gamma_1 - 1} \right] (A_R' + P_R') \tag{6.A.12}$$

This is the equation which produces the results reported in Table 6.1.

6.A.2. SIMULTANEOUS EQUATION MODELS

The primary virtue of equation (6.A.12) is its simplicity, easily estimable form, and readily interpretable coefficients. The model generating (6.A.12), however, embodies several strong assumptions: the elasticity of rural labor's average product with respect to labor supply (δ) is assumed to be zero, equilibrium conditions governing trade and demand and supply of agricultural output are ignored, and there is assumed to be no use of agricultural intermediate inputs by formal sector firms.

The introduction of a foreign exchange constraint necessitates the estimation of a simultaneous equations system. The foreign exchange constraint can be written as:

$$eP_R X_R (P_R, L_R) + eX_{other} + FKI = eP_M M_{UM} + eM_{FOOD} + eM_{OTHER} \tag{6.A.13}$$

That is, the value at world prices of rural and other exports plus the value of foreign capital inflows (FKI) must equal the pretariff value of urban formal sector imports, food imports, and all other imports. If the world price of manufactures is fixed, then the domestic price (P_M) becomes endogenous, depending upon the value of the exchange rate. To the extent that rural (mainly agricultural) exports depend on rural conditions, e and hence P_M will depend on Q_R and L_R via (6.A.10).

If imported intermediates are unimportant for formal sector production and if exports and foreign capital inflows are highly inelastic with respect to the exchange rate, then little error is caused by treating the exchange rate as exogenous. But if these conditions are not met, the exchange rate via its effect on $P_M{}^*$ will affect L_{UM} in equation (6.A.3) as well as the equilibrium rural labor force, and L_{UM} must be simultaneously estimated with L_R.

The second constraint, equating the demand and supply of food, also makes the exchange rate a function of the rural labor force and rural output:

$$X_R\,(P_R) + F(\overline{L}) = M_{FOOD}(FKI) + A_R L_R^{1+\delta} \qquad (6.A.14)$$

or

$$X_R\,(eP_R^W) + F(\overline{L}) = M_{FOOD}(FKI) + A_R L_R^{1+\delta} \qquad (6.A.15)$$

The right-hand side of the equation is total food supply (domestic production plus food imports), while the left-hand side is food exports plus domestic demand for food. Assuming FKI and the world price are exogenously fixed, (6.A.14) determines e (and hence P_R) as a function of L_R. The exchange rate will also be a function of L_R if F depends on P_R—even if X_R is constant.

Incorporation of rural intermediates into urban modern production adds a P_R term to equation (6.A.3), the demand for formal sector labor. If P_R is regarded as an exogenous policy variable, then the only effect is to add terms with a negative sign in front of the $P_R{}'$ term in (6.A.12) and other growth equations. But explicitly recognizing that P_R depends on L_R and A_R, and replacing informal sector inputs into the urban modern sector with inputs from the rural sector yields:

$$L_{UM} = \rho^{\beta_1}\left(\frac{\alpha_1}{W_{UM}}\right)^{\beta_1\beta_2}\left[\frac{\alpha_3}{P_R\,(A_R,\,L_R)}\right]^{\beta_3}K_{UM}^{\alpha_4\beta_1\eta}\left[\frac{\alpha_2}{P_M^*}\right]^{\alpha_2\beta_1\eta} \qquad (6.A.16)$$

and

$$L_R = \overline{L} - L_{UM}\left\{1 + \left[\frac{P_R(A_R,\,L_R)\,A_R L_R^\delta}{W_{UM}}\right]^{\frac{1}{\phi}}\right\} - \left[\frac{\gamma_1 A_T K_T^{\gamma_4}}{P_R\,(A_R,\,L_R)\,A_R L_R^\delta}\right]^{\frac{1}{1-\gamma_1}} \qquad (6.A.17)$$

Totally differentiating (15) and (16) yields a 2×2 matrix in which $[L'_{UM}, L'_R]$ are dependent on $[W_{UM},\,A_R,\,GDP',\,GOV',\,K'_{UM},\,(1 + ARP)',\,\overline{L'},\,K'_T]$. Incorporating P_M's dependence on L_R via the foreign exchange constraint alters the coefficient terms but not the vector of explanatory variables. The resulting matrix can be estimated empirically using two-stage least squares (2SLS). A glance at the equation indicates that it satisfies the rank and order conditions for 2SLS estimation.

Appendix 6B. Data Sources and Definitions

Variable	Definition	Source
POP_T	national population	World Bank (1984a)
POP_R	rural population	United Nations (1981), Cour (1985)
POP_U	urban population	United Nations (1981), Cour (1985)
POP_i	city i's population	United Nations (1980), Cour (1985)
L_{um}	urban modern employment	World Bank (1983)
GDP	gross domestic product	World Bank (1983)
$GOVEXP$	central government expenditure	IMF (1984)
K_{um}	urban modern capital stock	IMF (1984)
$LFPR$	labor force participation rate	World Bank (1983)
$URBL$	urbanization level	United Nations (1981)
CAL	caloric intake	World Bank (1983)
K_T	urban traditional capital stock	World Bank (1983) IMF (1984)
P	domestic price of urban formal sector goods	UNCTAD (1984) IMF (1984)
$SIZE$	habitable land area	FAO (1982)
ARP	average rate of protection	IMF (1984)

Appendix 6C. Derivation of the Rent-seeking Model.

Production and output demand conditions in the rent-seeking model are identical to those in the neoclassical model, but formal sector labor demand is not. The rent-seeking model begins with the assumption that workers in the urban modern sector are able to capture a portion of that sector's value added:

$$W_{UM}L_{UM} = \theta\,[P_{UM}Q_{UM} - P_M^*M_{UM} - P_TT_{UM}] \qquad \text{(6.C.1)}$$

In addition, while labor cannot unilaterally determine both the wage and employment level, it is able to constrain firm hiring decisions:

$$L_{UM}(t) = \phi L_{UM}(t-1); \ \phi \geq 1 \qquad \text{(6.C.2)}$$

In effect, (6.C.2.) says that firms cannot reduce employment.

Equation (6.C.2.) can be substituted into (6.C.1) (after specifying an appropriate functional form for ϕ and θ), and this new equation can be solved for L_{UM}:

$$L_{UM} = f(P_{UM},\ P_M^*\overline{W_{UM}},\ P_T,\ \overline{K_{UM}},\ A_{UM},\ L_{UM}\,(t-1),\ \phi,\ \theta) \qquad \text{(6.C.3)}$$

Once the demand-sided condition determining P_{UM} is specified (see equation [6.A.2]), we have:

$$L_{UM} = f(\rho, \overline{W_{UM}}, P^*_M, P_T, \overline{K_{UM}}, A_{UM}, L_{UM} (t-1), \phi, \theta) \qquad \textbf{(6.C.4)}$$

Note the similarity between this specification of the rent-seeking model and equation (6.A.3) of the neoclassical model. The only difference between the two are the lagged urban modern labor employment, and the two parameters ϕ and θ, which describe labor's ability to fix employment and capture rents, respectively.

The technique for solving the rent-seeking model is the same as that for the neoclassical model. The labor force constraint is imposed (see equation [6.A.8] of Appendix 6A), and the equation is solved for the change in urban population (see equation [6.A.12]). Not surprisingly, the only differences in the reduced form equation *or* in the simultaneous equations system (if equilibrium constraints are imposed) are the new variables present in equation (6.C.4).

Finally, we need to specify the rent-share term. We assume that formal sector workers' ability to extract rents depends on:

$$\theta = g\left(\frac{G}{Y}, \frac{BD}{Y}, TB, FKI, PROT, U\right); g_1, g_3, g_4, g_5, g_6 > 0 > g_2 \qquad \textbf{(6.C.5)}$$

where G/Y is the share of government produced goods and services in GDP, BD/Y is the government budget deficit as a share of GDP, TB is the trade balance, FKI are foreign capital inflows, $PROT$ is a measure of the degree of protection conferred on the domestic formal sector, and U is the unemployment rate. To derive an estimating equation similar to (6.A.12), we then assume that firms seek to maximize profits given labor's bargaining position. While this assumption is obviously simplistic, it is apparent that most modifications of this assumption (regarding monopolistic, monopsonistic, satisficing, or general output maximizing behavior) will yield labor demand functions that are monotonically related to the labor demand function derived from profit maximization.[25]

7

Development Policies from an Urban Perspective: Strategies for the Future

We have concentrated thus far on analyzing forces that have generated Africa's exceptionally rapid urban growth, especially in its largest cities. The analysis for the most part has been positive: that is, we have examined the causes of the existing state of affairs, rather than suggesting what the world *should* look like. On the other hand, we have pointed out suboptimal policies. In this concluding chapter, therefore, we switch largely to normative analysis and offer a set of policy suggestions.

The first section sums up a few salient findings of the preceding chapters. These central conclusions serve as the bases for the recommendations that follow. Section 7.2 then sketches a set of proposals for urban decentralization and fiscal reform. Our viewpoint is similar but hardly identical to that advanced by the World Bank and other international agencies; our relative emphases often differ sharply. The third section turns to a brief discussion of economy-wide policies that will be conducive to rapid urban employment and income growth. The final section suggests the most immediate steps.

Before turning to normative analysis, we should reemphasize an essential point: situations differ from country to country. Nigeria is quite different from Namibia; Senegal hardly faces the same conditions as Kenya. Obviously, we believe there are economic and demographic similarities as well: if not, it would be unacceptable to write a book purporting to analyze "African urbanization." But simplification and abstraction are essential in theoretical and accompanying empirical analysis. On the other hand, general economic analysis and the general normative recommendations that follow require thoughtful modification before they form the basis for policy in any specific situation. Otherwise, country-specific constraints and idiosyncrasies that are fairly unimportant for most nations are likely to result in unanticipated, unique consequences in any application. To repeat: theory is inherently more general than policy.

7.1 Urban Growth in the Coming Decades

It is an inappropriate stereotype that little is known about African economies or cities. In reality, we have been able to establish a rather large set of conclusions. A few are briefly repeated here to serve as the basis for the following sections, but we do not seek to provide a lengthy summary of findings.

Urban growth in most African countries is likely to diminish in the next decade or two. This finding is driven in large part by the demographic cohort shifts taking place, though it must be emphasized that these are not permanent. That is, equilibrium population pyramids eventually will be restored. In addition, shifting terms of trade in favor of rural activities and the contractions of governments and urban formal sector activities also serve to discourage rural out-migration. The dramatic decline in real formal sector wages, which we believe reflects an underlying loss of rents (and labor's share of those rents), again discourages urban in-migration.

These adverse shocks are, one hopes, temporary. If structural adjustment policies are (eventually) successful in moving African nations to high-growth paths, there is little doubt that rapid economic growth will be accompanied by rapid urbanization. Economic growth will include rising formal sector labor demand; at the same time, income growth will imply surging demands for informal sector goods and services. While agricultural incomes will rise as well, Engels effects imply that they will hold labor back less strongly than the urban pull effects. Furthermore, trade liberalization in the long run will mean more agricultural imports in many countries. Economic growth also will be accompanied by a resumption of rapid gains in education and health care, leading to a renewed surge in the proportion of the population most likely to live in cities. In short, urban growth rates in the near future are likely to diminish. But unless there are considerable declines in fertility rates, African cities will resume their rapid growth in the event that economic fortunes are reversed.

Declining rural-urban migration will mean slower total real gross domestic product (GDP) growth. This result stems from the fact that migration involves movement from low- to high-productivity occupations. There can be little doubt, however, that some and perhaps a large proportion of the recorded GDP gain from migration does not reflect welfare gains, due to vestiges of urban bias in pricing policies and the negative externalities caused by migrants. In any event, this further decline in GDP growth simply reflects the process of structural adjustment, and should be expected. Thus, at least a portion of the decline does not reflect further deterioration in economic performance.

Nonetheless, cities generate much of Africa's GDP. We saw earlier that between 25 percent and 75 percent of GDP in various African countries was probably generated in urban areas. A unique social accounting matrix (SAM) recently estimated for Madagascar (World Bank [1991d]) contains careful information on rural and urban incomes; it finds that urban activities account for 45 percent of 1988 GDP, and 70 percent of likely GDP growth in the 1990s. The current estimate is that Madagascar's population is only 26 percent urban, implying an urban/rural per capita income ratio of 2.34. This figure is again very close to the estimates presented earlier for other African nations; it also appears that *rural/urban income gaps have declined* in Madagascar as well as in most of the continent. But even in the face of declining interregional inequality, it is virtually certain that urban areas will generate half or more of the Africa's additional output in the coming decades.

Like cities throughout the world, *Africa's cities are capital- and import-intensive.* Evidence surveyed in earlier chapters points to these phenomena, and in fact indicates that there are vast differentials in capital and import intensities between the largest urban centers and rural areas, and even main and secondary cities. Again, some specific estimates are available for Madagascar (World Bank [1991d]). Turning first to the trade balance, urban areas generated 56 percent of all 1988 exports (much of which were processed agricultural goods) but consumed 73 percent of imports. Rural Madagascar ran a fifty-six million dollar trade surplus with the rest of the world, and a sixty-seven million dollar surplus with urban Madagascar; urban Madagascar ran a ninety-two million dollar trade deficit with the rest of the world, so that the national trade balance was negative. Even more strikingly, the Antananarivo metro area alone was responsible for 32 percent of all imports, leading to a ninety million dollar foreign trade deficit. Without its capital city, Madagascar ran a fifty-three million dollar trade surplus; urban Madagascar outside the capital nearly balanced its account with the respect to external trade. Urban households accounted for 85 percent of all household imports, and 33 percent of all imports were attributed to the urban "elite" alone.

Turning to investment, urban Antananarivo received 26 percent of national investment (and 32 percent of public investment); urban Madagascar as a whole received 66 percent of total investment and 77 percent of public investment. Ironically, though, urban areas were responsible for slightly less than half of national savings, implying, as we have seen, net resource flows from rural to urban areas. Overall, rural Madagascar's ratio of savings to gross regional product in 1988 was 9.5 percent; the ratio for Antananarivo was 13.2 percent; and the ratio for other urban areas was 10.7 percent.

Urban growth in Africa is not and has not been "runaway." Rather, growth both of individual cities and total urban populations appears to reflect the effects of demographic and economic factors. The process is far from mysterious—the driving forces, on the contrary, are quite apparent. Furthermore, the forces driving urban growth in Africa are virtually identical to those that drive urbanization elsewhere. Africa is unique because the forces driving urban growth have been stronger than in most other places. In particular, these forces include total fertility, demographic shifts, deteriorating agricultural performance, and growth of government. It also appears that these forces have begun causing decelerating urbanization in many countries, including Zambia and Kenya, and (based on very tentative population estimates) Madagascar.

Africa's demographic shifts have had a side effect of great importance to policymakers. Urban adult populations have become much more clustered in the fifteen to twenty-nine year age groups since 1970. This shift has meant increasing demands for services, especially primary schooling for children, secondary schooling for teenagers, and maternal health care services. Thus, already rapidly growing pressure for more public services in the cities of Africa has been accentuated by an increase in the proportion of young adults.

Let us now turn to our findings with regard to African urban labor markets. *No model to date adequately explains migration behavior.* The neoclassical models that can be estimated fit cross-country data well, but do not do a good job either of explaining the tremendous declines in real wages in many countries during the 1980s, nor of accounting for the apparent slowdown in rural-urban migration in Kenya, despite continued agricultural deterioration. Rent-seeking models strike us as being inherently more plausible, and are consistent with time series trends, but do not fit well across countries. The demographic explanations clearly are important but, equally clearly, do not tell the whole story. Our view is that some combination of the models is needed to understand the process of migration and wage adjustment, and that future econometric work should be based on such multi-explanation models.

Labor market studies also indicate that *wage differentials within urban areas are due more to human capital differences than institutional barriers.* This is particularly true in the current economic environment, since protected sectors are far less protected than in the past. The immediate policy implication is that restricted access to education, barriers to skill and experience acquisition, differential access to credit, and forces that make it difficult for women to enter occupational tracks that permit upward mobility should be combated, while sectoral effects alone are generally less important. Secondly, the distinction between formal and informal sectors is important for understanding sources of economic growth, but may no longer be of great importance for understanding sources of earnings' inequality (once one corrects for differences in skills, full- or part-time labor market participation, and access to credit). On the other hand, if rent-seeking models remain more appropriate for formal sector analysis while competitive neoclassical economic paradigms are appropriate in the case of the informal sector, it will still be necessary to distinguish them conceptually in labor market studies.

It also appears most unlikely that further formal sector wage declines of the magnitude experienced since the late 1970s will take place. Part of the reason is that the gap between formal sector and urban informal sector or agricultural earnings has greatly narrowed, and will no longer permit huge formal sector wage declines without commensurate falls elsewhere. As incomes are already extremely low, great declines elsewhere are unlikely. Secondly, countries that have implemented structural adjustment programs (SAPs) do seem to have stabilized (especially as international credit flows have resumed), and the available evidence suggests that wages have at least stabilized. On the other hand, it is probably also unlikely that large rises are looming on the horizon.

SAPs also will affect urban structure. *Public policy prior to the imposition of SAPs tended to favor the relatively rapid growth of large cities (and hence of urban concentration), but the macroeconomic components of SAPs favor deconcentration.* The shrinking of government is perhaps the most important force here; focus on export production also should encourage the growth of secondary towns that engage in weight-losing processing of primary products. The decline of parastatals and rise of private sector production may have a mixed effect, although the efficiency of locational choices is almost certain to improve. In general, as Table 3.5 demonstrates, the shift away from state-sponsored industrialization is likely to generate urban deconcentration. Just as the models of migration and city growth suggested that standard economic and demographic forces were at work, so the study of urban concentration suggests that the relative availability of factors of production and comparative advantage can explain much of the differences in patterns of city systems.

On the other hand, *the current infrastructure rehabilitation, financial sector reform, and local government strengthening components of SAPs all have a big-city bias.* The reason for this is simple. Rehabilitation and decentralization needs are so vast, and financial sectors so stunted in many countries, that African governments and international institutions have little option but to concentrate first on restoring basic infrastructural services and creating viable institutions in the center rather than in smaller towns or rural areas. Only in countries such as Guinea, where rehabilitation of the major city is well underway (and, in Guinea's case, towns other than Conakry lack basic services as well as public sector management capability to introduce them) is attention now being turned even partially to building capacity in secondary cities (see World Bank [1990e]).

Again, the long run may look very different. In the near future, successful implementation of SAPs is likely to result in the rise of 1) resource-based processing cities, 2) agricultural marketing and supply towns, and 3) ports and towns at points of goods' transfer. Ultimately, though, economic growth will be accompanied by industrial growth and skills' deepening, and hence by forces that increase urban concentration. As we found in Chapter 3, if one of the accomplishments of SAPs is to reduce the balance of payments constraint, that too will induce greater urban concentration, since large cities tend to be foreign exchange intensive.

Chapter 2 discussed a set of problems that together greatly hampered urban output, employment, and productivity growth. *Disintegrating infrastructure and living conditions* are among the most visible problems. The examples cited earlier in this book are hardly atypical and cannot be said merely to reflect conditions from a passing era. In Addis Ababa, for example, the number of persons per room rose from 1.9 to 3.3 between 1984 and 1988 (World Bank [1990g]). In Ghana, the ratio of urban housing prices to income are possibly the highest in the world—about 12:1 (World Bank [1990f]), more than twice the ratios found even in Japan and India, and reflecting the virtual paralysis of the domestic construction industry. Basic urban sanitation and transport services in urban Ghana also collapsed between the mid-1970s and mid-1980s. The same can be said of urban Madagascar, where real public service expenditures fell by 60 percent between 1979 and 1988,[1] and where a World Bank (1991d:59) team was moved to comment that "the quality of the services provided by local governments has continually eroded, so that it often appears that the main function local governments perform today is to pay their employees' wages."

While conditions in capital cities are bad, matters typically are far worse in secondary cities. Moreover, insofar as infrastructure rehabilitation takes place, it will favor urban areas in general and the largest cities in particular, mainly because these have been the sites of most initial infrastructure. In many countries in recent years (for example, in Benin during the late 1980s), institutions charged with infrastructure maintenance have had virtually no resources at their disposal beyond staff salaries.

Weak land and capital markets clearly affect urban production as well, though the magnitudes are not well established. Unclear property rights greatly discourage the construction of large structures, as the threat of confiscation exists.[2] The risk is especially great for private sector concerns (governments can always change the rules), and for those without political pull. Presumably, private entrepreneurs who are not too small (as they must have access to capital) but who are not so big as to be politically powerful are those who suffer the most from unclear property rights. In a country such as Ghana, where "there is no effective market for land" (World Bank [1990f:8]), the absence of the most available collateral and difficulty of obtaining clear title represent binding constraints on the functioning of a viable housing construction sector.[3] Not only is the total volume of housing and other urban investment reduced by land market failures, limited transactions and large numbers of "squatter" settlements also ensure that urban densities in most if not all large African cities are suboptimally low—and hence that unit costs of service provision and urban transport are excessive.[4]

Another finding that has appeared continuously throughout this book is that *rural and urban households maintain strong linkages*.[5] One cannot have a set of urban or rural policies in isolation. Spillover effects are often complex and surprising. We know that remittances are extremely important, but only recently have micro studies of migration established the great extent to which rural-urban migration is a risk-minimizing strategy. The focus of the migration literature on expected returns thus misses an important and policy-relevant aspect to migration: the extent to which it is driven by the uncertain nature of rural incomes.

Taken together, these findings and others reported throughout the book suggest that policymakers should reassess the way they approach urban issues. Indeed, the five urban policy themes presented in Chapter 1 are largely irrelevant today, and certainly provide no guide to designing further urban policies. Of the themes and objectives, we have argued in this book that *combating big city primacy* is an inappropriate goal, mainly because spatial concentration itself is determined by various economic forces, and has little independent impact on welfare. Furthermore, spatial patterns are not easily influenced by public policy unless huge public infrastructure and parastatal investments are made. Few African countries are in a position to make such commitments today. Moreover, the next decade is likely to be one of greater spatial deconcentration.

Many of the same remarks apply to *overurbanization*. Not only is reducing the proportion of the population living in cities at best a second tier objective, it is our strong belief that urban growth rates will slow greatly in many countries during the 1990s. It is not likely, however, that urbanization rates will actually decline—that is, that rural population growth rates will exceed urban population growth rates. The *decentralized physical structure* of many African cities is again a second tier problem, and one that is best addressed by tackling the underlying impediments to more rapid increases in urban densities. Chief among these barriers in many cities are land use restrictions and an absence of clear property rights.

Nor is the concern about *maintaining (high) standards* particularly relevant to the 1990s. Idealized standards cannot be maintained; rather, the key debates concern what is feasible. But the temptation to excessively "rehabilitate" national capitals once SAPs have been adopted and foreign capital inflows have picked up must be resisted if recovery is not to be slowed. On the other hand, some basic rehabilitation must be achieved in countries that have experienced an almost complete collapse of transport and other economic services (as in Uganda: see World Bank [1990d]). The creation of a healthy economic growth environment also means that *distrust of the informal sector* must truly cease. Of all the policy tenets, this may be the most damaging, and anecdotal evidence suggests that many African governments remain hostile.

In summary, the major debates of the past decades have passed by. While policymakers may not always follow practices conducive to rapid income and welfare growth—especially of the poor—there is little disagreement among researchers or policy analysts about the assertions in the preceding paragraphs. Rather, the present policy debates are focused on fiscal reform and the strengthening of local governments, and on appropriate macro and industrial policies.

7.2. Fiscal Reforms and Strengthening Local Governments

A major component of structural adjustment programs has been a commitment to raise tax revenues, especially for public services. Many countries also have been encouraged to strengthen their local governments by decentralizing responsibility for providing public services, and also transferring some fiscal authority from central governments. The World Bank, with the concurrence of other international organizations and major donor countries, has been instrumental in promoting these elements of SAPs. In countries with highly centralized systems, such as Mozambique or Ethiopia, only very preliminary steps are being taken to decentralize; elsewhere, progress has advanced much further.

These objectives are highly desirable, though they entail costs as well. The most important constraint is that government decentralization may increase the demand for skilled civil servants. As few governments are capable of expanding their real manpower budgets, the alternative may be to have untrained or skeleton staffs to man various local government authorities. This is particularly true if local authorities have fee or tax-collecting responsibilities. Nevertheless, there is a compelling case for strengthening local governments. Unfortunately, donors have continued to shy away from funding restoration of local civil service positions at remotely attractive salaries in advance of other reforms, and in general have not clearly integrated urban and manpower development programs.[6]

While most World Bank and other international agency projects do have "institutional support components," our reading of specific project appraisal reports is that the resources devoted are not clearly connected to long-term needs. Nor are fallback positions identified in case local governments do not rise to the tasks assigned them, either because the optimistic local tax revenue projections are not realized or because skilled civil servants cannot be attracted even given rapid revenue growth and pay hikes. These problems are especially severe when projects are aimed at secondary cities. These points should not be taken as criticisms of the World Bank or other agencies, which clearly cannot solve all problems, and must start somewhere. Rather, the manpower issue is one that must be tackled by African governments, with whom responsibility lies for renewing secondary and higher education. To put it differently, *structural adjustment programs require skill intensities not greatly different from that needed for (failed) planned economies, and the international community's assistance with soft loans and institutional advice may prove useless unless African nations rise to the challenge and increase their supply of two complementary inputs—skilled labor and a willingness to truly decentralize.*

These points are made unusually bluntly in a World Bank (1990f:46) staff appraisal report of Ghana's Urban II Project:

> In the medium term (3-5 years), there is no substitute for restructuring civil service organizations, restructuring parastatals and training qualified staff . . . restructuring salaries and incentives and *developing special postgraduate programs to train both public and private sector managers.* Such programs do not exist in Ghana at present, and their importance has been lost in the recent focus on primary education. The problem will become worse if action is not taken now.

Looking back over roughly three decades of independent government across Africa, a widely applicable generalization can be made fairly: central governments attempted to extend control over all aspects of economic life in an effort to enforce their vision of development against the "whims" of other sources of initiative. But instead of success, there has been a decline of institutional infrastructure matched by a growth of parallel channels of activity for which the state has become increasingly irrelevant.[7]

In particular, municipal government has been a major victim of central government attempts to stifle independent initiative. As withdrawal into parallel markets obviously was not an option for these local public authorities, they simply withered:

> top government officials took authority away from local governments, under the illusion that they were thereby acquiring more power. They discovered instead that they had acquired the *negative* power to prevent other political actors from taking independent initiatives, but not the *positive* power to implement policies that would improve social welfare. (Kasfir [1983])

Where they were relatively strong, local governments had their financial autonomy curtailed and their freedom of action severely circumscribed. In some cases, such as in Tanzania, local government actually was abolished during part of the 1970s. In others, such as in Nigeria, municipal governments saw many of their functions taken over by parastatals and state governments. Some municipalities, such as Monrovia (Liberia), were given few internally generated revenues:

> Central Government has pre-empted most significant sources of local revenue including the property tax, typically the most common source of municipal revenue elsewhere. City income includes minor fees for marketing stalls, burials, trash collection, and city court fines totalling only about $164,000. . . . These are the only funds [the local government] . . . has authority to spend directly. (World Bank [1981a])

In Francophone and Lusophone Africa, local government at Independence was embryonic to begin with, and remains subject to the capriciousness of highly centralized decision making. Even in Anglophone countries, like Kenya, which maintained a commitment to local authority, some traditional sources of revenue dried up even as new responsibilities were added.

In countries driven by revolutionary socialist ideology, there has typically been a confusion of egalitarianism with centralization of state authority— especially where wars have exacerbated the need for centralization. In countries such as Mozambique, there is virtually no local autonomy, given the system of "dual subordination," which in practice means that urban authorities are heavily responsible directly to the central government (World Bank [1991f]). While modern socialist thought has come to recognize that both empowerment of the citizenry and economic success requires true decentralization, most African socialist experiments first undertook disastrous experiments with extreme centralization. Although they are now reversing themselves, the FRELIMO and other socialist governments have lost a great deal of legitimacy, and also have wrecked already weak local institutions.[8]

Creating local, autonomous governments under such circumstances will be difficult. Local decision-making capability in a country such as Mozambique is very limited: central control (or, in its absence, near paralysis) is still great. So is dependence on central government transfers. While cities like Beira and Maputo no longer receive 70 percent or so of their budgets from the central government, 40-60 percent in the larger cities was standard as of 1989.[9] In Ghana (World Bank [1990f]), the central government pays all local civil service salaries, and, while the nation has taken admirable and striking steps toward political decentralization, extreme financial and administrative centralization remains.

And yet, *the process of structural adjustment*, with its commitment to central government retrenchment, greater resource mobilization by public bodies, encouragement of private initiative, and the preservation of existing assets, *cannot succeed without the simultaneous strengthening of local government, especially in Africa's cities and towns*. It is in these urban areas that a significant share of economic activity occurs, and it is also at the local level that all alternatives to viable autonomous local government have long reached the limits of their competence. These alternatives include the overextended national authority, but also private voluntary organizations which readily admit that, given the magnitude of local governance requirements, much of what they do in this field is more symbolic than substantive.

Municipal governments must have the ability to govern Africa's cities and towns. They must plan investment programs, implement them, and maintain the resultant infrastructure and services. For this, municipalities must have autonomy as well as institutional competence. The central government's role should not be negligible, but must be trimmed back and refocused. Specifically, central governments must retain important oversight functions, including auditing of accounts, prescribing standards for staff qualifications, providing periodic inspections by central supervisors, and reviewing procurement processes. Central governments also must administer infrastructure development loan funds, incentive grants, and other funds. And central governments must show patience with newly empowered autonomous bodies, as they will certainly take time to become efficiently functioning entities, especially given the manpower shortages in countries with the greatest degree of deterioration.

Of current government systems in Africa, perhaps the strongest system is in Zimbabwe—where, not coincidentally, municipal facilities and services are the best in the region. As of the mid-1980s,

> Government financial assistance to local authorities . . . is quite limited. There is no system of revenue sharing, with only modest grants for general administrative purposes which are being gradually phased out. There are no subsidies for local public services.

> Government loans are made to local authorities for capital projects. . . .
> Funds are provided on a project-by-project basis, with the Government
> appraising the projects financed. The Central Government . . . exer-
> cises . . . financial control over local authorities, including approval of
> budgets and all borrowing powers. . . .
> Zimbabwe's cities have well-developed public services and are in sound
> financial conditions. They produce detailed budgets and accounts and
> maintain strict control over expenditure. The principal of cost recovery
> is stringently applied to services that can run commercially . . . and tar-
> iffs are raised as necessary to keep pace with costs. Revenue collections
> operate well and the accounts do not show substantial arrears. (World
> Bank [1985]).

The gap between this model and reality elsewhere is large. Sustained external
support will be needed as local institutions are rehabilitated and developed. But
examples of increased municipal self-reliance exist, in World Bank–funded projects
from Mali to Burundi to Ghana to Madagascar to Nigeria (see Hamer [1986]). Bamako's tax revenue tripled in U.S. dollar terms between 1979 and 1985. This has
come about through better enforcement of existing tax codes and through new
taxes. In Bujumbura, local revenues (in terms of U.S. dollars) rose fourfold between
1980 and 1985; in the latter year, 80 percent of revenues were generated by taxes
approved during the first World Bank urban project. Accra, benefiting from a re-
evaluation of its property tax base, had expected to triple locally generated revenues in real terms between 1984 and 1989; in fact, this goal was actually achieved
a year early.[10] Antananarivo, whose receipts fell 30 percent in real terms during
the 1970s, is forecast to double real revenues between 1983 and 1994, despite a decline from roughly one-third to one-sixth in the share financed by central government transfers. Lagos sought in the mid-1980s to nearly quadruple in one year its
property tax collections. Conakry's tax resources per capita doubled between 1986
and 1988; the second urban plan with the World Bank envisions a more than tripling between 1990 and 1995. And with World Bank (1992) assistance, Benin is also
undertaking a major push to increase local resources in Cotonou and Porto Novo.

Part of the benefit from increased autonomy is automatic. If central governments are paralyzed and failing to provide essential services, then greater local autonomy can only improve matters. Strengthened local governments are certain as
well to be responsive to local needs and priorities, and can hardly fail to be more
successful in collecting tax revenue.

Public sector devolution of authority also represents an important step in
achieving greater economic efficiency. Towns with comparative advantages in production will experience more rapid growth than other urban areas, more rapidly
growing local government tax revenue, and therefore more rapid growth in the
provision of public services. These towns will therefore attract more firms and
workers. Consequently, factors of production will be induced to go to relatively efficient towns, or towns with particular cost advantages. In the presence of various
externalities (such as added congestion costs not borne by migrating capital or labor), such an outcome cannot be guaranteed to improve social efficiency. But in
practice, it seems overwhelmingly likely that there will be considerable efficiency
gains realized relative to the existing, largely arbitrary central allocation of public
services and infrastructure.

On a somewhat more speculative plane, it is also possible to envision different cities and towns competing for (at least relatively wealthy) workers and firms. This competition (first modeled in the U.S. context by Tiebout [1956]) will generate improvements both in the efficiency of production of local public goods and services, and also in the desirability of the mix provided. While serious equity concerns unquestionably exist, it still seems highly likely that such competition would bring considerable social benefits, given the potential growth that would be unleashed simply by the creation of responsive local authorities.

7.2.1. A Selective Agenda for Local Governments

With increased self-reliance comes the possibility of fulfilling a key macroeconomic objective: the preservation and rehabilitation of existing infrastructure and services, along with efforts to make more effective use of these existing assets. Many examples of this type can be found among World Bank urban projects. In Accra, a project was developed in the mid-1980s to support the government's economic recovery program (see World Bank [1984b], [1990f]); it entered a second phase and was extended to five other cities in 1990. It provided for selective new investments to remove infrastructural bottlenecks constraining the road transport of exports and imports, along with a maintenance program for Accra's road and drainage networks. Economic rates of returns ranging from 45 percent to 155 percent were calculated for the various road sections being completed or rehabilitated. Rates of return for the periodic and routine maintenance work were estimated to vary from 30 percent to 46 percent. Similar results are likely to obtain in other African cities, especially in countries beset by wars or which have experienced dramatic declines in GDP and public sector capacity.[11] These rates of return tend to be higher than for other urban investments (again, for Uganda, see World Bank [1990d]), and for many if not most nonurban investments. Economic efficiency thus indicates that they should be given high priority in Africa's least developed countries, and especially in countries with great rehabilitation needs.

There are also examples where better use of existing facilities has made planned new investments unnecessary. A good example emerged in Abidjan during the implementation of the World Bank's first urban project. Better use of roads and bridges, by employing traffic management measures and introducing preferential lane treatment for buses, allowed the government to defer new investments totalling more than US$ 400 million (Tager [1985]).

The challenge to urban governments in Africa does not end there. *They must ease the adjustments to rapid urban growth by increasing serviced land development and tapping latent private initiative.* At the rates of urban growth forecast over the next decade (4.0 percent seems to be a likely lower bound; 6.0 percent is a plausible upper bound), urban Africa's population will grow by an average of 7.7 million to 11.6 million residents annually, or the equivalent of replicating Kinshasa plus Lagos. This, in turn, will call for annual growth of 77,000 to 116,000 serviced hectares of urban land for all uses (assuming a minimum of 100 square meters per new resident, for all purposes). The costs of not responding to this challenge are evident across Africa—as both Kinshasa and Lagos demonstrate vividly.

This task requires the coordinated introduction of affordable infrastructure across thousands of cities and towns. It must be unsubsidized as well, since no funds exist for massive subsidies.[12] Massive infrastructure provision requires that certain other conditions be met as well: 1) the public sector must *disengage* from activities that subsidize the city dweller; 2) new infrastructure standards are needed that are lower than those that prevailed during the construction of colonial towns; 3) there must be a serious effort to conserve public resources by encouraging private investments (as is underway in Benin); 4) a new system of intergovernmental relations should focus on the creation of consolidated, self-financing infrastructure development funds which allow cities and towns to compete against one another for investment capital on equal terms; and 5) institutional reforms are needed that will permit the creation of coherent city-wide development strategies and greater managerial capacity.

The case for progressive *central government disengagement* is as easy to justify economically as it may be difficult to implement politically. Misguided and unaffordable efforts at equating equity with subsidies, rather than with access to services, have failed across Africa. Fortunately, in country after country, central governments are beginning to face up to the hemorrhaging of public funds that is caused by any attempt to maintain high levels of public service provision for select, favored groups.

From the building codes in Nairobi to the sites and services developments in Bamako and Bauchi State (Nigeria), significantly lower and more appropriate standards have become increasingly acceptable across urban Africa. This has affected not only the quality of residential developments, but also the efficiency of the productive sectors, especially informal activities, that function in their midst. The small-scale businesses so prominent in these local economies require careful tending: for the informal entrepreneur, unaffordable infrastructure standards are as damaging as no services at all, and the end result is that most neighborhoods are neglected because cost recovery strategies are made impossibly burdensome.

The stage is now set to introduce, on a wide scale across the continent, the remaining components needed to ensure the success of a strategy of rapid growth of serviced land development.[13] The World Bank is continuing to fund these projects, but it alone can hardly meet Africa's needs. We now know that the private sector and individual households will respond (at least under the right conditions) as intended, carrying out investments on serviced land. On the initial sites and services projects in Senegal, for example, more than eight CFA francs were invested by households benefiting from the project for every CFA franc invested by the Senegalese government and World Bank (Tager [1985]). Furthermore, this multiplier effect encouraged the growth of sectors with relatively high domestic value added, and diverted funds that otherwise would have been spent in part on imported goods. This has obvious macroeconomic implications, and supports the structural adjustment process.

In Zimbabwe, the government has engaged the energies and financial resources of private savings and loans building societies to help finance serviced land development. Where once municipalities were mortgage holders as well as developers of serviced plots, now the building societies hold the mortgages, financing up to two-thirds of recoverable development costs. Because local governments can now immediately recover most investment costs attributable to serviced land development, the same resources can finance up to one-third more infrastructural development than before (World Bank [1985]). More recently, the World Bank has committed resources to establishing a viable formal sector housing finance institution in Ghana.

Kenyan authorities have gone one step further. As part of the World Bank's third urban project, a subdivision owned by a private developer in Eldoret is ceding rights of way and land for public facilities to the municipality, which, in turn, provides the requisite infrastructure. The developer then gets private financing for plot development costs and repays the municipality at the time of sale. Similarly, in the portion of the current World Bank urban project in Benin aimed at the Cotonou suburb of Godomey-Sud, local beneficiaries will be expected to cede part of their land for public infrastructure, as well as to provide labor for secondary drains construction and pay a share of survey and engineering fees.

Turning to infrastructure construction, in Ethiopia and several other countries, bids for civil works contracts for street maintenance, urban waste management, and other infrastructure will be solicited in small units (an average value of $200,000 is estimated), thus aiming to attract bids from medium-scale local contractors. In this way, the initial rehabilitation projects are aimed at increasing local capacity, and hopefully increased demand for domestic production of construction materials (which remains problematic in Ethiopia). Infrastructure rehabilitation, with an emphasis on contracting to the informal and semiformal sectors (a part of the current urban rehabilitation and management projects in Benin and Guinea, and, in the case of the most recent Ghanaian project, including a small pilot specifically training women in construction), together with efforts to strengthen housing finance markets, appear to be taking precedence over sites and services schemes today, though some of the latter continue to be included in various projects.

These mechanisms in effect are preparatory steps for the more ambitious effort to establish consolidated revolving infrastructure development funds. Ideally, funding agencies would appraise both project proposals and local government financial and institutional capacity when municipalities make fund requests, whether for commercial, private housing, industrial, or mixed infrastructural development projects. Weaker municipalities then would be provided with technical assistance in the initial phases of such an operation. Eventually, municipalities would self-select for participation in fund proceeds by competing with one another in terms both of projects and municipal government performance. This concept already has been adopted in several developing countries.

One final item remains on the agenda: an improved urban management process.[14] Administrative and institutional reform at the local level must parallel conventional infrastructure project efforts. As new local resources are mobilized, more attention must be paid to creating a local development strategy that sets priorities for municipal development, the policies required to implement them, and the investments needed to ensure their realization. This framework also should enable coordination with strategic frameworks for other sectors, so that they can be mutually supportive.

In the past, governments and donors have emphasized the preparation of physical investment projects by agencies often at best tenuously connected to the local government whose responsibility it is to coordinate local development and maintain the resulting works. The result has been a proliferation of weak or missing links between conventional project investments and the rest of the area's infrastructure. Many of the problems identified in the discussion of infrastructure deficiencies in Chapter 2 are symptoms of weak local urban management capacity.

It is also important to install a systematic strategy to manage urban assets and services, including the development of measures to monitor, assess, and modify operations and maintenance performance. To date, inadequate attention has been given by central governments and donors alike to these issues. Yet the conventional approach to development projects is often guilty of triggering a management crisis at the local level by failing to coordinate the creation of assets with the definition of responsibilities and revenue sources to preserve them thereafter. A similar failure to ensure adequate local skilled manpower to manage the projects during their lives is equally or more damaging, as it leads to dependence on expatriates or rapid deterioration of the assets created.[15]

Over time, these issues can only grow more important. Many cities in sub-Saharan Africa can be expected to grow very large over the next decade or two. Capital investments will proliferate in number and grow in size as more cities begin to experience the problems of a Lagos or a Kinshasa, an Accra or a Dar es Salaam. With the prolonged economic crisis, even cities in relatively prosperous and well-managed countries like Zimbabwe have experienced severe urban management problems in the face of accelerating demands and often stagnant or dwindling real resources. In short, the ability of local governments to select, coordinate, and preserve infrastructure service packages will be tested continuously, and the results will greatly influence whether African countries are able to develop efficient, vibrant economies in the coming decade.

7.2.2. The Need for Improved Factor Markets

Many of the measures discussed thus far require that attention be paid to factor markets, especially those for land. There is a serious need to develop land information systems that not only will make urban land mobilization more effective, but also will allow entrepreneurs and households to freely trade land whose ownership is not in question.

Progressively upgradable land information systems can be devised. At its simplest, officials can record just the information needed for property taxation. The name of the owner, owner's agent, or occupant can be assigned to each plot, along with the rough size class corresponding to the land area occupied. A size class and quality of construction category can be assigned to any structure on the lot. But throughout Africa in the near future, more elaborate systems must be implemented as well. This includes a survey and ownership registry of all urban (and, eventually, rural) property, with courts or other referees making final assignments. These must then be followed by the establishment of permanent ownership records. Limitations on the number of co-owners of plots, or of those with the legal right to halt plot transfer, also may be important in many societies—as will be clear delineation of and restrictions on the state's eminent domain.

More modest, but also interesting, are the efforts underway from Bamako to Kampala (and virtually all World Bank urban project sites in between) to survey substantial portions of the city, and to provide tenure regularization, through the systematic registration and compilation of all occupancy permits.[16] But the importance of these achievements should not be underestimated, for efficient land use cannot occur without adequate mechanisms for property transfer, which in turn requires clear titles. At the same time, real property is the most important source of loan collateral by small enterprises seeking formal sector loans; the absence of clear property rights is thus a major impediment as well to the development of a nation's financial system. Finally, property registration is prerequisite for the establishment of a viable property tax system, which must be one of the main sources of local public finance.

Such efforts deserve more support from governments and the international community alike. As with land market issues, those involving loans to smaller-scale enterprises can be tackled if accumulated experience is used as a guide (for useful reviews, see von Pischke [1991]; Adams, Graham, and von Pischke [1984]; Harper [1984]; and Blayney and Otero [1985]). Improvements in capital market access for smaller firms begin at the macroeconomic level. As with most forms of subsidization in poorer countries, subsidization of interest rates on loans to small business constrains access to funds by making such loans unremunerative to the supplier. Interest on such loans will have to be higher than those for larger businesses, at least initially, because the administrative costs involved are higher. Per unit of funds lent, more applications must be reviewed, more approvals must be granted, and more legal titles to collateral must be confirmed. Small loan borrowers also face serious problems. The formalities involved in loan applications are formidable, and generating acceptable collateral is extremely difficult. Moreover, countless visits must be made to the banks by the owner-manager, thus disrupting production.

Once the interest rate issue is resolved, however, there are many low cost ways of dealing with the problems cited. Referrals and formalities can be filtered through local extension services (which will be needed in any case), community bank managers, and trade groups or other nongovernmental organizations. Collateral bottlenecks can be alleviated by the development of guarantee or insurance funds to cover such loans. Financial institutions also can use self-selected mutual security group loans, where funds are guaranteed against default by several potential borrowers. Other features of loans can be adapted to encourage a good credit record. The initial loans can be both small and short-term (the best collateral is the need for a future loan); larger, longer-term loans can follow, based in part on prior repayment performance. Problems with arrears can be dealt with by the use of substantial penalties and aggressive follow-up, leading to restructuring, rescheduling, or a foreclosure of the loan.

The record of carefully crafted microenterprise loan schemes is generally very good, with high rates of return and substantial employment effects. Indeed, the emphasis on risk of lending to new, small-scale borrowers (largely women in many cases) is offset by their systematic overappreciation of lending institutions' ability to collect bad loans (which is often very limited). As Becker and Lubuele (1991) have found in The Gambia, "familiarity breeds contempt" for larger, more powerful and informed borrowers, who consequently have greatly inferior repayment records relative to those less well connected. In any event, developing functional capital markets that extend to the informal sector is a critical component of a viable development strategy in nearly all African nations, and capital market development will proceed alongside the development of urban land markets.

7.3. Toward New Economy-Wide Strategies

In the preceding section, we sketched a set of urban policies that would improve the efficiency of African cities while simultaneously contributing to real GDP growth. We turn now to the converse topic: a brief examination of macroeconomic policies conducive to or at least compatible with increasingly efficient urban production and overall spatial division of production.

Let us begin by offering our own formal definition of *urban bias*. We define sectoral bias *to encompass all policies that raise a sector's unit value added at domestic prices above that which would prevail at international prices.* This definition obviously includes protective tariffs. It also includes government infrastructural or other subsidies that reduce costs. The concept is also a net one: controlled prices and taxes work to reduce the favorable bias toward a factor. One can define a bias toward a particular factor of production in a given sector (namely, urban formal sector labor) analogously.

Given this definition, we advocate implementation of a balanced development *policy.* This advocacy is seemingly inconsistent with Hirschman's (1961) notion of unbalanced development as a spur to the development of various linkages, but, in fact, imbalances should be determined by market forces. It is inappropriate for governments to designate "leading sectors," mainly because they are so likely to be wrong. It is inevitably the case that rapid growth environments will involve considerable growth disparities across sectors, but government should maintain a level playing field rather than trying to spur growth further by tilting toward those sectors with alleged agglomeration economies, economies of scale, or dynamic comparative advantages.[17] In our view, the extra growth achieved by such favoritism is likely to be more than offset by inaccurate forecasting and inappropriate biases driven by political considerations. This almost certainly has been the record to date. The only biases that may be warranted are, first, those that compensate for clear social externalities or market failures, as in the case of the nascent capital markets discussed above. Secondly, ostensible biases stemming from production externalities across sectors will be merited, but only if the linkages can be clearly established.

Static productive efficiency is achieved when marginal revenue products at world prices are equalized in all productive activities for factors such as capital and labor. Thus, not only is an urban bias as defined above likely to be inegalitarian, for the most part it is also inefficient. Increases in output could be achieved if both public and private capital were moved from low to high rate of return sectors. In addition to realizing gains in productive efficiency, removal of urban formal sector biases probably would redistribute incomes to poorer groups, thus further increasing any reasonable notion of social welfare.

The previous paragraph's framework is that of static microeconomic theory. Defenders of policies with urban biases often point to their dynamic qualities: in particular, profits are increased for modern sector activities with high savings propensities; hence, national investment rates rise. Yet this justification has little validity. First, there are virtually no conclusive studies of savings patterns in African urban informal sectors or rural economies to justify the central savings assumption.[18] Second, it is difficult to avoid the impression that most African internal pricing structures have failed to promote high savings rates largely *because* the potential profits generated have been dissipated through unduly high formal sector wage rates, government consumption, price controls, and taxes on imported goods for urban consumers.

Even ignoring these criticisms, it is still likely that African governments, prior to the imposition of rigorous SAPs, have imposed an excessive urban bias. Maximization of formal sector savings rates requires sufficient rural investment to keep down the costs of food and rural-supplied intermediates (Dixit [1969]). The solution to a dynamic optimal growth problem thus indicates some rural investment even if government were unable to realize any returns from such expenditures (i.e., if capital were essentially given away to the peasantry).

Intuitive consideration of the rural-urban linkages discussed in Chapter 2 and the figures for Madagascar cited in Section 7.1 also make clear the cost of neglecting the rural economy. Rural consumers are a major source of demand for urban products; rural producers are essential sources of urban intermediates and consumption goods. The urban economy is similarly critical for the rural sector. The imposition of policies that cause rural stagnation therefore will lead to shortages or higher prices of rural goods, thus transmitting stagnancy to the cities. In particular, growing productivity in food crop production is essential for urban and national development as well as rural prosperity. Many traditional export crops face deteriorating demand conditions, and, at any given instant, fairly price and income inelastic demands. On the other hand, growth in productivity of agricultural goods produced domestically will create a vibrant market for urban exports—which, as the outstanding World Bank (1991d) multiregion SAM study of Madagascar shows, is likely to be a market characterized by high income elasticities of demand, and which will certainly be far larger than the market for exports from urban areas to the rest of the world. At the same time, growth in food productivity will raise the offer curve for unskilled labor and cause the price of food to decline, thereby raising welfare of rural middle- and upper-income groups, and, in some cases, the rural poor.

At any rate, many aspects of the urban bias are neither statically nor dynamically efficient. Until recently, all but a handful of African nations neglected their rural economies, and the consequence has been stagnation in both *rural and urban* areas. To some extent, reductions in urban biases are inevitable, both because the historic biases are unsustainable, and because reductions are implied in the design of structural adjustment programs. It must be understood, however, that removing urban bias is not the same as slowing urban growth. Indeed, diminution of urban bias that fosters economic growth and reduces foreign exchange constraints is likely to increase urbanization rates in the long run. Not only is the process of economic growth an inherently urbanizing one, but there will be shifts from capital- to labor-intensive urban activities with the removal of capital and import subsidies. On the other hand, an infusion of investment capital and physical and social infrastructure into rural areas may reduce out-migration rates, especially in the short run.

As an aside, it also must be understood that many of the standard rural-urban distinctions are no longer viable, especially in the poorest African nations, or those that have experienced the most upheaval. Earlier in the text, we found that a significant proportion of the urban population, especially in smaller cities and towns, engaged in farming activity. In countries suffering the greatest deterioration (which have received relatively little attention in this volume, mainly because reliable economic data are, almost by definition, unobtainable), the situation is more striking still. Indeed, a recent report on Mozambique (World Bank [1991f:2]) emphasizes a new phenomenon:

> The urbanization of Mozambique is peculiar; the process has been one of ruralization of the urban centers rather than urbanization of the rural populations. The change from urban to rural lifestyles among the people coming to the cities is at best incomplete. Peasants try to replicate on urban land the subsistence system they left behind. Food crops are planted on any available soil; women and children plow and plant in backyards and in neighborhood pathways, empty lots, and on the unpaved sidewalks, meridians, and slopes of major streets and roads.

Thus, the concept of "urban bias" is mislabeled—it is really a bias toward a limited part of the urban economy. Coherent development policies must encourage (and, in some cases, restore viability to) rural regions, for surely cities do not have a comparative advantage in food production.

A second macroeconomic policy focus must involve *raising national savings rates*—again, a major objective of SAPs. Output gains can be achieved both by increasing the efficiency of use of current resources and from accumulating factor stocks. Our comments on the need to remove price distortions that together comprise an urban bias reflect the need to achieve efficiency gains stemming from resource reallocation. However, it is also critical to address the role of the urban sector in increasing stocks of human and physical capital.

We are aware of no study—other than for Madagascar (World Bank [1991d])—that estimates the proportion of savings generated by urban activities in an African economy. It is quite likely, however, that capital formation in urban activities is likely to outweigh considerably urban savings in countries in which government appropriates a large portion of agricultural value added. In view of the need to promote rural development emphasized above, it is apparent that growth or even maintenance of present rates of urban capital formation will necessitate an increase in urban savings (or borrowing from abroad).

In fact, the picture is an extremely grim one. Between 1965 and 1987, total gross domestic savings (GDS) declined from 14 percent to 13 percent of GDP in sub-Saharan Africa—and from 15 percent to 11 percent when Nigeria is excluded. If the latest figures are accurate, 1990 saw a rise in the GDS rate to 16.6 percent (12.5 percent without Nigeria), but when one considers *national* savings, excluding the effect of savings by foreign-owned entities operating in Africa, the savings rate even in 1990 is only 8 percent, with or without Nigeria. Indeed, these aggregates hide great intercountry disparities: 1985 GDS rates were 20 percent for oil exporters and 16 percent for all middle-income countries—but averaged only 7 percent for low-income countries (excluding Nigeria) and 5 percent for Sahelian countries. Of the non-oil exporting countries of mainland sub-Saharan Africa with GDS rates above 10 percent, only Kenya experienced a large rise in its GDS/GDP ratio during 1965–87 (see World Bank [1989a] and UNDP/World Bank [1992]).

In many respects, the situation is even worse than these figures suggest. *Net savings* (gross savings less depreciation) will of course be lower, and it is net savings that count for capital accumulation. A gross savings rate of 12–15 percent is likely to translate into a net savings rate of 3–6 percent (thereby implying a capital stock growth rate of 1–2 percent, assuming an aggregate incremental capital/output ratio of roughly 3) under normal circumstances. But circumstances are not normal: neglected maintenance expenditures, especially of public sector capital stock and infrastructure, will accelerate real depreciation. Consequently, real net savings are zero or negative for much of the continent—and so may be real net investment, since net foreign capital inflows as of the late 1980s amounted only to 3–4 percent of GDP.

In view of the unfavorable and, until recently, deteriorating situation, it is imperative that measures be taken to increase national savings, and urban savings in particular. A wide variety of policies can be followed to this end, and most are integral components of SAPs. Declining formal sector wages and layoffs of redundant workers have taken place in many countries during the past fifteen years, and can be expected to increase formal sector surpluses. But further wage declines and layoffs would be inegalitarian and, in many countries, difficult to achieve. In addition, many of the other measures of SAPs—removal of tariff protection, devaluation, liberalized foreign exchange control mechanisms, capital market liberalization, decreased subsidies, privatization of parastatals, and price decontrols—are unlikely to improve formal sector net retained earnings in the near future. Firms are likely to face some pressure to limit price increases, so that rising costs are likely to prevent margins from rising greatly. Furthermore, many firms will find themselves unable to face international competition in a liberalized environment. It is hardly surprising that the near future looks bleak for a sector plagued with plants geared to inappropriate input and output price structures, burdened with expenses imposed for political reasons, and realizing few scale economies. In fact, liberalization moves in many African economies have been met by continued industrial decline.

If formal sector profits are likely to remain low or even fall during the era of structural adjustment, other sources must be tapped. Inevitably, recurrent central government expenditures must decrease, and, hopefully, tax revenues must rise—again, standard SAP components. Indeed, all macroeconomic SAPs or proposals for infrastructure rehabilitation contain domestic resource mobilization components.

Financial incentives providing positive real interest rates may increase private savings, but empirical evidence is lacking. At the very least, however, such a move is likely to channel private savings from investments in unproductive activities to more productive uses. Furthermore, local finance of social infrastructure projects will reduce recurrent central government expenditures, thereby raising its savings rate. Total public savings will rise if local governments are able to recover a larger share of project costs than national governments have done to date—a plausible outcome.

Removal of subsidies on housing, food, education, and health care also could increase public savings. But maintaining many of these subsidies can be defended on social equity, collection cost, and externality grounds, and the blanket removal in SAPs hardly can be optimal policy.

A largely untapped savings pool may be available from the small enterprise sector. If efforts to extend the financial sector to microenterprises are successful, the ultimate effect may include healthier national savings rates. Formalization of property rights also makes investment more attractive; as much of it will be self-financed, national savings rates again will increase.

Efforts to increase national savings rates and achieve greater intra- and inter-sectoral efficiency cannot stand alone. Inequality and un- or underemployment are problems that cannot await trickle-down solutions, especially given the surge in young urban dwellers. The appropriate policy response to rapid urbanization is to generate new employment and earnings opportunities in both urban and rural areas. Increased agricultural investment and farmgate prices, improvements in the rural marketing structure (starting with public decontrol), and extensions of rural social services all will raise peasants' welfare and reduce incentives to migrate to the cities. Of course, better rural education and communication, and further commercialization of rural agriculture ultimately will lead to further urban growth. But such an event is not undesirable, particularly as much of it will be in secondary towns.

Simultaneously, it is essential to pursue policies that will reduce the cost of capital goods. Increasing savings alone is insufficient; the purchasing power of the savings pool also must increase. This can be done most readily by increasing the supply of domestic capital goods industries—farm implements, construction and, in some cases, engineering. As most sophisticated capital goods are imported, increasing the purchasing power of savings also means improving balances of payments (before capital imports are considered) and strengthening real exchange rates.

The reorientation of industrial policy away from capital-intensive import substitutes (which, ironically, often tend to be import-intensive as well, since they use many imported intermediates and capital goods) in principal should result in formal sector employment expansion. Gains are most likely to occur in agricultural processing, mass consumer durables and semidurables, and rural intermediate goods. In more developed African economies, some potential also exists in the engineering, construction, and more advanced intermediate goods industries. Equal or greater employment growth potential may be achieved from promoting informal sector development, but the absolute and relative magnitudes of employment gains remain highly speculative. Improvements in the export orientation of urban industries also will help reduce foreign exchange constraints, thereby enabling renewed formal sector employment growth (but, of course, also urbanization). The empirical work in Chapters 3 and 6 indirectly suggests that foreign exchange constraints are one of the central, and perhaps in some countries *the* most important, constraints to formal sector employment and output growth.

A major weakness of many African countries has been a lack of integrated planning of agricultural, industrial, and institutional development, and infrastructural policies. To the extent that governments should be engaged in any planning (and some planning will continue, as governments will remain responsible for infrastructure, education, and the overall economic environment), they must plan to provide supporting infrastructure where private demand exists. As growth is likely to take place in agricultural marketing, processing, and intermediate goods sectors, which often will locate in towns very different from those that have historically received relatively good roads, electricity, and water supplies, careful coordination is all the more important.[19] This market-driven decentralization of production will be reinforced by the evolution of Africa's industrial sectors from being producers of import substitutes to being more integrated with rural economies. Briefly, the production of import substitutes is "market-oriented" (to the extent that rational location decisions have been permitted in the past), and the main markets are the few large cities in each country. In contrast, as most primary products are weight-losing (in the sense that their weight declines with processing and the addition of ubiquitous inputs), agricultural processing plants are "material-oriented," and can be expected to locate in smaller towns close to important agricultural and mining areas.

Taken together, a focus on labor-intensive industrialization, the promotion of rural growth and especially food production (largely by removing urban formal sector biases), and an increase in national and urban savings rates all will benefit urban sectoral development. Without these economy-wide policies, and without the concurrent development of financial markets and local governments, urban sectoral policies in isolation will fail. Taken together, these macro policies will help tackle urban and rural poverty, while simultaneously enabling countries to establish or reestablish economic growth not entirely dependent on the whims and good will of the international community. Further, they will make the resumption of minimal provision of urban services more likely to be achieved and will provide the resources that make the development of local governments and establishment of viable capital and land markets possible. In summary, the urban sector objectives outlined above are most unlikely to be realized in isolation—but, at the same time their realization will contribute to macroeconomic stability and growth.

7.4. Next Steps

Most African nations today have made commitments, albeit with varying degrees of enthusiasm, to economic liberalization. In effect, this liberalization removes many of the previous urban biases. The extent to which urban-rural gaps have narrowed, for instance, has been detailed in earlier chapters.

SAPs imply declining central government expenditures and control over the economy. Such shrinkage also implies a decline in the level of social services provided by the central government relative to the levels provided prior to the advent of economic crisis. It also suggests that local governments will become more important. Cities whose residents desire services will have to generate their own resources. Low cost housing programs will be viable, but will require the mobilization of resources by those that occupy the sites. The success in designing local tax mechanisms will be a critical determinant of the success of public service decentralization.

Many services also can be provided by the private sector. Urban transport and large-scale housing projects both offer the possibility of greater private participation in many countries. Small communities also can contract with private firms for specific services (sewage, water lines, road maintenance, or construction). But private participation in urban infrastructure provision will be impossible in the absence of an effective local government authority structure, along with clear property rights (including the right to seek redress from local governments!). *Thus, structural adjustment must include the development of local government administrative capacity and fiscal authority, along with plans to permit private sector development, if urban infrastructure is to improve in the coming years.*

Secondly, national regional policy will become even more important than it is now, and the need for coherent policies must be recognized. Liberalization implies strengthened rural-urban ties, but deteriorated transport infrastructure means that bottlenecks may impose important constraints on future development. Neither rural producers nor urban suppliers will flourish if there are few passable roads or operating vehicles. Instead, transport sector plans must be consistent with both agricultural and industrial plans.

Third, because of the strategic importance of urban areas in Africa's economies—bearing in mind that the urban sectors' *marginal* shares of GDP and investment will exceed 50 percent in most of Africa—it is essential that the sector be considered in major analyses of investments by countries and international organizations. The absence of a spatial dimension has been and continues to be a major problem. The World Bank reports discussed in Hamer (1986) are typical in this regard; investment plans appear to take place on a featureless plain, so that geographical linkages are missed. Thus, for example, there is no effort (possibly excluding very recent projects in Benin, Guinea, and Ghana) to coordinate urban investments with the expected geographic focus of rapid agricultural growth.[20] Today, there is growing recognition in some countries and international and bilateral organizations (notably USAID and the urban and infrastructure groups at the World Bank) of the need to design policies that exploit these linkages. It is less clear, however, that macroeconomic policymakers in Africa or in the World Bank have begun paying much attention to how all the pieces of the regional puzzle fit together.

Both countries and donor agencies need to spend more effort identifying which cities and towns have key developmental potential in support of agriculture; which policies and institutions help or hinder efficient symbiosis between town and country; and what bottlenecks exist that prevent the more efficient functioning of these towns in support of rural areas, especially with regard to infrastructure and services. This approach has been the core of a large USAID-funded program in Kenya (see Gaile [1988a], [1988b]), but it must become more widespread.[21] Indeed, the emphasis of structural adjustment policies on macroeconomic reforms may well have delayed the implementation of integrated regional programs.

These remarks do not contradict our earlier exhortation for governments to avoid tilting the playing field. Rather, as public sectors cannot implement all possible programs simultaneously given the enormity of the tasks they face, and as there exist substantial fixed costs and scale economies in infrastructure and public service provision, governments must inevitably establish priorities. In doing so, the appropriate ranking is by estimated rate of return (which still does not seem to be an accepted procedure among African governments or international or bilateral aid donors), including social returns reflecting productivity improvements in sectors other than the one directly involved. Thus, recognizing intersectoral linkages is central to proper policy formation.

The same conclusion can be reached about linkages between urban areas and industrial, service, and artisan activities in general. With some but relatively few exceptions (currently Benin, and possibly Madagascar in the near future), these ties are ignored in the preparation of macroeconomic SAPs, even when major urban bottlenecks to the efficient operation of these subsectors are explicitly identified. In addition, the heavy volume of investments in interregional transportation facilities appears to be taking place in ways that are delinked from any urban development strategy.

Today, the most critical conceptual sectoral problems facing African economic policymakers do not involve whether to adopt adjustment and liberalization policies: there is virtually no choice in the matter. Nor are the urban policies outlined in Section 7.2 (along with important programs not treated there in detail, such as sites and services schemes) the focus of much debate, since two decades of experience in their implementation has generated considerable knowledge of technical solutions and appropriate microeconomic designs. Rather, the most critical problems are ensuring the adoption of "structural adjustment with a human face," along with integrating an urban perspective into the process of structural adjustment and the renewal of economic growth. Though most national governments and international agencies are afflicted by sectoral myopia (and asectoral macro policies), the time has come to creatively experiment with cross-sectoral approaches.

But while explicit spatial perspectives are needed, *the explicitly spatial instruments advocated in the past have proven bankrupt*. Growth poles, migration controls, infant region promotion, and optimal city-size controls—all these have been tried and found wanting. A new approach must be taken. Policy relevant regional models must be used to answer questions about how different urban initiatives might help to achieve objectives of rural development, transport networks, industrial development, export promotion, resource mobilization, and rehabilitation of infrastructure.

By incorporating a broader perspective into the process, planning for economic recovery and growth in Africa would be more realistic and more rewarding. It would no longer be possible for "gatekeepers" to assign to the "urban sector" a percentage of national or international agency investment funds based on past shares or on the relative priority given narrow sectoral objectives taken in isolation. Instead, investment priorities should be determined first by the contribution each proposed project makes, *regardless of sector of origin*, toward attaining critical development objectives. Urban (and other) development initiatives should be judged on the basis of their immediate effects as well as their demonstrable impacts on the success of investment programs and public policies in other, apparently unrelated sectors.

Neither governments nor the international community can ignore Africa's urban sectors. Their levels of efficiency affect the operations of most other conventionally defined sectors. To set urban issues aside as an "unnecessary complication" is to deny the importance of intersectoral and geographic linkages. In addition, such inattention threatens the otherwise strategic contribution that the better management of cities and towns can make to a host of SAP objectives. Africa cannot recover unless its cities and towns are made partners in the process. Africa will not develop unless the economic role of cities is recognized.

NOTES

CHAPTER 1
African Economic Development and Urbanization

1. For a thorough descriptive review of policies in eastern and southern Africa, see *Southern African Economist* (1990).

2. Unless otherwise stated, data provided in this chapter are taken from UNDP/World Bank (1992). Throughout this book, "Africa" will refer exclusively to sub-Saharan Africa, excluding the Republic of South Africa.

3. We resist use of the term *subsistence agriculture*, since most agricultural production in Africa is monetized, or involves the production for own consumption of crops for which established prices exist.

4. In The Gambia, fertility in rural areas does not appear to vary greatly with educational achievement, while it does in the country's sole urban area, Banjul (and nearby towns). As of the 1983 census, for example, the average woman age twenty to twenty-four in the Banjul metro area with no education or primary schooling had given birth to 1.35 children; those with secondary or higher education had given birth to only 0.75 children. The comparable figure for rural Gambian women aged twenty to twenty-four was 2.27 children. See Becker (1991:128) or Republic of The Gambia (1987) *Census of The Gambia 1983.* Banjul: Government of The Gambia Central Statistical Development (CSD).

5. The rate implied by the latest World Bank (1989a:33) graphical projections is 5.0 percent.

6. This possibility, and conditions under which it may arise, are analyzed in Becker, Williamson, and Mills (1992).

7. This is unlikely to have been important in Africa, however. Output gains in Côte d'Ivoire, for example, have been due almost exclusively to expansion of cropped area. Even mechanization associated with hybrid maize expansion in eastern and southern Africa is likely to have been offset by yield growth induced labor demand for activities such as weeding and harvesting. See Gahi and Radwan (1983).

8. It is important to recognize, though, that current urban patterns also reflect the spatial consequences of colonial policies. In many cases, colonial policies were indifferent or hostile to development of the indigenous population, and the city-size and spatial distributions would have been nonoptimal from the point of view of the African population. Consequently, some public intervention in the city formation process may be justified to alleviate earlier inappropriate policies.

CHAPTER 2
Urban Centers in African Economies

1. See, for example, the World Bank's (1982) *World Development Report, 1982* succinct statement of the Lewis (1954) framework: "The transfer of labor from agriculture (where the

amount of capital per worker is relatively low) to industry and services (where capital per worker and average productivity are relatively high) is the key to raising incomes and output. The higher average productivity of labor in the non-agricultural economy is reflected in income differences between it and agriculture. . . . This income difference provides the incentive for people to move out of agriculture into non-agricultural activities in urban centers. The agricultural shares of output and employment are roughly equalized only at a comparatively late stage of development."

2. The link is particularly important when one moves from abstract concepts such as "economic welfare" or "real income" to measured gross domestic product (GDP). GDP measures tend to omit many nonmarketed activities and undervalue many of the rest; they also are relatively likely to understate rural marketed activities. Therefore, the contribution of modern urban activities to recorded GDP growth will be very high in virtually all African countries, even if (as is often the case) recorded modern urban sector growth rates have little impact on the welfare of most of the population.

3. These assumptions are roughly consistent with Indian data (see Becker, Williamson, and Mills [1992]), which provide both locational and functional breakdowns, but probably *understate* the urban contribution in most African countries.

4. See Becker (1987). The ratio of unskilled urban formal sector wages to rural wages is probably above 8:1 in many countries; Dumont and Mottin report a ratio of 15:1 for Zambia. As only a portion of workers are wage earners, and rural labor force participation rates exceed urban rates, these wage differentials translate into smaller per capita income gaps. In much of Africa, however, rural-urban income gaps have diminished greatly in recent years, reflecting the economic crises that have hit the modern sector with particular force. For evidence of a narrowing gap, see Jamal and Weeks (1988). Also see Dumont and Mottin (1983) for a discussion of Zambia, and Berry and Sabot (1978) for a general discussion of labor market gaps.

5. Cour's (1985:92–93) estimates of the ratios of nonprimary production to primary production are consistent with this claim, but his ratios tend to be smaller than the shares reported in Table 2.1. Given his even higher degree of aggregation, however, it seems likely that our figures are slightly more accurate.

6. The recorded gaps are also likely to be biased in favor of urban households to the extent that rural production activities are less completely measured than urban economic activities.

7. For that matter, prices are rarely market-determined at all in the case of government services (a large portion of modern services in African economies). For the bureaucracy and army, national income accounts statistics define value added to equal the sum of wage payments. The price index used to determine a general deflator, though, will be based on a basket of privately produced goods and services that are only remotely related to government services. The deflator also may be biased downward (and hence "real output growth" statistics biased upward) if goods in the basket are subject to price controls that bind with increasing severity over time.

8. The choice of base and terminal years has limited impact on this downward trend for the continent as a whole, but matters considerably for particular countries. For the entire continent, the decline from 1969–71 to 1977–79 was 1.4 percent. In general, it is highly inappropriate to estimate trends without correcting for weather quality, either by estimating running averages, estimating trends from the coefficients of the time trend from a regression equation, or by adjusting annual output series by a weather-quality factor.

9. See Table 2.4 for trends in food imports. The percentage of import spending devoted to food items quoted above is an unweighted average computed from Table 2.4.

10. The term *forward linkages* refers to the connections between a good and other sectors that may purchase it as an input. If productivity gains in industry A result in cost savings that

are passed on to another sector B, and A is an important input in B's production process, so that production of B expands rapidly in response to productivity gains in A, then A is said to have an important forward linkage with respect to B. Conversely, if growth in output of industry C results in growth in demand for inputs produced by industry A, and that demand growth in turn leads to productivity gains in A (through realizing scale economies) and hence cost decreases, then C is said to have important *backward linkages* with respect to A.

11. The importance of these demand shifts remains to be verified empirically but can be addressed by the construction of highly detailed social accounting matrices that include information on consumer demand and investment good composition.

12. The dollar value of exports continued to decline, at a rate of 1.3 percent per annum over the period 1980–87, although excluding Nigeria, export values actually grew at a rate of 1.7 percent (World Bank [1989a]).

13. Time series figures on capacity utilization for the aggregate manufacturing sector are available only for a few African countries (UNDP/World Bank [1992: 254]), but these series are telling. Tanzanian capacity utilization was 55 percent in 1980, but declined to 30 percent by 1987. In Niger, the series oscillates, but capacity utilization rates appear to be on a slow upward trend, and averaged 56 percent in the late 1980s. Nigeria's capacity utilization was almost constant around 40 percent between 1985 and 1990. The "success" story is Ghana, which enjoyed a rise in its capacity utilization rate from 18 percent in 1984 to an average of 38 percent in 1988–90, in large part because of Bank-Fund encouraged capital inflows. As a whole, though, these rates are extremely low by international standards.

14. Engel's effect refers to the virtually universal tendency for expenditure shares on food to diminish as incomes rise, and hence for the share of nonfood goods in total expenditures to rise.

15. Such a pattern is found by Colclough and Fallon (1983) for Botswana. For further confirming evidence and theory, see Lucas and Stark (1985) and Stark (1991).

16. The basis for the downward revisions presumably lies with the appearance of some of the censuses around 1990. As more of these become available, further revisions will be made. The considerable difference in projections made by recently published documents is provided as a sobering example—the true urban population growth rate is unknown, and all estimates carry considerable uncertainty.

17. SCET International, SCET AGRI, SEDES (1984). The cited data exclude the Republic of South Africa. The study identifies all settlements with five thousand or more residents as urban.

18. The relatively low *level* of African urbanization is still found in the most recent World Bank (1989a, 1989b) studies. For all low-income countries, the weighted average proportion of the population living in urban areas in 1987 was 30 percent; for low-income Africa the proportion was 27 percent. For middle-income countries, the figures are 57 percent for all countries, 51 percent for lower-middle income countries, and 37 percent for African countries.

19. Other examples include Swaziland and Lesotho, which appear to rely on South Africa's cities for the "missing" urban functions.

20. World Bank (1983a). For Kenya, the World Bank's *Kenya: Growth and Structural Change* (1983a) notes, "Even if nonagricultural employment were to quadruple from 1976 to 2000, agricultural employment would have to more than double . . . simply to prevent unemployment from growing."

21. In terms of employment, these tend to be small enterprises having fifty or fewer employees, with most having fewer than ten.

22. Today, roughly 60 percent of total rural transactions in sub-Saharan Africa are monetized. See Haggblade, Hazell, and Brown (1987).

23. These and related data are presented in Anderson (1978) and Chuta and Liedholm (1979).
24. See Chuta and Liedholm (1979) for a discussion of available evidence.
25. That microenterprise employment is far more important relative to total employment in smaller towns is clearly documented in Kilby (1987) (also see Gaile [1988b]). In Kenya in 1985 there were 26 microenterprise employees *per hundred residents* in town of fewer than eight thousand people; this number fell to 15 for towns of eight to twelve thousand, 9.5 for towns of twelve to forty thousand, and continued to decline until it reached 6.5 for Nairobi and Mombasa.
26. For a review of the literature on agglomeration effects see Moomaw (1981), Henderson (1988a), Wheaton and Shishido (1981), Mera (1977), and Mera and Shishido (1981).
27. SCET International (1978); somewhat lower estimates were arrived for earlier, incomplete surveys. See Joshi, Lubell, and Mouly (1976). More recent estimates suggest that far higher proportions of Abidjan's labor force work in the informal sector, ranging from 69 percent on up (Kannappan [1988]).
28. As noted earlier, the *share* of Africa's labor force working in industry appears to have stagnated (UNDP/World Bank [1992]) since 1980. To the extent that parastatal employment is more closely associated with the "protected" formal sector, the pattern is even more striking. Specifically, the series provided by the UNDP/World Bank (p.262) suggests that of sixteen countries for which more than one observation is available in the 1980s, ten had stagnant or declining *absolute numbers* of parastatal employees—implying even greater declines in employment shares.
29. The estimate for the urban "low-income" group in Lesotho, a middle-income country, implied by Carvalho's (1998) social accounting matrix is 40 percent. For The Gambia, poor household's food expenditure shares ranged from 47 percent to 64 percent in various parts of the Banjul metro area, with the latter figure being much more representative. For rural Gambian areas, food expenditure shares ranged from 62 percent to 79 percent (Jabara [1990]).
30. For a detailed theoretical rationale, see Henderson (1988).
31. It is likely that these shares have fallen somewhat in the past five to ten years (cf. Table 2.1). For Lagos, see Wilbur Smith Associates et al. (n.d.); for Nairobi, see Nairobi Urban Study Group (n.d.); for Abidjan, see Groupement SCET International (1978); for Bamako, see Direction du Projet Urbain de Mali (1984); for Dakar, see Ministere du Plan et de la Cooperation, EPVRY (1983). The Kinshasa estimates are based on private conversations between Andrew Hamer and officials of the Bureau d'Etudes d'Amenagements Urbains (Kinshasa).
32. In Lagos, for example, the unregulated sector provides 57 percent of the employment but produces only 14 percent of the value added (Wilbur Smith Associates et al. [n.d.]).
33. This statement does not imply that total government will shrink, since African local governments need to be strengthened, to gain further autonomy, and to grow significantly in the coming decades. Nor does it imply that the central government has an unimportant role to play in promoting development. Rather, we believe that government has many central roles, but also that development of a vibrant private economy and a reduced bureaucracy is essential in most African countries.
34. For a detailed description of conditions in major eastern and southern African cities, see *Southern African Economist* (1990).
35. But while colonial governments left decent infrastructure in central cities and elite suburbs, they typically built limited infrastructure elsewhere. Of equal importance is the long-term impact of European-designed master plans for major cities that have resulted in excessive decentralization and unsustainable levels of public services, as well as extremely strong segregation by race and income class (Mabogunje [1990]).
36. The collapse of the Lagos State Transport Corporation (LSCT) is detailed in Barrett (1988:95). As of the late 1980s, the LSCT owned 540 buses, of which an average of 215 were

operating on any given day. This number represented a marked improvement over 1985, however, when only an average of 70 were in service.

37. Barrett (1988) reports that a ten kilometer cross-city bus trip involving two interchanges can take up to one and a half hours—implying very high average commuting times.

38. Stren (1989:41), citing Jean Saint-Vil, reports that the share of Abidjan's residents with water connections declined from 57 percent in 1977 to 47 percent only six years later. The reason for the decline was the mushrooming of unserviced "spontaneous settlement areas," whose residents bought water from private vendors at a cost about five times the rate paid for by those with pipe connections.

39. This section draws on the work of Kahnert (1985).

40. Anderson (1987) provides an excellent exposition of this theme.

41. Elkan (1988) never mentions the issue. Marsden and Belot (1987) devote two short paragraphs to the issue in sixty-six pages.

42. This point is emphasized by Stren (1989) and others in the Stren and White (1989) volume. A rule of thumb appears to be that squatter settlements pay private suppliers five to ten times the rate charged those with public hookups for water; they also pay high costs for transport when time costs are considered, and simply do without many other services.

43. Part of the problem stems from fragmentation within bilateral and multilateral development agencies. Sections in charge of infrastructure or in the implementation of specific projects are acutely aware of infrastructural limitations in African cities (and elsewhere) and issue research and policy documents that stress infrastructural development (such as World Bank [1988a] and Barrett [1988]). But their pronouncements frequently do not represent agency consensus, and other groups may implement policies that ignore infrastructural needs and realities.

44. As always, the problem is especially severe for those outside the formal sector. As Stren (1989:61) writes, "The gradual restriction of the formal urban land market to the wealthy and well-connected is a feature of almost all large African cities." A stunning example recently observed by the authors of the importance of connections occurs in the rapidly developing regions of Kanefing, Serre Kunda, and Fajara in the greater Banjul metropolitan area. Here the Gambian government gives out long-term rights-of-use on plots without charge to those (both citizens and foreigners) who request the land. Not surprisingly, there is excess demand for choice sites, and those with cash and connections come away with fine prizes.

45. For a review of World Bank experience in this area, see Bernstein (1985). A more detailed exposition of land issues can be found in Dunkerley (1983).

46. "In the Côte d'Ivoire, self-employed labor is not unproductive, though marginal returns are somewhat less than the wage rate of equivalent salaried workers. Capital yields extremely high returns, possibly 100 percent per month. Assuming that the financial market is hard to access for an Ivorian with some but only little funds, such person may be well off to establish his own enterprise and gain the large returns to capital that offset the somewhat lower returns to labor" (Vijverberg [1988]). Evidence in support of this claim— albeit in a rural setting—is provided by Graham et al. (1988).

47. Evidence can be found in, among others, Van Dijk (1980), Fowler (1981), Fapohunda (1981), Mabogunje and Filani (1981), and Aryee (1981). For eastern Africa, see International Labour Office (1982), Ghai, Godfrey, and Lisk (1979), and Livingstone (1981).

48. The pioneers include Johnson (1970); Johnston and Kilby (1975); and Rondinelli and Ruddle (1978). Within the World Bank, an early attempt at tackling these issues is Cohen (1979). Among the bilateral donors, the earliest work was done under the auspices of USAID. A quick review of this work is given in Belsky (1985).

49. Indeed, Fleuret and Greeley (cited in Clark [1985:9]) go so far as to assert that one cannot even treat "urban population" as a separate category. While we do not go that far, their point is not entirely without merit. Nor is it surprising given the fact that the overwhelm-

ing majority of urban African adults were born in rural areas. In Kinshasa, only 7 percent of household heads were born in Kinshasa, 60 percent came directly from rural areas, and the remaining 33 percent came from other cities and towns—though many of them must have been born in rural areas as well. See Mbuyi (1989:151).

50. Among others, see Caldwell (1969); Moller (1978); Johnson and Whitelaw (1974); Adepoju (1974); and Sabot (1979).

51. It is also apparent from this survey that remitters had far higher incomes than those that did not remit, and, from the econometric estimates provided, that many nonremitters were recent (presumably unsettled) migrants.

52. One should be wary about using such data, however, because sample selection bias problems abound. To put it briefly, correlation does not imply causality.

53. As Gaveau and Monnier (1984) note in their study of Zaire: "The large cities find it simpler to import foreign food products paid with the earnings from copper exports, than to take advantage of the national potential for agricultural production" (translation by the authors).

54. This point is made forcibly in the World Bank's (1983f) *Tanzania Agricultural Sector Report*, in its (1982a) *Zaire Economic Memorandum*, in its (1983e) *Zimbabwe Agricultural Sector Study*, in its (1985b) *Ghana Agricultural Sector Review*, and in its (1984d) *Nigeria Agricultural Sector Memorandum*.

55. The eighteen hundred kilometer drive from Zaire's Atlantic coast to its eastern border, which once took two days, now requires three weeks (Greenhouse [1988]).

56. Société d'aménagement et d'exploration des terres du delta, du fleuve Sénégal et des vallées du fleuve Sénégal et de la Falémé.

57. "From the Government's point of view," reports the World Bank's (1983f) *Tanzania Agricultural Sector Report*, "the substantial donor support for parastatals has probably been seen as supporting evidence of their suitability as a form of agricultural organization."

58. These conclusions are sometimes overshadowed by the lively controversy over what units of what average size will play this vanguard role. Whatever size categories take the lead, the results should be similar.

Chapter 3
African City Systems and Urban Growth

1. The rank size rule suggests that the size of each city or town bears a fixed relationship to both larger and smaller urban centers. Specifically, the "rule" states that each urban area's population roughly equals that of the largest city, divided by the smaller city's rank in terms of population. Thus, the second largest city is roughly one-half of the size of the largest, the third largest city is roughly one-third the size of the largest, and so on. Of course, this rule is actually a testable hypothesis; statistical estimates have found some validity for it, but it is generally a rather imperfect approximation to actual city size distributions. See Ledent (1990) and Rosen and Resnick (1980).

2. Data are extremely unreliable, and the concept of unemployment can be difficult to define in many African settings. Detailed surveys were carried out in Tanzania in the late 1970s, and unemployment in Dar es Salaam was found to be somewhat *lower* than in smaller cities (Ishumi [1984]).

3. Empirical evidence is provided in Kahnert (1985), Collier and Lal (1980), Collier (1979), Fallon (1985), and Direction du Projet Urbain de Mali (1984).

4. This is not meant to minimize the role of family support structures present in most African societies, which provide an important safety net, as well as a structure that permits higher open unemployment and quasi-unemployment than in many Asian countries with comparable per capita incomes. Whether or not the private welfare system and the underlying social relations will survive a prolonged period of "structural adjustment"

remains to be seen, but they seem to have held up to date. Interestingly, though, long-distance temporary immigrants (e.g., Guineans in The Gambia) who make less use of this safety net generally are more successful and have higher savings rates than local ethnic groups. While selection bias certainly plays a role (in that migrants are not typical of the population in origin regions), the most frequently offered explanation is that as distance from home increases, the number of relatives who will show up and share in one's success decreases. But the policy implications are unclear: steps that break down social obligations may increase private production incentives and savings rates, but they would be both profoundly unpopular and would risk social catastrophe in a very poor society with no social safety net.

5. Mazumdar (1976) disputes the claim that most migrants enter the informal sector, citing contrary evidence from Bombay. But African patterns appear to be different. Given African cities' rapid growth rates, slow formal sector employment growth, and stable labor force participation rates, it is clear that African informal sectors must have absorbed the majority of migrants.

6. For example, see Jabara's (1990) work on The Gambia, as well as Jamal and Weeks (1988).

7. It would be quite inappropriate to conclude that all African policymakers or others in influential positions favor removal of squatters. This is certainly not the case; one example from the influential *Southern African Economist* (Oesman [1990:6]) is revealing:

> What then can governments and others do about the urban crisis? The short answer is that there is no possibility of a quick fix. One option should be ruled out from the beginning: that of compulsory repatriation of people from town to country, or what the racist government of South Africa used to call influx control. . . . Wherever such action has been tried, the result has always been an initial flurry of police bullying, with people being harassed and being picked up more or less at random, followed shortly by an official acknowledgement that the exercise is to be discontinued.

8. India, Becker, Williamson, and Mills (1992) have found that incomes policies that drive up unskilled formal sector workers' incomes by one rupee reduce gross domestic product GDP by roughly 1.5 rupees. Chapter 5 details trends in wage gaps between urban formal sector unskilled wages and informal sector unskilled incomes. Briefly, the gap has declined over time in many countries.

9. Empirical evidence indicates (see Chapter 5) that African governments typically buy few goods and services from informal sector firms.

10. See, for example, the discussion on urban areas in World Bank (1984) and Wheaton and Shishido (1981).

11. This criticism does not apply to Shukla and Stark (1990) or Henderson (1988).

12. The Tiebout model assumes utility-maximizing individuals who freely decide to live in cities with other individuals possessing similar tastes vis-à-vis levels of taxation and public services. It may not be relevant to African settings where a politically powerful class imposes taxes on other groups in order to pay for the level of infrastructure desired by that powerful class, or where central rather than local governments bear service costs, since the link between level of service and cost is thus broken. When central governments provide services, there is no connection between the level of services a household receives and the taxes it pays. And unfortunately, virtually throughout Africa there actually is very little obvious connection between local taxes and levels of urban public services. In the absence of such a connection, there is no incentive for households to demand remotely optimal levels of services (given society's ability to pay for them).

13. For a detailed discussion of the practical issues involved, see Linn (1982).

14. For the case of Kenya see Gaile (1990) and World Bank (1985c). In 1982, for example, Nairobi accounted for 42 percent of Kenya's urban population, but had 56 percent of urban wage employment, and generated 66 percent of urban wage earnings.

15. Figures are taken from World Bank (1984a) and (1989a), except that corrected population data for Benin, Guinea, Senegal, Lesotho, Botswana, and Nigeria which were taken from Cour (1985).
16. For formal models of this process, see Henderson (1988).
17. Documentation of the trends in the concentration of urban population is given in Parr (1985).
18. While it is not certain (though certainly plausible) that in-migrants to the largest cities represent more of a "brain drain" than do migrants to smaller towns, there is little doubt that rural out-migrants to towns and cities are generally better educated than those who stayed. Evidence for this is provided by Zachariah and Conde (1981) and Sabot (1979).
19. For a discussion of Kenya's Rural Trade and Production Centers (RPTC) program, see Gaile (1988a).
20. The estimates for UP, taken from World Bank data, and for the share of the first four cities in the urban population, taken from Ledent (1990), are not always consistent. Indeed, the World Bank actually reports a larger share for the biggest city than Ledent does for the biggest four in Benin, Guinea, and Mozambique. On the other hand, the share of the largest city in Malawi is less than one-fourth of the share of the largest four reported by Ledent. These inconsistencies point out the uncertainty surrounding the estimates, as well as differences in definitions of "urban areas."
21. Concentration also appeared to fall in Cameroon, but in this case it reflects the growth of the capital, Yaounde, relative to the main port and oil city, Douala.
22. This is certainly the case for India. For the entire country, the Pareto value was 1.13 in 1971 and 1.10 in 1981 (see Mills and Becker [1986:56]). When India is divided into five regions (each with a larger population than nearly all African countries), however, the average regional Pareto coefficient falls to 0.95 in 1971 and 0.99 in 1981.
23. However, both we and Ledent (1990) have found such a relationship in regression analyses reported in section 3.5.
24. Other examples could easily be cited. For a particularly clear discussion of the role of the British-constructed railway on the diffusion of economic growth in Sierra Leone, see Riddell (1969).
25. Mills and Becker (1986: Ch. 5) test such a model for the Indian state of Madhya Pradesh and find that small city growth rates are in fact increased by proximity to a major urban center at small distances, but that the effect reverses as distance increases.
26. A simple extension of Abiodun's (1981) work is needed. She ran three bivariate ordinary lease squares (OLS) regressions with city size and distance variables. A multiple regression with the same variables in a simultaneous equations system would more realistically model the process of innovation.
27. The theoretical part of this section is based on Henderson (1988).
28. Documentation of trade barriers imposed by countries is compiled by the International Monetary Fund and published in their *Exchange Arrangements and Exchange Restrictions: Annual Report* (various years).
29. Note that the familiar Stolper-Samuelson theorem result obtains as well. As productive factors move out of the labor-intensive sector, this causes an excess supply of labor and excess demand for capital at given wage and capital rental rates. Consequently, the value of labor's marginal product must fall, and capital's marginal product must rise. If one assumes that capital is mobile internationally, then the increased return to capital will attract capital inflows from abroad until risk-adjusted rates of return to capital are again equalized internationally. At the same time, this increase in the country's capital stock will shift out the national transformation (production possibilities) curve.
30. Heteroskedasticity refers to an econometric problem caused when the accuracy of the prediction generated by the regression varies greatly and systematically across observations. The underlying problem is that either the dependent variable varies greatly in

magnitude for different observations or the explanatory power of the model differs greatly across observations. The observations were ranked according to the value of the independent variable, and the middle seven observations were dropped. Separate ordinary least squares (OLS) regressions were then run on the two subsamples. The null hypothesis of identical variances in the errors—the unexplained portions of each observation—in the two subsamples was soundly rejected: the F-statistic was significant at the 1 percent level.

CHAPTER 4

The Role of Migration in African Urbanization

1. *Externalities* are said to take place when the actions of one economic agent affect the welfare of others in ways that are not compensated for by market transactions. For example, if one purchases an automobile, payment to the previous owner means that no externality occurs at that point. But when one drives the car, one creates pollution that adversely affects others who are not compensated for their loss in utility by the driver, thus creating a negative externality.

2. Whether per capita cost increases or decreases depends on public sector technology and the "taxability" of the migrants. If there are large economies of scale in the provision of public services, migration may create a positive externality.

3. Roughly put, the theory of the second best states that moves toward efficiency in one market may not increase overall economic efficiency if there are inefficiencies elsewhere in the economy.

4. National accounts statisticians would be more precise. The value of the flow of final products equals gross national product (GNP). Subtracting from GNP the values for depreciation and indirect taxes yields national income.

5. The case has been made for a number of regions in the world by Lipton (1976). For Africa, see Bates (1981). For a different view, emphasizing the degree of deprivation found in urban Africa, and challenging Lipton's assumptions about the political foundation of "urban bias," see Sandbrook (1982).

6. This applies to internationally traded commodities. For "nontradable" goods one would expect to find otherwise unexplained departures from the world prices of traded goods and services that use similar factor inputs.

7. As noted in more detail in the concluding section of this chapter, this ranking is based on policies in place in the 1970s, before recent structural adjustment programs.

8. This experience is reviewed in the World Bank (1980a), Cohen (1982), and Lemer (1985).

9. An extremely detailed description of rural and urban informal sector activities is provided in Livingstone (1991); see also Haggblade and Brown (1989) and Ellis (1984:29–30).

10. These references are to *real* per capita income or output differences. Nominal measures would vary even in long-run equilibrium because different regions will have different price structures.

11. For example, in Senegal, with one of the largest formal sectors, 48.4 percent of the urban labor force worked in the informal sector, while 17.3 percent was openly unemployed in 1980 (Terrell and Svejnar [1989]). The modern sector share, 34.3 percent, actually declined slightly from its 35.0 percent share in 1960—while open unemployment rose from 6.8 percent.

12. For a careful analysis of the variants of the HT model, see Blomqvist (1981).

13. For a study examining population density as a cause of migration, see Udo (1982). Udo urges consideration not solely of population density, but of population pressure on available resources.

14. There are some interesting cross-sectional data on the education characteristics of migrants, if not on the time trends of these characteristics. See Section 4.2.7 for these data.

15. It also should be obvious that this system is ideal for petty political manipulation (that is, foremen will be under pressure to pick as permanent employees kin, fellow villagers, and people from their own ethnic group).
16. Duration of schooling also varies greatly. It is positively but imperfectly correlated with past performance, so that length of schooling L also is a proxy for Z. But L is also determined by one's family's wealth and social standing, and it will be in the interest of the wealthy to continue schooling even low Z children.
17. Greenwood (1985:527) makes this point in the U.S. case. For extensive surveys of the migration literature from both economic and demographic standpoints, see Greenwood (1985) and (1975).
18. This is done using data on age- and education-specific migration rates estimated by Barnum and Sabot (1977) for neighboring Tanzania. Restrictions were also imposed that ensured that cohort-specific migration rates generate observed aggregate migration patterns.
19. But the larger negative rural outmigration rate for the educated also reflects a lower initial base of educated individuals. While the link between education and migration is confirmed when urban population is used as the base, the case is less striking.
20. Huntington uses the number of group members in rural areas times the number in urban areas as a rough measure of the number of potential urban contacts.
21. Some suggest that the household—an imprecise term everywhere, and in need of precise delineation from society to society in Africa—is the correct unit, but even the household is probably too limited a definition of the relevant decision-making group, as kinship ties and obligations are often very broad. On the other hand, individual household members' interests often diverge, and decision-making is frequently an individualistic event. We prefer to model individuals as the unit of analysis but view utility functions as containing the consumption of other kin as arguments. See Caldwell (1969) and Guyer (1981).
22. Since the young are both the most productive rural workers and the most likely to migrate, argue Hedlund and Lundahl, migration in Africa will tend to lower the real agricultural wage (or more precisely, the average product). They fail to note that in some of the more traditional African societies it is women who are almost exclusively responsible for agricultural activities. See also Lipton (1980).
23. Part of the following is drawn from Findley (1976).
24. Collier and Rempel (1977) report an average income gain in the first year of migration from urban migration in 1964–68 Kenya of 182 percent over previous rural income (and 230 percent for those who found regular employment). Presumably, this differential grew in subsequent years as well. Rempel (1981:100) finds that migrants with primary education experienced average income increases of 45 percent in their first two years in towns; those with secondary education enjoyed 16 percent gains. His Kenyan data from the early 1970s also suggest an average income increase from rural-urban migration of 105 percent. These figures are probably reasonable for much of pre-1973 Africa, but are likely to be considerable overstatements of present earnings and productivity gaps.
25. See Chapter 5 for a fuller discussion of the informal sector and its training functions.
26. Clearly, the type of employment creation envisaged cannot refer to greater numbers of high-wage positions in capital-intensive activities.
27. This policy also allowed capitalists (or state enterprises) to reap higher profits; the effect on income distribution is clear.
28. National product is the planner's (or the World Bank's) simplest maximand—certainly not the best.
29. Some authors have argued that such a distribution would be uneconomic and would spread resources too thinly. See, for example, Ligale (1982:183).
30. Potts charges that these self-serving motives played some part in President Banda's decision to move the Malawian capital.

31. The section draws heavily on Becker (1991).
32. Detailed discussion of Bank policy are available in Bamberger et al. (1982) and Keare and Parris (1982). A very detailed description of the Dakar sites-and-services projects is given by Adepoju (1991), while Seibolds and Steinberg (1982) offer a comprehensive description of the programs in Tanzania.
33. Strictly, this result depends upon the general equilibrium elasticities of factor input substitution and output supply. It is possible that growth in skilled labor will lead mainly to falling skilled wages and, in aggregate, skilled incomes.
34. In total, there were eighteen projects; they were ranked by date of appraisal and every second project was selected for review.
35. World Bank and United Nations Development Program (1989). A further assessment of reform efforts can be found in May (1988).
36. The comparison is limited to countries that did not suffer severe external shocks during the mid-1980s.
37. World Bank and United Nations Development Program (1989). The report lists the following countries as reformers: Burundi, Central African Republic Congo, Côte d'Ivoire, The Gambia, Ghana, Guinea, Guinea-Bissau, Kenya, Madagascar, Malawi, Mauritania, Mauritius, Niger, Nigeria, Senegal, Tanzania, Togo, and Zaire. Of these, the following experienced severe (positive or negative) external shocks in the mid-1980's, in the form of abnormally large extremes in the range of annual agricultural growth rates and/or exceptionally large changes in the index of export prices, during 1985–87; Burundi, Congo, Malawi, Niger, and Nigeria.
38. As an example, World Bank forecasts for Côte d'Ivoire predict that for the period 1986–95, disposable household incomes per capita, in real terms, will grow by 4.6 percent per annum in the rural north of the country and 3.5 percent in the rural south, while falling at a rate of 1.3 percent per annum in urban areas. Nevertheless, population growth rates for the same three areas are predicted to be: 0.1 percent, 3.2 percent, and 5.5 percent, respectively. See World Bank (1987a).

CHAPTER 5
Employment Growth and the Wage Structure
in Urban Africa

1. The increasing price of oil obviously cannot explain decreasing employment in Cameroon, an oil exporter.
2. Recent estimates (Swanson and Wolde-Semait [1989:53]) are that 80 African parastatals were sold (that is, their shares were privatized) between 1983 and 1987; the largest number of privatizations (with the exact number in parentheses) were in Guinea (19), Côte d'Ivoire (14), Niger (12), Uganda (7), and Togo (6). Some 60 privatizations were underway in Senegal (18), Guinea (11), Niger (6), Nigeria (6), Uganda (5), Ghana (5), and other countries. In addition, 78 parastatals had been liquidated (their assets were sold); most were located in Côte d'Ivoire (24) and Senegal (18). Another 52 parastatals were in the process of liquidation, with the largest number being in Guinea (15). Overall, of all 270 planned and completed privatizations and liquidations, 204 were in Francophone countries; only 55 were in Anglophone nations.
3. Valentine (1982) provides the wage sequence from 1961 through 1975. Assuming that he and Weeks used the same deflator (and that Valentine's wage sector earnings mirrored Weeks' nonagricultural wage sector earnings), the implication is that real wages in 1983 and 1961 were virtually identical, having gone through a tripling rise and then fall during the interim. Valentine also points out that by the mid-1970s, at least 70 percent of the modern sector wage bill in Tanzania was under direct government control.

4. We have ignored this point otherwise, mainly in the interest of greater readability of the text. The pattern of general real wage decline is sufficiently clear that it does not depend on deflators—though the mild recoveries under SAPs might well, as Radelet claims is the case in The Gambia. It is essential, however, that formal statistical work or economic forecasts be consistent in their choice of deflator.
5. This pattern represented a change from Tanzania in 1971, when private sector wages were clearly lowest, whether or not one controlled for workers' characteristics (Knight and Sabot [1990:147]).
6. Estimates of returns typically show private returns greater than social returns, since the positive social externalities generated by education are difficult or impossible to measure. In effect, the difference between private and social returns is the public expenditure on education which, while included in the calculation of social returns, is not included in the calculation of private returns.
7. In terms of total compensation, parastatals and non-French MNCs pay much more; Syro-Lebanese firms pay considerably less.
8. Indeed, van der Gaag, Stelcner, and Vijverberg (1989), again using switching regressions, estimate that public sector wage offers are actually below private offers, on average. In reality, of course, the public sector will make some higher wage offers and some lower offers, depending on an individual's characteristics. The switching methodology assumes that workers sort themselves into the sector in which they will receive the higher wage.
9. There are some dissenting voices on this topic. Pack (1972) argues that manufacturing plants in Kenya in 1964 were *not* particularly capital intensive by world standards. Of course, such comparisons of factor intensities should only be made with countries that have similar wage-rental ratios.
10. House and Rempel (1976) also conclude that unionization has little impact on Kenyan wages, while ability to pay does positively influence wages.
11. A more detailed discussion is provided in Palmer (1991). But the patterns can be gleaned from virtually any of the major surveys reported in this chapter.
12. For a summary of these studies see Liedholm and Mead (1987:69). Capital productivity is measured as the value of gross output divided by the value of a firm's capital stock.
13. There is another important criticism of partial efficiency measures. As Liedholm and Mead (1987:61 and ff.) correctly point out, the validity of a partial measure is dependent on there being only one scarce factor of production. In developing countries this is commonly assumed to be capital, so output-capital ratios are often used as partial efficiency measures. To the extent that other resources such as management skills and skilled labor are scarce and have nonzero opportunity costs, a partial efficiency measures will yield misleading results.
14. For more details see Liedholm and Mead (1987).
15. In addition to the Liedholm and Mead work discussed below, see Wayem (1983).
16. A detailed discussion of measurement problems is provided by Knight and Sabot (1982).
17. This section draws extensively from Becker (1990).
18. The worst-case scenario in the Population Council's model generates a population growth decline of about 1 percent per annum in the early twenty-first century. See Merritt et al. (1988:119).
19. Waite (1988) reports total health care expenditures per capita for the mid-1980s of $2.00 in Uganda and $1.67 in the Central African Republic. Even corrected for the fact that expenditures converted at official exchange rates do not closely reflect "purchasing power parity" expenditures in very poor countries, there is no doubt that health care expenditures are very small. For the continent as a whole, public health expenditures accounted

for 4.7 percent to 5.0 percent of government expenditure and lending less repayments. In terms of constant 1987 U.S. dollars, these per capita amounts ranged from $0.40 in Nigeria (which, however, has substantial private health care) and $0.20 in Somalia to $36.90 in Lesotho, $28.30 in Mauritius, $22.20 in Botswana, and $16.60 in Zimbabwe; the median figure was $4.10 in Ghana (UNDP/World Bank [1992]).

20. This is particularly true of capital cities. Urban/rural per capita income differentials range widely, as we have seen, but appear to be large in many AIDS belt countries. Per capita incomes in the capital city may be as high as five to ten times that of rural areas.

21. Actually, since the loss of labor would depress returns to other factors and reduce tax revenues, these figures are underestimates for that reason. Nonetheless, the orders of magnitude are not unreasonable. These numbers are much smaller than the $350 million loss per year to Zaire from AIDS deaths by 1995 estimated by the Harvard Institute for International Development (cited in Mann et al. [1988]): this figure is roughly 8 percent of Zaire's 1984 GNP.

22. While savings rates tend to be higher in mineral-rich economies, even in these there has been a dramatic downturn since the first OPEC shock. For the continent as a whole, the ratio of gross domestic savings to GDP declined from 22 percent in 1980 to 13 percent in 1987. For low-income countries (excluding Nigeria), the fall was from 9 percent to 7 percent; for oil exporters the fall was from 30 percent to 20 percent. It also fell in most other mineral exporters, though surprising increases were recorded in Sierra Leone (from 1 percent to 10 percent) and Mauritania (from 7 percent to 14 percent). (World Bank [1989a]).

CHAPTER 6
Classical Models of Urbanization
and Competing Paradigms

1. This chapter draws heavily from Becker and Morrison (1993).

2. Chapter 4 presents a sample of previous migration function estimates (Table 4.6). Virtually all of these are in the neoclassical or spatial interaction spirit, and they appear to support these hypotheses.

3. These rates did not fall in all countries during the 1980s. As the data below indicate, however, there was at the very least a slowing in the rate of mortality *decline* and in the rate of *increase* in educational levels in almost all countries.

4. This section is based on a model presented in Becker and Morrison (1988).

5. National participation rates (labor force divided by population aged fifteen to sixty-four) appear to have declined in every African nation between 1960 and 1980. This phenomenon is likely to be associated with the extension of schooling, among other factors, and may be particularly pronounced in urban areas, given the urban bias characterizing African nations' public service expenditures during this period.

6. The anticipated effects of these factors, that is, the expected signs on the coefficients in the regression equation, are discussed in Appendix 6A.

7. The urban formal/modern (UM) sector equilibrium labor demand equation depends on the exchange rate, which depends on the distribution of the labor force. In turn, the reduced form for rural labor demand also depends on labor force distribution; in both cases, the forms are sufficiently complex to prevent us from substituting one equation into the other to derive an ultimate single equation reduced form. Consequently, a simultaneous, multiple equation quasi-reduced form must be estimated.

8. Or the public enterprises posted losses for the only year for which results were reported in this period. Net financial results are profits less losses, where profits and losses are determined before transfers, subsidies, and taxes, and after interest. In some cases the losses were a significant share of GDP: over 1 percent and 3 percent in Malawi and The Gambia, respectively.

9. These numbers should be interpreted with caution. Productivity declines certainly did occur, but the effects may be exaggerated due to lagged adjustments of wages to inflation, poor agricultural performance in terminal years, or other factors.

10. If production functions were estimated for the set of countries with productivity increases, these increases would be attributed to labor-saving technological change. In fact, however, new technologies are not driving this result. Redundant labor in the urban modern sector simply has been reduced.

11. Lack of data for particular variables prevents the actual sample in any given regression from exceeding twenty-four even in the neoclassical model regressions, though.

12. Since this is the case, it makes little sense to proceed to the next step, testing the hypothesized determinants of labor's share presented in section 6.5.

13. For the continent as a whole, infant mortality rates fell from 152 in 1965 to 115 in 1983, but then only to 107 in 1989; child mortality fell from 34 per thousand in 1965 to 20 per thousand in 1983. Kenya, the country for which the DCS model is estimated, experienced an infant mortality decline from 124 to 81 (1983) and 66 (1990), and a child mortality decline from 25 (1965) to 14 (1983). Data here and elsewhere in this section are taken from United Nations (1989a) and UNDP/World Bank (1992).

14. The best data are available for Kenya using the 1978 and 1982 Statistical Abstracts, and for Côte d'Ivoire based on Dupont (1986) and Dureau (1987).

15. The use of net—rather than gross—migration rates will underestimate the impact of age/ education cohort effect in creating a "bubble" of extremely rapid urban population growth in the 1960–85 period. The explanation is simple: initially Kenya was an overwhelmingly rural country, with few individuals migrating (often return migration) to the countryside. Over time, however, the proportion of the population living in the cities rises considerably, so that return streams will be greater. Thus, if gross migration rates were constant over time, the net migration rate would necessarily be declining. See Rogers (1990) and the discussion earlier in section 6.4 of this chapter.

16. The migration rates are from World Bank (1983a). Clearly, it would be preferable to stratify these migration streams using the educational characteristics of Kenyan internal migrants, but no such data are available. Thus, estimates of differential migration rates by educational attainment are taken from Barnum and Sabot's (1977) estimates for a structurally similar country (Tanzania).

17. United Nations (1979) and Hayase (1986) are used for mortality data. Fertility rates are from various editions of the United Nations *Demographic Yearbook*.

18. This division is somewhat arbitrary, and is used primarily because it was available in all components of the data set.

19. Negative population entries occur in two cases when the impact of death and migration results in a larger withdrawal from older rural skilled cohorts than were present in the first place. There is nothing wrong with the model; migration rates simply were not constant at all times.

20. Thus, if international data collections focused on rural out-migration or rural population growth rates rather than urban population growth rates (which are, of course, opposite sides of the same coin), researchers would come away with very different impressions of which countries are undergoing the most rapid population shifts.

21. There is also something of a partial tautology in the economic models. To the extent that urban price levels are higher and rural incomes are underestimated, rural-urban migration will cause counted GDP to rise without any changes in welfare taking place. In this sense, spurious correlation between migration and GDP growth will be observed.

22. Some terms, such as provincial and city modern sector employment growth, properly are endogenous, and should be estimated simultaneously. Absence of suitable instruments and small sample problems prevent us from conducting simultaneous estimation, however.

23. The *DIND* variable is a public enterprise project location dummy that takes the value one if a town with base period population below 100,000 had a new parastatal founded during the period.
24. Residuals were used since employment data were available for only some cities, and because we wished to examine growth determinants for specific periods.
25. For a more detailed derivation, see Becker and Morrison (1993).

CHAPTER 7

Developmental Policies From an Urban Perspective:
Strategies for the Future

1. Somewhat contentiously, the World Bank (1991d) urban survey suggested that a consequence of service collapse was for the population to decreasingly view cities as centers of "profit, growth and structural change." This study argues that the loss of confidence in cities to provide basic amenities causes migrants to settle in peri-urban areas on the outskirts, where it is possible to undertake subsistence farming—but which also causes an acceleration of urban sprawl.
2. The importance of establishing land registration, primarily for property tax purposes but also for enabling land transfers, is emphasized in the World Bank's (1990d) appraisal report for Kampala, Uganda's urban project loan, as well as in loans for urban Ghana (1990f), Benin (1992), and Guinea (1990e).
3. Alas, other constraints also bind, including inflexible and excessive standards, tiny and virtually bankrupt formal sector housing finance institutions, and control (and inefficient allocation) by government of much existing housing stock.
4. The term squatter is not appropriate when the ultimate ownership of land is unclear. Rather, we prefer the term "nonlegal" to characterize the vast majority of urban housing in countries such as Guinea, as formal recognition of land title remains ambiguous.
5. Again, the Madagascar SAMs are suggestive. In particular, 59 percent of all urban formal sector households' consumption is food; the figure rises to 79 percent for informal sector urban households. But the flow is not all one way: rural Madagascar "imports" twice as many goods from urban areas as from the rest of the world, and these imports from the cities amount to 18.2 percent of gross regional product (GRP). Urban imports from rural Madagascar amount to 29.3 percent of GRP (38.9 percent for urban areas other than Antananarivo).
6. The World Bank (1990d) and other lenders have committed to a substantial urban rehabilitation and development project in Kampala, and have included in that a major increase in the authority and responsibilities of the Kampala City Resistance Council (KCC). Their plans envision growth in KCC funding along with increases in local taxes. But given that only 1,166 (44 percent) of 2,643 city government posts were filled at the time of the loan, it is unlikely that the training programs envisioned will be adequate.
7. Instructive case studies include Chazan (1983) and Hyden (1983).
8. Creation of multilayered political institutions to encourage mass participation in countries such as Madagascar combines with strong central oversight to create virtual paralysis of local government structures—especially when resource transfers from the center diminish sharply, as they did during the 1980s.
9. But not for smaller towns, which tended to run either balanced budgets or received only small (4–17 percent) subsidies: World Bank (1991f:16).
10. The Accra District Rehabilitation Program appears to have been quite successful overall. In addition to property tax revaluation, successful slum upgrading, road construction, rehabilitation projects, and—strikingly for the past decade—a five-year corporate plan for the Accra City Council were completed.

11. In the second Ghana urban project, road rehabilitation and traffic management economic rates of return (ERRs) were estimated to be 105 percent for Accra, 33 percent for Kumasi, and an incredible 345 percent for the first stage in the smaller city of Sekondi-Takoradi. The ERR for rehabilitation of Kumasi's central market was 107 percent; the ERR for the Tema sewerage rehabilitation component was at least 200 percent. The pilot land administration ERR came in at only 2 percent, but its small initial nature inherently means high fixed costs. Overall, the expected ERR for the most recent Ghana project is 44 percent— higher than for most African (or other) urban projects, given the extraordinarily great urban housing, transport, and sanitation problems of urban Ghana. In Ethiopia (World Bank [1990g]), projected economic rates of return to the Addis Ababa sites and services scheme is 17–19 percent; the ERR to low-income neighborhood infrastructure upgrading is 14 percent, the ERR for street maintenance is 18 percent; and the ERR is 9.6 percent for water supply expansion in the industrial city of Akaki. In Benin, the rate of return on road pavement was estimated to exceed 24 percent (World Bank [1992]). In Guinea (World Bank [1990e]), ERRs for road improvements were estimated to be 32 percent. In general, projected ERRs are biased downward because they exclude benefits that are not easily quantified (and all second round, general equilibrium benefits); optimistic assumptions and an ignorance of some costs create an upward bias. There is no way to tell which bias is stronger *ex ante*.

12. Concentrated subsidization is unlikely to be successful in any event and certainly is inequitable.

13. The combination of policies to encourage private enterprise and formalize land titles has had a dramatic impact in Guinea. World Bank (1990e) estimates are that Conakry's annual housing stock rose from 78,000 units in 1983 to 110,000 in 1987. Conakry's housing investment alone during these years was thus about 3 percent of GDP. This sort of housing boom has important employment effects, especially for the small-scale construction industry.

14. These remarks draw heavily on Williams (1985).

15. An apparent exception to the standard limited manpower development side of urban projects is the new program in Benin. This project contains 1) training of urban management staff, 2) formulation and preparation of teaching materials, 3) preparation of a national training strategy for urban management, 4) establishment of technical units for urban management, and 5) funds for a general urban sector strategic plan that would interact and be compatible with the national public investment program.

16. In Bamako's case occupancy permits can be bought and sold on the market as elementary titles.

17. Most African economies have very small industrial sectors, and these and other urban activities certainly will grow more rapidly than rural ones. Moreover, productivity gains in urban activities will be the major source of long-run growth, particularly given the harsh realities of agriculture in much of Africa. Rather, balanced development refers to an aggregate growth-maximizing path in which relative factor and product prices continually reflect true scarcities. Put differently, rural growth must be adequate to prevent bottlenecks in food and foreign exchange from crippling "modern sector" development.

18. The Madagascar study certainly does not support this claim: rural savings are surprisingly high, given the general lack of support for rural areas (and likely underestimation of rural autoinvestment, and hence savings).

19. To reiterate our earlier comments, secondary towns are not the main beneficiaries of current infrastructural rehabilitation and institution building loans from international or bilateral sources. For successful industrial and agricultural growth to take place, though, decentralization of international loans and domestic infrastructure investments must commence as soon as the most chaotic problems of the center are addressed. Good

models for quick decentralization include the World Bank's Second Urban Projects in Guinea and Ghana (World Bank [1990e] and [1990f], respectively), which take a major step toward beginning basic infrastructure provision in several secondary cities.

20. This occurs even where agricultural parastatals are being dismantled, as in the case of northeast Senegal's irrigated rice zones. In another example (World Bank [1985h]), Mauritania's agricultural investments in the mid- and late-1980s were directed at one set of regions (Gargol and Guidimaka), while new urban infrastructure was largely assigned to other areas. Similarly, discussions concerning agricultural development projects supported by the World Bank in Nigeria and Ghana make no reference to the urban centers in their midst which will exercise important marketing and service roles.

21. Within the World Bank, a regional development project was designed in the mid-1980s for Kivu Province, Zaire. The anticipated interventions in each sector complement one another, and include the rehabilitation of market areas and feeder roads, as well as technical and financial assistance to private cooperative savings and loan associations in the area. Nonetheless, much more remains to be done in a much broader range of countries.

Sources

Abate, Yohannis. 1980. "Demographic Factors in Africa's Development: The Nature of Population Policy in Africa." *Rural Africana*.
———. 1980. "Population Growth and Urbanization in Africa." *Current History* 78.
Abiodun, Josephine. 1983. "Accelerated Urbanization and the Problems of Urban Peripheries: The case of Nigeria." *Indian Journal of Regional Science*, 15, no. 1.
———. 1981. "Aspects of the Spatial Impact of Development Efforts: A Case Study of Nigeria." *Tijdschrift voor Economische en Sociale Geografie* 72, no. 2.
Aboagye, A. 1986. *Informal Sector Employment in Kenya*. Addis Ababa:ILO/JASPA.
Adalemo, A. 1977. "Towards a Model of Planned Urban Development in African Countries." In A. Mabogunje and A. Faniran, eds., *Regional Planning and National Development in Tropical Africa*. Ibadan, Nigeria: Ibadan University Press.
Adams, Dale W., Douglas H. Graham, and J.D. von Pischke, eds. 1984. *Undermining Rural Development with Cheap Credit*. Boulder: Westview.
Adedibu, Afolabi A. 1981. "The Impact of Government Policy on Indigenous Housing In Iorlu, Nigeria," *Ekistics*, 48, no. 287.
Adepoju, Aderanti. 1991. "Urbanization Policy in Senegal." In IUSSP, *Population Policy in Sub-Saharan Africa: Drawing on International Experience*. Liege: IUSSP.
———. 1984. "Migration and Rural Opportunities in Nigeria." *Labour and Society* 9(1).
———. 1983. "Issues in the Study of Migration and Urbanization in Africa South of the Sahara." In Peter Morrison, ed., *Population Movements: Their Forms and Functions in Urbanization and Development*. Liege, Belgium: Ordina Editions.
———. 1982. "Selected Studies on the Dynamics, Patterns, and Consequences of Migration, IV. Medium-Sized Towns in Nigeria: Research and Policy Prospects." UNESCO, Reports and Papers in the Social Sciences, no. 53.
———. 1982a. "Population Redistribution: A Review of Governmental Policies." In John Clarke and Leszek Kosinski (eds.), *Redistribution of Population in Africa*. London: Heinemann Educational Books.
———. 1978. "Migration and Rural Development in Tropical Africa." *African Urban Studies* 2.
———. 1974. "Between Urban Migrants and Their Home Communities in Nigeria." *Africa* 44.
Adewuyi, Alfred A. 1985. "Intergenerational Change in Family Size Among the Urban Residents in Ibadan, Nigeria," Paper Contributed to Fertility Session during the IUSSP XX General Conference, Florence, Italy.
African Farmer. 1990 (July). "Helping Farmers Resist the Pull of the City." New York: The Hunger Project, no. 4: 5–15.
Agarwala, Ramgopal. 1983. "Price Distortions and Growth in Developing Countries." World Bank Staff Working Paper no. 575.

Ajaegbu, H. I. 1976. *Urban and Rural Development in Nigeria*. London: Heinemann Educational Books.

Alchian, A.A., and H. Demsetz. 1972. "Production, Information Cost, and Economic Organization." *American Economic Review* 62.

Amis, Philip. 1984. "Squatters or Tenants: The Commercialization of Unauthorized Housing in Nairobi." *World Development* 12, no. 1.

Anderson, D. 1978 (January). *Rural Enterprise and Non-Farm Employment*. Washington, DC: World Bank.

————. 1987 (November). *The Public Revenue and Economic Policies in African Countries: An Overview of Issues and Policy Options*. Washington, DC: World Bank Discussion Paper no. 19.

Antonio, Philippe, and Claude Henny. 1983. "Urbanisation et Dimension Du Menage: Le ras d'Abidjan." *Cahiers ORSTOM*, Serie Sciences Humaines 19(3).

Appleton, Simon, Paul Collier, and Paul Horsnell. 1990. "Gender, Education, and Employment in Côte d'Ivoire." Washington, DC: World Bank SDA Unit Working Paper no. 8.

Arnaud, M. 1985. "Esquisse de Schéma d'Aménagement de la Région du Bas-Zaire: Contexte Spatiale et Evolutions à Long Terme." Kinshasa: République du Zaire, Departement des Travaux Publics et d'Aménagement du Territoire.

Aryee, George. 1981. "The Informal Manufacturing Sector in Kumasi." In S. Sethuraman, ed., *The Urban Informal Sector in Developing Countries*. Geneva: International Labour Office.

————. 1976. "Effects of Formal Education and Training on the Intensity of Employment in the Informal Sector. *World Employment Programme Research, Working Papers*. Geneva: International Labour Office.

Asabere, Paul. 1981. "The Determinants of Land Values in an African City: The Case of Accra, Ghana." *Land Economics* 57, no. 3.

Asabere, Paul K., and K. Owusu-Banahene. 1983. "Population Density Function for Ghanaian (African) Cities: An Empirial Note." *Journal of Urban Economics* 14.

Austin, Ralph. 1987. *African Economic History*. London: James Currey, and Portsmouth, NH: Heinemann.

Bamberger, Michael, Bishwara Sanyal, and Nelson Valverde. 1982. "Evaluation of Sites and Services Projects: The Experience of Lusaka, Zambia." Washington, DC: *World Bank Staff Working Paper* no. 548.

Barber, G. M., and W. J. Milne. 1986. "Modeling Internal Migration in Kenya: An Econometric Analysis Using Limited Data." Toronto: University of Toronto, unpublished manuscript.

Barbier, J. C., G. Courade, and P. Gubry. 1981. "L'exode rural au Caméroun." *Cashiers ORSTOM: Série Sciences Humaines* 18(1).

Bardhan, Pranab K. 1979. "Wages and Unemployment in a Poor Agrarian Economy." *Journal of Political Economy*.

Barnum, H. N., and R. H. Sabot. 1977. "Education, Employment Probabilities and Rural-Urban Migration in Tanzania." *Oxford Bulletin of Economics and Statistics* 39(2).

Barrett, Richard. 1988. *Urban Transport in West Africa*. Washington, DC: World Bank, Technical Paper no. 81, Urban Transport Series.

Bates, R. H. 1981. *Markets and States in Tropical Africa: The Political Basis of Agricultural Policies*. Berkeley: University of California Press.

Beals, R. M., M. Levy, and L. Moses. 1967. "Rationality and Migration in Ghana." *Review of Economics and Statistics* 49.

Becker, Charles M. 1991. "Poverty in The Gambia: Country Assessment and Policy Issues." Washington, DC: World Bank (AF1SD) restricted.

————. 1991a. "Migration and Urbanization in Sub-Saharan Africa: International Agency Influences." In IUSSP, *Population Policy in Sub-Saharan Africa: Drawing on International Experiences*. Liege: International Union for the Scientific Study of Population.

————. 1990. "The Demo-Economic Impact of the AIDS Pandemic in Sub-Saharan Africa." *World Development* **18**:12 (December): 1599–1619.

————. 1989. "Dependency Theory: A Neoclassical Exposition." Boulder, CO: University of Colorado, Economics Institute Working Paper.

————. 1987. "Urban Sector Income Distribution and Economic Development. *Journal of Urban Economics* **21**: 127–45.

————. 1985. "Public Industrial Enterprises in Zambia." Washington, DC: The World Bank (INDSP), restricted document.

————. 1985. "The Effect of Government Policy on Urban Population Growth in Sub-Saharan Africa." Nashville, TN: University working paper.

Becker, Charles M. and Lubuele Luan'Sende. 1991. "Are Women Better Credit Risks in Developing Countries? Evidence from Small-Scale, Formal Sector Loans in The Gambia, West Africa." Boulder, CO: Economics Institute working paper.

Becker, Charles M., and Andrew R. Morrison. 1993. "Observational Equivalence in the Modeling of African Labor Markets and Rural-Urban Migration." *World Development*. 21:4, pp. 535–554.

————. 1988. "The Determinants of Urban Population Growth in Sub-Saharan Africa." *Economic Development and Cultural Change* **36,** no. 2.

Becker, Charles M., Jeffrey G. Williamson, and Edwin S. Mills. 1992. *Indian Urbanization and Economic Development*. Baltimore: Johns Hopkins University Press.

Belsky, E.S. 1985. "Review of Selected Documents on Rural-Urban Dynamics." Worcester, MA: Clark Unversity, Cooperative Agreement on Settlements and Resource System Analysis.

Bernstein, J. 1985 (September). "Review of World Bank Lending for Land Registration and Property Tax Improvements in Urban Projects, FY 1972–82." Washington, DC: World Bank (Water Suppply and Urban Development Department), unpublished manuscript.

Berry, R. Albert, and Richard H. Sabot. 1978. "Labour Market Performance in Developing Countries: A Survey." *World Development* 6.

Berry, Robert, and John Sommer. 1976. "Freetown: Images of the Urban Environment." *Pan-African Journal* 9, no 2.

Bevan, D.L., A. Bigsten, P. Collier, and J.W. Gunning. 1988. "Incomes in the United Republic of Tanzania during the 'Nyerere Experiment.' " In Wouter van Ginnekin, ed., *Trends in Employment and Labour Incomes:Case Studies on Developing Countries*. Geneva: ILO.

Bissiliat, J., and J. Fenet-Rieutord. 1984 (March). *Les Villes Secondaires en Afrique: Leur Role et leurs Fonctions dans le Développement National et Régional, Phase 1, Sénégal*. Paris: Agence Française pour l'Aménagement et le Développement à l'Etranger.

Blayney, R. and M. Otero. 1985. "Small and Micro-Enterprises: Contributions to Development and Future Directions for AID's Support." Washington, DC: USAID.

Blomqvist, A. G. 1981. "Urban Job Creation and Unemployment in LDCs: Todaro vs. Harris and Todaro." *Journal of Development Economics* 5.

Boaden, B. G. 1980. "A Laizzez-Faire Approach to the Housing of Urban Blacks." *The South African Journal of Economics* 48: 28–44.

————. 1979. "Economic Aspects of Black Housing in South Africa with Particular Reference to the New 99-Year Lease Hold legislation." *The South African Journal of Economics* 47(4): 442.

Bohra, D. M. 1979. "Patterns of Urban Settlements in Somalia." *GeoJournal* 3, no. 1.

Boserup, Ester. 1981. *Population and Technology: A Study of Long-Term Trends*. Chicago: University of Chicago Press.

Bricker, Gary, and Sounana Traore. 1979. "Transitional Urbanization in Upper Volta: The Case of Ougadougou, a Savannah Capital." In R. A. Obudho, and S. El-Shakhs, eds., *Development of Urban Systems in Africa*. New York: Praeger.

Brown, B. B. 1983. "The Impact of Male Labor Migration on Women in Botswana." *African Affairs* 82(328).

Brueckner, Jan. 1990. "Analyzing Third-World Urbanization: A Theoretical Model with Empirical Evidence." *Economic Development and Cultural Change* 38:3, pp 587–610.

Bryant, Coralie. 1980. "Squatters, Collective Action, and Participation: Learning from Lusaka." *World Development* 8.

Bryceson, Derek. 1984. *Urbanization and Agrarian Development in Tanzania with Special Reference to Secondary Cities*. London: International Institute for Environment and Development.

Bulatao, Rodolfo. 1987 (June). "Initial Investigation of the Demographic Impact of AIDS in One African Country." Washington, DC: World Bank, unpublished manuscript.

Bureau d'Etudes d'Aménagements Urbains (Kinshasa). 1984 (January). "Programme de Recherche Croissance Urbaine et Gestion des Villes, Rapport d'Analyse Générale, Kinshasa." Kinshasa: BEAU.

Byerlee, Derek. 1974. "Rural-Urban Migration in Africa: Theory, Policy, and Research Implications." *International Migration Review* 8.

Byerlee, Derek, Joseph L. Tommy, and Habib Fatoo. 1976. "Rural-Urban Migration in Sierra Leone: Determinants and Policy Implications." Michigan State University, African Rural Economy Program, African Rural Economy Paper no. 13.

Caldwell, John C. 1977. "The Economic Rationality of High Fertility: An Investigation Illustrated with Nigerian Survey Data." *Population Studies*.

———, ed. 1975. *Population Growth and Socioeconomic Change in West Africa*. New York: Columbia University Press.

———. 1969. *African Rural-Urban Migration: The Movement to Ghana's Towns*. New York: Columbia University Press.

Calvert, Albert F. 1969. *South-West Africa During the German Occupation, 1884–1914*. New York: Negro Universities Press.

Carvalho, Joe William. 1988. *Agriculture and Economic Development in Lesotho: Analysis Using a Social Accounting Matrix*. Pullman, WA: Washington State University, Department of Agricultural Economics, unpublished Ph.D. dissertation.

Chambers, Robert. 1969. *Settlement Schemes in Tropical Africa: A Study of Organizations and Development*. London: Routledge and Kegan Paul.

Champand, J., J. Lombard, and M. Sivignon. 1984 (December). *Les Villes Secondaires en Afrique, Leur Role et leurs Fonctions dans le Développement National et Régional, Phase 2, Etude de Cas Régional: Sénégal*. Paris: Agence Française pour l'Aménagement et le Développement à l'Etranger.

Chapman, Murray, and R. Mansell Prothero. 1983. "Themes on Circulation in the Third World." *International Migration Review* 17(4).

Chatterji, Manas, et al. (eds.) *Spatial, Environmental, and Resource Policy in the Developing Countries*. Brookfield, VT: Gower Publishing.

Chazen, N. 1983. *An Anatomy of Ghanaian Politics: Managing Political Recession, 1969–1982*. Boulder: Westview.

Chilivumbo, A. 1985. *Migration and Uneven Rural Development in Africa: The Case of Zambia*. New York: University Press of America.

Christiansen, Robert. 1984. "The Pattern of Internal Migration in Response to Structural Change in the Economy of Malawi, 1966–77." *Development and Change* 15(1).

Christopher, Garland. 1979. "Urbanisation, exode rural vers les centres urbains et politiques de développement en Côte d'Ivoire." *Cahiers Ivoiriens de Recherches Economiques et Sociales* no. 22.

Chuta, E., and C. Liedholm. 1979. *Rural Non-Farm Employment: A Review of the State of the Art*. East Lansing, MI: Michigan State University Department of Agricultural Economics, Rural Development Paper no. 4.

Clark, Mari H. 1985 (February). "Household Economic Strategies and Support Networks of the Poor in Kenya." Washington, DC: World Bank (Water Supply and Urban Development Department) Discussion Paper UDD-69.

Cleaver, Kevin. 1985. "The Impact of Price and Exchange Rate Policies on Agriculture in Sub-Saharan Agriculture." Washington, DC: *World Bank Staff Working Paper* no. 728.

Cliffe, Lionel. 1978. "Labour Migration and Peasant Differentiation: Zambian Experiences." *Journal of Peasant Studies* 5(3).

Cochrane, Susan H., and Samir M. Farid. 1989. "Fertility in Sub-Saharan Africa." Washington, DC: World Bank Discussion Paper no. 43.

Cohen, Michael A. 1982. "The Political Economy of Urban Reform in Africa." Paper presented at meeting of Canadian Association of African Studies.

———. "The Senegal Sites and Services Project: A Case Study of Project Experience" for use in the EDI/AABITAT course Abidjan.

———. 1979. "Urban Growth and Economic Development in the Sahel." *World Bank Staff Working Paper* no. 315.

Colclough, Christopher, and Peter Fallon. 1983. "Rural Poverty in Botswana: Dimensions, Causes and Constraints." In Dharam Ghai and Samir Radwan, eds., *Agrarian Policies and Rural Poverty in Africa.* Geneva: International Labour Office.

Cole, William E., and Richard D. Sanders. 1985. "Internal Migration and Urbanization in the Third World." *American Economic Review* 75(3).

Collier, Paul. 1985 (July). "An Analysis of the Nigerian Labor Market." Washington, DC: World Bank, West African Programs Department.

———. 1983. "Oil and Inequality in Rural Nigeria." In Dharam Ghai and Samir Radwan, eds., *Agrarian Policies and Rural Poverty in Africa.* Geneva: ILO.

———. 1979. "Migration and Unemployment: A Dynamic General Equilibrium Analysis Applied to Tanzania." *Oxford Economic Papers* 31(2).

Collier, Paul, and A. Bigsten. 1981. "A Model of Educational Expansion and Labor Market Adjustment Applied to Kenya. *Oxford Bulletin of Economics and Statistics* 43(1).

Collier, Paul, and Deepak Lal. 1986. *Labour and Poverty in Kenya 1900–1980.* Oxford: Clarendon Press.

———. 1984. "Why Poor People Get Rich: Kenya 1960–1979." *World Development* 12, no. 10.

———. 1980. "Poverty and Growth in Kenya." World Bank Staff Working Paper no. 389.

Collier, V. C., and H. Rempel. 1977. "The Divergence of Private from Social Costs in Rural-Urban Migration: A Case of Nairobi, Kenya." *Journal of Development Studies* 13(3).

Conyers, Diana. 1981. "Decentralization for Regional Development: A Comparative Study of Tanzania, Zambia, and Papua New Guinea." *Public Administration and Development.*

Coulibaly, Sidiki, Joel Gregory, and Victor Piche. 1980. *Les migrations voltaique.* Ottawa: Centre de Recherches pour le Développement International.

Cour, Jean-Marie. 1985 (September). *Macroeconomic Implications of Urban Growth: Interaction Between Cities and Their Hinterlands.* Washington, DC: World Bank (Eastern and Southern Africa Region, Water Supply and Urban Development Region).

Davies, Hywel. 1969. "Lusaka, Zambia: Some Town Planning Problems in an African Capital City of Independence." *Zambia Urban Studies* no. 1.

Davis, Diana, and Prothero R. Mansell. 1982. "A Bibliography of Population Mobility in West Africa." Liverpool Papers in Human Geograpy, Working Paper no. 6.

Davis, Kingsley. 1981. "International Inequality and Migration to the Middle East and North Africa." In K. Srinivasan and S. Makerji, eds., *Dynamics of Population and Family Welfare.* Bombay: Himalaya Publishing House.

De Cola, Lee. 1985. "Lognormal Estimates of Macroregional City-Size Distributions, 1950–1970." *Environment and Planning A* 17.

———. 1984. "Statistical Determinants of the Population for a Nation's Largest City." *Economic Development and Cultural Change* 33, no.1.

———. n.d. "A Path Analysis of World Development and Urbanization." Burlington, VT: University of Vermont Department of Geography, unpublished manuscript.

Deble, Isabelle, and Phillipe Hugon, eds. 1982. *Vivre et survivre dans les villes africaines*. Paris: Presses Universitaires de France.

Diallo, Yacine Marius. 1981. "Les conséquences de la sécheresse sur les migrations dans les pays du Sahel: L'exemple du Mali." In *International Population Conference (1981): Solicited Papers*. Liège, Belgium: International Union for the Scientific Study of Population.

Direction du Projet Urbain de Mali. 1984 (March). *Etude du Développement Urbain de Bamako: Rapport Socio-Economique*. Bamako: Direction du Projet Urbain de Mali.

Dixit, Avinash. 1969. "Marketable Surplus and Dual Development." *Journal of Economic Theory*.

Doebele, William. 1983 (July). "Why Cadastral Systems Are Important for Less Developed Countries." Washington, DC: World Bank (Urban Development Department).

Dow, Thomas E., Jr., and Eugene Benjamin. 1975. "Sierra Leone: Demographic Trends and Implications." In John C. Cladwell, ed., *Population Growth and Socioeconomic Change in West Africa*. New York: Columbia University Press.

Dow, T. 1971. "Fertility and Family Planning in Africa. *Journal of Modern Studies* 8(3).

Due, John F. 1983. "Trends in Rail Transportation in Four African Countries: Zimbabwe, Zambia, Tanzania, Sudan." University of Illinois Bureau of Economic and Business Research, Faculty Working Paper no. 937.

Dumont, Rene, and Marie-France Mottin. 1983. *Stranglehold on Africa*. London: Andre Deutsch.

Dunkerly, H., ed. 1983. *Urban Land Policy: Issues and Opportunities*. New York: Oxford University Press.

Dupont, Veronique. 1986. *Dynamique de Villes Secondaires et. . . . Processus Migratoires en Afrique de l'Ouest*. Paris: ORSTOM.

Dureau, Francoise. 1987. *Migration et Urbanisation: le Cas de la Côte d'Ivoire*. Paris: ORSTOM.

Ebong, M. O. 1982. "Spatial Dynamics of Population in Nigeria: Implications for Rational Migration Policies." In A. Findlay, ed., *Recent National Population Change*. Durham, England: University of Durham, Department of Geography.

Eglin, R. 1978. "The Oligopolistic Structure and Competitive Characteristics of Direct Foreign Investment in Kenya's Manufacturing Sector." In R. Kaplinsky, ed., *Readings on the Multinational Corporation in Kenya*. Nairobi: Oxford University Press.

Eke, E. Feral. 1982. "Changing Views on Urbanization, Migration and Squatters." *Habitat International* 6(2).

Elkan, W. 1988 (July). "Entrepreneurs and Entrepreneurship in Africa." *World Bank Research Observer* 3, no. 2.

———. 1980. "Labor Migration from Botswana, Lesotho, and Swaziland." *Economic Development and Cultural Change* 28(3).

———. 1976. "Is a Proletariat Emerging in Nairobi?" *Economic Development and Cultural Change* 24.

———. 1963. "Circular Migration and the Growth of Towns in East Africa." *International Labour Review* 96 no. 6.

Ellis, Frank. 1984. "Relative Agricultural Prices and the Urban Bias Model: A Comparative Analysis of Tanzania and Fiji." *Journal of Development Studies* 20, no. 3.

El-Shakhs, S., and R. A. Obudho, eds. 1974. *Urbanization National Development and Regional Planning in Africa*. New York: Praeger Publishers.

Essang, Sunday M., and Adewale F. Mabawonku. 1974. "Determinants and Impact of Rural-Urban Migration: A Case Study of Selected Communities in Western Nigeria." Michigan State University African Rural Employment Research Network, African Rural Employment Paper no. 10.

Fadayomi, T. O. 1979. "Rural Outmigration in Nigeria: Its Determinants and Policy Implications." *Rural Africana*, no. 6.

———. 1978. "Rural Migration and Rural Development: An Exploratory Study of Return Migrants in Selected Rural Communities of Nigeria." *Journal of Rural Economics and Development* 12(2).

Fallon, Peter. 1985. "The Labor Market in Kenya: Recent Evidence." Washington, DC: The World Bank, Development Research Department, Labor Market Division (August).

Fapohunda, O. J. 1981. "Human Resources and the Lagos Informal Sector." *The Urban Informal Sector in Developing Countries*. Geneva: ILO.

Fargures, Philippe. 1981. "Les migrations en Côte d'Ivoire d'après le recensement de la population de 1975." *Cahiers Ivoiriens de Recherche Economique et Sociale* no. 31–32.

Faruqee, Rashid, and Ravi Gulhati. 1983. "Rapid Population Growth in Sub-Saharan Africa: Issues and Policies." World Bank Staff Working Paper no. 559.

Faruqee, Rashid, et al. 1980. *Kenya: Population and Development*. The World Bank.

Findlay, Allan. 1982. "Migration Planning: The Case for Tunisia." *Applied Geography* 2(3).

Findley, Sally. 1976. *Planning for Internal Migration: A Review of Issues and Policies in Developing Countries*. U.S. Department of Commerce, Bureau of the Census.

Finnegan, Gregory. 1980. "Employment and Migration Among the Mossi of Upper Volta." In George Dalton, ed., *Research in Economic Anthropology, a Research Annual* (3).

Food and Agriculture Organization (United Nations). 1982. *Production Yearbook*. Rome: FAO.

Foot, David, and William Milne. 1984. "Net Migration Estimation in an Extended, Multiregional Gravity Model." *Journal of Regional Science* 24, (1).

Fowler, D. A. 1981. "The Informal Sector in Freetown: Opportunities for Self-Employment." in S. Sethuraman, ed. *The Urban Informal Sector in Developing Countries*. Geneva: ILO.

Franke, Richard W. 1980. *Seeds of Famine: Ecological Destruction and the Development Dilemma in the West African Sahel*. Montclair, NJ: Allenheld and Osmun.

Franqueville, André. 1979. "Croissance démographique et immigration à Yaounde." *Cahiers d' Outre Mer* 32(128).

Van der Gaag, Jacques, and Wim Vijverberg. 1988. "Wage Determiants in Côte d'Ivoire." Washington, DC: World Bank, Living Standards Measurement Study, Working Paper no. 33.

Van der Gaag, Jacques, Morton Stelcner, and Wim Vijverberg. 1989. "Public-Private Sector Wage Comparisons and Moonlighting in Developing Countries: Evidence from Côte d'Ivoire and Peru." Washington, DC: World Bank, Living Standards Measurement Study, Working Paper no. 52.

Gaile, Gary L. 1988a (March). "Kenya's Rural Trade and Production Centers." Cambridge, MA: Harvard University, Harvard Institute for International Development, Development Discussion Paper no. 263.

———. 1988b (July). "Choosing Locations for Small Town Development to Enable Market and Employment Expansion: The Case of Kenya." *Economic Geography* 64(3): 242–54.

———. 1976. "Processes Affecting the Pattern of Rural-Urban Development in Kenya." *African Studies Review* 19, no. 3.

———. 1990 (March). "Improving Rural-Urban Linkages Through Small Town Market-Based Development." Boulder, CO: University of Colorado, Institute of Behavioral Science, Population Program working paper WP-90-3.

Gaile, Gary L., and Helen Ruth Aspaas. 1991. "Kenya's Spatial Dimensions of Development Strategy." *Urban Geography* 12(4): 381–86.

Gaude, Jacques, ed. 1982. *Phenomene migratoire et politiques associees dans le contexte africain*. Geneva: International Labour Office.

Gaveau, G., and C. Monnier. 1984. *Les Villes Secondaire en Afrique: Leur Role et leurs Fonctions dans le Développement National et Régional: Le Zaire*. Paris: Agence Française pour l'Aménagement et le Développement à l'Etranger.

Gerry, Chris. 1974. "Petty Producers and the Urban Economy: A Case Study of Dakar," Geneva: International Labour Office, World Employment Programme working paper.

Ghai, Dharam, and Samir Radwan, eds. 1983. *Agarian Policies and Rural Poverty in Africa*. Geneva: International Labour Office.

———. 1983a. "Growth and Inequality: Rural Development in Malawi, 1964–1978." In Dharam Ghai and Samir Radwan, eds., *Agarian Policies and Rural Poverty in Africa*. Geneva: International Labour Office.

Ghai, D., M. Godfrey, and F. Lisk. 1979. *Planning for Basic Needs in Kenya: Performance, Policies and Prospects*. Geneva: ILO.

Glewwe, Paul. 1988. "The Distribution of Welfare in Côte d'Ivoire in 1985." Washington, DC: World Bank, Living Standards Measurement Study Working Paper no. 29.

Glewwe, Paul, and Dennis de Tray. 1988. "The Poor During Adjustment: A Case Study of Côte d'Ivoire." Washington, DC: World Bank, Living Standards Measurement Study, Working Paper no. 47.

Godfrey, E.M. 1973. "Economic Variables and Rural-Urban Migration: Some Thoughts on the Todaro Hypothesis." *Journal of Development Studies* 10.

Goldsheider, Calvin. 1983. "Modernization, Migration, and Urbanization." In Peter A. Morrison (ed.), *Population Movements: Their Forms and Functions in Urbanization and Development*. Liege, Belgium: Ordina Editions.

Gore, Charles. 1984. *Regions in Question*. London: Methuen.

Gozo, M.K. 1985. "Le Secteur Non-Structuré de Kinshasa." Addis Ababa: International Labour Office.

Graham, Douglas H., Nelson Aguilera, Michel Keita, and Kifle Negash. 1988. "Informal Finance in Rural Niger: Scope, Magnitudes and Organization." Columbus, OH: Ohio State University, Department of Agricultural Economics and Rural Sociology, Studies in Rural Finance Occasional Paper no. 1472.

Greenhouse, S. 1988 (May 23). "Zaire, The Manager's Nightmare: So Much Potential." *New York Times*.

Greenwood, Michael. 1985. "Human Migration: Theory, Models and Empirical Studies." *Journal of Regional Science* 25 (4): 521–43.

———. 1975. "Research on Internal Migration in the United States: A Survey." *Journal of Economic Literature* 13: 397–433.

Gregory, Joel W., and Victor Piche. 1983. "African Return Migration: Past, Present, and Future." *Contemporary Marxism* (7).

Grimes, Orvile F., Jr. 1976. *Housing for Low-Income Urban Families*. Baltimore: The Johns Hopkins University Press.

Gugler, Josef. 1991. "Life in a Dual System Revisited: Urban-Rural Ties in Enugu, Nigeria, 1961–87." *World Development* 19(5): 399–409.

Gugler, Josef, and William G. Flanagan. 1978. *Urbanization and Social Change in West Africa*. Cambridge: Cambridge University Press.

Guhr, Ingo. 1980. "Co-operative Housing in Urban Tanzania." *Habitat International* 4(3).

Guichaoua, Andre. 1982. "Population migrante et types de mobilite au Burundi." *Cahiers d'Outre-Mer* 35(138).

Gulhati, Ravi, and Gautam Datta. 1983. "Capital Accumulation in Eastern and Southern Africa." Washington, DC: *World Bank Staff Working Paper* no. 562.

Gulhati, Ravi and Uday Sekhar. 1982 (November). "Industrial Strategy for Late Starters: The Experience of Kenya." *World Development* 10(11).

Gupta, Desh B. 1979. "Regional Imbalance and Migration in Kenya." *Journal of African Studies* 6(1).

Guyer, Jane. 1981. "Household and Community in African Studies." *African Studies Review* 24, no. 2/3.

Haan, Hans C. 1982. "Some Characteristics of Informal Sector Businessmen in Lusaka and Kitwe, Zambia," Lusaka: International Labour Office, World Employment Programme SATEP working paper.

Haeringer, Philipps. 1983. *La recherche urbaine à l'Orstom: Bibliographie analytique, 1950–1980.* Paris: L' Office de la Recherche Scientifique et Technique Outre-Mer (ORSTOM).

Haggblade, S., and J. Brown. 1989. "Farm-Nonfarm Linkages in Rural Sub-Saharan Africa." *World Development* 17: 1173–1201.

Haggblade, S., P. Hazell, and J. Brown. 1987 (December). *Farm/ Non-Farm Linkages in Rural Sub-Saharan Africa and Empirical Evidence and Policy Implications.* Washington, DC: World Bank (Agricultural and Rural Development Department, Agricultural Policies Division) AGRAP Economic Discussion Paper no. 2.

Haggblade, Steven, and Carl Liedholm. 1991. "Agriculture, Rural Labor Markets, and the Evolution of the Rural Nonfarm Economy." E. Lansing, MI: Michigan State University (Department of Economics), unpublished manuscript.

Hake, Andrew. 1977. *African Metroplis.* New York: St. Martin Press.

Hamer, Andrew M. 1986 (April). "Urban sub-Sarahan Africa in Macroeconomic Perspective." Washington, DC: World Bank, Water Supply and Urban Development Department discussion paper no. UDD-96.

Hanna, William J., and Judith I. Hanna. 1981. *Urban Dynamics in Black Africa.* New York: Aldine Publishing Company.

Hansen, Bent. 1979. "Colonial Economic Development with an Unlimited Supply of Land: A Ricardian Case." *Economic Development and Cultural Change* 27(4).

Hansen, Karen Tranbert. 1982. "Lusaka's Squatters: Past and Present." *African Studies Review* 25, nos. 2 and 3: 117–236.

Haq, Cynthia. 1988. "Data on AIDS in Africa: An Assessment," in Norman Miller and Richard Rockwell, eds. *AIDS in Africa.* Lewiston, NY: Edwin Mellen.

Harper, M. 1984. *Small Business in the Third World: Guidelines for Practical Assistance.* New York: John Wiley.

Harris, John, and Richard Sabot. 1982. "Urban Unemployment in LDC's: Towards a More General Search Model." In R.H. Sabot, ed., *Migration and the Labor Market in Developing Countries.* Boulder, CO: Westview.

Harris, John, and Michael Todaro. 1970. "Migration, Unemployment and Development: A Two-Sector Analysis." *American Economic Review* 60(1).

Haugeraud, Angelique. 1984. "The Consequences of Land Tenure Reform Among Small Holders in the Kenya Highlands." *Rural Africana* 15/16.

Hay, Michael J. 1980. "A Structural Equations Model of Migration in Tunisia." *Economic Development and Cultural Change* 28(2).

Hayase, Yasuko. 1986. *Changes in Mortality and in Its Cause Structure Among Developing Countries.* Tokyo: Institute of Developing Economies.

Hedlund, Hans, and Mats Lundahl. 1983. "Migration and Change in Rural Zambia." Scandinavian Institute of African Studies Report, no. 70.

Heisel, Don. 1968. "Attitudes and Practices of Contraception in Kenya." *Demography* 5 (2).

Henderson, J. Vernon 1988. *Urban Development: Theory, Fact and Illusion.* New York: Oxford University Press.

———. 1988a. "General Equilibrium Modeling of Systems and Cities." In P. Nijkamp and E. Mills, eds., *Handbooks in Regional and Urban Economics, Vol. II.* Amsterdam: North-Holland.

———. 1980. "A Framework for International Comparisons of Systems of Cities." World Bank, Urban and Regional Economics Division, Urban and Regional Report no. 80–3.

———. 1979. "The Economics of Systems of Cities." Brown University Working Paper no. 78–22.

————. 1977. *Economic Theory and the Cities*. New York: Academic Press.

Henderson, J. Vernon, and Yannis M. Ioanides. 1981. "Aspects of Growth in a System of Cities." *Journal of Urban Economics* 10.

Hervitz, Hugo. 1985. "Selectivity, Adaptation, or Disruption? A Comparison of Alternative Hypotheses on the Effects of Migration on Fertility: The Case of Brazil." *International Migration Review* 19:2.

Hervouet, J. P. 1981. "Mobilité sahelienne dans le triangle frontalier Mauritanie-Sénégal-Mali." *Cahiers Géographiques de Rouen*, v.e. frontalier 15.

Hirschman, Albert. 1961. *The Strategy of Economic Development*. New Haven, CT: Yale University Press.

Hocking, J. A., and N. R. Thomson. 1981. *Migration and Urbanisation in West Africa*. Moray House College of Education.

Hoddinott, John. 1992 (August). "Modelling Remittance Flows in Kenya." *Journal of African Economies* 1:2.

Van der Hoeven, R. 1984. "Zambia." In Wouter van Ginnekin and Jong-goo Park, eds., *Generating Internationally Comparable Income Distribution Estimates*. Geneva: International Labour Office.

House, William. 1987. "Labor Market Differentiation in a Developing Economy: An Example from Urban Juba, Southern Sudan." *World Development* 15(7): 877–97.

————. 1984. "Nairobi's Informal Sector: Dynamic Entrepreneurs or Surplus Labor?" *Economic Development and Cultural Change* 32, (2).

————. 1981. "Nairobi's Informal Sector: An Exploratory Study." In Tony Killick, ed., *Papers on the Kenyan Economy: Performance, Problems, and Policy*. London: Heinemann.

House, William, and Henry Rempel. 1980. "The Determinants of Interregional Migration in Kenya." *World Development* 8(1).

————. 1976. "The Impact of Unionization on Negotiated Wages in the Manufacturing Sector in Kenya," *Oxford Bulletin of Economics and Statistics*, no. 5.

Hoyle, B. S. 1979. "African Socialism and Urban Development: The Relocation of the Tanzanian Capital." *Tijdschrift voor Economische en Sociale Geografie* 70(4).

Hoyuma, A. M. 1983. "The Growth of Population and Employment in the Dar es Salaam City Region, Tanzania." *Ekistics* 50(301).

Hugon, P., ed. 1980 (April–June). *Secteur Informel et Petite Production Marchande dans les Villes du Tiers Monde*, a special number of *Revue Tiers-Monde* 21, no. 82.

Hunter, Guy. 1972. "Employment Policy in Tropical Africa." *International Labor Review*: 35–59.

Huntington, Hillard G. 1977. "An Empirical Study of Ethnic Linkages in Kenyan Rural-Urban Migration." Institute for Development Studies, University of Nairobi, Discussion Paper no. 260.

Hyatt, Douglas E., and William J. Milne. 1990 (October). "Urban and Rural Fertility Differentials in Kenya: An Econometric Analysis Using Micro Data." Toronto: University of Toronto, Institute for Policy Analysis Working Paper.

Hyden, Goran. 1983. *No Shortcuts to Progress: African Development Management in Perspective*. Berkeley: University of California Press.

International Labour Office, Jobs and Skills Programme for Africa. 1976. *Economic Transformation in a Socialist Framework: An Employment and Basic Needs Oriented Development Strategy for Somalia*. Addis Ababa: ILO/JASPA.

————. 1982. *Basic Needs in Danger: A Basic Needs Oriented Strategy for Tanzania*. Addis Ababa: ILO/JASPA.

International Monetary Fund. 1984. *Government Finance Statistics Yearbook*. Washington, DC: IMF.

————. 1983. *Financial Statistics Yearbook*. Washington, DC: IMF.

————. 1983a. *Government Finance Statistics Yearbook*. Washington, DC: IMF.

———. Various years. *Exchange Arrangements and Exchange Restrictions: Annual Report.* Washington, DC: IMF.

Ishumi, Abel G. M. 1984. *The Urban Jobless in Eastern Africa.* Uppsala: Scandinavian Institute of African Studies.

Jabara, Cathy. 1990. "Economic Reform and Poverty in The Gambia: A Survey of Pre- and Post-ERP Experience." Washington, DC: International Food Policy Research Institute for USAID.

Jackman, M. E. 1979. "School Leaver Migration in Zambia." University of Zambia, Institute of African Studies. Manpower Research Reports no. 2.

Jackson, Dudley. 1979. "The Disappearance of Strikes in Tanzania: Incomes Policy and Industrial Democracy." *Journal of Modern African Studies* **17**:2.

Jamal, Vali. 1984. "Rural Urban Gap and Income Distribution: Synthesis Report of Seventeen African Countries." Addis Ababa: International Labour Office/JASPA.

Jamal, Vali, and John Weeks. 1988. "The Vanishing Rural-Urban Gap in Sub-Saharan Africa." *International Labour Review* 127(3).

Jimenez, Emmanuel. 1982. "The Economics of Self-Help Housing: Theory and Some Evidence from a Developing Country." *Journal of Urban Economics* 11.

Johnson, E.A.J. 1970. *The Organization of Space in Developing Countries.* Cambridge, MA: Harvard University Press.

Johnson, G. E., and Whitelaw, W. E. 1974. "Urban-Rural Income Transfers in Kenya: An Estimated Remittance Function." *Economic Development and Cultural Change* 22(3).

Johnston, Bruce F., and Peter Kilby. 1975. *Agriculture and Structural Transformation: Economic Strategies in Late-Developing Countries.* New York: Oxford University Press.

Joshi, Heather, Harold Lubell, and Jean Mouly. 1976. *Abidjan: Urban Development and Employment in the Ivory Coast.* Geneva: International Labour Office.

Kahnert, Felix. 1985. "Improving Urban Employment and Labor Productivity." Washington, DC: World Bank, Water Supply and Urban Development Department.

Kalabamu, Faustine T. 1984. "A Review of Tanzania's New National Housing Policy." *Habitat International* 8.

Kamarck, Andrew M. 1976. *The Tropics and Economic Development: A Provocative Inquiry into the Poverty of Nations.* Baltimore: The Johns Hopkins University Press.

Kannappan, Subbbiah. 1988 (July). "Urban Labor Markets and Development." *World Bank Research Observer* 3, (2).

———. 1983. *Employment Problems and the Urban Labor Market in Developing Countries.* Ann Arbor, MI: University of Michigan, Graduate School of Business Administration, Division of Research.

Karmiloff, Igor. 1990. "Cameroon." In R. Riddell, ed. (1990c).

———. 1990a. "Zambia." In R. Riddell, ed., (1990c).

Kasfir, N. 1983. "Designs and Dilemmas: An Overview." In P. Mahwood, ed. *Government in the Third World: The Experience of Tropical Africa.* New York: John Wiley.

Katz, Eliakim, and Oded Stark. 1986. "On the Shadow Wage of Urban Jobs in Less Developed Countries." *Journal of Urban Economics* **20**.

Keare, Douglas, and Scott Parris. 1982. "Evaluation of Shelter Programs for the Urban Poor." Washington, DC: *World Bank Staff Working Paper* no. 547.

Keesing, Donald. 1985. "Bank Operations for Industrial Development in Sub-Saharan Africa." Washington, DC: World Bank (Industry Department).

———1984. "Industrial Policy Issues in Eastern Africa." Washington, DC: World Bank.

Kelley, Allen C. 1991 (September). "African Urbanization and City Growth: Perspectives, Problems, and Policies." Durham, NC: Duke University, Department of Economics, unpublished manuscript.

Kelley, Allen C., and Jeffrey G. Williamson. 1984. *What Drives Third World City Growth? A Synamic General Equilibrium Approach.* Princeton: Princeton University Press.

Khasiani, Shanyisa A. 1982. *Social and Psychological Factors Influencing Migration Dispositions in Kenya.* Unpublished Ph.D. dissertation, Florida State University.

Kilby, Peter. 1981. "Small-Scale Industry in Kenya." Washington, DC: World Bank, Development Economics Department, Employment and Rural Development Study 69.

Kliest, T. J., and H. R. Scheffer. 1981. "John Turner's Theory of Intra-Urban Mobility and the African Reality: Examples from East and West Africa." *Tijdschrift voor Economische en Sociale Geografie* 72(5).

Kloos, H. 1982. "Farm Labor Migrations in the Awask Valley of Ethiopia." *International Migration Review* 16(1).

Knight, J. B. 1981. "The Role of the Firm in Wage Determination: An African Case Study." World Bank Discussion Paper no. 81–10.

Knight, J. B., and R. H. Sabot. 1982. "From Migrants to Proletarians: Employment Experience, Mobility, and Wages in Tanzania." *Oxford Bulletin of Economics and Statistics* 44(3).

———. 1981 (March). "From Migrants to Proletarians: Employment Experience, Mobility and Wages in Tanzania." Washington, DC: World Bank, Population and Human Resources Division Discussion Paper 81–12.

———. 1981a. "The Role of the Firm in Wage Determination: An African Case Study." Washington, DC: World Bank, PHRD Discussion Paper no. 81-10.

———. 1981b (February). "The Returns to Education: Increasing with Experience or Decreasing with Expansion?" *Oxford Bulletin of Economics and Statistics* 43(1): 51–71.

———. 1990. *Education, Productivity and Inequality: The East African Natural Experiment.* Oxford: Oxford University Press.

———. 1988. "Lewis Through a Looking Glass: Public Sector Employment, Rent Seeking and Economic Growth." Williamstown, MA: Williams College Center for Development Economics, Working Paper RM-108.

Knotts, Mary A. 1977. *The Social and Economic Factors Associated with the Rural-Urban Migration of Kenyan Women.* Unpublished Ph.D. dissertation, Johns Hopkins University.

Knowles, J. C., and Anker R. 1981. "An Analysis of Income Transfers in a Developing Country: The Case of Kenya." *Journal of Development Economics* 8(2).

Koehn, Peter, and Effgehia F. Koehn. 1979. "Urbanization and Urban Development Planning in Ethiopia." In P. H. Obudho, and S. El-Shakhs, eds., *Development of Urban Systems in Africa.* New York: Praeger.

Kossoudji, Sherrie, and Eva Mueller. 1983. "The Economic and Demographic Status of Female Headed Households in Rural Botswana." *Economics Development and Cultural Change* 31(4).

Kozel, Valerie. 1990. "The Composition and Distribution of Income in Côte d'Ivoire." Washington, DC: World Bank, Living Standards and Measurement Study Working Paper no. 68.

Krumm, K. July 1985. "The External Debt of Sub-Saharan Africa: Origins, Magnitude, and Implications for Action." Washington, DC: *World Bank Staff Working Paper* no. 741.

Kudiabor, C. D. K. 1977. "Urbanization and Growth Pole Strategy for Regional Development in Ghana." In A. Faniran, ed., *Regional Planning and National Development in Tropical Africa.* Ibadan, Nigeria: Ibadan University Press.

Kulaba, Saitiel. 1989. "Local Government and the Management of Urban Services in Tanzania." In Richard Stren and Rodney White, (1989).

Lahuec, J. P., and J. Y. Marchal. 1979. "La mobilité du peuplement Bissa et Mossi." Paris: Office de la Recherche Scientifique et Technique Outre-Mer (ORSTOM), Travaux et Document no. 103.

Ledent, Jacque. 1990. "The Distribution of City Sizes in Subsaharan Africa: A Cross-Sectional Analysis." Montreal: Universite du Quebec au Montreal, INRS-Urbanisation, unpublished manuscript presented at the 1990 North American meetings of the Regional Science Association.

—————. 1982 (April). "Rural-Urban Migration, Urbanization, and Economic Development." *Economic Development and Cultural Change.* **30**(3): 507–38.

Lee, Kyu Sik. 1981. "Intra-Urban Location of Manufacturing Employment in Colombia." *Journal of Urban Economics* 9.

Lemarchands, Guy. 1978. "An Urban Housing Project in Upper Volta." *Habitit International* 3, no 2.

Lemer, A. 1985. "Resource Mobilization, Cost Recovery, and Replicability." Washington, DC: World Bank, Water Supply and Urban Development Division, Eastern and Southern African Projects Department

Lemer, Andrew C. 1982. "Strategy for Meeting Housing Needs in Nigeria's Urban Centres: Methods and Recommendations." *Housing Science* 6, no 1.

LeNoir, Rebecca G., and David F. Sly. 1983. "Demographic Consequences of Short-Term Mobility in the Rural Population of Kenya." Florida State University, Center for the Study of Population, Working Paper no. 83-03.

Lewis, W. Arthur. 1954. "Economic Development with Unlimited Supplies of Labour." *The Manchester School* **22**(2): 139–91.

Liedholm, Carl, and Donald Mead. 1987. *Small Scale Industries in Developing Countries: Empirical Evidence and Policy Implications.* East Lansing, MI: Michigan State University, Department of Agricultural Economics, MSU International Development Paper no. 9.

Ligale, Andrew Ndooli. 1982. "The Role of Small and Intermediate Cities in National Development in Africa." In Mathur, ed., *Small Cities and National Development.* Nagoya, Japan: United Nations Centre for Regional Development.

Lillydahl, Jane. *Economic and Demographic Influences on Household Saving in Urban Kenya.* Durham, NC: Duke University Department of Economics, unpublished Ph.D. dissertation.

Linn, Johannes F. 1982 (April). "The Costs of Urbanization in Developing Countries." *Economic Development and Cultural Change* 30(3).

—————. 1979. "Policies for Efficient and Equitable Growth of Cities in Developing countries." World Bank Staff Working Paper no. 342.

Lipton, Michael. 1980. "Migration from Rural Areas of Poor Countries: The Impact on Rural Productivity and Income Distribution." *World Development* **8.**

—————. 1976. *Why Poor People Stay Poor: Urban Bias in World Development.* Cambridge, MA: Harvard University Press.

Livingstone, Ian. 1991. "A Reassessment of Kenya's Rural and Urban Informal Sector." *World Development* **19**(6): 651–70.

—————. 1981. *Rural Development, Employment and Incomes in Kenya.* Addia Ababa: ILO/JASPA.

Loewinger, A. 1979. "Labor Migration in Southern Africa Among the Lakeside Tonga of Malawi." *Journal of International Affairs* 33(2).

Loser, Hans. 1979. "Wanderarbeit und Soziale Mobilisierung: Das beispiel des Senegal". *Arbeitern*, v. 15. Renner Universitat zu Gottingen, Institut fur Volkerkunde.

Lubell, Harold. 1978. "Urban Development and Employment: the Third World Metropolis." *International Labour Review* 177(6).

Lucas, Robert. 1982. "Determinants of Migration Decisions." In *Migration in Botswana: Patterns, Causes, and Consequences. Final Report of the National Migration Study.* Gaborone, Botswana: Government Printers.

Lucas, Robert E. B., and Oded Stark. 1985. "Motivations to Remit: Evidence from Botswana." *Journal of Political Economy* **93.**

Mabogunje, Akin. 1990 (September). "Urban Planning and the Post-Colonial State in Africa," *African Studies Review* 33, no. 2.

—————. 1983. "The Case for Big Cities." *Habitat International* 7, (5/6).

—————. 1981. "Effectiveness of Population Redistribution Policies: The African Experience." In *International Population Conference (1981): Solicited Papers.* Leige, Belgium: International Union for the Scientific Study of Population.

——. 1977. "Regional Planning and the Transformation of African Economies." In A. Mabogunje and A. Faniran, eds., *Regional Planning and National Development in Tropical Africa.*
Ibadan, Nigeria: Ibadan University Press.

——. 1976. "The Urban Situation in Nigeria." In Sidney Goldstein and David F. Sly, eds.,
Patterns of Urbanization: Comparative Country Studies. Dolhain, Belgium: Ordina Editions.

Mabogunje, A. L., and M. O. Filani. 1981. "The Informal Sector in a Small City: The Case of
Kano." In S. Sethuramen, ed., *The Urban Informal Sector in Developing Countries.* Geneva:
International Labour Office.

MacLiver, Sherry. 1977. "Gaborone Migration Survey Follow-up." Botswana National Institute for Research in Development and African Studies, Documentation Unit, Working
Paper no. 9.

McNulty, M. 1985 (September). "Ghana/Nigeria: Rural-Urban Linkage Case Study." Washington, DC: World Bank (Water Supply and Urban Development Department).

Maitha, J. K. 1973. "Capital-Labour Substitution in Manufacturing in a Developing Economy:
The Case of Kenya." *Eastern Africa Economic Review.*

Mali, Nompilo Zukiswa. 1983. *Size Distribution of Urban Areas of Africa.* Unpublished M.A.
Thesis, Vanderbilt University.

Malpezzi, Stephen, and Stephen K. Mayo, with David J. Gross. 1985. "Housing Demand in
Developing Countries." World Bank Staff Working Paper no. 733.

Mamalakis, M. J. 1971. "The Theory of Sectoral Clashes and Coalitions Revisited." *Latin American Research Review* 6(3).

——. 1969. "The Theory of Sectoral Clashes." *Latin American Research Review* 4(3).

Mann, Jonathan M., James Chin, Peter Piot, and Thomas Quinn. 1988 (October). "The International Epidemiology of AIDS." *Scientific American* **259:4.**

Marguerat, Yves. 1981–82. "Des éthnies et des villes: Analyse des migrations vers les villes
de Côte d'Ivoire." *Cahiers ORSTOM: Série Sciences Humaines* 18(3).

Marsden, K., and T. Belot. 1987 (July). *Private Enterprise in Africa: Creating a Better Environment.*
Washington, DC: World Bank, Discussion Paper no. 17.

Mathieu, Renee. 1982 (November). "Locational Analysis of Bank-Funded Projects in Ivory
Coast, Cameroon, and Mali." Washington, DC: World Bank, Water Supply and Urban
Development Department Discussion Paper UDD-28.

Mathur, Om Prakash. 1982. "The Role of Small Cities in National Development Reexamined." In Mathur (ed.), *Small Cities and National Development.* Nagoya, Japan: United
Nations Centre for Regional Development.

May, D. 1988. *Africa: Heading for Tomorrow.* Washington, DC: The Bretton Woods Committee.

Mazumdar, Dipak. 1988. "Rural-Urban Migration in Developing Countries." In *Handbook of
Regional and Urban Economics,* vol. 1. New York: Elsevier Science Publishers.

——. 1976. "The Urban Informal Sector." *World Development* 4(8).

Mazur, Robert E. 1982. "Migration and Rural Socio-Economic Structure in Sub-Saharan Africa: The Case of Mali." Unpublished Ph.D. dissertation, Brown University.

Mbuyi, Kankonde. 1989. "Kinshasa: Problems of Land Management, Infrastructure and Food
Supply." In Richard Stren and Rodney White, (1989).

McKim, Wayne. 1979. "Patterns of Spatial Interaction in Kenya," in R. Obudho and D. Taylor,
eds. *The Spatial Structure of Development: A Study of Kenya.* Boulder, CO: Westview.

Mera, Koichi. 1977. "The Changing Pattern of Population Distribution in Japan and Its Implications for Developing Countries." *Habitat International* 2.

Mera, Koichi, and Hisanobu Shishido. 1981. "A Cross-Sectional Analysis of Urbanization and
Socio-Economic World." Washington, DC: World Bank (Water Supply and Urban Development Department) Discussion Paper no. 40.

Merritt, Gary, William Lyerly, and Jack Thomas. 1988. "The HIV/AIDS Pandemic in Africa:
Issues of Donor Strategy." In Norman Miller and Richard Rockwell, eds. *AIDS in Africa.*
Lewiston, NY: Edwin Mellen.

Mills, Edwin S. 1983. "The Concept of Urbanization." *Nagarlok* 15(2), April-June.

Mills, Edwin, and Charles Becker. 1986. *Studies in Indian Urban Development*. New York: Oxford University Press.

Mills, Edwin S., and Bruce W. Hamilton. 1989. *Urban Economics* (ed. 4), Glenview, Ill.: Scot Foreswan and Company.

Mills, Edwin S., and Jee Peng Tan. 1980. "A Comparison of Urban Population Density Functions in Developed and Developing Countries" *Urban Studies*, 17.

Ministere du Plan et de la Cooperation, EVPRY. 1983 (May). *Secteur Urbain, Preparation d'un Credit d'Engenerie, Rapport Intermediare*. Dakar: Government of Senegal.

Miracle, Marvin, Diane Miracle, and Laurie Cohen. 1980. "Informal Savings Mobilization in Africa." *Economic Development and Cultural Change*, 28(4).

de Miras, C. 1980. "Le Secteur de Subsistence dans les Branches de Production à Abidjan." In P. Hugon, ed., (1980).

Mitra, A. 1977. *Terms of Trade and Class Relations*. London: Frank Cass.

Mlay, W. F. I. 1977. "Rural to Urban Migration and Rural Development." *Tanzania Notes and Records*.

Moller, V. 1978. *Urban Commitment and Involvement among Black Rhodesians*. Durban, RSA: University of Natal Press.

Montgomery, M., and E. Brown. 1985 (April). *Migration and Urbanization in Sub-Saharan Africa*. Washington, DC: The World Bank (Population, Health, and Nutrition Department).

Moock, Joyce. 1973 (October). "Pragmatism and the Primary School:The Case of a Non-Rural Village." *Africa* 43(4): 302–16.

Moock, Peter. 1976. "The Efficiency of Women as Farm Manager: Kenya." *American Journal of Agricultural Economics* 58, (5).

Moomaw, R. 1981. "Productivity and City Size: A Critique of the Evidence." *Quarterly Journal of Economics* 96, (4).

Morrison, Andrew K. 1993. "Unproductive Migration Reconsidered: A Stochastic Frontier Production Function Framework for Analyzing Internal Migration." *Oxford Economic Papers* 45 (July).

———. 1994. "Are Institutions or Economic Rents Responsible for Wage Differentials in LDCs? Evidence from Ecuador." *World Development* 22(3).

Muludiang, Venasio T. 1983. *Urbanization, Female Migration and Labor Utilization in Urban Sudan: The Case of the Southern Region*. Unpublished Ph.D. dissertation, Brown University.

Murray, C. 1980. "Migrant Labor and Changing Family Structure in the Rural Periphery of Southern Africa." *Journal of Southern African Studies* 6(2).

Muth, Richard. 1969. *Cities and Housing*. University of Chicago Press.

Muwonge, J. W. 1980. "Urban Policy and Patterns of Low-Income Settlement in Nairobi, Kenya." *Politics and Development Review*.

Muyoba, Godfrey. 1983. "Labor Recruitment and Urban Migration: The Zambian Experience." Unpublished Ph.D. dissertation, University of Washington.

Mwanza, Jacob M. 1979. "Rural-Urban Migration and Urban Employment in Zambia." *Developing Economies* 17(2).

Nafziger, E. Wayne. 1988. *Inequality in Africa*. Cambridge, UK: Cambridge University Press.

Nairobi Urban Study Group. n.d. *Nairobi: Metropolitan Growth Strategy, Vol. 2: Technical Appendices*. Nairobi: NUSG.

Ndongko, Wilfred A. 1977. "A Note on Problems and Prospects of Labour Mobility within African Regional Groupings." *Nigerian Journal of Economic and Social Studies* 19(2).

Ndubizu, Gordian A. 1984. "Hypertrophy and Economic Development: The Case of Lagos in Perspective." *Journal of African Studies*.

Nellis, J. 1985 (June). "Public Enterprises in Sub-Saharan Africa," Washington, DC: World Bank, Public Sector Management Unit, Projects Policy Department, unpublished manuscript.

Niedercorn, J. H., and B. V. Bechdolt, Jr. 1969. "An Economic Derivation of the 'Gravity Law' of Spatial Interaction." *Journal of Regional Science* 9(2).

Nihan, Georges, Erik Demol, and Comlavi Jondoh. 1979. "The Modern Informal Sector in Lomé." *International Labour Review* 118, (4).

Nihan, Georges, and Robert Jourdain. 1978. "The Modern Informal Sector in Nouakchott." *International Labour Review* 117 (6).

Nkambwe, Musisi. 1982. "Change in Urban in Urban Areas in Nigeria." *Urban Studies* 19.

Nolan, R. W. 1979. "Migrants to the City in Africa: The Search for a Conceptual Framework." *African Urban Studies* 5.

Nwabueze, R. O. 1980. "Socio-Economic Effects of Rural-Urban Migration: A Critical Analysis of the Nigerian Experience." *Indian Journal of Labour Economics* 23(3).

Obudho, R.A. 1983. *Urbanization in Kenya,* Lanham: University Press of America Inc.

———, ed. 1981. *Urbanization and Development Planning in Kenya.* Nairobi: Kenya Literature Bureau.

Obudho, R. A., and D. R. F. Taylor, eds. 1979. *The Spatial Structure of Development: A Study of Kenya.* Boulder, CO: Westview Press.

———. 1976. "City, Urbanization and Regional Planning in Africa. An International and Intranational Problem." *Pan-African Journal* 4, no. 2.

Obudho, Robert A., and Peter P. Walder. 1976. *Periodic Markets, Urbanization, and Regional Planning: A Case Study from Western Kenya.* Westport, CT: Greenwood Press.

O'Connor, Anthony. 1983. *The African City.* New York: Africana Publishing Company.

———. 1981. *Urbanization in Tropical Africa: An Annotated Bibliography.* Boston: G. K. Hall and Co.

Odetola, T. O. 1978. "National Integration and the Creation of States in Nigeria." *Journal of Black Studies* 9, no. 2.

OECD Development Centre. 1979. "Migration in West Africa: Report of the Seminar held in Ouagadougou, Upper Volta on 16th–19th January."

Okojie, C. E. E. 1984. "Female Migrants in the Urban Labor Market: Benin City, Nigeria." *Canadian Journal of African Studies* 18(3).

Okpala, Donatus G. I. 1978. "Housing Standards: A Constraint on Urban Housing Production in Nigeria." *Ekistics* 240.

Olayemi, Olusegun A. 1979. "Movements of Population from Urban to Rural Areas of Yoruba Towns, Nigeria: A Case Study of Ibadan." *Geneve-Afrique* 17(2).

Olenja, C. K. 1980. "Patterns and Trends of Migration in Nairobi up to 1978." University of Nairobi, Institute of African Studies Paper no. 141.

Onibokun, Adepoju G. 1989. "Urban Growth and Urban Management in Nigeria." In Richard Stren and Rodney White, (1989).

Onokerhoraye, Andrew Godwin. 1977. "The Spatial Pattern of Residential Districts in Benin, Nigeria." *Urban Studies* 14.

———. 1976. "The Spatial Aspects of Urban Growth in Nigeria: Some Planning Implications for National Development." *Cultures et developpement: revue internationale des sciences du d'eveloppement* 8.

Over, Mead, et al. 1988. "The Direct and Indirect Cost of HIV Infection: The Cases of Zaire and Tanzania." Paper Presented at the IV International AIDS Conference, Stockholm, June 12–16.

Oyekanmi, F. D. 1985. "Population Pressure and Housing Conditions in Lojos, Nigeria." Paper Presented at International Population Conference, Florence, Italy.

Pack, Howard. 1977. "Unemployment and Income Distribution in Kenya." *Economic Development and Cultural Change* 26.

———. 1974. "The Employment-Output Trade-Off in LDC's—A Micro-economic Approach." *Oxford Economic Papers.*

————. 1972. "Employment and Productivity in Kenya Manufacturing." *Eastern Africa Economic Review.*

Page, John M., Jr. 1979. *Enterprises in African Development: A Survey.* World Bank Staff Working Paper, no. 363.

Page, John M. Jr. and William F. Steel. 1984. "Economic Issues of Small Enterprise Development in Africa." Washington, DC: World Bank, unpublished manuscript.

Palmer, Ingrid. 1991. *Gender and Population in the Adjustment of African Economies: Planning for Change.* Geneva: International Labour Office.

Parr, J. 1985. "A Note on the Size Distribution of Cities over Time." *Journal of Urban Economics* 18.

Pedersen, P. O. 1970. "Innovation Diffusion Within and Between National Urban Systems." *Geographical Analysis* 2, no. 3.

Peil, Margaret. 1981. *Cities and Suburbs: Urban Life in West Africa.* New York: Africana Publishers.

————. 1979. "Housing the Poor in West Africa, Public and Private Provisions." *Institute of Development Studies Bulletin* 10(4): 28–32.

————. 1976. "Demographic Change in A Ghanaian Suburb." *Ghana Social Science Journal* 3(1): 63–78.

————. 1976. "African Squatter Settlements: A Comparative Study." *Urban Studies* 13.

Pfister, Francois. 1982. "Housing Improvement and Popular Participation in the Upper Volta." *Habitat International* 6, (2): 209–14.

Phillips, D. A. "Industrialization in Tanzania: The Case of Small Scale Production." In Kwan Kim et al., eds. *Papers on the Political Economy of Tanzania.* London: Heinemann.

Piche, V., J. Gregory, and D. Derosiers. 1981. "Migration et sous-développement en Haute-Volta: essai de typologie." *Cahiers Québecois de Démographie* 10(1).

Plange, N. 1979. "Opportunity Cost and Labor Migration: A Misinterpretation of Proletarianization in Northern Ghana." *Journal of Modern African Studies* 17(4).

Potts, Deborah. 1985. "The Development of Malawi's New Capital at Lilongwe: A Comparison with Other New African Capitals." *Comparative Urban Research* **10**:2.

Prindle, D. 1984. *Zaire: Rural-Urban Profile.* Washington, DC: USAID (Office of Housing and Urban Programs).

Prothero, R. Mansell. 1981. "The Need for Historical Perspective on Population Mobility in West Africa." In *African Historical Demography, Vol. II* (Proceeding of Seminar Held in the Centre of African Studies, University of Edinburgh): 24–25.

Prud'homme, Rémy. 1985 (November). "Le Financement des Services Publics Urbains à Kinshasa: Institutions et Méchanismes." Washington, DC: World Bank, unpublished manuscript.

Pryor, Frederic L. 1988. "Income Distribution and Economic Development in Madagascar." Washington, DC: World Bank, Discussion Paper no. 37.

————. 1988a. "Income Distribution and Economic Development in Malawi." Washington, DC: World Bank, discussion paper no. 36.

Quigley, John M. 1979. "What Have We Learned About Urban Housing Markets?" *Current Issues in Urban Economics*, eds. Peter Miezkowski and Mahlon Straszheim. Baltimore: The Johns Hopkins University Press.

Quinn, T.C. 1986 (November). "AIDS in Africa: An Epidemiologic Paradigm." *Science* No. **234**.

Rabevazaha, C. 1981. "Control of Development by the People: Regional Planning and Basic Needs in Madagascar." *International Labour Review* 120(4).

Radelet, Steven C. 1990. *Economic Recovery in The Gambia: The Anatomy of an Economic Reform Program.* Cambridge, MA: Harvard University, Kennedy School of Government, unpublished Ph.D. dissertation.

Ranis, Gustav, and John C. H. Fei. 1961. "A Theory of Economic Development." *American Economic Review* 51.

Renaud, Bertrand. 1979. "National Urbanization Policies in Developing Countries." World Bank Staff Working Paper no. 347.

Rempel, Henry. 1981. *Rural-Urban Labor Migration and Urban Unemployment in Kenya*. Laxenburg, Austria: International Institute for Applied Systems Analysis.

Rempel, Henry, and William House. 1978. *The Kenyan Employment Problem*. Nairobi: Oxford University Press. Republic Of Kenya. 1991. *1991 Economic Survey*. Nairobi: Government Printer.

————. 1982. *Statistical Abstract—1982*. Nairobi: Central Bureau of Statistics, Ministry of Economic Planning and Community Affairs.

————. 1978. *Statistical Abstract—1978*. Nairobi: Central Bureau of Statistics, Ministry of Economic Planning and Community Affairs.

Republic of Zambia, Central Statistical Office. Various years. *Monthly Digest of Statistics*. Lusaka: CSO.

Republic of Zimbabwe. 1985 (June). *Quarterly Digest of Statistics*.

Rhoda, Richard. 1980. "Migration and Employmnent of Educated Youth in Ghana." *International Migration Review* 14(1).

Richardson, Harry. 1982. "Policies for Strengthening Small Cities in Developing Countries." In Mathur, ed., *Small Cities and National Development*. Nagoya, Japan: United Nations Centre for Regional Development.

————. 1980. "An Urban Development Strategy for Kenya." *Journal of Developing Areas* 15.

————. 1977. "City Size and National Spacing Strategy in Developing Countries." World Bank Staff Working Paper no. 252.

————. 1977a. "City Size and National Spatial Strategies in Developing Countries." Washington, DC: *World Bank Staff Working Paper* no. 252.

Riddell, J. Barry. 1981. "Beyond the Description of Spatial Pattern: The Process of Proletarianization as a Factor in Population Migration in West Africa." *Progress in Human Geography* 55(3).

————. 1980. "Is Continuing Urbanization Possible in West Africa?" *African Studies Review* 23.

————. 1978. "The Migration to the Cities of West Africa: Some Policy Considerations." *Journal of Modern African Studies* 16.

————. 1969. *Structure, Diffusion, and Response: The Spatial Dynamics of Modernization in Sierra Leone*. Ph.D. Dissertation, Pennsylvania State University.

Riddell, Roger C., ed. 1990c. *Manufacturing Africa*. London and Portsmouth: James Currey and Heinemann Educational Books.

————. 1990a. "Côte d'Ivoire." In R. Riddell, ed. (1990c).

————. 1990b. "Zimbabwe." In R. Riddell, ed. (1990c).

Rodney, Walter. 1981. *How Europe Underdeveloped Africa*. Washington, DC: Howard University Press.

Rogers, Andrei. 1990 (October). "Requiem for the Net Migrant." *Geographical Analysis* 22(4): 283–300.

————. 1985. *Regional Population Projection Models*. Beverly Hills, CA: Sage.

————. 1982 (April). "Sources of Urban Population Growth and Urbanization 1950–2000: A Demographic Accounting." *Economic Development and Cultural Change* 30(3): 483–506.

Rogers, Andrei, and Jeffrey G. Williamson. 1982 (April). "Migration, Urbanization, and Third World Development: An Overview." *Economic Development and Cultural Change* 30(3): 463–82.

Rondinelli, Dennis. 1983. *Secondary Cities in Developing Countries*. Beverly Hills: Sage.

————. 1982. "Intermediate Cities in Developing Countries: A Comparative Analysis of their Demographic, Social and Economic Characteristics." *Third World Planning Review* 4.

Rondinelli, D., and K. Ruddle. 1978. *Urbanization and Rural Development: A Spatial Policy for Rural Growth.* New York: Praeger.

Rosen, Kenneth T., and Mitchel Resnick. 1980. "The Size Distribution of Cities: An Examination of the Pareto Law and Primacy. *Journal of Urban Economics* 4: 165–86.

Rosing, K. E. 1966. "A Rejection of the Zipf Model (rank-size) in Relation to City Size." *The Professional Geographer* 18.

Rothman, Norman C. 1979. "Housing and Service Planning in Lusaka Zambia." In Obudho, R. A., and El-Shakhs, eds., *Development of Urban Systems in Africa.* New York: Praeger.

Ruane, Francis. 1981 (November). "On Modelling the Influence of Sectoral Policies on the Spatial Concentration of Industrial Activities." Washington, DC: World Bank, Urban and Regional Economics Division, Development Economics Departmentl Urban and Regional Report no. 81–28.

Rweyemanu, Justinian. 1973. *Underdevelopment and Industrialisation in Tanzania.* Nairobi: Oxford University Press.

Sabot, Richard H., ed. 1982. *Migration and Labor Market in Developing Countries.* Boulder, CO: Westview Press.

Sabot, Richard H., et al. 1981. "The Structure of Wages in Kenya and Tanzania: What Role has Pay Policy Played?" World Bank, Population and Human Resources Division. Discussion Paper No. 81–55, Washington DC: World Bank.

———. 1979. *Economic Development and Urban Migration: Tanzania, 1900–1971.* Oxford: Clarendon Press.

Sabot, Richard, Albert Berry, A. Hazlewood, and John Knight. 1982 (March). "Urban Employees in Kenya and Tanzania: Educational Attainment and Its Relation to Jobs, Pay, Mobility, and Rural Links." Washington, DC: World Bank, Population and Human Resources Division discussion paper.

———. 1981a. "Does the Expansion of Education Compress the Structure of Wages and Reduce the Inequality of Pay?" Washington, DC: World Bank, PHRD Discussion Paper no. 81–23.

———. 1981b. "The Structure of Wages in Kenya and Tanzania: What Role Has Pay Policy Played?" Washington, DC: World Bank, PHRD discussion paper no. 81–55.

Sada, P., and A. Onokerhoraye. 1984 (April). "The Emergence of Secondary Cities and National Development in Nigeria." Dakar: paper presented at the Ninth (USAID-Sponsored) Conference on Housing in Africa.

Safa, Helen. 1986. "The Urban Informal Economy and the State in Latin America." *Urban Anthropology* 15.

Salau, Ademola T. "Nigeria's Housing Policies and Programmes: A Preliminary Assessment."

Sandbrook, R. 1982. *The Politics of Basic Needs: Urban Aspects of Assaulting Poverty in Africa.* London: Heinemann.

Sanyal, Biswapriya. 1981. "Who Get What, Where, Why and How: A Critical Look at the Housing Subsidies in Zambia." *Development and Change* 12.

Sautter, G. 1980. "Migrations, société et développement en pays Mossi." *Cahiers d' Etudes Africaines* 20(3).

Sawers, Larry. 1989 (July). "Urban Primacy in Tanzania." *Economic Development and Cultural Change* 37(4): 841–59.

SCET International, SCET AGRI, SEDES. 1984 (January). *Une Image à Long Terme de l'Afrique au Sud du Sahara.* "ILTA." Paris: Commission des Communautés Europeenes et Caisse des Dépots et Consignations.

SCET International. 1978 (February). *Perspectives Décennales de Développement d'Abidjan, Vol. 4: Annexes du Rapport de première Phase.* Paris: SCET.

Schmidt, A. 1978. "Labour Migration and Structural Heterogeneity in West Africa." *Verfassung und Recht in Ubersee* 11(2).

Segal, Edwin S. 1975. "Urban Development Planning in Dar es Salaam." In Obudho, R. A.,
and El-Shakhs, S., eds., *Development of Urban Systems in Africa*. New York: Praeger.

Seibolds, P., and F. Steinberg. 1982. "Tanzania: Sites and Services." *Habitat International* 6(1/2).

Sethuraman, S.V. 1981. *The Urban Informal Sector in Developing Countries*. Geneva: International
Labour Office.

Shapiro, Carl, and Joseph Stiglitz. 1984. "Euqilibrium Unemployment as a Worker Discipline
Device." *American Economic Review* 74(3).

Sharpley, Jennifer, and Stephen Lewis. 1990. "Kenya." In R. Riddell, ed. (1990c).

Sheppard, Eric. 1982. "City Size Distributions and Spatial Economic Change." *International
Regional Science Review* 7, (2).

Shields, Nwanganga. 1980 (April). "Women in the Urban Labor Market in Africa: The Case
of Tanzania." *World Bank Staff Working Paper* no. 380.

Shukla, Vibhooti, and Oded Stark. 1990. "Policy Comparisons with Agglomeration Effects—
Augmented Dual Economy Model." *Journal of Urban Economics* **27.**

———. 1989 (June). "Why Are Urban Formal Sector Wages Above the Market-Clearing
Level?" Cambridge, MA: Harvard University, Center for Population Studies, Migration
and Development Program, Discussion Paper no. 44.

Siebolds, Peter, and Florian Steinberg. 1982. "Tanzania:Sites-and-Services." *Habitat International* 6(1/2): 109–30.

Simon, David. 1982. "Recent Trends in Namibian Urbanization." *Tijdschrift voor Economische en
Sociale Geografie* 73, (4).

Soja, E. W., and Weaver, C. E. 1976. "Urbanization and Underdevelopment in East Africa."
In B.J.L. Berry, ed., *Urbanization and Counter-Urbanization*. Beverly Hills, CA: Sage.

Southern African Economist. 1990 (April/May). "A Toll of Many Cities." Harare 3(2): 5–22.

Speake, Graham, ed. 1981. *Cultural Atlas of Africa*. New York: Facts on File.

Standing, Guy. 1982. "Circulation and Proletarianisation." International Labour Office,
World Employment Programme Research. Population and Labour Policies Programme,
Working Paper no. 119.

Stark, Oded. 1991. *The Migration of Labor*. Cambridge, MA, and Oxford, UK: Basil Blackwell.

———. 1980 (April). "On the Role of Urban-to-Rural Remittances in Rural Development."
Journal of Development Studies 16, no. 3.

———. 1979. "On the Political Economy of Constraining Rural-to-Urban Migration in LDCs."
Tel Aviv University, David Horowitz Institute for the Research of Developing Countries,
Paper no. 10/79.

Steel, William F., and Jonathan Evans. 1984. "Industrialization Experience in Africa: Objectives, Strategies, Results and Issues." Washington, DC: World Bank Paper Prepared for
the High-Level Industrial Policy Seminar for Africa.

Steel, William F. 1981. "Female and Small-Scale Employment Under Modernization in
Ghana." *Economic Development and Cultural Change*.

———. 1979. "Development of Urban Artisanal Sector in Ghana and Cameroun." *The Journal
of Modern African Studies* 17, (2).

Steel, William F., and Yasuoki Takagi. 1983. "The Intermediate Sector, Unemployment and
the Employment-Output Conflict: A Multi-Sector Model." *Oxford Economic Papers* 35 (3).

Steele, David. 1975. "The Theory of the Dual Economy and African Entrepreneurship in
Kenya." *Journal of Development Studies*.

Stern, Claudio. 1984. "Population Growth, Migration, and Rural-Urban Problems in Developing Countries." *World Futures* 19(3–4).

Stevens, Christopher. 1990. "Nigeria," in Roger Riddell (1990c).

Stiglitz, Joseph. 1982. "The Structure of Labor Markets and Shadow Prices in LDCs." In R.H.
Sabot, ed., *Migration and the Labor Market in Developing Countries*. Boulder, CO: Westview.

———. 1976. "The Efficiency Wage Hypothesis, Surplus Labor, and the Distribution of Income in LDCs." *Oxford Economic Papers* 28(2).

——. 1974. "Alternative Theories of Wage Determination and Unemployment in LDCs: The Labor Turnover Model." *Quarterly Journal of Economics* 88, (2).

——. 1969. "Rural-Urban Migration, Surplus Labor, and Relationship Between Urban and Rural Wages." *East African Economic Review.*

Stren, Richard E. 1989. "The Administration of Urban Services." In Richard Stren and Rodney White, (1989).

——. 1982. "Underdevelopment, Urban Squatting and the State Bureaucracy: A Case Study of Tanzania," *Canadian Journal of African Studies* 16 (1).

——. 1978. *Housing the Urban Poor in Africa.* Institute of International Studies University of California, Berkeley.

——. 1975a. "Urban Policy and Performance in Kenya and Tanzania." *Journal of Modern African Studies* 13, no. 2.

——. 1975b. *Urban Inequality and Housing Policy in Tanzania.* Institute of International Studies, University of California, Berkeley.

Stren, Richard, and Claire Letemendia, eds. 1986. *Coping with Rapid Urban Growth in Africa: An Annotated Bibliography.* Montreal: McGill University.

Stren, Richard E., and Rodney R. White, eds. 1989. *African Cities in Crisis: Managing Raid Urban Growth.* Boulder, CO: Westview.

Summers, Robert and Alan Heston. 1991. "The Penn World Table (Mark 5): An Expanded Set of International Comparisons, 1950–1988." *Quarterly Journal of Economics* 106(2).

——. 1988. "A New Set of International Comparisons of Real Product and Price Levels: Estimates for 130 Countries, 1950–1985." *Review of Income and Wealth* 34(1).

Svejnar, Jan. 1984. "The Determinants of Industrial-Sector Earnings in Senegal." *Journal of Development Economics* **15**: 289–311.

Swanson, Daniel, and Teferra Wolde-Semait. 1989. "Africa's Public Enterprise Sector and Evidence of Reforms." Washington, DC: World Bank, Technical Paper no. 95.

Swindell, Kenneth. 1982. *Pre-Colonial and Colonial Labour Migration in West Africa: The Gambia and Northwest Nigeria, 1850–1980.* International Sociological Association.

——. 1979. "Labour Migration in Underdeveloped Countries: The Case of Sub-Saharan Africa." *Progress in Human Geography* 3(2).

Tabi, James, Wayne H. Howard, and Truman Phillips. 1991. "Urbanization and Food Imports in Sub-Saharan Africa." Guelph, Ont.: Department of Agricultural Economics and Business, unpublished manuscript.

Tager, C. 1985 (November). "Sub-Sarahan Urban Africa in Macroeconomic Perspective: West Africa Project Evaluations." Washington DC: World Bank, Water Supply and Urban Development Department, draft report.

Ta-Ninga, Yongoro O. R. 1978. "Paysages urbains et phénomène de claustration spatio-temporelle et sociologique dans les villes africaines." *Developpement Voltaique,* no. 56–57.

Taylor, Lowry. 1982. *A Dynamic Model of Rural-Urban Migration and Job Allocation in Kenya.* Unpublished Ph.D. Dissertation, Northwestern University.

Terrell, Katherine, and Jan Svejnar. 1989. *The Industrial Labor Market and Economic Performance in Senegal.* Boulder, CO:Westview.

Thadani, V. N. 1982. "Social Relations and Geographic Mobility: Male and Female Migration in Kenya." Population Council, Center for Policy Studies, Working Paper no. 85.

Tiebout, Charles. 1956. "A Pure Theory of Local Public Expenditures." *Journal of Political Economy* 64, pp. 416–24.

Todaro, Michael P. 1980. "Internal Migration, Urban Population Growth, and Unemployment in Developing Nations: Issues and Controversies. *Journal of Economic Development* 5(1).

——. 1971. "Income Expectations, Rural-Ruban Migration and Employment in Africa." *International Labour Review.*

Udo, Reuben K. 1982. *The Human Geography of Tropical Africa.* Ibadan: Heinemann Educational Books (Nigeria) Ltd.

————. 1975. "Migration and Urbanization in Nigeria." In John Caldwell, (ed.), *Population Growth and Socioeconomic Change in West Africa*. New York: Columbia University Press.

United Nations. 1989. *African Economic and Financial Data*. Washington: World Bank.

————. 1989a. *UNESCO Yearbook 1988*. New York: United Nations.

————. 1988a. *World Population Trends and Policies: 1987 Monitoring Report*. New York: United Nations.

————. 1984. *Population and Vital Statistics Report: 1984 Special Supplement*. New York: United Nations.

————. 1982. *World Population Trends and Policies, 1981 Monitoring Report*. New York: United Nations.

————. 1982a. *World Population Prospects: Estimates and Projections as Assessed in 1981*. New York: United Nations.

————. 1982b. *Model Life Tables for Developing Countries*. New York: United Nations.

————. 1981. *Population Distribution Policies in Development Planning*. Population Studies, no. 75.

————. 1980. *Patterns of Urban and Rural Population Growth*. New York: United Nations.

————. 1979. *Demographic Yearbook*. New York: United Nations.

United Nations Conference on Trade and Development (UNCTAD). 1984. *Handbook on International Trade and Development Statistics*. New York: United Nations.

————. 1983. *Handbook of International Trade and Development Statistics*. New York: United Nations.

United Nations Development Programme (UNDP). 1991. *Human Development Report 1991*. New York: Oxford University Press.

————. 1989. *African Economic and Financial Data*. Washington, DC: World Bank.

United Nations Development Program and The World Bank. 1992. *African Development Indicators*. Washington, DC, and New York: UNDP/World Bank.

United Republic of Tanzania. 1969. *Tanzania Second Five Year Plan for Economic and Social Development*. Vol. 1. Dar es Salaam: The Government Printer.

Uyanga, J. 1981. "African Mobility: A Source Paper." *International Migration Review* 15(4).

Valentine, Theodore R. 1982. "An Evaluation of Post-Independence Wage Policy in Tanzania: Its Objectives, Impact on Price Levels, Employment and Price Effects." Nashville, TN: Vanderbilt University Department of Economics Working Paper no. 82–W06.

Van Dijk, M. 1980. "La Réussite des Petits Entrepreneurs dans le Secteur Informel de Ouagadougou (Hate Volta)." In P. Hugon, ed., (1980).

Van Donge, Jan K. 1984. "Rural-Urban Migration and the Rural Alternative in Mwase Lundazi, Eastern Province, Zambia." *African Studies Review* 27(1).

Vaugelade, Jacques. 1982. "Stocks et flux dans l'analyse des migrations de retour." *Population* 37(6).

Venard, J. 1985 (July). "Senegal: Urban-Rural Linkages Study." Washington, DC: World Bank.

Venetier, Pierre. *Les villes d'Afrique tropicale*. New York: Masson.

Vijverberg, W. 1988 (April). *Profits from Self-Employent: A Case Study of the Ivory Coast*. Washington, DC: World Bank, Living Standards Measurement Study No. 43.

Vijverberg, W., and Jacques van der Gaag. 1991 (October). "The Private Wage Sector in Côte d'Ivoire: Homogeneity or Heterogeneity?" *Southern Economic Journal* 58(2):.

Voirin, M. 1983. "Social Security for Migrant Workers in Africa." *International Labor Review* 122(3).

Von Pischke, J. D. 1991. *Finance at the Frontier*. Washington, DC: World Bank, Economic Development Institute.

Waite, Gloria. 1988. "The Politics of Disease: The AIDS Virus and Africa." In Norman Miller and Richard Rockwell, eds., *AIDS in Africa*. Lewiston, NY: Edwin Mellen.

Wasow, Bernard. 1981. "The Working Age-Sex Ratio and Job Search Migration in Kenya." *Journal of Developing Areas* 15(3).

Wayem, John Atsu. 1983. "Infant Industry, Protection and Import-Substitution Industrialization: An Economic Analysis of the Textile Industry in Ghana." Nashville, TN: Vanderbilt University, Department of Economics, unpublished M.A. dissertation.

Weeks, John. 1986 (December). "Income Distribution and Its Implications for Population Trends in Sub-Saharan Africa." Paper presented at the IUSSP/University of Nairobi Seminar on Consequences of Population Trends in Africa, Nairobi.

Wetheimer, M., B. Becq, and G. Gaveau. 1984. *Secondary Towns in Africa: Their Role and Functions in National and Regional Development*. Paris: Agence Française pour l'Aménagement et le Développement à l'Etranger.

Wheaton, William C., and Hisanobu Shishido. 1981. "Urban Concentration, Agglomeration Economies, and the Level of Economic Development." *Economic Development and Cultural Change* 30 (1).

———. 1981. "Housing Policies and Urban 'Markets' in Developing Countries: The Egyptian Experience." *Journal of Urban Economics* 9.

Whitney, Vincent H. 1983. "Planning for Migration and Urbanization: Some Issues and Options for Policymakers and Planners." In Peter Morrison, ed., *Population Movements: Their Forms and Functions in Urbanization and Development*. Liege, Belgium: Ordina Edition.

Wilber Smith Associates et al. n.d. *Lagos Master Plan*.

Williams, D. 1985 (October). "The Role of the Bank in Urban Management." Washington, DC: World Bank, Water Supply and Urban Development Department.

Williamson, Jeffrey G. 1988. "Migration and Urbanization in the Third World." In Hollis Chenery and T.N. Srinivasan, eds., *Handbook of Development Economics*. Vol. 1. Amsterdam: North-Holland.

Wood, A.P. 1982. "Population Trends in Zambia: A Review of the 1980 Census." In A. Findlay, ed., *Recent National Population Change*. Durham, UK: University of Durham, Department of Geography, Population Study Group.

World Bank and the United Nations Development Program. 1989. *Africa's Adjustment and Growth in the 1980s*. Washington, DC: World Bank.

World Bank. 1992. *Staff Appraisal Report: Republic of Benia Urban Rehabilitation and Management Project*. Washington, DC: World Bank, Infrastructure Operations Division, Occidental and Central Africa Department.

———. 1991. *World Development Report 1991*. Washington, DC: World Bank.

———. 1991a. *Madagascar: Beyond Stabilization to Sustainable Growth*. Washington, DC: World Bank, Africa Region, Country Operations Division.

———. 1991b. *Public Choices for Private Initiatives: Prioritizing Public Expenditures for Sustainable and Equitable Growth in Uganda*. Washington, DC: World Bank, Africa Region, Country Operations Division.

———. 1991c. *Tanzania Economic Report: Towards Sustainable Development in the 1990s*. Washington, DC: World Bank, Southern Africa Department, Country Operations Division.

———. 1991d. *Madagascar Urban Sector Review*. Washington, DC: World Bank, Africa Region, Infrastructure Operations Division.

———. 1990e. *Staff Appraisal Report: Republic of Guinea Second Urban Project*. Washington, DC: World Bank, Infrastructure Operations Division, Occidental and Central Africa Department.

———. 1991f. *Mozambique: Urban Local Government and the Environment Sector Review*. Washington, DC: World Bank, Infrastructure Operations Division, Southern Africa Department.

———. 1990g. *Staff Appraisal Report: Ethiopia: Second Addis Ababa Urban Development Project*. Washington, DC: World Bank, Infrastructure Operations Division, Eastern Africa Department.

———. 1991h. *Staff Appraisal Report: Republic of Ghana Urban II Project.* Washington, DC: World Bank, Infrastructure Operations Division, Western Africa Department.

———. 1990a. *Republic of Guinea Country Economic Memorandum.* Washington, DC: World Bank, Africa Region, Country Operations Division.

———. 1990b. *Kenya Stabilization and Adjustment: Toward Accelerated Growth.* Washington, DC: World Bank, Africa Region, Country Operations Division.

———. 1990c. *Mozambique: Restoring Rural Production and Trade.* Washington, DC: World Bank, Southern Africa Department, Country Operations Division.

———. 1990d. *Staff Appraisal Report: Uganda: First Urban Project.* Washington, DC: World Bank, Infrastructure Operations Division, Eastern Africa Department.

———. 1989a. *Sub-Saharan Africa: From Crisis to Sustainable Growth.* Washington, DC: World Bank.

———. 1989b. *World Development Report.* Washington, DC: World Bank.

———. 1989c. *World Tables, 1988–89 Edition.* Baltimore: Johns Hopkins University Press.

———. 1989d (November). *Social Dimensions of Adjustment Country Assessment Paper: Cameroon.* Washington, DC: World Bank, Africa Region, SDA Unit.

———. 1989e (June). *Mauritania Country Assessment Paper: Etude d'Evaluation de la Pauvrete en Mauritanie,* Washington, DC: World Bank, Africa Region, SDA Unit.

———. 1989f (September). *Adjustment and Poverty in Côte d'Ivoire 1980–89.* Washintgon, DC: World Bank, Africa Region, SDA Unit.

———. 1989g (June). *Poverty Alleviation in Madagascar.* Washington, DC: World Bank, Africa Region, SDA Unit.

———. 1989h (April). *Poverty Profile of Togo.* Washington, DC: World Bank, Africa Region, SDA Unit.

———. 1989i (December). *Poverty Alleviation in Central African Republic.* Washington, DC: World Bank, Africa Region, SDA Unit.

———. 1989j (October). *Social Dimensions of Structural Adjustment Country Assessment Paper: Senegal.* Washington, DC: World Bank, SDA Unit.

———. 1989k (September). *A Poverty Profile for Ghana, 1987–88.* Washington, DC: World Bank, Africa Region, SDA Unit.

———. 1988 (March). *Zaire Urban Sector Mission Report: Annex vii: Regional Development of Kivu.* Washington, DC: World Bank (Africa Region, South Central, and Indian Ocean Department, Infrastructure Operations Division) Report no. 6930-ZR.

———. 1988a. *Road Deterioration in Developing Countries.* Washington, DC: World Bank.

———. 1988b (May). *Nigeria: The Structiral Adjustment Program: Policies, Impacts, Prospects.* Washington, DC: World Bank, Africa Region.

———. 1987. *Ghana: Policies and Issues of Structural Adjustment.* Washington, DC: World Bank (Western Africa Region).

———. 1987a (March). *The Ivory Coast in Transition: From Structural Adjustment to Self-Sustained Growth.* Washington, DC: World Bank (Western Africa Region).

———. 1985 (February). *Zimbabwe Urban Sector Review.* Washington, DC: World Bank (East Africa Projects Department) Report no. 4171–ZIM.

———. 1985a (January). *Mali's Urban Sector: A Financial Investent Strategy for Mali's Capital City, Bamako—1985–95.* Washington, DC: World Bank (West Africa Projects Department, Urban Projects Division).

———. 1985b (August). *Ghana Agricultural Sector Review.* Washington, DC: World Bank (Western Africa Region) Report no. 5366-GH.

———. 1985c (December). *Kenya: Economic Development and Urbanization Policy.* Washington, DC: World Bank (Eastern and Southern Africa Projects Department) Report no. 4148-KE.

———. 1985d (June). *Sudan: Prospects for Rehabilitation of the Sudanese Economy.* Washington, DC: World Bank (Eastern and Southern Africa Regional Office, Division EA2NE) Report no. 5496.

———. 1985e (March). *Zaire Economic Memorandum: Economic Change and External Assistance.* Washington, DC: World Bank (Country Programs Department II, Eastern and Southern Africa), Report no. 5417-ZR.

———. 1985f (June). *Ivory Coast: Third Structural Adjustment Loan.* Washington, DC: World Bank.

———. 1985g (August). *Ghana: Priorities for Public Expenditures, 1986–1988.* Washington, DC: World Bank (Country Programs I, Western Africa), Report no. 5824-GH.

———. 1985h (May). "Republique Islamique de Mauritania: Development Urbaine: Elements Pour Une Strategie Sectorielle," Washington, DC: World Bank, West Africa Projects Department, Urban Division.

———. 1985h (October). *Malawi: Economic Recovery: Resource and Policy Needs.* Washington, DC: World Bank (Country Programs K, Eastern and Southern Africa Region). Report no. 5801-MAI.

———. 1984. *World Development Report 1984.* Washington, DC: World Bank.

———. 1984a. *Toward Sustained Development in Sub-Saharan Africa: A Joint Program of Action.* Washington, D.C.: World Bank.

———. 1984b (September). *Ghana: Accra District Rehabilitation Project.* Washington, DC: World Bank (West Africa Projects Department, Urban Projects Division).

———. 1984c (February). *Cameroon: Douala Infrastructure Development Project: Initiating Project Brief.* Washington, DC: World Bank (West Africa Projects Department, Urban Projects Division).

———. 1984d (June). *Nigeria Agricultural Sector Memorandum.* Washington, DC: World Bank (Western Africa Projects Department, Agriculture Division B).

———. 1984e (January). *Kenya Agricultural Sector Report.* Washington, DC: World Bank (Eastern Africa Projects Department, Central Agricultural Division).

———. 1983. *World Tables,* 3d edition, vol. 1. Baltimore: John Hopkins University Press.

———. 1983a (December). *Kenya: Growth and Structural Change.* Washington, DC: World Bank (Eastern Africa Projects Department, Southern Agriculture Division).

———. 1983b. *Kenya: Growth and Structural Change. Annex II: Issues in Kenyan Agricultural Development.* Washington: World Bank.

———. 1983c (June). *Senegal: Urban Sector Memorandum.* Washington, DC: World Bank (West Africa Region, Urban Projects Division) Report no. 4537-SE.

———. 1983d (September). *Nigeria: Lagos Urban Sector Review.* Washington, DC: World Bank (West Africa Region, Urban Projects Division) Report no. 4479-UNI.

———. 1983e (December). *Zimbabwe Agricultural Sector Study.* Washington, DC: World Bank (Eastern Africa Projects Department, Southern Agriculture Division) Report no. 4401-ZIM.

———. 1983f (August). *Tanzania Agriculture Sector Report.* Washington, DC: World Bank (Eastern Africa Projects Department, Southern Agriculture Division) Report no. 4052-TA.

———. 1983g. (July). *Sierra Leone: Prospects for Growth and Equity.* Washington, DC: World Bank (Western Africa Region) Report No. 3375-SL.

———. 1982. *World Development Report 1982.* Washington, DC: The World Bank.

———. 1982a. *Zaire Economic Memorandum: Recent Economic and Sectoral Development and Current Issues.* Washington, DC: World Bank (Eastern Africa Country Programs Department II) Report no. 4077-ZR.

———. 1982b. *Malawi: Growth and Structural Change.* Washington, DC: World Bank, Eastern Africa Regional Office. Report no. 3082a-MAI.

———. 1981. *Accelerated Development in Sub-Saharan Africa: An Agenda for Action.* Washington, DC: The World Bank.

———. 1981a (November). *Staff Appraisal Report: Monrovia Urban Development Project.* Washington, DC: World Bank (West Africa Region, West Africa Projects Department) Report no. 3384-LR.

——. 1980. *Kenya: Population and Development*. Washington: World Bank.

——. 1980a. "A Review of Project Development and a Look Ahead." Washington, DC: World Bank, Urban Projects Division, West Africa Department.

——. 1977. *Tanzania: The Second National Sites and Services Project*. Report no. 1513a-TA.

——. n.d. *Cameroon: Urban Sector Review and Sector Assistance Strategy*. Washington, DC: World Bank (West Africa Projects Department, Urban Projects Division) Report no. 4540-CM.

World Health Organization (WHO). 1988 (June 30). *Update: AIDS Cases Reported to SFI Assessment Unit*. Geneva: WHO.

Yap, Lorene. 1977. "The Attraction of Cities: A Review of the Migration Literature." *Journal of Development Economics* 4, (3).

Yeager, Rodger. 1982. "Demography and Development Policy in Tanzania." *Journal of Developing Areas* 16.

Zachariah, K. C., and Julian Conde. 1981. *Migration in West Africa: Demographic Aspects*. New York: Oxford University.

——. 1980. *Demographic Aspects of Migration in West Africa, Volumes 1 and 2*. World Bank Staff Working Papers no. 413–5.

Zachariah, K.C., and My T. Vu. 1987 (December) (revised). *Africa Region Population Projections 1987–88*. Washington, DC: World Bank, Population and Human Resources Department, PHN Technical Note 87-19a.

INDEX

289